# NOT / GLORY!

## True Accounts of RAF Airmen Taken Prisoner in Europe, 1939–1945

### Victor F. Gammon

*Sunday 3 September 1939, 11.20 a.m., RAF Yatesbury*

'Don't imagine you'll be up there all glamour and heroics,' asserted the 'old sweat' Drill Sergeant to the trainees, indicating a Tiger Moth flying overhead. 'It's not all glory y'know.' Then, pointing hs finger towards the ground, he declared grimly, 'That's where you'll be, mates, down in the bloody trenches with a rifle – just like last time.'

ARMS AND
ARMOUR

**Arms and Armour Press**
An Imprint of the Cassell Group
Wellington House, 125 Strand, London WC2R 0BB

Distributed in the USA by Sterling Publishing Co. Inc.,
387 Park Avenue South, New York, NY 10016-8810.

Distributed in Australia by Capricorn Link (Australia) Pty. Ltd,
2/13 Carrington Road, Castle Hill, NSW 2154.

British Library Cataloguing-in-Publication Data:
a catalogue record for this book is available from
the British Library

ISBN 1-85409-337-1

Designed and edited by DAG Publications Ltd.
Designed by David Gibbons; edited by Jonathan
Falconer; printed and bound in Great Britain.

# CONTENTS

# Introduction

Here are the true experiences of named men from all Commands of the Royal Air Forces who fought and literally fell into enemy hands but never gave up the fight. Their adventures, always hazardous from their capture to their liberation, range from acts of matchless courage to moments of hilarity when the innate humour of the Serviceman surfaced

Blenheims and Wellingtons were in the thick of battle on the second day of the war, when the Royal Air Force took the war to the enemy. During the fraught period when the continental nations were thrust aside by the all-conquering Wehrmacht it was the crews of Fairey Battles of the Advanced Air Striking Force that fought to the last plane. When the enemy surveyed the British coastline from just twenty one miles distant and prepared to invade, it was pilots of the Royal Air Force's Spitfires and Hurricanes that made this powerful, ruthless, determined enemy think again and postpone his plans indefinitely. Then, during the years when Germany had Europe at its feet the Royal Air Force and US Air Force Heavy Bombers crews hammered at the enemy homeland, tying up vast numbers of men and resources. When the Allies prepared to invade France it was the men of the Royal Air Force and US Air Force Bombers and Fighters that prepared the way and were fighting to the last days of the war. From all these operations in the European theatre less than ten thousand Royal Air Force men were taken prisoner.

These were the survivors of fierce battles and the ratio of one man taken for every five or six aircrew men killed in action is an indication of the narrowness of the margins with which they cheated death. As prisoners of the enemy they had to summon up their courage and steadfastness for up to six years of constant struggle.

I knew that the exploits and experiences of these men, young when they lived their lives at full stretch, would be lost forever unless preserved for posterity.

To members of the Royal Air Forces Ex-Prisoner of War Association, my friends and colleagues to whom this book is dedicated, I give my grateful thanks for your help and encouragement. I am honoured and proud to be one of you.

Vic Gammon

# —— Acknowledgements ——

The author wishes to acknowledge the help of the contributors listed below and apologises for any inadvertent omissions.

Ron (Ackers) Akerman, R. (Jock) Alexander, W. (Tex) Ash, MBE, George Atkinson, Bill Baird, John Banfield, George Barrowman, H. (Batch) Batchelder, DFM, John (Jock) Bell, Ron Bence, Bill Bennett, Air Vice Marshal D.C.T. Bennett, CB, CBE, DSO, William (Bill) Bloxham, Brian (Porky) Booth, George Booth, Cas de Bounevialle, Don (Fritz) Boutle, John (Jack) Boyes, Albert Bracegirdle, DFM, Roy (Lofty) Bromley, Stan (Lemmy) Brooks, John (Jack) Broughton, Don Bruce, Ron Buckingham, Alec Burton, Maurice Butt, George Calvert, C. (Ken) Campbell, DFC, Percy Carruthers, DFM, H. (Bert) Carter, Lt. Cdr. John Casson, OBE, E. (Ted) Chapman, Ken Chapman, J.R. (Nobby) Clark, Allen (Nobby) Clarke, John F. (Jack) Clarke, Len Clarke, Reg Cleaver, Bob (Smudge) Coles, MBE, E. Hugh Collins, Tom Cooksey, Henry (Roger) Coverley, Stan Croft, MBE, Hal Croxson, V. (Bob) Cutts, Ron Damman, Gp. Capt. Harry (Wings) Day, GC, DSO, OBE, James (Dixie) Deans, MBE, H. David Denchfield, John Dennis, A.J. (Tubby) Dixon, J. (Bas) Downing, Bert Dowty, R. (Jack) Dunn, Desmond Dunphy, Wg. Cdr. L. Edwards, RNZAF, Dennis (Pinky) Emes, Ron Esling, Ron Fermor, Geoff (Charlie) Fletcher, C. (Wally) Floody, Leslie Ford, John Forward, A. (Fris) Frisby, Denis (Freddie) Fry, Doug (Junior) Fry, W.V. (Bill) Garfield, Bill Garrioch, Ron Gibson, E. (Goldie) Gold, Bill Goodall, Ken (Marmaduke) Goodchild, W. (Bill) Goodman, Reg Gould, G. Greenfield, John (Gristle) Grimer, Ray Gulliford, A. (Ron) Gunton, Roy (Happy) Hale, E.L.Graham (Knobby) Hall, MBE, L. Harcus, Marshal of the Royal Air Force Sir Arthur Harris, Bt., CGB, OBE, AFC, LL.D, Gerry Harris, W. (Peachy) Harrison, W. (Bill) Hart, Tom Harvey, Benny Hayward, Walter Hedges, Ray (Tin Bashing Tom) Hedley, Peter Hewitt, Bill (Shiner) Higgs, Paul Hilton, CGM, Geoffrey Hobbs, Eric Hookings, Maj. J. (Jimmy) Howe, MBE, Frank Hunt, W. Jim (Red) Hunter, Stan Hurrell, W. (Wilf) Hurst, Gp. Capt. Frank Jensen, CBE, DFC, AFC, AE, R. (Johnnie) Johnston, Ivan Kayes, Alex Kerr, Archie King, John Knott, John Leakey, W. (Bill) Legg, Norman (Len) Leonard, E. (Doc) Libbey, Len (Lindy) Lindridge, Denis Lloyd, Dan London, Bert (Rosie) Long, Len Ludlam, Mike Ludlow, George Luke, H. Lloyd Lyne, Jack (Tiger) Lyon, J. Alistair Macdonald, OBE, John Mahony, Jack Marsden, Air Marshal Sir

Harold Martin, KCB, DSO, DFC, AFC, Peter Mason, Air Cdr. H. Massey, CBE, DSO, MC, H. (Mac) McLean, Alex (Dusty) Miller, James (Jack) Mills, Arthur (Arf-a-mo) Minnitt, Reg Moffat, Ron Mogg, Arthur (Chester) Morris, Don Morrison, DFC, DFM, Bob (Snowball) Morton, Vic Munnings, John Murrell. Sydney Murrell, Tom Nelson, Wg. Cdr. G. (Bill) Newby, Reginald (Dick) Newdick, C. (Nick) Nichol, Alec (Nicky) Nicholas, Neville Northover, H.J. Noy, N.F. Oates, Gordon (Oggie) Ogden, Ian Osbourne, MBE, S. (Jim) Padgham, Jim Palmer, Norman (Bill) Panter, Geoff Parnell, D. (Jack) Paul, DFM, Roger Peacock, Gwilym (Taffy) Peake, John Pickering, Deryck Polley, Leslie Poole, Phil Potts, Edgar (Eddie) Poulter, Max (Zaba) Rech, Stan Reed, Wg. Cdr. Ken (Shag) Rees, George Rex, Ian Robb, Mike Roberts, Bill Rolfe, C. (Cec) Room, Eric (Sandy) Sanderson, Ron Scales, Percy Sekine, Geoff Shepherd, Leslie (Sid) Sidwell, Larry Slattery, Arthur (Smudge) Smith, F.G. Smith. J. (Chip) Sparrow, R. (Bobby) Stark, Maurice (Moggie) Stretton, Marian Jozef (Joe) Stule, Archie Sulston, Johnnie Sutton, Wilf Sutton, Alec Taylor, James (Jim, Schneider) Taylor, W. (Buck) Taylor, Peter Tebbutt, H. (Tommy) Tomkins, Peter Tomlinson, Ken Townsend, Ken Trott, Frederick Turner, MM, J. (Jim) Verran, Len (Titch) Walker, Brian S. Walley, R. David Ward, Bernard Warren, Doug Waters, John Weston, W. (Bill) Williams, Alan (Tug) Wilson, Ernest Winfield, Harry Wink, Roy Witham, George Woodhead, David Young, Mrs J. Bowerman, Mrs K. Chapman, Mrs M. Marsden. Special thanks are due to Desmond Dunphy M.I.L. for his advice and help with the German language also to R. (Bob) Anderson and Dave Westmacott for permission to use cartoons from *Handle with Care*.

Vic Gammon

*That makes 1,500 guys in this camp with an Auntie Winnie and an Uncle Joe.*

# Glossary

**Aber wir haben viel von solchem Holz in Deutschland!** But we have plenty of such wood in Germany

**Abwehr** Armed forces secret & counter-intelligence service

**Anschluss** German union with Austria (1938)

**Arzt** Doctor

**Barbarossa** Codename for the German invasion of Russia (1941)

**Dolmetscher** Interpreter

**Endlösung** Final solution, used chiefly about the 'Jewish question'

**Ersatz** Imitation

**Ferret** Prisoners name for camp security guards

**Gefreite** Lance-corporal

**Gestapo** Geheime Staatspolizei, Secret State Police

**Hände Hoch!** Hands up!

**'He, Sie dort Stehen bleiben!'** 'Oi! You there. Stop!'

**Kripo** Kriminalpolizei, Criminal Police

**M.A.N.** Maschinenfabrik Augsburg – Nürnberg AG

**Oberfeldwebel** Sergeant Major

**Oberst** Colonel

**Oberstleutnant** Lieutenant Colonel

**OKH** Oberkommando des Heeres, Army High Command

**OKW** Oberkommando der Wehrmacht, Armed Forces High Command

**Ordnungspolizei** Uniformed police

**Räder müssen rollen für den Sieg** Wheels must roll for victory

**SA** Sturmabteilung, Nazi paramilitary arm

**Sanitäter** Medical Orderly or First Aider

**SAO** Senior American Officer

**SBO** Senior British Officer

**Schadenfreude** Malicious joy (at another's misfortune)

**SD** Sicherheitsdienst, (SS) Security Service

**Sondermeldung** Special Announcement

**SS** Schutz Staffeln, literally Protection Units

**Totenkopf** Death's Head

**Volkssturm** The peoples' army or home defence units

**Waffen SS** SS field troops

**Wehrmacht** Armed Forces, but usually applied to the German Army by Kriegies

Note that the German Authorities numbered Prisoner of War camps by Roman Numerals. For convenience they have been converted here to Arabic Numerals – for example, Stalag VIIIB is given as Stalag 8B or just 8B, and Stalag Luft III as Stalag Luft 3 or merely Luft 3. The prisoners invariably referred to the camps in this fashion.

# PART 1
# 1939–1940

### FLYING START

The sudden clearing of haze startled Sergeant Prince's Blenheim crew. There, ahead and below, at anchor at Wilhelmshaven, four German warships with flak guns blazing were covering the air around the attacking aircraft with black smoke puffs of exploding shells. Where lines of tracer criss-crossed the sky Sergeant Booth, the navigator, saw a Blenheim explode in a flash of boiling flame. Anti-aircraft fire was concentrated on the 110 Squadron aircraft which had left four minutes before Prince's 107 Squadron flight. All chances of surprise were now lost.

Within hours of the declaration of war on 3 September, the passenger ship SS *Athenia* had been sunk by a U-boat. The War Cabinet felt that a warlike gesture was needed so an attack on the German Fleet was planned. Poor weather prevented action that day but now, the 4th, 15 Blenheims had been sent.

Booth peered forward from his navigator's table as Prince called, 'Going in'. Prince dived to near sea level. Aircraftsman Second Class (AC2) Slattery's machine guns blasting from the dorsal turret added to the roaring din as Prince levelled the Blenheim, the airscrews almost churning the water. Booth's nervous joke about remustering to the submarine service from the RAF was stifled in his throat as the Blenheim bounced like a skimming stone on the sea surface, shot forward over the waves and suddenly slapped down on to the water, stopping dead. Booth was thrown forward as the sea gushed in through the smashed bottom panels and stove-in nose perspex. The cacophony of screaming engines and chattering guns had ceased but the quiet slopping as the fuselage filled with sea water was as menacing. Booth had to move fast. Throwing open the top hatch he leapt out on to the port wing shouting, 'Princey, Princey, get a move on'. Booth steadied himself, looking back to help, but Prince remained in his seat, strangely still and silent.

A sudden lurch of the flooding Blenheim threw Booth into the sea. He had subconsciously rid himself of his flying boots and inflated his Mae West life jacket. Now he was floating in the comparative peace of a quiet and misty sea. He felt no pain; he was just cold, wet and miserable. Then men were calling to each other, the language was unfamiliar but the meaning clear: he had been seen. Minutes later he was hauled over the gunnels to lie squelching in the bottom of a rowing boat. Regaining his breath, Booth's first thoughts were for Prince and Slattery. His rescuers told him that both men had been picked up but were seriously hurt.

Transferred to a pilot pinnace Booth found that he could only stand on the toes of his left foot. In a far corner another figure lay huddled motionless on the deck. 'Is that you Princey?' he called. There was an indistinct, almost inaudible reply, but George Booth knew that accent, it was Larry Slattery. Slattery's jaw had been fractured in several places and his nose had been almost severed when his face smashed into his turret gun. He could hardly speak but Booth was relieved, Larry was alive.

Bandages seemed to be holding Slattery's head together. Booth reckoned they had been applied with maximum enthusiasm and minimum experience, but despite his injuries Slattery's Irish courage and sense of humour surfaced later as the two men lay on bunks in a cabin. Slattery muttered, his brogue muffled by the bandages, 'I think I shall be a lot better looking when I get over this'. Booth was sure that Slattery would have been smiling beneath the swathing dressings.

Sergeant A.S. Prince's name was added to the 'Missing' on the first casualty list issued in Britain but he was already dead, as were all the 11 other ranks, NCOs and three officers listed as 'Missing'. For Booth and Slattery, the first RAF prisoners-of-war, it was the beginning of long years of what seemed an interminable wait for victory in Europe and their freedom.

The second day of the Second World War had been a disaster for the RAF. Five of 10 attacking Blenheims had been lost and the only damage done to the *Kriegsmarine* had been when one aircraft had crashed on the cruiser *Emden*.

The next day New Zealander Pilot Officer Laurie Edwards of 206 Squadron, Coastal Command, flew his Avro Anson from RAF Bircham Newton, on his second reconnaissance over the North Sea. Edwards' 'Faithful Annie' was intercepted by a German floatplane near the Dogger Bank. The Anson's armament was no match for the enemy's 20mm cannon and machine guns. Soon the 'Annie' was ablaze and diving towards the sea. Edwards fought to hold the plane up to enable his crew to escape, but with flames roaring around him he was already too low and the ensuing impact with the sea knocked him unconscious.

Edwards' head cleared slowly as he drifted among floating wreckage. As the floatplane landed nearby his hopes plummeted for he could see no other survivors. Burned and barely conscious, he was thrown roughly into the floatplane's rear compartment and flown to the *Luftwaffe* hospital on the East Friesian island of Nordeney. Edwards was sent for burns treatment to the *Kriegsmarine* hospital at Wesermünde where Booth and Slattery were both patients. Edwards was the third airman and the first RAF officer to be taken prisoner in the Second World War.

On the fifth day of his captivity George Booth awoke to sudden activity in the hospital room occupied by him and Slattery. They had been well treated but found it difficult to attune their rebellious stomachs to the black bread, rice, prunes and sausage served on one plate. Booth still found it hard to believe that he was a prisoner-of-war. It was just a week since he had said goodbye to his wife Stella and baby son; now he was in a foreign country and about to be served more of their unpalatable food.

But it was not for a meal that the hospital staff were bustling around. The small ward was quickly polished to showroom condition, Booth was shaved and Slattery's bandages tidied. Booth guessed that the 'bull' was for some propaganda purpose. His hunch was confirmed when burns-scarred Edwards was ushered in and the small room began to fill with photographers, foreign correspondents and radio men wielding microphones. By keeping their answers non-committal the prisoners were able to make the interviews innocuous, although Booth, with typical North Country astuteness, managed to mention 'Yorkshire Pudding' and so conveyed via 'Lord Haw-Haw' the first coded message from a prisoner-of-war. His relatives now knew that Booth was alive and kicking, albeit with a broken ankle.

As the interviews closed and the party was leaving, an American correspondent hung back. Leaning over, apparently still asking routine questions, the American's soft whisper was like a shout of triumph to Booth: 'Cheer up,' he breathed quietly and then, as if denying the recent US neutrality declaration, he murmured, 'we shall be with you soon'.

George Booth's ankle strengthened and Larry Slattery improved daily. Slattery was taken away for treatment, his jaw was wired and his nose 'trimmed'. In the hurry to fix his nose back to his face it had not been replaced 'squarely'.

The weather turned colder and the countryside settled with a peaceful blanket of snow. Red Cross parcels began to arrive for Booth and the Germans had to open a special store. He was living well in the hospital but was losing all sense of the passing of time and was sad that he would not be at home in Yorkshire for Christmas.

## THE FIRST SBO

'His generation was the one between the wars;
the thirties were his stamping ground.' — *Bradbury*

No 57 Squadron had flown its short-nosed Blenheims from RAF Upper Heyford to France as part of the Air Component of the British Expeditionary Force. Since his return from leave Wing Commander Harry 'Wings' Day had been impatient for action. Reconnaissance was a task for which 'Wings' thought the Blenheim I highly unsuitable, but his squadron had been ordered to undertake a photo-recce of the Ruhr and rather than ask someone else to take on the dangerously deep-penetration operation he had decided to go himself.

Cloud had been forecast throughout Germany so he planned to drop down briefly through the overcast and take overlap photographs with the belly camera of the Hamm–Ruhr rail traffic, while navigator Sergeant Hillier took an oblique angle film with a small hand-held cine camera. Then they would race back into the clouds and belt for home. It was Friday 13 October.

Calling to gunner Leading Aircraftsman (LAC) Moller to keep a sharp lookout during their below-cloud jaunt, Day lowered himself into the pilot's seat. Stretching out his long legs, his feet feeling for the rudder bar, he showed no sign of strain. The etching of vertical face lines was his normal appearance, breaking up only when swapping carefree banter or leading a raucously roared chorus whilst standing on a Mess table, a glass of whisky waving dangerously in his hand. There had been occasions when senior ranks had looked askance at Harry Day's exuberant outbursts, but he was popular and few knew as many verses of *The Bold Aviator* or could equal the ribaldry of his version. But now he was serious, lifting the Blenheim into the sunshine above the clouds, and in his element.

His mood changed rapidly to one of alarm when the Blenheim unexpectedly 'ran out of cloud'. The Rhine below glistened in the sunshine; the crew felt naked and vulnerable. Within seconds Moller was calling out, 'Flak ahead – flak ahead!'. But Day suspected fighters. Three Messerschmitt Bf109s turned in to attack from port and, despite throwing the Blenheim through every defensive manoeuvre, the unequal fight was lost from the moment Day felt his aircraft shudder as cannon shells smashed home. Flames roared up around him and back into the fuselage. Moller screamed in agony. Day saw Hillier buckling on his parachute and signalled him to jump. Searing flames were already blinding Day when with a supreme effort he heaved his body through the top escape hatch, drew his legs out and kicked away from the blazing plane.

As he parachuted down through the sudden quiet, Day could see people running to the spot where they judged he would land. Surrounding him, but standing back as he thumped heavily to the ground, the gathering crowd stared at this wild-looking sight. Day, his face swollen and blackened with blister-burns across his forehead, looked a frightening mess but he knew his wounds were not serious. His concern was for his crewmen. One of the crowd told him in halting English that they had been seen falling with their parachutes blazing. Two bodies lay just a short distance away near the village of Langweiler.

'Wings' Day was stricken when he saw them. As he raised a saluting hand to his blistered forehead, tears ran slowly down the smoke-grimed channels of his face. The *Luftwaffe* was delighted to have captured the highest ranking RAF officer so far, and a squadron commander to boot.

### NEW YEAR GLOW

In the depths of the snowy Polish countryside, one prisoner-of-war, an RAF corporal, was involved in moments of high comedy. Ron 'Gunner' Gunton, had been the wireless operator and 'dustbin' gunner of a Whitley that was showering Munich with leaflets when it was blasted by flak on 16 October 1939. Gunton always searched for a means of escape and from the early days the Germans realised that he was a special case to be watched. They despatched him from Spangenberg direct to the Napoleonic Fort 8 near Posen where it was reckoned a sharp eye could be kept on him. Gunton was paraded for each guard to know and recognise and given the job of camp electrician so that he could earn a few *Lagergeld* marks.

On New Year's Eve 1939, a cold wintry night, the lights in Fort 8 flickered and dimmed. Gunton was not surprised when within five minutes the German guard commander, accompanied by six guards, strode into his room and ordered him to accompany them to an electrical sub-station outside the camp. At the substation the *Stabsfeldwebel* opened the door and indicated to Gunton that he should have a look to see if he could find the fault. Gunton hardly wanted to get deeply involved so, with a look of authority, he studied the substation's intricate interior and announced confidently that the fault lay at the main power station. That was exactly what the *Stabsfeldwebel* wanted to hear. Slapping Gunton happily on the back he turned to the other guards and collected his winnings from the bets he had placed about the source of the electrical fault.

Turning back to Gunton the *Stabsfeldwebel* said, 'Give me your word of honour that you will not try to escape for the next 24 hours.'

15

Looking at the two feet of snow in which they were standing, Gunton readily agreed. Then indicating that he should follow, the German led the way to where a riotous party was in progress. When he was seated, a full bottle of Schnapps was pushed into his hand and several bottles of beer banged down on the table before him. His orders were to join the party and start drinking.

Six hours, the bottle of Schnapps and a dozen bottles of beer later, it was decided that Gunton should return to the Fort. A *Feldwebel* carrying a sub-machine gun, another guard and Corporal Gunton began their faltering walk back to the prisoners' compound. The combination of the drink and the icy road surface was too much and all three collapsed in a slithering, laughing heap. They picked themselves up, brushed down their clothes and staggered onward. The trio arrived unsteadily at the camp gate, said their jovial 'goodnights' and turned to go their different ways when Gunton realised that he had the German's sub-machine gun slung over his shoulder. Calling him back Corporal Gunton handed over the gun to the now red-faced *Feldwebel*. Thereafter, whenever the *Feldwebel* saw Gunton an involuntary rosy glow spread over his face as he recalled New Year's Eve.

That only some 30 RAF men were prisoners-of-war towards the year's end was indicative of the large number of crewmen killed. Yet these few were now distributed all over Germany in hospitals, camps, castles, prisons, and fortresses, but by December the Germans began to segregate Air Force prisoners. A party of five airmen were sent to an interrogation centre at Oberursel, four miles north-west of Frankfurt. The camp, as yet incomplete, was to become familiar as Dulag Luft.

——————————————— **1940** ———————————————

### IMPRESSING THE NATIVES

When the German doctors decided the time had come for George Booth to leave the Wesermünde *Kriegsmarine* Hospital he was sent in February to Oflag 9/AH at Spangenberg. To Booth the *Unterlager* where the NCOs and ORs were housed looked more like a holiday home. It had been used as a Hitler Youth and 'Strength through Joy' hostel and Nazi slogans proliferated. The officer Kriegies lived in the grim looking castle crowning a nearby 500ft hill. Life in the *Unterlager* was dull so the men readily accepted an invitation to a Church Parade in the castle and determined to 'Show The Flag'. They turned out 'bulled up' and with a smart step they marched up the steep hill, the castle appearing and disappearing with each turn of the track. The German guards were unable to match their military appearance or step. They were shabby and disorganised compared with the upright, striding, singing Britishers. When guards tried to stop the singing at the front of the column it broke out again at the rear. Running frantically to the rear of the column and shouting at the prisoners to be silent they then had to hurriedly reverse as the Serviceman's own version of *Colonel Bogey* resumed at the head. Crossing a bridge over a dry moat the contingent marched into the cobbled courtyard, halting on command with the guardsmen-like crash of their boots echoing and re-echoing from the surrounding high walls. 'That'll show 'em,' smiled Booth.

In April Germany invaded Denmark and Norway and on 10 May the *Luftwaffe* pounded a path for the *Panzer* divisions to roll across Holland, Belgium, Luxembourg and France. It was thought necessary to continue the daylight attacks to halt the *Blitzkrieg* so the Air Staff were forced to throw Battles and Blenheims into the land war.

### 'HÄNDE HOCH!'

On the sunny afternoon of 14 May, French General Billotte asked the RAF to destroy the pontoon bridges that German engineers had thrown across the Meuse near Sedan. The remaining Battles of 12 Squadron at Amifontaine were detailed for the task, two from B Flight were to attack a bridge south of Sedan and the three from A Flight were to bomb the bridge to the west.

When gunner AC2 Len 'Lofty' Clarke climbed into his rear cockpit gun position he had few illusions about the desperate nature of the mission: 12 Squadron losses two days earlier when four out of five aircraft had been lost in a similar attack left little hope of success. Clarke knew that despite their airy banter, observer Maurice Smalley and pilot Reg Winkler shared similar forebodings.

The two B Flight aircraft were intercepted by Bf109s and efficiently destroyed. It was agonising for the other crews to see the Battles' flaming paths to earth, leaving only hanging smoke trails. As the three A Flight Battles sped toward Sedan the fighters turned away. Clarke could see below the familiar harrowing scenes of war, the bombed trains, burning houses and the unending stream of refugees.

Heavy anti-aircraft fire buffeted the Battles. Len Clarke despaired as one of the accompanying planes dived towards the ground trailing smoke. Just two remained. As Clarke twisted to look in all directions a shell passed through the starboard wing of his aircraft and exploded above with a crump like a boxer's punch to the head.

17

Following the leader, Winkler threw the Battle down in a steep dive. As they pulled out of the dive, dust and smoke straddled the Meuse and houses blazed by the old bridge. As he swung his machine gun round in the heavy anti-aircraft fire, Clarke saw that pieces were falling from the leading Battle as it dived. Seconds later a direct hit heaved his aircraft upwards. Smoke, oil, glycol and flames swept around Winkler forcing him to stand to keep control. It was useless, Winkler shouted, 'Bale out!'. Len Clarke jumped first from the storm of noise and fire. Looking back he saw the smoke trail left by the blazing plane and nearby, close to the ground, two billowing parachutes.

Clarke crumpled on to a towpath, his canopy collapsing behind him. Staggering to his feet, he was collecting his wits and thanking providence for keeping him out of the canal when a dozen Bf109s roared past above, coolly demonstrating their complete mastery of the air. It was 16.00hrs, half an hour since the remnants of 12 Squadron, the 'Dirty Dozen', had left their base. Now all were lost.

*'Hände Hoch!'* Len Clarke needed no translation, the upward jerking muzzles of the sub-machine guns carried by two *Wehrmacht* soldiers conveyed their meaning explicitly. Searched and ordered into the sidecar of a motorcycle combination, Clarke was driven down a tree-lined road, there he saw row upon row of hidden tanks, sheltering beneath the trees, visibly primed and ready for battle. At a café, German infantrymen were surprisingly sympathetic. Clarke was the first British airman they had encountered and they were prepared to be magnanimous, plying him with fruit, cigarettes and coffee whilst dressing a cut on the back of his head. Laughingly they told him that he would not be a prisoner for long, within weeks the Germans would invade England and the war would be over. They were supremely confident.

Escorted by a young *Unteroffizier*, Clarke walked to the main street of a village. At the roadside a French soldier lay dying in the arms of another who cradled the wounded man's head in his lap and placed a lighted cigarette to his lips. A German medical orderly attended the Frenchman's massive injuries. Cattle and a fully harnessed horse ran up and down aimlessly. Amid all the chaos the one steady and orderly sight was German infantry moving through the street. Len Clarke had parachuted into the front line.

Shells burst around them when Clarke and his escort reached the middle of the village. The characteristic whistling scream and din of explosions added to the turmoil but the German troops calmly dropped into the ditches at the side of the road in orderly ranks. Clarke and the

*Unteroffizier* sheltered in a house doorway as the building opposite was deafeningly demolished by a direct hit. A splinter skidded across the road and bounced off Clarke's flying boot. He picked up the piece of hot metal and slipped it into the pocket of his Sidcot suit.

As the shelling increased and the explosions drew closer the pair scrambled to join the troops in the ditches. Clarke lay huddled in a ditch beside a German soldier who asked in faultless English, 'Haven't you got a helmet?'. When Clarke said he had not the German shouted, 'Get underneath me'. He moved over, making room for Clarke to be sheltered. Five minutes later when the shelling had stopped and the troops had climbed out of the ditches, Clarke thanked the German who answered, a little ruefully: 'It was nothing, you are a lucky one and will survive the war, but for me and my comrades no-one knows what the future holds. I wish you good luck and a safe return to your home.' The German turned away to carry on with his war.

Clarke's waking hours had been crammed with incident. When, in the early hours of the next morning, he was thrust into a barn holding French prisoners, Clarke plumped on to the straw, his head swimming with exhaustion. All his multitude of aches, pains, cuts and bruises forgotten, he lay back in the straw and slept. It had been a long day.

The RAF had suffered its heaviest losses for an operation of comparable size. Two pontoon bridges had been destroyed and two damaged but this had a minimal effect on the German advance. Of the 71 bombers sent to demolish the bridges, 40 had been shot down. Seventeen crew members had made their way back from enemy held territory and 103 had become prisoners-of-war or were dead.

By the end of May the defeat of France was certain and Britain was soon to come under severe air attack. The Air Staff decided it must conserve the crews and aircraft remaining and concentrate on night bombing.

### LOOKING DOWN THE BARREL

Shot down in May while bombing a bridge at Dinant, Wellington wireless operator Stan Brooks found the vaunted chivalrous behaviour of captor to captive showing cracks. Parachuting from his blazing plane into the waiting arms of the *Wehrmacht* he was seated on the pillion of a motorcycle combination with an armed guard in the sidecar and driven on a hair-raising journey. The combination careered bumpily across fields and tracks and hurtled through farm yards, scattering chickens and feathers in all directions.

19

The motorcycle combination screeched to a halt at a flight of steps in front of a chateau. With a sub-machine gun muzzle prodding his back Brooks was hustled past armed guards at the entrance and into a side room where a *Hauptmann* roughly demanded information. The *Hauptmann*'s temper increased with Brooks' stonewall reply of name, rank and number until choleric with rage he snatched open a desk drawer, whipped out a pistol, pressed it hard against Brooks' chest and threatened to shoot. Just as his finger was tightening on the trigger the door was flung open and two *Luftwaffe* officers burst in loudly demanding that the gun be turned away. The *Hauptmann* slowly relented and lowered the pistol. Stan Brooks took a deep breath as he was led away thanking Heaven for the intervention of the *Luftwaffe*.

## DULAG, BARTH AND GLEMNITZ

During the spring of 1940 the steadily increasing number of RAF prisoners were being brought together at Dulag Luft, Oberursel, near Frankfurt-am-Main. Here prisoners were to encounter the bogus Red Cross form and its unanswerable questions concerning squadrons, airfields, aircraft equipment and commanders. Some were also presented with a card to be filled in with details of previous employment and qualifications. The purpose was to assess the kind of work to which a prisoner might be directed by Germany when they had won the war. Many occupations entered on the cards would be of little use in reconstruction. For example, there were a surprising number of 'lion tamers'. Another prisoner listed an occupation for which there was likely to be a limited call: he claimed that he was a 'planer and re-shaper of square heads'.

The gathering together of prisoners was a slow process. Once the interrogation was completed they, apart from those forming a kind of semi-permanent staff, were sent to camps such as those at Schubin and Lamsdorf, but from July 1940 captured aircrew began to be assembled in one permanent camp administered by the *Luftwaffe*, Stalag Luft 1 Barth, near Pomerania's Baltic shore. Some of the earliest prisoners to arrive there were transferred from Stalag 8B Lamsdorf.

Around Barth the landscape was dreary and flat but the nearby coastline was popular with Germans for yachting. The tips of sails could just be seen from one point in the camp. To the south-east, rising high above the town roofs, was the steeple of the Marienkirche, carrying at night a red light as a warning to aircraft. On the other side of the camp was a brick-built training school for *Luftwaffe* anti-aircraft recruits which afforded some amusement for the prisoners as they watched the trainees

20

throwing themselves in the mud, jumping up and dashing forward only to be ordered down flat into the mud again and again.

By Christmas 1940 there were three single-storey huts in the NCOs' compound in which lived between 2–300 prisoners. In that confined space they soon came to know each other well. A single-strand barbed wire fence with a small gate, usually open, separated the huts from the rest of the compound which contained the cookhouse, the *Appell* or parade ground, and the main gate to the *Vorlager*.

The *Vorlager* at Stalag Luft 1 contained the German Headquarters or *Kommandantur*, various administrative huts and the *Arrestlok* or 'Cooler'. Prisoners in their compound would frequently shout encouragement to a man in 'solitary' and sometimes a face would appear at the high bars as an inmate leapt up, hung on the bars and shouted in reply. The guards would menacingly unsling their rifles while the Kriegies innocently sauntered away. Communication would often be established with a prisoner in the *Arrestlok* by shouting and simultaneously pretending to be barracking players in a football game on the *Appell* ground. Few of the ordinary guards understood English and even had they been interpreters they would probably have found the mixture of RAF slang and obscenities quite beyond their understanding.

But here at Barth the Kriegies were to meet one German who had to be constantly watched. The casual air and friendliness of chief 'ferret', *Oberfeldwebel* Glemnitz, was such that one could be misled into believing that this highly professional soldier was capable of relaxing on duty. Glemnitz had travelled the world, fought as an infantryman in the Great War and later became a pilot, a ship and plough company machinist, and a competent linguist. Very soon every Kriegie realised that Glemnitz was always 'on duty'; as were his team of ferrets. The complete senior NCO, Glemnitz was not an unkindly man and his ready sense of humour was well understood by the Kriegies. He was respected and feared because his excellent knowledge of colloquial English made him a dangerous adversary. If there was one German who could fathom the Britisher's mind and discover any subterranean or other questionable activity it was the prying, probing, listening Hermann Glemnitz, who was to stay with them at one camp or another until the end of the war.

### TAKING HIS TIME

News of the promotion in May of lower aircrew ranks to sergeant reached the prisoners from new arrivals but, as far as the Germans were concerned, it was unofficial and unconfirmed. The 'Erks' had to continue working. Among them was LAC Joe 'Nobby' Clark who had been on operations with 37 Squadron, RAF Feltwell, since the outbreak of war. By chance he had missed becoming a statistic in the December daylight raids but by late March 1940 his luck had run out. On yet another 'Nickel' and recce flight with a new crew, his was the next 37 Squadron aircraft to go missing. The Wellington, hit by flak, crash-landed in Germany. Clark suffered minor injuries and concussion and was sent first to Dulag Luft and then to Limburg. As yet unused to German arrogance he argued with a guard who raised his rifle as if to hit him with the butt. Clark ducked, seeing as he did so that the German had a gold watch in an open fob pocket. In the ensuing scuffle, Clark, using two fingers, removed the watch with the skill of an expert pickpocket. Clark was transferred to Barth.

Upon arrival he had been put to work on the local railway where the chance of obtaining extra food was remote. The thought of hard work outdoors on minimum rations during the winter ahead was an unattractive prospect. Conditions were obviously better among the officers. Clark, carefully concealing the gold watch he had 'lifted' from the German's fob, volunteered to be an orderly and moved into the officers' compound where he became orderly to Flight Lieutenant Harry Burton.

During a morning search, Joe Clark was lost in admiration as Squadron Leader Roger Bushell went 'hammer and tongs' for a guard who had pushed him. In perfect *Hochdeutsch*, Bushell 'tore a strip' from the German, he cursed and ranted, leaving the German shaken. Bushell, Joe Clark decided, was a very tough man indeed, whose mercurial moods changed with staggering rapidity. As he finished berating the German, Bushell calmly walked over to Clark, sat down beside him and began chatting. Clark later told a friend, 'If you could have seen that guard's red face you'd have reckoned he was in two minds whether or not to pack up and go home'.

Later when a request was sent round the camp for anyone with gold jewellery to voluntarily give it up for bribing the guards for radio equipment, Bushell sent for Clark and said:

'I know you have got a gold watch, where did you get it?' Handing over the watch for Bushell to see, Clark replied with a straight face:

'It was a present from a rich uncle.'

'Clarkie, you are a lying bastard,' replied Bushell, 'this is a German watch – but if you will give it up now I will get in touch after the war and buy you any watch you would like to mention.'

'You have it sir,' said Clark resignedly, 'I might get shot tomorrow or lose it in a search.'

August 1940 saw the first serious struggle in the Battle of Britain. *Adlertag* or Eagle Day, 13 August, was when the *Luftwaffe* launched its huge air offensive. Throughout that month the *Luftwaffe* threw aircraft against the Spitfires and Hurricanes of Fighter Command and suffered enormous losses but the RAF was fighting a battle of desperation. Airfields were being very severely damaged, many temporarily put out of action. When a fighter-harassed *Luftwaffe* pilot jettisoned his bomb-load on London the course of the air war changed. The RAF bombed Berlin in retaliation and Hitler ordered the immediate cessation of the bombing of Britain's fighter airfields and instead demanded the bombing of London. On Saturday afternoon, 7 September, the *Luftwaffe* made its first big fire attack on London, the huge conflagration easily visible to a Wellington crew as they took off from Marham in Norfolk. Watching the burning East End from the Air Ministry roof Air Marshal Sir Arthur Harris remarked to his chief, Air Chief Marshal Sir Charles Portal, 'Well, they are sowing the wind'. Portal agreed.

## MAN OF CONFIDENCE
'He was a man, take him for all in all,
I shall not look upon his like again.' — *Shakespeare*

Despite the danger of invasion, the urgent necessity to destroy German landing craft in the Channel ports, and the now almost continuous air attacks on England, it was decided that some bomber aircraft must be used to attack German targets, in particular, Berlin. Hitting back was all important. A Whitley bomber flying home from a Berlin raid on 10 September was hit by flak and badly damaged. The pilot, 26-year-old Sergeant James Deans, fought tenaciously to keep the crippled aircraft flying but the Whitley crash-landed near the Dutch–German border and soon Deans joined those behind the wire of Stalag Luft 1.

Deans' exceptional qualities were quickly recognised by the airmen prisoners. NCOs of higher rank in the camp were not always suitable for the job of Camp Leader, or, like Flight Sergeant Graham 'Nobby' Hall, because he had been branded a persistent escaper and troublemaker by the Germans, was not really in contention. Deans had an air of calm authority, a wide knowledge of colloquial German and, above all, the men believed him capable and that he would do his utmost on their behalf. By overwhelmingly popular consent the NCOs and airmen at Barth made Deans their *Vertrauensmann*, their 'Man of Confidence' or leader. A cultured Glaswegian, Deans was the right man in the right place at the right time. Aptly described as 'nuggety' by fellow prisoner Calton Younger, Deans was respected and not a little feared by the Germans running the camp. They knew they needed his natural control of their recalcitrant captives but found it difficult to understand the democratic process that could put one of junior rank in command. It just could not happen in the German forces. Deans had the goodwill and faith of the men under his voluntary command. Provided he thought it right and proper to do so, the aircrews, who were not usually amenable to discipline, would do as he asked. He was a buffer between them and the German authorities and would brook no nonsense from either.

Deans became a leader of RAF prisoners in situations fraught with danger. Throughout their captivity 'Dixie' Deans was their champion and guide. He made them feel safe.

## FOUR-POSTER TO DOUBLE BUNK

Major-General Josef Kammhuber was determined to make his night-fighter defence line a near impenetrable barrier for RAF bomber crews. Nightfighting was in its infancy; the only method known was the use of 'Big Ear' audio detectors and 'illuminated nightfighting' when fighters waited for searchlights to highlight the bombers against the darkness of the sky. Kammhuber knew that by using this First World War method, successes were few. He worked to establish a system based on the latest techniques.

The *Himmelbett* or 'Four-Poster Bed' system divided the sky into approximately 20-mile wide boxes in which a nightfighter patrolled alone; all other aircraft were prohibited from entering the area. To control each box Kammhuber installed one *Freya* (early warning) and two *Würzburg* (directional) radars. The *Freya* directed a *Würzburg* on to the target bomber whilst the other *Würzburg* tracked the nightfighter. The *Himmelbett* ground controller brought the fighter pilot into visual range by radioing 'intercept vectors'. As the controller positioned the fighter outside but near the searchlight belt, there was a second chance of intercepting the bomber with the 'lit-up' method.

A master searchlight, radar-controlled, was introduced and later recognised by bomber crews as the light with the blue-tinted beam. This searchlight would point vertically upwards, apparently immobile, then with a sudden swing it would fasten on to the bomber. Despite desperate weaving by the bomber pilot the master light would invariably hold the bomber until all other searchlights were switched over and the aircraft became 'coned', transfixed as securely as a butterfly with a pin. By late September 1940 Kammhuber was ready to test his 'Line'.

The moonless but starlit night of 30 September was warm and still from the Indian summer that Britain was enjoying. It was as if nature was trying to compensate for the awful events that had been happening since the spring. RAF Marham, Norfolk lay tranquil and lethargic until the huge roar of the Pegasus engines of Wellington Q-Queenie tore the quiet air apart like grounded thunder. Then slowly taxying to the far end of the field Queenie turned and faced down the flarepath like a sprinter toeing the start line.

Her lumbering roll belied the enormous power of the now screaming engines, but gradually she picked up speed. The heavy fuel and bomb-load made her progress slow and flying speed was only reached near the boundary hedge and trees. Watchers on the tarmac at Marham saw Queenie disappear as she rolled down the far side of Marham's hump and then re-appear with her undercarriage retracting as she banked slowly to the east.

Pilot Officer D. Maclean, known only as 'Mac', corrected the Wellington's course at navigator Sergeant Gerry Tipping's instructions, and soon they were heading in an almost straight line towards the vast synthetic oil manufacturing plant *Leunawerke* near Leipzig. With no fuel to spare there was little chance of deviation on such a long flight.

Four of the crew, front gunner Sergeant John 'Jock' Hamilton, second pilot Sergeant Stan 'Bill' Williams, wireless operator Sergeant Vic Gammon and navigator Sergeant Gerry Tipping had carried out 20 operations together but Maclean was fairly new to the crew as captain. Rear gunner Pilot Officer W. Mathieson was on his first trip over hostile lands. Mathieson had been posted to 38 Squadron as Armament Officer and was a firm believer that he would be in no position to instruct others what to do on operations unless he had personal experience. When a vacancy as rear-gunner occurred Mathieson quickly took the chance to fly on this trip.

The crew were not happy about the long haul to Leuna, especially as their instructions were to find the pumping house near the middle of several square miles of the huge petro-chemical complex. They were to destroy the pumping house, so bringing the whole works to a standstill. Had the Intelligence Officer ever flown at night, they wondered? It was going to be hard enough to find Leuna itself at near the 'point of no return', without 'stooging' around looking for a small building among hundreds.

As they drew near the coast of Holland the tension increased although only occasional light flak curled up prettily some distance away and the odd searchlight aimlessly fingered its way across the sky. It was not until approaching the Dutch/German border that the crew saw ahead, some 10 miles away, a massed, stationary curtain of searchlight beams which seemed to stretch right across the eastern horizon. Steadily the

Wellington flew on towards the searchlights. Sergeant Gammon had wondered why no diversion had been attempted but now that they were so close there seemed little alternative but to fly onwards. Gammon's duties on the radio set meant that he had taken little part in the intercom conversation.

The suddenness of being the focus of blinding light and of the aircraft taking violent evasive action made Gammon quickly plug into the intercom system. The Wellington was thoroughly and dazzlingly coned. He heard Mathieson shout, 'He's coming in again,' and then he screamed, 'I've been hit – I've been hit!'

Through the side windows Gammon could see that wing fuel tanks on both sides were blazing and tracer from the nightfighter was still flashing past. The Wellington had not long to last. Bullets clanged against the armour plating near his head as Gammon heard Mac, with firm calmness as if on a practice, order, 'Abandon aircraft – abandon aircraft'.

Reaching for his parachute and ramming it on his harness dogclips, Gammon saw that Williams and Tipping were already leaving, that Hamilton had climbed out of his front turret and was kneeling over the open bottom hatch about to dive out head first. Gammon quickly glanced up at Mac just as Hamilton disappeared. Mac, his face white and set was struggling to hold up the blazing aircraft to enable the crew to escape. At that moment a tremendous blow threw Gammon backwards and the escape hatch, which had been below, was now above his eye level. Guessing that the starboard wing had been blown off, Gammon threw himself up and forward, grasped the edge of the hatch and dragged himself over.

As he fell into the quiet, cool, night air he was thankful he had missed the thrashing port airscrew. The aircraft was on its side and diving rapidly, the prop must have been close. Ineffectual pulling of the cloth carrying handle of the parachute pack forced Gammon to think coolly and feel for the cold steel of the 'D' ring. The parachute opened but the smooth descent was immediately and violently disrupted by the blast of the huge orange-coloured ground explosion of the crashing aircraft and its detonating bomb-load. The blast swung Gammon from side to side and around like a madly gyrating pendulum. Attempting to slow the swings by pulling the opposite shroud lines resulted in the parachute canopy 'candling'. The descent became a headlong rush towards earth. The welcome sound of the canopy snapping open like a whiplash made Gammon decide to leave well alone and continue with his slower, if swinging, descent.

The ground rushed towards him and Gammon fell heavily against a small fence which pumped the air from his lungs. He knew his furious gasping was creating noise that could attract attention, but he did not care – he had to breathe. Looking up through a mist of panting, Vic Gammon saw two parachutes held in the searchlight beams. 'So I've beaten some of them down,' he thought. He had been the last out of the aircraft and the first on the ground but Maclean and Mathieson, he was sure, would have gone down with the plane.

It was open country and a still night. In the distance he could hear cheering and dogs barking. The searchlight crews were celebrating and other parties were clearly searching for downed airmen. It was 10 minutes before Gammon could summon enough breath to stand and push his parachute into a ditch. Locating the Pole Star he set off in a vaguely westerly direction knowing only that he was somewhere in North West Germany, the enemy's homeland. There was little likelihood of help.

As he crept away he heard the engine throb of another aircraft and prayed that it would not fall into the same searchlight and fighter trap. Inevitably the searchlights locked on to a Wellington and were quickly followed by the glowing trace and sound of cannon shells from the invisible fighter outside the cone of searchlight beams. That soon-to-become-familiar whining scream of a stricken aircraft came from the Wellington as it dived flaming to the ground. One parachute appeared this time, held steadily in the beams until almost to the ground. The Kammhuber Line had claimed a second victim.

Walking along a dark, hedgeless country lane Gammon saw swinging lanterns and torchlights, heard voices and barking dogs. A search party was just ahead. He turned quickly and started to run into a field but the dogs had sensed him. When he saw and heard another search party coming from the opposite direction he knew that it was time to give-up. Cries of 'Halt!' and 'Hände Hoch!' and the muzzle of a shotgun in the small of his back were decisive. There was some argument among the searchers about whose prisoner he was, but finally the combined parties with the airman in the centre marched triumphantly to the hall of a village school. Despite it being the early hours of the morning it seemed that the population of the village, young and old, had risen from their beds and gathered in the hall to stare at and chatter excitedly about this apparition from the sky in a strange uniform.

Vic Gammon's reception by the German people had been surprisingly gentle and generally one of curiosity and concern for his well-being. 'Are you wounded?' asked the village schoolmaster in French. 'Are you hungry, would you like some whisky?' Gammon accepted the proffered black bread and garlic sausage sandwich and the glass of neat, colourless methylated spirits, not knowing when or where he would eat or drink again.

27

The excited chatter ceased abruptly as a tall, monocled *Luftwaffe* officer strode into the hall. As with one movement the arms of the assembled villagers shot out at a forty-five degree angle and, as with one voice, the cry of *'Heil Hitler!'* reverberated around the walls. Gammon thought the situation, although of deadly seriousness, had a slightly ludicrous overtone of comic opera.

Seated with an armed guard on either side in the back of a car, Gammon gripped the remains of his carefully wrapped garlic sausage, while driven to the headquarters of the nightfighter group. Again his reception was a kind of patronising gallantry.

'Would you like to meet the man who shot you down?" he was asked, and a white jacketed orderly was sent for *Oberleutnant* Werner Streib. Streib asked about the rest of the crew and when told that the captain was believed to have gone down with the plane, he commented with a shrug of regret:

'I am sorry – *c'est la guerre.*'

'Would you like a cup of coffee?' asked another young *Luftwaffe* officer. 'This is real coffee,' he emphasised, 'we know you cannot get this in England so enjoy it.'

Sergeant Gammon smiled for the first time since he had been shot down. Drinking the coffee gratefully he studied the young German airman. He had absorbed Göbbels' propaganda.

The survivors of the crew of Q-Queenie had been rounded up and assembled in a guardroom cell at Venlo *Luftwaffe* base. The parachute Gammon had seen falling from the second aircraft was that of Sergeant Ron Mogg, navigator and only survivor of his 115 Squadron Wellington. Mogg was known to all the 38 Squadron men when he joined them in the cell – 115 Squadron was also based at Marham. The men from Mogg's crew had not left the burning aircraft. The five airmen sitting in the straw in the guardroom cell were the survivors of 12 or perhaps 18 men. Streib claimed a third Wellington that night but there was no news of more captives.

# PART 2

# 1941

### THE LONELY TOMB

The 10th of February 1941 was cold yet clear. A bright moon with some cloud cover was forecast. Two hundred and twenty of Bomber Command's heavies were to attack Hanover. One of these aircraft took off from RAF Alconbury in Cambridgeshire, a Wellington piloted by Dubliner Sergeant Bill Garrioch and crewed by NCOs. The outward leg had been comparatively uneventful but ...

Banking the Wellington on to a course for Alconbury, Bill Garrioch was reasonably pleased with the operation. It had been a cold wintry trip but now they were on their way home, leaving the Hanover target area blazing. Opposition had been comparatively slight. Garrioch and his crew were experienced and for such a target the flak had been almost too light for comfort. Each man knew the build-up of brilliantly moonlit white cumulus beneath the Wellington made it a highly visible nightfighter target. Garrioch ordered the crew to keep a sharp lookout. The flight against a strong headwind continued for some minutes, the silence on the intercom indicating the intensity of each man's search of the surrounding sky and the bright, white desert of cloud below.

As the Wellington passed over the east coast of the Zuider Zee, the intercom's silence was shattered by a shout from rear gunner Sergeant 'Jock' Hall, 'Fighter below and behind!'. Wrenching the Wellington into a tight steep turn to starboard to face the attacker, Garrioch found himself momentarily staring at a Messerschmitt Bf110. Forcing the Wellington back into a violent port turn he heard 'Jock' Hall's rear turret guns firing a long burst, but still the Messerschmitt came on and shells and bullets struck home in the port engine and behind in the fuselage. Garrioch lowered the flaps and the Messerschmitt overshot but within seconds it was back. Shells were striking home again and navigator Bob Beioley was calling out the flyer's most feared words, 'We are on fire!'.

The anguished calls for help from 'Taffy' Reardon in the front turret and 'Jock' Hall in the rear, both of whom had been hit, had to be ignored as cannon shells exploded among George Hedge's radio equipment and slammed against the armour plating. Amid the blinding smoke that filled the fuselage Garrioch could just see second pilot Jordan struggling to open the front turret doors, trying to release Reardon. Garrioch

29

raised the flaps again and ordered the crew to prepare to bale out but the fighter pilot was still not prepared to let them go; he was coming in for the kill. Lowering the flaps again Garrioch throttled back and side slipped almost into a stall. Cannon shells, a stream of machine gun tracer and the Messerschmitt passed above. Garrioch called to Reardon to shoot the fighter down as it passed before him but there was no answer from the front turret. Reardon's quiet moans of 'Get me out' had died away.

Jordan had fought unsuccessfully to open the turret doors and prepared to follow the Captain's orders and jump through the nose hatch when Garrioch signalled him to stay. Garrioch had decided to crash-land the Wellington. Reardon was trapped in the front turret and Hedge, Beioley and Hall were behind in the smoke-filled fuselage. Garrioch did not know if they were alive but it was certain they would stand no chance if he abandoned the aircraft. Also, unless they got out very quickly they would all be roasted.

The Wellington was now diving fast to port with the port engine and inner wing burning furiously. Garrioch cut off the fuel, put the starboard engine on full throttle and tried to level off but the elevators were sluggish and the frozen expanse of the Zuider Zee still hurtled up towards them.

Thumping down on her belly the Wellington careered erratically across the ice, spraying a wave of slush. Garrioch could only grip the control column grimly and wait for the mad rush to end. As the Wellington slowed and stopped it broke through the thin ice surface and began to sink. Ice and water poured through the bottom hatch as Garrioch wrenched open the top cockpit hatch and pulled himself through to the roof. He slid down the fuselage on to the thin, brittle ice, thankful that there had not been the explosion he had feared. Followed quickly by George Hedge, the two took the rear gunner 'Jock' Hall from Beioley and Jordan as he was lowered down the fuselage side. Hall was badly hurt and burned.

Leaving Hall on the ice, the four crunched and crashed their way across the crumbling surface to the front turret. It looked undamaged but the aircraft was tilted down slightly at the front and already sinking. Garrioch could see 'Taffy' Reardon inside, quite still, unconscious or dead. In desperation the crew tried to smash the perspex cover with their bare fists. For one moment Garrioch thought he saw Reardon's arm move. The four men fought against the unyielding perspex, they were desperate to save their helpless comrade whom they could see so clearly but could not reach. Now up to their knees in water, they struggled to force open the turret.

It was hopeless, despite their herculean efforts and bloodied hands the four were forced to watch with horror and stunned anguish as the water quenched the flames of the still burning nose end of the aircraft and the turret sank beneath the ice of the Zuider Zee. The Wellington's front turret was to be 'Taffy' Reardon's lonely tomb.

Looking back Garrioch could see that the still burning centre and rear of the Wellington was melting the thin ice. Ammunition was spraying noisily and there was the danger of the plane exploding and killing them all or it would sink beneath the ice taking the survivors with it. Quickly the airmen dragged wounded 'Jock' Hall away, constantly lifting each other out of the water as they sank through the black patches where the ice was perilously thin.

When Garrioch calculated that they were a safe distance from the crackling wreck he stopped to look more closely at 'Jock's' wounds. They were bad. 'Jock's' left foot seemed to be almost severed, bullet holes had seared his burned flying clothing and his face and hair were burned where he had torn off his helmet. A parachute harness was cut to improvise a tourniquet to staunch the blood and 'Jock's' wounded leg was strapped to the good one. He was weak but conscious. Garrioch tore his scorched scarf from his throat and wrapped it around 'Jock's' head to help him retain some warmth. It was impossible for 'Jock' to walk so the airmen, using more harness as a trace, dragged him along on his back.

Pausing to take stock, Garrioch saw that it was 20 minutes to midnight and almost an hour since they had crashed on to the ice. There was no doubt that the ice had saved them, such a crash on to solid land or into the sea would undoubtedly have wiped out the entire crew. Even as he turned to look back at the Wellington a series of explosions wracked the plane and it sank, bubbling and hissing, beneath the surface of the Zuider Zee, leaving a cloud of smoke hovering over the spot. Garrioch felt strangely reluctant to leave Taffy. Now, as he looked around at the unending sea of ice, Garrioch understood how Arctic wastes must have appeared to lonely explorers. The sound of RAF planes returning home, invisible in the darkness above, increased the feeling of the utter hopelessness and desperation of their plight. Then, there in the far, dark distance, the four airmen saw a small, winking white light. That tiny beacon was their only hope. With a few words of encouragement to 'Jock' they set off, three dragging him and another gingerly treading and testing the ice ahead.

The freezing wind and spindrift ripped about them as they staggered on soaked to the waist, stopping only for brief rests of five minutes in every hour, always sitting in a sheltering circle around 'Jock' and loosening the tourniquet around his leg. Gradually as wan daylight spread across the ice they saw that seagulls were diving to pick small pieces of flesh that had dropped from 'Jock's' shattered foot.

Garrioch looked more closely at the foot and leg. He had been forced to give up loosening the tourniquet for fear of 'Jock' dying from loss of blood but his leg was turning a strange colour. It looked gangrenous. 'Jock' moaned a lot, saying that he wanted to sleep, that they should leave him and try to get help – but the crew knew that was the way of certain death. It was the fear of 'Jock' dying and of them all falling through the melting ice that spurred them on towards the distant light.

With daylight the winking light had disappeared but Garrioch saw a slight rise in the horizon and they made for that. All were desperate to be found before 'Jock', who was now delirious, should die. Relief swept over them when figures were seen running along a shore, they knew they had been seen. Garrioch and Bob Beioley, a non-swimmer, decided to wade or swim ashore. Despite their conditions all the men checked their pockets to make sure that nothing could connect them with 15 Squadron or Cambridgeshire.

As they neared the shore the ice gave way. Garrioch and Beioley sank up to their waists in the freezing water. Two German soldiers shouted and waded out to help. Others appeared with a small boat to bring in Bill Jordan, George Hedge and the wounded 'Jock' Hall.

At a flak unit they were given a drink of Schnapps as a warmer whilst 'Jock', because of the seriousness of his injuries, was given as much as he wished. Later at the Queen Wilhelmina Hospital in Amsterdam 'Jock's' leg was amputated beneath the knee, the doctor assuring the crew that he would be fine. They were sincerely grateful, it was their reward for the agonising struggle to bring 'Jock' in.

As he sat in a cell in Amsterdam jail, Garrioch saw that his wristwatch, though wet, was still working. He wondered how his parents in Dublin would react to the 'Missing' telegram – they had been expecting him home for a few days' leave. Now, 26 hours after taking off from Alconbury, one of his crew was dead, another seriously hurt and the remainder faced with imprisonment. He grieved for 'Taffy' and hated leaving him dead and alone in that alien place. But he was proud of his surviving crew. They had not lost their heads for a second, they had saved 'Jock' and each other in appalling circumstances by sheer courage. Despite suffering the misfortunes of war Garrioch felt that he was a lucky man.

Later, lying in one of Dulag's cell-like rooms, Garrioch went over in his mind all that had happened since they had flown from England: he remembered with pain, 'Taffy' dead in his turret beneath the Zuider Zee; he wondered how 'Jock' would now face life with his leg amputated; and how would they all face life as prisoners-of-war? He thought back to the hectic journey through Amsterdam to the station and how the German van driver had deliberately knocked down two cyclists. Of how the guards pushed the Dutch people away with rifle butts and of how those same gallant people had pushed forward to slap the prisoners on the back, shouted 'Good Luck' and had tried to pass sweets to them. When the prisoners were on the train the Dutch had crowded around the window, giving the thumbs-up. Then there was the platform trolley vendor who tried to pass the prisoners chocolate, was hit by a guard who then knocked the trolley over spilling the contents to the concrete. The Nazi jackboot stamped heavily in Holland but the people were far from subdued, shortly afterwards, rioting in Holland forced the occupying Germans to declare Martial Law.

When *Leutnant* Heinrich Eberhardt brought the fake Red Cross form Garrioch was amazed at the naiveté of the approach. The form was now well known in England and Eberhardt, for all his smooth English, gained nothing more than name, rank and number. Neither did the suave and persuasive Rumpel.

That evening Bill Garrioch and his crew were taken down to the main camp. The double rows of frosted barbed wire glistened beneath the glaring boundary lights as they were counted and passed through the main gate. They were instantly in a small, confined world of RAF men who welcomed them as friends anxious to know the 'gen' from home.

### 'GEBEN SIE MIR EIN DOPPELBETT'
On 8 May, Flying Officer Ted Chapman eased his 64ft Scott-Paine Air/Sea Rescue launch out of Dover's East Dock while brooding on his cancelled embarkation leave. He had been due to open a new base in Gibraltar as a squadron leader; instead he was going to sea in someone else's boat to try to rescue a Messerschmitt pilot downed off Boulogne. Gibraltar, he mused, would have been pleasant in the spring. The high-speed launch roared off at nearly 45kts, the thrust of its 1,500hp engine throwing up a huge bow wave.

Later, calling off the search Chapman observed dryly, 'We are nearly in Boulogne High Street'. At that moment seven Messerschmitt Bf109s flew near, peeled off and made three attacks on the launch. Within seconds the wooden craft was blazing from stem to stern, a cannon shell smashed into the Cox's right shoulder, an engineer was killed and the wireless operator shot through the lung. The others were all badly wounded in the legs, only Chapman, the captain, and the second wireless operator were unharmed. In the midst of the havoc Chapman saw that the 109s were turning for another attack. He abandoned ship but his dinghy was like a colander and down to the gunnels in the water. A German boat coming close alongside prevented another Messerschmitt attack. The German crew swung their boat round to make a lee but capsized the dinghy in doing so. Chapman saw the unconscious and badly wounded members of his crew into the German boat and then, exhausted and almost drowned, he was dragged on board.

On shore the fighter leader and a one-armed Prussian liaison officer asked Chapman to join them in a 'victory celebration' in the Officers' Mess. They were angry when he refused and quite oblivious to his feelings or the loss of some of his crew.

In the Hotel Bristol, Boulogne, and at the *Gestapo* headquarters at St Omer, Chapman was closely questioned about the high-speed launch being some kind of secret weapon. The Germans were particularly concerned about the launch's bright yellow deck and the large roundel on the foc'sle. Chapman reckoned the Germans believed it concealed some devilish English stratagem.

Chapman studied the surrounding motley collection of young German liaison officers. Every kind of uniform seemed represented. Looking at a photograph of Chapman's blonde daughter one exclaimed, 'Ach, she is a true Aryan and will go to our stud farm and you,' indicating Chapman, 'you are the squire class and will be castrated.'

'Who told you all that guff?' asked Chapman with disgust.

'Adolf Hitler,' the herd screamed as one and went into a spasm of *'Heil Hitlers'*. Had it not been such a desperate and dangerous situation it would have been hilarious, but Chapman found their brainwashed, infantile beliefs frightening and nauseating.

The officer in charge of the rescue boats was meanwhile arguing vehemently with the Prussian one-armed liaison officer. He was angry and although Chapman could not understand a word it was obvious they were talking about him. Suddenly the Prussian turned to Chapman and asked, 'You understand German?'. Then menacingly he leaned over Chapman and hissed, 'What German do you know?'

Chapman thought quickly and remembered a phrase he had learned for a planned pre-war visit to Germany with his wife.

*'Geben Sie mir ein Doppelbett,'* he said quietly, with aplomb.

There was a momentary silence before the Prussian exploded with glaring fury, snatching up his hat he stormed from the room, slamming the door behind him. There was another silence before the young German officers around Chapman burst into near hysterical laughter, such behaviour towards a major was unheard of and they thoroughly enjoyed his discomfiture. So too did the officer in charge of the rescue boats. Dismissing the youths he telephoned his friends, meanwhile slapping his thigh and repeating to himself with relish, *'Geben Sie mir ein Doppelbett!'*. He ordered the removal of the *ersatz* and told the waiter to bring real coffee, white bread, butter, cream and strawberry jam.

Expressing concern about Chapman's wounded crew and hearing that they had been separated, the officer ordered that they all be put together in one ward. Satisfied that he was behaving in a civilised manner the officer turned to the food and switched on the radio to listen to the BBC news. But first Victor Sylvester and his Orchestra were playing 'Night and Day'. Chapman wondered when he would hear that again.

## POLES APART

It was inevitable that the influx of angry men from countries occupied by Germany should provide the British armed services, in particular the RAF, with a flood of volunteers anxious to get at German throats. In the early months of 1941 there were four Polish squadrons in Bomber Command manned by men willing to risk all to drive the enemy from their homeland. One of the first all-Polish crews to be shot down and taken prisoner was that of a Wellington 1c attacked over Holland by a Messerschmitt Bf110. The rear gunner and observer were killed in the cannon and machine gun attack and the remaining four members of the crew parachuted from the blazing plane. They were quickly rounded up by waiting flak and searchlight crews but the 'Poland' shoulder flash on their RAF uniforms singled them out for 'special treatment' as *'Polnische Schwein'*. In particular the youngest member of the crew, wireless operator Tadeusz or 'Teddy' Zuk, was picked upon because he could speak English.

All the Poles were subjected to prolonged, and frequently violent, questioning at a *Luftwaffe* station. The interrogations were repeated during three weeks of solitary confinement at Dulag Luft. Washing or shaving were not allowed, they were visited day and night by *Luftwaffe* interrogators who demanded details of the Polish units in England. Polite questions gradually changed into angry shouts of *'Polnische Schwein'* and 'Gangster' followed by beatings.

Zuk was surprised when he was granted a request to send a letter to a girlfriend, but if the Germans had hoped to glean information that way they were to be disappointed. Teddy's letter was, the Poles believed, inadvertently sent on by the German authorities. It was bland, carried no hidden message but was of vital importance. Now the International Red Cross knew of the Poles' existence and whereabouts. The crew believed that the postcard saved their lives.

The NCOs Tom Kasprzyk and Teddy Zuk were sent to Stalag 11B, at Fallingbostel, at that time a penal camp for prisoners of nationalities other than British. It was a hard régime camp but again their uniforms saved them from the worst excesses although the *Volksdeutsch* guards treated them roughly. The *Kommandant*, however, told them the wearing of RAF uniform meant that he was unable to keep them and four weeks later the two Polish NCOs were sent to Stalag 8B at Lamsdorf. Still the Germans seemed unable to make up their minds about the status of the Poles and they were forced into a penal barracks with Ukrainians in Polish uniform, in a part of the camp separated from the British prisoners. The Ukrainians were awaiting release to become volunteer units with the *Wehrmacht*. The barrack *Führer* was a man who was to become a notorious figure in the camp, a Ukrainian *Volksdeutsch*, *Unteroffizier* Küssel.

Küssel would deliberately antagonise the two Poles. They would never get out of the prison until Germany had been rebuilt he would shout. They were forbidden to leave the barracks except during roll calls, or to communicate with British prisoners in any way.

It was Teddy Zuk's 21st birthday, 7 July 1941 when the prisoners were parading outside their barracks, that *Unteroffizier* Küssel ominously unbuckled his leather belt and advanced on Zuk. Hanging from the belt were his pistol and bayonet but that did not prevent him from brandishing the belt and raining a succession of blows on Zuk, punctuated only by the raging yells of the usual *'Polnische Schwein'*, *'Schweinhund'* and *'Gangster'*. There was nothing Zuk could do but collapse under the blows and pray for it to stop. British prisoners could see what was happening and crossed over the forbidden zone, shouting to Küssel to stop. To everyone's surprise, Küssel, panting with the exertion, dropped his arm, replaced his belt and glowering darkly, walked away. Teddy Zuk staggered back to his barrack helped by Tom Kasprzyk.

The two Polish NCOs had to endure two further weeks of Küssel's harassment until they were transferred from his 'care' to that of the 35 RAF men in their compound. There their lives changed. Away from Küssel's fanatically intolerant and brutal behaviour, his continually abusive language and deliberate victimisation, it seemed to be Heaven. From near starvation the Polish airmen went to the comparative opulence of a parcel of Red Cross food each week. Even more importantly they were with men who immediately accepted them as one of themselves. Henceforth Poles, and the nationals of other German-occupied countries who wore

RAF uniform, were afforded some protection against being sent to the concentration or death camps. James Deans and other camp leaders sometimes had a struggle to keep Jewish flyers, but the precedent that an RAF man was entitled to protection, no matter what his race, creed or colour, had been established by Teddy Zuk and the Poles.

### UNREHEARSED SOLO

No 38 Squadron operated from RAF Marham until late 1940 when it was sent to the Middle East, while 115 Squadron carried on from Marham with its bombing raids in Europe. Their Wellington bombers attacked targets in Hamburg on the night of 10 May 1941, exactly one year from the shock of the *Blitzkrieg* across the Low Countries and France.

That night, whilst Deputy *Führer* Rudolf Hess was flying towards Britain, an all-NCO crew captained by experienced Sergeant 'Jock' Anderson set off towards Germany at 23.17hrs. The second pilot was Australian Alex Kerr, a classmate of Sergeant Ron Damman shot down just two weeks before. The navigator was tall Sergeant Bill Legg, an optimistic and happy natured native of Weymouth, the front gunner was Sergeant Bernie Morgan, the rear gunner Sergeant Dave Fraser and the wireless operator Sergeant Geoff Hogg. They were a crew of friends and this was their third operation together.

It was a clear night and the outward flight fairly uneventful, but the occasional flak had not prepared them for the massive barrage and the mass of blueish searchlights which concentrated on them in the Hamburg area. Bill Legg, stretched out horizontally in the bomb-aiming position, peered through the bomb-sight as the target slowly came into view. His six-foot frame felt a mile long and horribly vulnerable as the aircraft was held in a searchlight cone. All the flak seeming to head straight towards him. Legg would have been much happier had he been lying on a strip of solid armour plate. His run-up instructions to the captain and the final cry of 'Bombs gone. Go! Go! Go!' brought a welcoming cheer from the crew. 'Jock' Anderson swung the Wellington round on full boost to the homeward course as a voice muttered over the intercom, 'Let's get the hell out of it'. There was complete agreement.

Legg had been temporarily out of contact with the rest of the crew as he climbed back up to the navigator's table and rammed his jackplug into the intercom socket. He was then startled to hear the rear gunner Dave Fraser calling to Anderson.

'My turret's on fire and I don't think my extinguisher is man enough for the job.' There was no panic in his voice, only urgency. Grabbing an extinguisher, Legg answered:

'Hang on, I'll be right down.'

As Legg climbed over the main spar he was out of communication with the rest of the crew again and did not hear Fraser's warning call.

'Fighter on our tail!'

'More fumes than flames,' Legg thought, guessing that the hydraulic oil pipes had been shattered by the flak. Making his way back to the navigator's table he passed Alex Kerr peering from the astrodome and directing evasive action for pilot Anderson.

At that moment Kerr saw tracer bullets like fiery pinpoints racing towards him and felt a heavy blow as if he had been punched hard all over his body. He tumbled back on to the canvas bed. He knew he had been hit, hit hard and was overwhelmed by the stark fear of the helpless. An incendiary shell ignited a bright yellow fire which raged six feet away. Kerr was paralysed and unable to move.

Legg was hit at the same moment. A crashing blow on his lower back smashed him to the floor. As he fell bullets struck him again and again. Both men lay powerless and inert near the roaring inferno.

The nightfighter pilot, seeing that the Wellington was defenceless with the rear turret out of action, came in for the 'kill'. Anderson looked back at the fiercely roaring fire inside the aircraft. It was close to other flares and oxygen bottles. The aircraft could blow up at any moment. He gave the order to bale out.

Dave Fraser struggled from his wrecked rear turret and pulled his way forward to wounded Alex Kerr. Kerr just sat, his senses reeling, aware only of the brilliant intensity of the yellow, crackling and hissing flames, of the acrid smell of petrol and oil and that the aircraft itself was a great roaring, flying blow-torch.

Legg was slumped by the astro-hatch and as Kerr stirred he saw Legg move and turn towards him. Kerr tried to beckon with his left hand but the arm inside the ripped and bloody sleeve of his Irvin jacket would not move. Managing to raise his right hand he gestured to Legg to crawl towards him but Legg shook his head – he too was unable to move.

The left leg of Kerr's flying suit was ripped and he could feel the blood flooding into his flying boot. Suddenly Fraser was leaning over him, clipping a parachute to his harness, smiling and indicating that he should jump. Kerr tried, movement seemed impossibly slow until Fraser, clearing the way and untangling a harness clip at the kick-out emergency hatch, placed Kerr's hand on the parachute 'D' ring and pushed him into the darkness of space. As he fell Kerr vaguely saw two more parachutes descending and, passing near, the flying inferno of the Wellington.

Quickly Fraser climbed over to Legg who was bleeding profusely from his stomach and several other places, and was very still, as still as death. 'He's bought it,' Fraser quickly decided. There was nothing more he could do. Clipping on his parachute he raced to the hatch and jumped from the fierce fire around him into the cool night air.

Pilot 'Jock' Anderson saw Bernie Morgan and Geoff Hogg dive through the front hatch and as the fire was behind him he believed that the rest of the crew must have left from the mid-hatch. At the last moment, when he had no answer to his calls on the intercom and was sure that he was alone, he switched over to the automatic pilot and scrambled down to the escape hatch. The Wellington, shattered and burning but, remarkably, still operating under the influence of 'George', the automatic pilot, flew north like a fiery comet across the dark skies of Schleswig.

Bill Legg stirred. He struggled weakly to his feet, staggered forward away from the blistering heat of the fire, crawled across the main spar which crossed the fuselage and fell over to the far side. In his dazed state he was intent on asking Anderson what were his orders. Legg hardly noticed that the wireless operator was missing but when he reached the nose of the aircraft and found both pilots' seats empty the truth dawned. He was seriously wounded, weak from loss of blood and alone in a blazing Wellington at 9,000 feet over Germany. Survival instinct told him he must get out. Reeling back to his navigator's table he grabbed his parachute pack from the floor but he was dazed and weak. Instead of clipping the parachute to his harness, Legg struggled forward again where he stood over the open hatch. His strength ebbing, he relaxed his grip on the parachute pack handle and in mute dismay watched it disappear through the hole into the black void beneath. Stunned and brain muddled, Legg just stood there with the burning fuselage behind him, wondering vaguely what to do next.

Laboriously he heaved his body into the pilot's bucket seat. The parachute pack which normally raised the seat had gone when the pilot baled out, without this Legg sat too low. The aircraft's hydraulics had been cut making pumping the handle to raise the seat useless. Convinced that survival was now impossible Legg switched over to manual control and pushed the nose of the Wellington down, determined to crash the aircraft and take someone or something with him.

As the aircraft lost height Legg could distinguish fields, rivers and houses below. Then it was that the first glimmer of hope appeared and he suddenly levelled the aircraft at 600 feet, calculating the chances of putting the Wellington down in the larger of the fields below. He had previously flown the plane straight and level with the pilot beside him but his only landings had been as an observer. But this was now literally 'do or die'.

Turning in a wide circuit he selected 15 degrees of flap and turned the undercarriage switch to 'Down'. Neither worked but he turned the aircraft in towards the field at about 100ft, throttled back to what he thought was just above stalling speed, then closing the throttles completely, Legg grasped the control column firmly, braced himself and waited for the crash.

Three-quarters of the way across the field the Wellington smashed on to the ground. The aircraft, with Legg still in the pilot's seat, slithered across the remainder of the field, its erratic progress ending in the hedge of the back gardens of a row of terraced houses. Looking over his shoulder Legg saw that the fuselage area was still burning furiously. Reaching up, he released the top escape hatch but found it impossible to lift himself from the seat. His strength failing rapidly, Bill Legg resigned himself to knowing that this was as far as he could go. Now he was on the ground he was going to bleed to death or fry. So far he had felt no pain, just a dazed feeling and warm numbness in the lower part of his body. He sat back and waited for the end.

It was the sound of shouting that roused Legg from his warm, distant lethargy. Two members of a nearby flak battery had run to the wreck, hesitating just for a second until they saw Legg's crumpled and bloody form in the pilot's seat. They then climbed rapidly into the shattered and burning fuselage, quickly heaved the helpless man out and carried him a safe distance from the wreckage and laid him on the grass. Bill Legg wanted to thank his rescuers but no sound came from his throat, instead the welcome oblivion of unconsciousness washed over him just as there was a violent explosion on the burning Wellington.

Alex Kerr was still conscious when he collapsed to the ground, his parachute billowing around him. He lay there panting and then heard voices. He called out for help. There were muttered words and Kerr felt himself heaved up on to a broad back and carried to a hut. There he was laid on a wooden table and by the dim light of a single bulb Kerr saw the German soldier who had carried him wipe the blood from his hands. Kerr lay helpless as the soldier removed his flying jacket, he felt so dry and his breathing became increasingly laboured.

'I've been shot in the chest,' he thought and then he saw the tangled mess of bloody skin and leather that was his left arm. Dave Fraser and Bernie Morgan were brought in and hustled out again. Fraser's expression was very serious and Morgan seemed to be in a trance, just staring straight ahead. They were sure that Kerr was dying. Kerr wished he *could* die. In his confusion he tried holding his breath. Three attempts convinced him that he could not die that way. The following ambulance journey was agony. Perhaps, he thought, reciting the Lord's Prayer would help but that was no good either, he could not remember it with his mind and body in such wracked turmoil. He was just breathing when the ambulance arrived at a hospital near the Danish border. As he was lowered down to an operating table an anaesthetist's mask at last blotted out his pain.

Professor Rend Simony and a Polish colleague operated on the 10 wounds they found on Kerr's body. Efficiently they removed two bullets from his liver, stitched up a six-inch incision in his stomach and others in his leg, arm and chest, and finally removed a ricocheted, misshapen and twisted spent bullet which seemed to have toured around in his flying leathers until it came to rest half-an-inch deep in his flesh. Kerr had lost much blood, the surgeons shook their heads sadly, it was a desperate shame, they had tried hard to save him but held out little hope.

Kerr, thin, drawn and white, surprised the doctors by living. He recovered sufficiently to be moved, splinted and bandaged, into a smaller four-bed room at the *Lazarett*. On the morning of 7 June, a tall skinny figure with a large ragged moustache was lowered, flopping feebly, into the vacant bed. It was Bill Legg. Kerr had been certain that Legg was dead, shot to smithereens and crashing finally in the blazing aircraft. Neither man could sit up and see the other but Legg could raise his head slightly. Finding each other was such a joy that they exchanged tales and laughed with sheer relief until the tears rolled down their cheeks.

In a corner bed by the door lay an inert figure swathed in bandages.

'Who is our friend?' asked Legg quietly.

'It's Peter Hind, a Hampden pilot,' said Kerr, 'he baled out but his clothing was on fire and he is very badly burnt.'

Legg lifted his head slightly, looking with pity at the bandaged man. He knew what it was like to be trapped in the flames of a blazing aircraft. Sleep did not come easily to either man and at night they lay awake listening to the drone of RAF bombers passing above.

On 23 August both men were transferred to the *Lazarett* at Rendsburg. That month spent there was the toughest of Legg's life. Kerr's wounds were mostly healed but he had a stabbing pain in his right side and was daily massaging his right arm in an effort to straighten it. It did not seem to be working. Legg's operation had opened and the stomach wound was discharging regularly from a hole in his back. He was at a low ebb, undernourished and losing weight.

There were three men in the locked room and the use of a bed pan was an eternal problem. A Polish orderly provided each man with a stick with a hook at one end and placed a bed pan in the middle so that whoever needed to use it could drag the pan to his bed and lift it up. The not unexpected crisis came when Hind, the third man, had used the pan and Kerr needed it. With his hooked stick Kerr dragged the pan across the floor but in lifting it spilt the whole contents. When there was no reply to Legg's call for aid he raised his voice higher reflecting upon the parentage of the whole German race. This brought a swifter reaction than expected. The door burst open, the guard rushed in and pressed a Luger pistol hard against Legg's forehead.

'Don't you call me a bastard,' he shouted in English, 'I was a prisoner in the last war and I am only carrying out my orders.'

Legg, calmer when the guard left, was unable to decide whether the shock of the guard's action had left any deleterious effects. He, Legg, always smelt like a cesspit anyway.

The German doctor in charge of the hospital hated the flyers and did nothing to relieve their suffering. Dressings were changed infrequently causing acute discomfort and the food was terrible, consisting of thin potato soup and black bread. Legg was down from his normal weight of more than 13 stone to nine stone. A special treat of a cod's head, cut off immediately behind the gills did little to cheer him.

Kerr and Legg were desperately sorry for a Canadian pilot Don Bennett, brought in terribly injured after being brought down during the big raid on Frankfurt the previous night. He was conscious for only short spells before lapsing into oblivion again and was obviously dying. The airmen were horrified to see one of his feet hanging from a bloody stump held by only a thin piece of skin. Bennett's whole body was pitted with wounds and deep abrasions. His face, especially around the mouth was badly mutilated. Despite the seriousness of their own wounds the hearts of the two men went out to this dying flyer who had crashed in his plane and lay in the wreckage for eight hours. At 8.00pm that evening Don Bennett died, released from pain at last. Kerr and a naval airman who had joined them, attended Bennett's funeral three days later. *Luftwaffe* men fired a volley over the coffin.

The naval airman who had been wounded and taken prisoner in Norway, provided the only light relief during this period with his alleged sailor-like adventures with Norwegian nurses. The wounded men were glad when they were transferred to the hospital attached to Dulag Luft although Legg found the journey taxing in his weakened state, and collapsed on the second day. The open wound in his back was no better but the life and treatment in the Dulag hospital was more comfortable.

After six months at Frankfurt military hospital Bill Legg was moved to Stalag 8C. Transferred to the *Lazarett*, Legg was placed in the care of a French Army surgeon named Chatenay from Martinique. Chatenay was young, enthusiastic and eager for experience. He immediately took a close interest in the legacy of the wounds of Bill Legg. His Red Cross equipment was limited but it did not prevent Chatenay from removing several fragments of explosive bullet, a rivet from his arm and twelve inches of Legg's perforated intestine.

Legg's coughing split stitches that needed replacing but the doctor was concerned that there were still openings in Legg's stomach and back through which bowel movements were issuing. Scar tissue prevented operations in the same wounds so Doctor Chatenay worked hard and concentrated on getting Legg active. Eventually the abdominal hole healed over completely and the rear exit closed down to a small hole which served as a kind of safety valve.

During the period in which Bill Legg was gradually improving he was in the unfortunate position of having flatulent emissions from three separate orifices of varying sizes. Even this unusual situation produced a form of black humour when to everyone's amusement it was suggested that if he practised the correct fingering he could make a fortune on the Music Halls.


The fame of legless fighter pilot Wing Commander Douglas Bader had spread throughout his own Command and the *Luftwaffe* fighter squadrons, but he was less well known in the early days to the men of Bomber Command. There had been rumours of a legless RAF pilot but the bomber men knew the difficulty of flying a heavy, cumbersome aircraft and dismissed the story as propaganda and just another tall story from the 'silk-scarved', top-button-undone glamour boys. Bader was downed in August 1941 but it was to be a while before he was to reach a prisoner-of-war camp.

Late in September 1941, Alex Kerr was moved to a French prisoner-of-war camp near the city of Mainz and within a day Bader arrived and told his story. He had collided with a Messerschmitt when operating over France on daily Channel sweeps and had been taken to hospital at St Omer. Bader told Kerr that when he jumped from his aircraft one of his metal legs had been damaged beyond repair and that later a new leg was dropped by parachute in a well padded box. It was this box, heavy with Bader's kit, that they both had to struggle with for the three-day journey from Mainz to Lübeck.

Kerr was profoundly glad to leave the dank dungeons of Mainz where the granite walls oozed continuously and the surroundings were what he thought of as a classical 'Prisoner of Zenda' situation. Food there was repulsive and the 'eating irons' rusty. It was due to the vigorous and outspoken protests from Bader that they had finally been moved.

The NCOs continued on a five-hour ride to Berlin and a tortuous journey through Berlin's Underground. It was on the morning of 4 October that the weary and exhausted men dragged themselves through the gates of Stalag 3E near Kirchain. There was succour here, although there were only at that time 184 aircrew at 3E and it was cramped, lacked any facilities and had crude sanitary arrangements, but there was food and rest which the new arrivals badly needed.

## HOME RUN

Flight Sergeant Graham Hall, briefly senior NCO at Barth, was an enthusiastic escaper and encouraged others who were like-minded. Beneath the floor of the small office that he had persuaded the Germans to allocate to him, was the entrance to yet another tunnel. It was planned to be about 80 yards long and to break out in the gap between the earth and the raised floor of the *Kommandantur* hut. The exit would be well shielded, unlikely to be watched, infrequently examined and escapers would emerge in the more lightly guarded German compound. A constant watch was maintained by Hall on the *Kommandantur* hut from a small hole in the window shutters. From the same position the barred windows of the *Arrestlok* or 'Cooler' could be seen, and when Hall saw a movement behind the bars of one window he wondered vaguely who the occupant was and what he was doing. The Cooler was hardly the easiest place from which to escape but when at 2.00am Hall crawled wearily on to his palliasse to sleep, he wished the man, awake in the cells, good luck.

The next morning the prisoners issuing from the three huts of the NCOs' compound at Barth were amazed to see a complete set of cell bars leaning against the wall of the Cooler on the other side of the wire. It was soon learned that Flight Lieutenant Harry Burton was 'out and away'. Burton, who had seen the huge invasion preparations when he was near St Malo in the previous September, was now trying to get home to tell what he knew and what he had learned during his nine months' captivity.

Although the prisoners were happy to barrack and jibe at the camp Germans about Burton's escape, they also knew that it meant many hours in the compound while the huts were searched. There would inevitably be a review of security and loss of the few 'privileges' they had. But it was exhilarating to know that a Kriegie was beyond the wire.

44

Joe 'Nobby' Clark, orderly to Burton, had no idea that he had gone from the camp. He knew that Burton was due to spend a week in solitary for possessing escape equipment but his room-mates cheekily told Clark that Burton had left because, 'He had an appointment in Piccadilly'.

Harry Burton arrived in Trelleborg, Sweden, on 31 May 1941 and eventually word got back to the Kriegies that Burton had made a 'home run'. When a new prisoner was asked later in the year if he had heard about Burton, he replied: 'Oh yes, he's touring RAF stations lecturing to aircrews on how to escape from prisoner-of-war camps'.

Burton's escape was a tremendous boost to the prisoners' morale and helped to disperse a little of the gloom about the *Bismarck*'s sinking of HMS *Hood*. The German broadcasts were continually baying about the sinking between blasts of the *'Horst Wessel'* song, roared out by military male voices. 'Don't you worry,' said Leading Seaman Purchase, 'the Navy knows where the bugger is and they'll get it.' His confidence was justified within days and Germany's pride, KMS *Bismarck* went to the bottom taking with her more than 2,000 *Kriegsmarine* sailors. Soon after Burton left, another prisoner, Flight Lieutenant Shore, escaped from Barth through a tunnel and stowed away to Sweden but the Germans were learning too. Security was very much tightened and the guards were held personally responsible on threat of punishment for any escapes.

Graham Hall determined to push ahead with his tunnel. With Sergeant Fancy digging enthusiastically and engineer Sergeant Ruse keeping it straight and level it was soon under the barbed wire and in a position to break out into the *Vorlager*. But there was still as far again to be dug before they could come up, concealed, beneath the administration block.

The early morning shouts of *'Appell! Appell!'* roughly roused the Kriegies. After being counted they were still waiting on the dusty field at 10.00am when a company of overalled 'Ferrets' poured through the gate into the compound led by *Oberfeldwebel* Glemnitz. Making straight for Block 1 they tore the wooden side from the lower part of the wall and without hesitation made straight for the tunnel. Hall and his diggers were shocked and weak with disappointment. Had there been a security lapse, what had gone wrong? Accusations and recriminations followed the dashed hopes until John Bristow pointed to wires leading into the ground. In his opinion seismographs had monitored the digging and the Kriegies had been left to work in peace as long as they were not likely to be successful. A hard, bitter lesson had been learned.

Digging in the Dulag tunnel had re-started in March 1941 and the break made in early June. Eighteen had escaped including Buckley, Bushell and

45

'Wings' Day. All were eventually recaptured but the Germans were furious. Any more than five men out was considered a mass escape for which the full hue and cry was ordered and Hitler informed. 'Wings' expected to be sent back to Spangenberg but he, the ringleaders and most of the 'permanents' were sent to Barth.

Almost every prisoner who had passed through Dulag had complained when he reached Barth about the apparent 'rackets' indulged in by the RAF men of the permanent staff. The mud was sticking grimly to everyone from 'Wings' Day down. Some of the officers appeared to have been on close, friendly terms with the *Kommandant, Major* Rumpel, to have been seen the worse for drink and to have been on visits outside the camp. The NCOs had lived in small comfortable rooms and appeared to have been a well-fed clique who controlled the running of the camp. Their lifestyle had been a stark contrast to that of the transients and their reception by the Kriegies at Barth was hardly going to be a red carpet affair. There was satisfaction among the Barth men that now the Dulag 'permanents' were about to know what it was really like to be a prisoner. The Kriegies were beginning to understand the meaning of *Schadenfreude*.

### BOXING CLEVER

'If I can get into that box, could you get me out beyond the compound wire?' asked Fleet Air Arm Lieutenant Filmer. Joe Clark readily agreed. Filmer had made a false bottom to a large box with a hinged side, in which empty tins were transported by orderlies on a four-wheeled trolley and taken to a hut outside the wire. Plans were made for an attempt to be made on a day in May but they were escorted from the compound by *Oberfeldwebel* Glemnitz. He was sharp and any escape attempt whilst under his escort was doomed to failure.

The next try was in June and looked more promising. Their escort was to be an ordinary guard and Clark thought it worth the attempt. Filmer secreted himself in the false bottom and the empty tins were piled in on top. The box was placed carefully on the trolley with the hinged side on the left. Escorted by the unsuspecting *Gefreite* the orderlies wheeled it through the gates into the *Vorlager*.

When the party reached the hut where the tins were to be stored, Clark, having already instructed the other orderlies to make the emptying a slow job, wandered off to the other end of the hut and lit a cigarette. The guard shouted to him to come back and followed, as Clark hoped he would. Pausing there Clark offered the guard a cigarette explaining that it was dangerous to smoke near the open door of the hut because of the straw inside. For five minutes the guard was kept in conversation about the seaplane base along the Baltic Coast while the hinged side of the box was lifted so that Filmer could dive beneath the straw in the hut. A second guard appeared causing a momentary flutter but he merely threw a large piece of wood on to the straw where Filmer was hiding and left. A sign from one of the other orderlies gave Clark the all-clear and the box was lifted on to the trolley and back to the compound they went, the box being deposited in its usual place in the cookhouse.

Lieutenant Filmer escaped from the *Vorlager* and was two weeks on the run before being recaptured on his second attempt to enter Denmark. Throughout his escape he was not missed by the Germans. The elderly guard had merely glanced into the room where Filmer was supposed to be ill in bed, had seen the outline of a dummy, muttered, 'Poor Mr Filmer', and ticked his list.

### 'BARBAROSSA' AND BARBARITY

Operation 'Barbarossa', a year to the day from that on which the French Armistice had been signed, was a surprise to most in the Stalags but the Kriegies were delighted; an invasion of Britain was now plainly out of the question and the worst of the air attacks would surely cease.

That evening Churchill spoke to all peoples on the World Service of the BBC. After naming Hitler a 'bloodthirsty guttersnipe' and promising Russia all technical and economic assistance in Britain's power, he went on to say:

'We shall bomb Germany by day as well as by night in ever-increasing measure, casting upon them month by month a heavier discharge of bombs, and making the German people taste and gulp each month a sharper dose of the miseries they have showered upon mankind.'

The early successes of the *Wehrmacht* in Russia were disheartening for the Kriegies. So too was the sight of the prisoners from the Red Army suffering brutal and inhuman treatment at the hands of the Germans. The fragile protection of the Geneva Convention had saved most of the British from the utter savagery of the shootings, beatings and torture, but at Barth they had to watch helplessly as the first party of Russians, emaciated by starvation and forced marches of hundreds of miles in appalling conditions, was driven into the *Vorlager* in a horse-drawn cart. This was the last stage of their nightmare journey. The Kriegies threw bread over the wire to the Russians but any further attempt to pass food was immediately stopped, a levelled sub-machine gun from the other side of the barbed wire keeping everyone well back.

Brusquely ordered out of the carts, the weak and wasted Russians were unable to climb down; one by one the 10 in the cart fell the three feet to the ground, one on top of the other. There were tears, anger, boos and catcalls for the Germans from the British on the other side of the wire as one Russian, attempting to stand on his feet and then trying to help another of his comrades to rise, was kicked and fell again to the earth. To the shouts of *'Raus! Raus!'* from the guards, the Russians slowly gathered themselves together and holding on to each other, staggered away out of sight behind the *Vorlager* huts.

'Did you see their backsides?' a man with medical knowledge asked quietly. 'There was no fat on them at all, the hip bones were sticking through their buttocks. When a man reaches that state there is little hope for him.' If the Germans had intended to bring these Russian prisoners to Pomerania to work they were too late.

Sergeant Deans protested on behalf of the RAF prisoners to the *Kommandant*. Every German entering the compound was left in no doubt about the anger the Kriegies felt about the vicious treatment the Russians had received. An interpreter claimed that such treatment had been ordered by 'Higher Authority' and that in any case German prisoners of the Russians were badly treated by the Asiatic barbarian *Untermenschen* who were savages.

### 'SALMON AND GLUCKSTEIN'

The British High Command, worried about the *Kriegsmarine* ships *Scharnhorst, Gneisenau* and *Prinz Eugen* lying in the harbour of Brest. These powerful warships could create havoc to vital Atlantic shipping and a convoy was shortly expected containing many thousands of Canadian troops. Despite the decision not to mount major daylight raids it was thought essential, on this operation, for the bombers to see their target. Reconnaissance revealed that the *Scharnhorst* had been moved at the last moment to the smaller harbour of La Pallice so the bomber force was split, 15 unescorted Halifaxes going to La Pallice and the others to Brest.

Just after 10.00hrs on 24 July the 15 Halifaxes, each carrying fifteen 500lb armour-piercing bombs, set out for La Pallice and the *Scharnhorst*. To avoid their direction of flight giving a clue to their intended target, the five vees of three aircraft flew out to sea only turning towards La Pallice on the final dog-leg, but they passed over a German cruiser. Its captain would have sent a radio warning. Near La Pallice, Halifax rear gunner Gilbanks alerted the captain Flight Sergeant Stan Greaves to fighters on the port beam. Sergeant Gordon Ogden at a beam gun on the port side counted 36 Bf109s which curved round and took up position behind the Halifaxes and waited. Moving into line astern for attack, the crews of the Halifaxes could plainly see the *Scharnhorst.*

Flak was accurately synchronised at 16,000 feet, the height from which the Halifaxes were to bomb. Ogden could hear the red hot pieces of metal rattling on the fuselage and punching holes in the aircraft's skin. He watched transfixed as a pattern of little holes appeared on the aluminium bulkhead and a cannon shell made a bigger hole, inches from his nose. Ignoring the flak, the fighters came in again and again for 20 minutes. A near miss put one engine out of action and Greaves asked the crew if he should jettison their bombs. A unanimous 'No' decided him to go round again.

'Halifaxes are falling about all over the sky' groaned Ogden, 'and we have to go through all that flak again.' Once more he screwed up his courage for action.

When the second and third engines seized they knew they were not going to get home. The intercom had been destroyed so Ogden scrambled over the main spar to tell rear gunner Gilbanks to jump. On reaching the tail he was amazed that anyone could have survived. The turret was peppered with holes, the perspex smashed and Gilbanks had no features below his hairline, just a red pulp of blood. Ogden went to turn away thinking that Gilbanks was dead but he heard him groan. Looking closely he realised that Gilbanks had been hit by shrapnel in the forehead and a flap of skin had fallen down over his face. Ogden lifted the flap and put it back, underneath Gilbanks' face appeared untouched. He heaved the rear gunner out of the turret and they and the rest of the crew baled out within seconds of each other.

All the crew landed safely and became prisoners, only 'just my bloody luck' Ogden falling into the bay. He expected to have to swim but the water came to just above his knees. The Halifax exploded in a flash of red and orange flame. It was one of five destroyed from the 15 which took part in the raid and all the remainder were damaged. Greaves' crew had accounted for four Bf109s.

Despite the fierce opposition the Halifaxes had pressed home their attack and it was believed that the *Scharnhorst* had been severely damaged but reconnaissance showed that she was soon on the move out of La Pallice. The Germans knew that the RAF would return and decided that the ship should go to Brest where the flak defences were more powerful and the repair facilities more extensive. But the *Scharnhorst* had been holed and her movements were made sluggish by the thousands of tons of water slopping around inside.

Meanwhile the main body of bombers attacked the *Gneisenau* and *Prinz Eugen*. Among 100 aircraft sent to Brest was a Wellington from 218 Squadron on which Sergeant John Knott was the wireless operator. The main force of 79 Wellingtons was expected to fight its way to and from the target unescorted.

In the first vee formation to attack, Knott's Wellington made a hectic run up to the target. Flak shells burst and thundered around the aircraft and Bf109s pressed home their attacks. The rear gunner fired ceaselessly and gave a simultaneous commentary as the fighters' bullets ripped into the Wellington. Knott saw that the rear of the plane was on fire and when the second pilot tapped him on the shoulder it was time to go. Clipping on his parachute Knott was dismayed to find that the ripcord had been pulled by a snag on the exit hatch. Following the navigator out of the plane with the 'chute gathered in his arms Knott jumped, still convinced that the canopy had caught inside the aircraft. But it was free.

Floating gently down Knott inflated his Mae West but was unable to release his harness before plunging into the sea. As he went down beneath the surface he thumped the quick release plate and shot upwards where his parachute was floating at his side. A Bf109 flew low over him after circling and indicating his position in the water to French fishing boats nearby. When he was picked up Knott took off his shirt to dry his body in the warm sunshine but found himself shivering. The realisation that he was still alive after his ordeal was an almost unbelievable relief. A motor launch drew up manned by German Army men to take him back to the shore.

As the launch tied up at the beach Knott was surprised and sickened to see dozens of French girls and German officers sunbathing and taking photographs. It seemed incongruous when a life and death battle had taken place close above their heads.

It was midnight before local interrogation was finished and a meal eaten. Following countless repetitions of 'For you the war is over', the journey to Dulag began. Losses had been high among the Wellingtons, with 10 lost from the 79, but the *Gneisenau* had been damaged. Most of the survivors of the downed Lancasters, Halifaxes and Hampdens went from Dulag to Stalag 3E at Kirchain.

*Kapitän* Hoffmann knew that the *Scharnhorst* was still one of the most powerfully defended ships in the world. The crew of a 217 Squadron Beaufort found that to be true on the early morning of 25 July.

It was misty with rain showers when, at 06.45hrs, the torpedo-armed Beaufort S-Sugar sighted the *Scharnhorst* and her destroyer escort.

The RAAF pilot, Squadron Leader Les Collings, had taken off from St Eval determined to find the ship in spite of the foul weather. A whoop of joy went up from observer, Pilot Officer Jim 'Red' Hunter, as Collings circled round to beam position to drop his 'tinfish'. Apart from the shipborne flak, watch had to be kept on the destroyer's armament and the battle-cruiser's aircraft, one of which, a Heinkel He115 twin-engined seaplane was already in the air. Air gunner Sergeant Ted Taylor kept his fingers ready on the triggers as he scanned the sky.

Choosing his position Collings approached the ship low on its starboard side. As he did so the side of the ship appeared to burst into smoke and flame. Every gun that could be laid on the Beaufort opened fire. The accompanying destroyer *Erich Steinbrink* also brought every gun to bear but Collings knew that he would not have another chance and would not be deflected. Hits were felt from the flak as the Beaufort kept its steady height and course so that the torpedo would run correctly. It was with horror that Hunter saw the torpedo bounce on the water, turn somersault and enter the water again vertically, disappearing without trace. As the Beaufort attempted to climb away a heavy flak shell hit the lower rear fuselage followed by streams of tracer from the He115. There was no saving the Beaufort. One of the hits had killed wireless operator Sergeant 'Pip' Appleby and now, as the undercarriage involuntarily lowered, Collings put the aircraft down as gently as possible on the sea.

It had been a brave try against overwhelming odds and the irony was not lost on the surviving crew members as they were taken prisoner by men from their target. They discovered that the *Scharnhorst* had sustained damage sufficient to put her out of action for another six months.

### CONCEPTION OF A 'CANARY'

Although the delivery of Red Cross parcels to Barth in May meant that the body was being fed, there was, to quote Dave Young, 'A continual dearth of news'. The loudspeaker at the end of the block would frequently erupt with William Joyce's sneering voice, slow, oily and precise: 'Germany calling, Germany calling...'

On a couple of occasions, German newsreels entitled *'Die Deutsche Wochenshau'* were shown in the cookhouse-cum-dining room. To the crashing sound of Germanic military music, formations of *Luftwaffe* dive-bombers were seen roaring past overhead, tanks and armoured columns rolled non-stop across the steppes and the infantry always advanced from left to right or as on a map, from west to east.

For the Kriegies the news was depressing. Britain and Russia suffered ferocious defeats everywhere, and British cities were being obliterated by bombing. 'The *Führer's* Headquarters and the *Oberkommando der Wehrmacht'* continually announced a new *'Sondermeldung'* or special announcement of Russian cities overrun and thousands more prisoners taken. Tanks were destroyed in astronomical numbers. There was never a mention of British or Russian successes, few though there may have been.

The whole world outside the wire seemed to be under German control and the future for prisoners-of-war appeared to be bleak, with no promise ever of release. This naturally led to a resurgence and increase in those wishing to attempt to escape but 'Dixie' Deans, the 'Tally Ho' escape organisation, and indeed all the Kriegies, realised that chances were pitifully few. What was needed to prevent the spread of rumour and to give a lift to morale was news untwisted by Göbbels' propaganda.

Late in the summer of 1941 Dave Young met two Kriegies living in the same block who had similar ideas to himself: a radio receiver was necessary but the chances of obtaining one were nil. The guards were mainly incorruptible as yet and the penalty for them not being so was horrific. That avenue seemed closed.

John 'Curly' Bristow was a tall, fair, engaging young man with a talent for making something from nothing. In order to visit every room in the camp he announced when collections could be made from the cookhouse. Everyone in the camp now knew him and by regular daily visits he was able to scrounge any materials necessary for various schemes he had under way, the latest being the manufacture of a steam engine. Dave Young described Bristow as 'a meticulous craftsman of unlimited ingenuity and enthusiasm'.

Ex-reporter Peter Stubbs, in combine with Bristow and his partner in all the scrounging and manufacturing activities, had been the navigator in a Battle that had been shot down in May 1940 during the ferociously fought, low level, daylight attacks on German tanks near St Vith. A recently fitted forward-firing Vickers 'K' gun had wreaked havoc among the advancing Germans but the ground fire had been heavy and devastating. Machine gun and cannon fire had ripped through the Battle. Their accompanying aircraft had gone down and it was not long before Stubbs's riddled plane also crashed in a field, splattering flaming petrol everywhere and certain to ignite the bombs still on board. Seriously hurt, Stubbs nevertheless managed to climb and run from the fierce heat of the blazing wreckage. Although hit again by the still firing Germans, he, with the wireless operator and the badly burned pilot, watched as the Battle blew up taking several cheering *Wehrmacht* men with it who had been standing too close.

Now recovered from his wounds, Stubbs' enthusiasm to do anything to further the Allied war effort matched Bristow's. So when Dave Young joined this driving duo, their collaboration was certain to achieve a result. Quickly the three went through the possibilities. A plan to smuggle in a receiver had already been discarded and the simplest form of receiver, a crystal set, was also dismissed as being useless to pick up BBC broadcasts at that range. The acquisition of a valve was an absolute necessity. Bristow, with his usual confident optimism, believed they would somehow 'acquire' one. An earphone also seemed impossible to make with the very limited materials such as tins and small pieces of wood.

Then there was security. Frequent searches made a safe hiding place essential for the components and the final receiver. On their walks round the circuit of the compound, under the constant gaze of the patrolling and Posten tower guards, Young, Bristow and Stubbs wrestled with the problem they had set themselves: how to solve the insoluble.

One extraordinary, almost unbelievable piece of luck occurred when the camp officer, *Hauptmann* Buchwig, asked 'Dixie' Deans for five volunteers of suitable ability to help with a pre-Christmas rush of repairs in a local bicycle-cum-radio shop. Bristow could only think of it as 'a typical piece of Teutonic idiocy'. Such a request had never been imagined and it seemed to be a heaven-sent chance for the radio men to get the items they needed – but was it really fortuitous? What was Buchwig up to, was it a trap of some kind?

Sometimes he waxed over-friendly, showing a little too much leaning toward the Allied cause for a *Luftwaffe Hauptmann*. Buchwig, who spoke good colloquial English, was a plausible jokey Austrian who gave the impression that he had little time for the hard faced, ardent German Nazis with whom he was forced to work. He enjoyed a chat and a cup of tea with the Kriegies in their rooms and most of them, whilst letting him talk and picking up as much information as possible, mistrusted him. Buchwig was a smiling enigma – but the Kriegies in the know were not going to let such an opportunity pass. The 'Boffin' trio of Bristow, Stubbs and Young were well known to the Germans as being up to something, so it was decided that they would not go on this foraging party. It was feared that they would, to quote Young, 'ruin the whole thing by thieving the entire stock of spares on the first day'.

Instead, a party of five led by knowledgeable Sergeant Cunningham-Sands went to the repair shop for a week until some higher ranking *Luftwaffe* officer heard about the ploy, realised the dangers of letting these men loose among the very goods they were after and put an immediate shut down on the arrangement. It was too late; by then Cunningham-Sands had acquired a triode valve, a rectifying valve and a tubular electrolytic capacitor.

An enormous fuss and massive search of the camp was expected as soon as the shop owner notified the authorities of the losses, so Cunningham-Sands quickly and carefully buried his 'loot', choosing an exactly measured spot near Block 1 that was not overlooked by the guards. Everyone in the know waited and held their breath. There was a chance that the owner of the shop would either not know he had lost the components or, more likely, would be afraid to report the loss. The punishments for aiding or allowing prisoners to 'win' such items were severe.

Nothing happened. Bristow was fired with enthusiasm but Cunningham-Sands who had spirited the components away and buried them had other ideas. He was technically capable of building his own radio and wanted to do so. It seemed reasonable that he should but Deans considered that Bristow was the most likely to succeed and decided in his favour. So the undercover radio manufacturing 'Firm' of Bristow, Stubbs and Young was formed.

With the approach of Christmas came snow and the digging up of the components became an impossibility. The disturbed yellow sand would immediately arouse suspicion and snow on the North German plain would stay for three months. Now that they had those vital parts within yards, impatience would not allow the trio to wait that long. The parts had to be retrieved soon and without digging. 'Curly' Bristow had no hesitation: 'I'll tunnel,' he said.

Straight through the floor of the hut and through the airspace beneath into the sandy soil Bristow dug and burrowed. He was soon back with sand in his hair, a triumphant gleam in his eye and the sealed tin with its valuable contents in his dirty hand. They would not be home for this Christmas or the coming New Year but at least they would soon learn the truth from home and who knows – perhaps next Christmas.

December 1941 was to bring an even greater surprise to the Kriegies than the German attack on Russia. The Japanese, without warning, mounted a devastating air attack on the United States Pacific Fleet at anchor in Hawaii. There was incredulity when high ranking officers in Washington received a message from the anchorage which read: 'Pearl Harbor bombed. This is no drill!' The British Government declared war on Japan the following day, and a reciprocal declaration between Germany and Italy on one side and the United States on the other took place on 11 December. At last America was an active ally.

# PART 3

# 1942

### THE HATCHING OF A 'CANARY'

January brought a long, hard frost to Pomerania, halting the digging of tunnels. The desire to escape was further reduced by the death in the snow of Sergeant Johnny Shaw, shot whilst attempting to crawl through the wire beneath sheets of a white material. The clear intention of the Germans to make escaping a life or death challenge was evident as Shaw lay in state in the tiny chapel, fashioned by the Kriegies at the end of a cookhouse. The camp was scoured for smart uniforms, ceremonial belts and 'Cheesecutter' hats so that two smartly uniformed men could stand in silent homage before the open coffin.

On the cold, snowy morning of the funeral the cortège was led by the coffin borne on a flat, horse-drawn cart driven by a top-hatted undertaker. The cart and the two horses were draped in black and the coffin covered by two ribboned wreaths, one from the RAF, the other from the *Luftwaffe*. At the graveside a party of 20 *Luftwaffe* men fired rifles across the grave in salute.

The *Kommandant*, in making much of the funeral, emphasised his point. Although he was a kindly man who regretted the death of Sergeant Shaw, such attempts would be met by guards who had orders to shoot. Escaping would never be a sport; a matter of merely outwitting the Germans, it would always be a lonely, deadly gamble with the dice heavily loaded against the Kriegie.

During the long winter nights when the prisoners were bolted inside their huts at dusk, Bristow, Stubbs and Young continued working at their radio construction. Making a workable transformer was a problem overcome by the laborious winding of stripped lighting cable and adjusting the current by the addition of lamps until it was estimated that the secondary voltage was correct. When the transformer was finished Dave Young thought it resembled a welder rather than an integral part of a one-valve plus rectifier radio. It was obviously a piece of electrical equipment and would be confiscated at sight by any German. The hiding of the transformer was solved by making a circular wooden baseboard which would fit into a swill bin kept in the corridor. With a false bottom fitted to the bin only a little of its swill capacity was lost and searching 'ferrets' were so used to seeing the bin in the corridor it was felt that they would ignore it – and so it proved.

The trio switched their attention to the problem of earphones. It was decided that the best that could be hoped for was a telephone earpiece which would have to be made to work despite the difference in the desired impedance. There was no stopping Bristow, he talked his way on to one of the occasional volunteer *Vorlager* working parties and seizing an opportunity he dashed into an empty office, swiftly removed the coil and magnet assembly from the telephone earpiece and replaced the diaphragm to preserve the appearance. This was a serious German court-martial offence for which Bristow could have found himself in a concentration camp, but nothing could have dampened his joy as he made his way back to the compound with his valuable contraband.

A container was needed for the telephone coil and magnet so next day Bristow joined Vic Gammon on the 'circuit' around the compound. Coming straight to the point Bristow asked: 'Vic, I believe you received a personal parcel with some Calvert's Tooth Powder in a screw-top plastic box – could I have the box please?' The tooth powder was poured into an empty tin. The coil and magnet assembly was screwed to a small piece of wood and fitted inside the tooth powder box. A circular piece of tin supplied the diaphragm and neat holes in the screw lid completed the project. The new headphone then went into hiding in the false bottom of a dried milk tin.

An ice hockey puck and odd pieces of brass from a defunct trombone served as valve holders. On his daily cookhouse round Bristow collected tin foil, which, when melted and poured into suitable cracks in the floorboards formed usable sticks of solder. Resin for flux was scraped from knots in the hut's pine walls with an occasional boost to supplies from a violinist Kriegie.

The trio's toolkit was primitive and constantly in danger of sudden depletion by a 'snap' search. All efforts to make a satisfactory soldering iron failed so a blowlamp was formed from a margarine lamp (a pyjama cord wick with an end in melted margarine) and a piece of rubber tubing obtained from the sick quarters. Pieces of broken hacksaw blades had been brought in by sharp-eyed working party members; others had been secretly stitched into modified uniforms or hidden in the spines of books. Bristow's treasure was a pair of pliers which had been unearthed in the compound and restored to serviceable condition. The most used tool was an ordinary brass dart with the flights removed. Darts were used as scribers, centre-punches and with suitable grinding on the door steps, as drills.

Such was the interest now among the Kriegies that the 'Firm' was able to set up 'shadow factories' with a constantly willing workforce always available. Tedious jobs such as cutting the strips for the transformer core were gladly undertaken. Everyone was thrilled to know that they were playing a part in fooling the 'Squareheads'.

By mid-February a radio receiver was completed, wired and fitted into the bass section of an accordion. A test of the components was carried out and despite the lack of a voltmeter the calculations of the team seemed correct. A length of packing case wire was strung across the room to serve as an aerial. With a few towels hanging as if to dry, it was no different from dozens of clothes-lines elsewhere and was left permanently fixed. An earth connection was wired to the electrical conduits, so avoiding a visible rod running down through the floor. By an evening in late February they were ready to go.

It was assumed that the nine o'clock news (10.00pm Barth time) was still being broadcast so the trio began to assemble the radio on a trestle table in the centre of the room at 8.00pm. With a bank of lamps for ballast, the transformer on its circular wooden base and the end section of the accordion, Young, Bristow and Stubbs thought their 'baby' an impressive sight, rather like a picture of Marconi's first efforts in the early part of the century.

At 9.00pm they were ready and connected to the mains supply. One by one the ballast lamps were screwed into place and the valve warmed up. A hush settled on the other men in the room as Bristow held the earphone to his ear and adjusted the toothbrush handle. Watchers saw Bristow's expression slowly change; wide-eyed with wonder he looked at Young and Stubbs and whispered: 'I can hear music'. Young and Stubbs then listened, enthralled.

Young thought back to his teens when he had made radio sets as a hobby. None worked first time and some never. Within a few moments they had found the BBC with the condenser vane at mid-position, roughly where they had expected. The setting of the reaction coil was very critical and there was too much mains hum, also the signal faded from time to time but Stubbs thought he could get something out of it and armed himself with a paper and pencil. The tooth-powder box earphone was tied to his head with a bandage and he settled down to wait for 10.00pm.

For 10 minutes Stubbs' pencil raced across the paper in a mixture of shorthand and longhand. When the bulletin ended he retired to a corner to transcribe his notes before he forgot some of his shorthand. Bristow and Young took the radio to pieces and restored the various parts to their hiding places.

For all their efforts they heard little but bad news. Singapore had fallen to the Japanese. The British and their new American allies seemed to be in desperate trouble, their troops falling back everywhere. Several edited copies of the bulletin were prepared for selected news-readers to visit each room at noon next day. Thus began a service which was to continue, with a few unavoidable interruptions, until the end of the war. The current news had little to cheer the Kriegies but it did at least settle a lot of rumours. Now with the two-way coded letters and a daily news bulletin from the BBC, real contact had been made with home.

### REAPING THE WHIRLWIND

For hours, deep into the night of 29 March, the men in Stalag Luft 1, peering through cracks in the shutters, stared at a distant glow in the western sky and felt, rather than heard, the muted crump of distant bomb explosions. 'Some poor bastard's getting it,' murmured an awed voice in the darkness of Room 2. The distant but conspicuous glow drew eyes back, constantly reminding Gammon of the glow he had seen when London's Dockland was blazing in September 1940. This time the brilliant, flushed night sky was aglow from the flames of a German city.

An aircraft, invisible in the night sky, announced itself as an RAF plane by its de-synchronised engines. 'He's a bit off-course,' said Jock Hamilton. 'I hope he makes it home,' and then as an afterthought, 'wish I was going with him.'

The next day a guard told them that Lübeck, a city which had previously seemed remote from the war, had been bombed and burned. 'Large fires, great damage,' he said, adding quietly, 'many killed.'

The Kriegies also learned of the success of the St Nazaire raid on the Normandie Dock, the only dock capable of handling the German battleship *Tirpitz*. Her forays into the Atlantic would be severely restricted.

It was nearing Easter and things were looking up. Perhaps this time next year...

### POWER PROBLEM TRANSFORMED

During the spring the nightly radio session at Barth had become routine and Bristow was able to complete a tin steam engine in which some of the German interpreters took a lively interest. It was a good decoy, deflecting interest from more arcane matters.

Rumours of a move from Barth had been rife for some time and Bristow, Young and Stubbs were faced with the problem of secretly transporting their radio equipment. The transformer was the chief trouble because of its size and weight. The components hidden in the accordion and the dried milk tins would probably be secure enough, but the Kriegies could not reasonably travel with a large jam tin full of potato peelings. A discussion walk around the compound circuit sorted out the worries.

By careful probing, details of the move were elicited. The Kriegies were to travel by special passenger train and each man would have to carry his personal belongings. Heavy communal property and unissued Red Cross Parcels would be sent separately on the long journey south.

The *Luftwaffe* announced that the whole compound was to be moved to a new and well equipped camp. Rumour also had it that there they would have flush toilets, the epitome of luxury. Rooms would be small, each accommodating some four prisoners and there was a lake for swimming. No-one believed that. But it was the news of flush toilets that intrigued the Kriegies. Dave Young noted that *all* rumours about new camps specified flush toilets. In common with food and women, flush toilets obsessed Kriegies after the insanitary, primitive '*aborts*' at Barth.

A glance at the stage electrical system convinced Bristow and Stubbs that their mains transformer would not look out of place screwed to the switchboard and re-classified as a light-dimming reactor. They held on to the transformer until the last moment and the news service continued.

Even in a prisoner-of-war camp it was surprising how much personal property each man had acquired. Pockets were stuffed with small necessities. Food, clothing, tins, boxes containing valuables and perhaps a blanket or two were carried in a kitbag or made-up haversack. Cooking utensils and tin mugs hung from strings and belts. Rattling and clanging as he walked, a Kriegie resembled a noisy, Victorian tinker. The combined cacophony from a column of marching men could be heard a mile away.

One who saw any move as a chance to escape was Bill Garrioch. He and three others hid in the cookhouse roof, staying silent until the parties had left. But they were missed. Searching the empty camp on the second day after the parties had left, the guards suspected that the cookhouse might be the hiding place and fired shots through the ceiling to weed out any prisoners. Nobody was hurt but commonsense made the Kriegies give themselves up for the journey to Sagan and another spell in the *Arrestlok*.

For once the prisoners travelled in a passenger train and the passing countryside could be studied. The seats were of hard, polished wood and uncomfortable when one was forced to spend two days in one compartment. Sleep was almost impossible but an arrangement was made whereby two men climbed on the luggage racks, two lay on the seats and the other two lay on the floor, head to tail. It was cramped and dirty, but infinitely preferable to the usual cattle trucks. The waiting seemed interminable as their train was shunted repeatedly into sidings, making way for munitions trains speeding east and hospital trains rolling west with their loads of stretcher-borne wounded, but once the train had reached Frankfurt-on-Oder and passed through Sommerfeld, it quickly drew into Sagan station.

Hearts sank as the Stalag Luft 3 came into view: the area was thickly covered with young pines in which the camp occupied a clearing. Horizons were again to be limited. Everything was new, even the split pine logs holding the barbed wire were raw wood and the sharp wire barbs sparkled menacingly. The accommodation huts were unused and pristine. It was not to last.

Bristow's casual air belied his anxiety when during one of the last of many searches Grimm, a cheerful interpreter, looked at the accordion and squeezed out a few notes without discovering that it had no bass. Ron Damman looked on with trepidation as Grimm asked if a guitar would play. 'Certainly', he was told. He proceeded to play, of all things, 'Tipperary'. The radio component concealed inside the sound box did not seem to affect the tone.

The NCOs' centre compound at Sagan did not live up to expectations. The rooms were large but not large enough to contain 60 Kriegies in two-tier beds without cramming, the 'lake' was a small static-water fire pool and the *Aborts* were of similar construction to those at Barth, but were of a greater capacity and for the use of many more men. The one consolation was that the compound was larger, making the circuit more of a walk and the view to the eternal conifer forests a little further away.

However, the new camp was found to have lamentable hygiene arrangements. Although it had only been opened a short time the primitive lavatories and the warm weather had encouraged swarms of large black flies. The open pits into which ordure settled became a writhing mass of millions of white maggots. Dysentery spread throughout the camp. In the NCOs' compound Camp Leader 'Dixie' Deans relayed orders from the Senior British Officer (SBO): all food and drink was to be covered and personal hygiene maintained to as high a standard as was possible in the circumstances.

The German authorities were asked to supply disinfectant but they had little available. When the man with the horse-drawn suction tank came to empty the *Abort* and plunged the wide hose into the heaving mess, he was forced to wear a mask. The Kriegies retired as far from the *Abort* as the encompassing wire would allow.

When sitting at one of the plain wooden tables a Kriegie was immediately surrounded by huge buzzing flies. Flies alighting on the table would deposit live grubs and take off. Dysentery was agonising, with the stomach continually cramped with griping pains. It was one of the few times that Kriegies longed for cold weather.

The compound seemed to be merely a larger version of Barth. It had 12 barrack blocks, 4 toilet blocks and 2 cookhouses, all built from the omnipresent wood. Germany's shortages certainly did not include wood. Between the cookhouses was the square, brick-lined static water tank, with sides some 15 feet long and a depth of 5 feet. In clearing the compound for the two-acre parade area the trees had been cut, the stumps studding a regular pattern. One or two trees had been spared in the compound.

Barrack buildings were of a similar size to those at Barth, but here there were no small rooms. Each block was divided in two with accommodation for 60 men in two-tier bunks in each section. At the end of each large room was a small kitchen and a tiny closet for a 'night bucket'. The East compound had already been occupied by the officers from Barth and other POW camps, and there was to be a North compound.

The rooms were occupied in sequence as the Kriegies were released from searches into the compound. Vic Gammon quickly sized up the lighting arrangements and saw that those in the bottom bunks would have to provide themselves with margarine lamps if they wanted to read. Dave Young also noted the square pattern of nine ceiling lights and bagged himself a top bunk.

For a few days the few hundred men from Barth had the compound to themselves. It was a time for taking stock of the surroundings, of weighing up chances and of even the luxury of taking a *verboten* dip in the fire pool. One hut was scheduled for recreational purposes and was to be converted into a theatre. The hut was exactly like all the others and months of work lay ahead providing a raked floor, seating and stage.

Bristow, Young and Stubbs knew that all the stage equipment and scenery was to remain in German custody until the theatre was finished, it might be months – but they could not wait that long. The radio was an essential prop to morale and the transformer, disguised as a dimmer, would somehow have to be rescued.

There were occasional guarded working parties required to unload Red Cross parcels or coal in the *Vorlager*, and from them the exact location of the electrical theatre props was established. Bristow went on the next volunteer party armed with a forbidden screwdriver. He returned triumphantly that evening with the transformer. It was a major coup but there was one more problem to be solved before the radio could be operational again: it needed mains electrical power.

Compound lighting was controlled by the Germans from outside. They reluctantly switched them on at dusk and after a warning flick, switched them off at 10.00pm. There was then no electrical power anywhere in the compound. In summer the long evenings meant that the lights hardly came on at all. Even with mains electricity the earliest that the radio men could achieve any success was 10.00pm. The situation seemed hopeless, but a conference walk around the circuit brought one slender thread of hope. They had noticed that a transmission line straddled the north-west corner of the compound. It comprised three thick cables and a thinner one on top, all supported by wooden pylons, one of which was inside the camp. There were no connections to the camp electrical system and the cables were clearly part of the normal three-phase public electricity supply. The size of the insulators indicated that it must be low tension at not more than 415 volts between phases, which would give the normal 240 volts between any phase and earth. The radio trio decided to take a risk.

Most of the interpreters had come to Sagan from Barth and were well known to the Kriegies. Although it would have been unwise to ask for anything as forbidden as radio parts, a few avenues of trade had been opened. A Kriegie well known as a model maker was asked to try to get some thin wire, saying he needed it for the rigging of a ship. It worked, so the radio men now had a small quantity of enamelled thirty-gauge wire which they intended to use for their voltage confirmation test.

The electricity cables swept low over the roof of a hut between the supporting poles, on their way across the barbed wire and on through the countryside. Bristow thought they could reach the lower cable from the hut window with a 10ft pole. A suitable piece of batten was removed from the hut structure, a nail driven into the end and a length of their thirty-gauge wire taken from the nail to a lamp and thence to a suitable earth connection. The thin wire would act as an in-built fuse. Should they have underestimated the voltage there would be a momentary flash as the wire evaporated and the project would have to be abandoned. Because a flash would be visible at night it was necessary to experiment in daylight.

With lookouts unobtrusively posted and at a time when the compound was free of patrolling ferrets, Stubbs, at a signal, leaned from the window while Bristow and Young watched the lamp. Stubbs steadied the wobbling pole and gently touched the nail on the cable. Bristow and Young looked at each other in triumph as the lamp glowed, their power problem solved.

The old camouflage of jam tins and potato peelings was no longer viable, so a portable wind-up gramophone was pressed into service as a hiding place for the transformer and power supply parts. The gramophone motor was removed and the deck raised by an inch to make space for the components. The turntable had to be removed to get at the connections and rectifier valve holder. The added weight was partly compensated for by the removal of the motor, but with the lid closed there was nothing to arouse suspicion and the outfit could be carried about with impunity.

The workers were happy with the accordion and dried milk tins, so all that was needed was to make a light-proof box for the ballast lamps. At night after lights-out it was now possible to open the window shutters, but it was necessary to leave the wire hooked to the cable without its supporting batten and to be able to remove it with a sharp tug in the case of an emergency. To operate the receiver Bristow and Stubbs had to move into another block. At 1.00am local time they would take down the news and stay for the rest of the night. It was awkward and inconvenient – but it was working.

For two weeks all went well until the morning when a group of prosperous-looking men were seen in the compound taking a keen interest in the overhead power line. They were evidently from the local electricity board, probably engineers looking for a sporadic out-of-balance leakage of an amp or so in their system. Within a few days a new section of line was erected outside the compound and the old cables removed. The 'Firm' was back where they began.

In the meantime 'Dixie' Deans and Ron Mogg, the Camp Secretary, had been poring over the Geneva Convention as it applied to prisoners-of-war. They found an interesting section which decreed that there had to be a means of signalling for assistance should a sudden case of illness occur during the night and also that a light must be provided for the night latrines. Deans brought up the subject at the next routine meeting with von Lindeiner and obtained complete agreement. The Germans agreed to supply the materials, provided that six suitable volunteers would be drawn from the Kriegies to carry out the installation. They would be supervised by a German electrician. As the power would have to remain 'on' all night, the Block Leaders would be responsible for the prompt implementation of 'lights-out'.

*Oberst* von Lindeiner's naiveté was breathtaking, perhaps he was just hoping for a quiet life but he was playing right into the hands of the designing Kriegies. It was hardly surprising that the names of the six Kriegies selected for the installation job included Bristow, Young and Stubbs.

## 'I BEGAN TO WORRY ABOUT HAMPDENS'

Straight from Gunnery School, his sergeant's stripes and air gunner's brevet fresh and newly sewn on his uniform, George Rex reported one Saturday afternoon in June 1941 to the guardroom of the operational training unit at RAF Cottesmore. As he waited, a funeral party carrying coffins containing the remains of the crew of a crashed Hampden, passed through the main gate heading for the local cemetery.

Because of cramped conditions, Hampdens could not be equipped with dual controls. A flying instructor had to show a trainee pilot what to do and then sit behind him and pray. There were many mistakes. The new Sergeant Rex was witnessing a result. Two days later he was detailed to take part in a similar funeral party. Rex began to worry about Hampdens – but the day was a milestone in the Station Warrant Officer's career – it was his 100th service funeral from RAF Cottesmore.

By late August Sergeant Rex was on his way to a squadron posting at RAF Scampton. At a Lincoln bus stop he met an acquaintance who had been posted to Scampton a few weeks earlier. 'Last week was a bad week,' moaned the acquaintance. 'A Hampden returning from ops taxied out to dispersal, the pilot opened the bomb doors but a bomb had hung-up. It exploded, wiping out the crew and all the ground staff around. Following aircraft were unable to land for a time and while circling two more planes collided over the airfield.'

Operational losses had also been high. August had not been a good month for Scampton. Rex's girlfriend, who had travelled to Lincoln to see him off, could be forgiven had she thought she might be saying a last 'goodbye'.

Six months later and despite the unhappy omens, Rex had carried out several operations against Germany in Hampdens. Now the four-man crews had amalgamated to form seven-man crews for the new Manchesters. The two wireless operator/air gunners alternated between the front turret and the radio on each operation. On the night flight of 9 March 1942 it was Rex's turn to man the turret, a numbing and cold position in which a gunner felt thrust into the forefront of continuous action, and yet where the eyes must be restlessly searching the sky for fighters or flak and studying the ground ahead for landmarks and the target.

There is no position in an operational bomber crew in which a man can relax, but the turret men are the constantly alert eyes of the crew. No-one knew this better than *Luftwaffe* fighter pilots so they tried to approach a bomber from a 'blind spot', usually slightly behind and below, where they would be able to pour their cannon shells and machine gun bullets into the unprotected belly of the bomber. It happened like that on the night the Manchester flew over Holland, near Drenthe. A Messer-schmitt Bf110 slid unseen beneath the bomber and within seconds had it blazing furiously. Pilot Officer Bob Cooper gave the order to drop their 4,000lb 'Cookie' at 'safe', but the bomb nevertheless detonated on contact. The fire in the rear of the Manchester spread rapidly as it flew on with the pilot struggling to maintain height.

Sergeant Rex had been ordered to bale out and as he climbed down to the escape hatch he saw that the fire was fiercest towards the rear of the fuselage. Thrusting his parachute pack on to his harness clips he jumped through the hatch.

The people of the small Dutch town of Assen were jerked awake by the gunfire and the bomb explosion. The locals were used to bombers passing overhead but this action was close. One farmer and his wife leapt from their bed, ran to the window and saw the sky ablaze with lights and a fireball roaring through the night sky towards their home. Screaming, they threw themselves on the floor in terror but the fireball roared low over their farm and crashed in a spectacular, fiery explosion further on, lighting the sky for miles around. People were seen running towards the fire but it was impossible to get close.

Unhurt apart from some slight facial burns, Rex landed comfortably and was able to unhook his parachute canopy where it had snagged on a small tree. It was 2.20am. Snow covered everything, footprints would certainly be seen but Rex had to get away as quickly as possible from the site of the crash fire. The clear sky, the bright moon and the snow made visibility perfect so, crossing hard and frozen fields with difficulty, he headed west towards the Zuider Zee.

During daylight Rex hid in a hut and resumed his walk westward at nightfall. In one small village he walked along the towpath of a canal and was surprised when a group of people smiled at him in a friendly manner as he crossed a bridge. They appeared not to notice his flying clothing. Three Dutchmen gave Rex food and drink when he spoke to them in English, then he was off walking again. At dawn he searched for somewhere to hide during the daylight hours but a dog barked every time he neared a haystack. At midday he spoke to children playing by a lonely farmhouse. With the warm innocence of the young they led him to their farm home. Their mother quickly recovered from her shock at the entry to her home of this oddly dressed and famished stranger, and welcomed him with a hot meal and a bed by the fire. Rex slept, exhausted.

He awoke to find the woman telling her husband about the visitor. The farmer was worried and frightened for his family; the harbouring of an Allied airman was punishable by death. For him there was no alternative but to hand George Rex to the police. Even when the policeman took him to his home and later to the town hall at Oosterwolde, Rex had a feeling that the man might hide him – but it was impossible, too many townsfolk and others had seen him; someone would talk. At Dulag Luft he was reunited with Sergeant Alf Key. The remainder of the crew had perished in the flaming crash.

On the same day that Rex was taken away, the five members of his crew who had died in the action were buried. The wreckage of the Manchester was spread over several hundred yards and the bodies of James Mowat (second pilot), Michael Cross (navigator), George Dalby (wireless operator/air gunner) and Charles Broad (air gunner) were found within the crash area. The body of Pilot Officer Robert Ward Cooper was found nearly a mile away.

At Hoogerswilde cemetery the five crew members were interred, in the presence only of a *Wehrmacht* firing squad. A crowd of Dutch villagers had come to pay their respects to the airmen but the *Feldwebel* in charge, with typical and total 'occupying power' mentality, drove them away. The Dutch policemen were given strict orders by the Germans to prevent flowers being laid on the graves. As always such orders in occupied lands would be defied when German backs were turned.

Another huge bomber force passed over Holland again that night on its way to Essen. Two of the aircraft were Lancasters taking part in the first raid on Germany of that aircraft type.

### AGONY AT AUGSBURG

The city of Augsburg was named after its founder the Roman Emperor Augustus and lies at the confluence of the Bavarian rivers Wertach and Lech. Famous during the Middle Ages, during the Second World War the city had a modern double claim to fame – the MAN works which produced diesel U-boat engines and the nearby Messerschmitt aircraft factory.

The Bomber Operations Directorate wanted Air Chief Marshal Sir Arthur Harris to order the bombing of the ball-bearing factory at Schweinfurt, but Harris thought this a 'panacea' target and difficult to reach. Instead he decided on an experimental raid. Twelve Lancasters were to make a low level, deep penetration attack on the MAN factory. The plan was that although the outward trip would be in daylight, the return would be after dark. This comprised an unescorted round trip of more than 1,200 miles. Such a distant target, a 'fighting all the way' type of attack, was thought by aircrews to be near suicidal.

Weeks of special training were needed for the 12 selected crews from 44 (Rhodesia) Squadron at Waddington and 97 (Straits Settlements)

Squadron at Woodhall Spa. At 15.00hrs on 17 April, under the command of Squadron Leader John Nettleton, they took off and formed up in what was planned to be a powerful defensive formation. A diversionary attack merely roused the *Luftwaffe* fighters of *von Richthofen 5* and *12 Staffeln* and within 15 minutes of crossing the French coast an attack by some 30 Messerschmitts sent three Lancasters down in flames and caused another to crash-land. Three more Lancasters were lost to flak near and over the target but the remaining five, all severely damaged, staggered home to their bases. A VC was awarded to Nettleton and DFCs and DFMs to the remaining members of the crews. The RAF's losses from this operation amounted to more than 58 per cent.

The damaged Lancaster which had been skilfully crash-landed by its skipper, Warrant Officer 'Herbie' Crum DFM, was T-Tommy of 44 Squadron. All the crewmen survived although Sergeant Bert Dowty, who was trapped in the front turret before he was axed free from the distorted metal and perspex, had some terrifying moments believing the aircraft to be on fire. A fire in the port engine had died down and unlike the 'flamers', T-Tommy's crew were on the ground in France trying their hardest to ignite their crashed aircraft and destroy equipment of value to the enemy. Every effort to fire the plane came to nought until Dowty's – strictly forbidden – box of Swan Vestas sent the wreck up with a huge whoosh. Dowty staggered back, unhurt but saddened and pleased as, rubbing his singed eyebrows, he watched 2,000 gallons of flaming high octane fuel consume the Lancaster. Satisfied, the crew moved away as quickly as possible, their minds intent on evading capture. Crum set off on his own to find out what had happened to a friend whose plane was burning in the distance.

Within little more than two weeks they had all been captured. Dowty and Saunderson were on a train heading for the demarcation line to unoccupied France when they were picked up by the Vichy *Milice*. Crum was sent to Dulag but the six other crew members were sent to Fort de la Revére near Nice in France, a few miles from the Italian border. A relic of Napoleonic times, the fort was sited on the solid rock of a mountain top, dungeons had been carved into the rock and it was surrounded by a dry moat.

With the halting by the Red Army of German troops on the outskirts of Moscow, a shiver of doubt had been sent throughout Vichy France and the Germans were not placing quite so much reliance on the local people, feeling that they were now more likely to aid escapers. The escape lines were known to the Germans so an increasing number of prisoners were being sent into camps within Germany for secure custody. Escape while still in France became increasingly urgent for the prisoners.

There had been a previous unsuccessful scramble through a ventilation shaft in the rock but now, late in the summer of 1942, a new plan was devised. A short, shallow tunnel was cut through the soil above the rock surface which would break surface behind a sentry post and within the barbed wire. If the exit could be made during the time that the sentry ate his meal inside the sentry box, the planners reckoned they could squeeze and wriggle through the wire with an even chance of success.

Contact with the 'Pat O'Leary' escape line was achieved through a Polish priest who visited the fort every Sunday to celebrate Mass for the Roman Catholics. O'Leary was the codename of Dr Albert Guérisse who had been a surgeon in the Belgian Army but who now worked for the Special Operations Executive (SOE). On the evening of 5 September 1942, 58 prisoners escaped in pairs and joined the Pat O'Leary escape line. With them were six members of Crum's Lancaster crew.

One man failed to descend the dry moat surrounding the fort. Lance-Corporal McMillan was still inside an unoccupied part of the fort. The result of the evening *Appell* had caused the usual screaming panic among the Germans when prisoners were found to be missing and an immediate search was started. A sentry shouted as he saw McMillan trying to crawl away to hide. Realising that resistance was useless, McMillan rolled on to his back, preparing to get up just as the sentry fired. A bullet entered McMillan's mouth and exited through his cheek, removing part of his ear lobe.

A few days later many of the escapees had been recaptured, including the crew of Lancaster T-Tommy, but 23 others arrived home. They had been taken down the 'line' for a rendezvous with a boat at Carnet-Plage near Perpignan and thence on to Gibraltar. On arrival at Gibraltar they were taken from the ship in a closed van so that they should not be seen by any pro-German Spanish workers. Before more escapes could be engineered the Germans moved the whole camp to Italian jurisdiction, but not before Dowty served his 30 days' solitary confinement where he met Lance-Corporal McMillan, now fully recovered and about to serve his term of punishment.

Bomber Command's chief, 'Butch' Harris, did not consider the 58 per cent loss on the Augsburg raid excessive 'in proportion to the importance of the objective and the serious damage done to it'. About the damage there were doubts; despite some harm to the MAN works the same firm had five other factories doing the same job and production at the Augsburg works was only 'delayed'. The 49 dead, wounded and captured men were, like all aircrew, volunteers, and most could not be asked how they felt about the raid but Harris did say that daylight raids on Germany could only be carried out at a prohibitive casualty rate.

### TORPEDOED

In November 1940, 38 Squadron had flown to Shallufa, Egypt, for operations in the Middle East. The front turrets of its Wellingtons had been faired-in and the usual crew of six reduced to five. During February 1942, 'A' Flight was converted for torpedo operations. So far five aircraft had been fitted to carry torpedoes and extensive rehearsals and practising had been undertaken.

On 27 March an attack was ordered on shipping in the Greek harbour of Patras. As his Wellington approached in the clear, bright moonlight, wireless operator Jim Padgham could plainly see the anti-submarine boom as Flight Lieutenant Henry Buckingham banked the Wellington towards the harbour.

To prevent two aircraft attacking at low level simultaneously, they were to transmit the aircraft identification letter followed by 'i' for 'in' at the commencement of the run in. When the torpedo was launched and after pulling clear they were to transmit the aircraft letter followed by 'o' for 'out'. 'Padg's' finger was on the key. Dropping to 50 feet above the water the bomb doors were opened and the torpedo fused. Not hearing any other signal Padgham sent his own 'in' signal.

From below came machine gun fire and light flak and suddenly the port engine spluttered. At 50 feet there is no room for manoeuvre and to pilot Buckingham it seemed that the aircraft suddenly dropped into the sea. There was just time for Padgham to tuck his head into the crook of his arm and save his face from smashing into the radio. A screeching crunch ripped away the bomb doors. When he slowly regained consciousness, Padgham was in pitch darkness with water up to his waist.

Sergeant Vic Munnings, the navigator, had been in the astrodome at the moment of crash, ready to map-read the outward route. He regained consciousness in the 'office', having been propelled forward through a plywood door.

When Padgham's head cleared he was very much aware that a few feet below his seat was a massive charge of high explosive. The torpedo's nose cap would have spun off after a 40-foot travel, and from then on the torpedo became a percussion weapon. He waded back to the astrodome in time to see the rear gunner fall backwards four feet from his turret into the water. Looking forward, Padgham could see Buckingham helping

Munnings out through the pilot's escape hatch. Blood was gushing from severe cuts on Munnings' face and head. Opening the astrodome, Padgham climbed out and sat astride the fuselage facing the tail. The tailplane was rising and fearing that he might become entangled with the IFF aerial, Padgham slid down into the water, keeping afloat by holding the Mae West with one arm. By the time he had turned around the aircraft had disappeared.

Padgham could hear 'Bucky' call out, but just as he answered him a column of water shot up into the air and a wave rushed towards him. The torpedo had detonated on striking the harbour bed. All the crew except Lucan, the second pilot, were eventually lifted from the icy water and taken to hospital, prisoners of the Italians.

## MURDER BY THE TRACK

Sergeant Bill Bennett and others, who had suffered humiliation and stoning on the village green outside Stalag 9C at Bad Sulza, were told on 30 April 1942 that they were moving to Sagan. Barth and now Sagan were known to be efficiently run by the Kriegies and in the overall charge of the *Luftwaffe*. The 9C men hoped for better treatment and conditions.

The *Feldwebel* in charge at 9C was typical of one kind of *Wehrmacht* NCO selected for prison camp duties. Small, fat and short-tempered, he was given to frothing at the mouth when angry and frustrated. The Kriegies' laughter at this 'un-British' conduct drove him to draw his pistol and fire a shot at their backs as they ran for the huts. The bullet lodged in a window shutter. This was the man who was to supervise the move to Sagan.

The usual box-car type of train waited for them at the siding, with one passenger coach shunted on at the end for the guards. As always during a move there were escape plans forming and the Germans knew it. The Kriegies were roughly ordered into the trucks, the central sliding doors closed and barred on the outside, and the clanking, jerking, stop-start journey to Sagan began.

Escape seemed impossible, the guards were tense and trigger-happy, but in one truck a Kriegie pushed a stick through a small grille near the door and dislodged a pin holding the restraining bar. The door was rolled back and as the train climbed a hill it slowed sufficiently for two men to take a chance. Leaping from the train they swiftly regained their balance and ran.

A shout from a watching guard brought the slow moving train to a shuddering halt, armed soldiers poured from the passenger coach and lined up by the railway line, rifles at the ready. The *Feldwebel* ordered them to fire. The volley of shots brought the two Kriegies to a halt, their arms upraised in surrender. The guards continued to fire so the two men dropped to the ground. As the guards ran forward the fat *Feldwebel*, consumed with choleric anger, continued to fire his pistol. As he reached the prostrate men he fired again.

All the truck doors were then opened in preparation for a count. Bennett saw the two escapers dragged back to the side of the track and spreadeagled. One was obviously severely wounded and bleeding but still he and the other man were mercilessly beaten with rifle butts until even the guards tired and threw the two bleeding men into the box-car. At the count that followed outside the trucks, the Kriegies were fiercely threatened on the consequences of further escape attempts. There were none. The train left again for Sagan.

'Dixie' Deans at Sagan protested vigorously to the *Kommandant* and the Protecting Power about the treatment of the men, one of whom died from loss of blood and shock from the beating. It was said that the *Feldwebel* was arrested, reduced to the ranks and sent to the dreaded *Ostfront*. The Kriegies felt, that if true, it was the least punishment which the sadistic German richly deserved for cold-blooded murder.

Despite the horrors of the journey, Bill Bennett was happier when he looked around him. He decided that Stalag Luft 3 Sagan was a holiday camp compared to Bad Sulza.

### THE 'KICK ACTION' GAIT

In late 1941 a group of officer prisoners at Warburg had seen a man coming towards them who walked with a characteristic kick-action gait. They assumed that here was another airman who had landed a bit too heavily. There were quite a few of those about but this pilot's bad landing had occurred many years earlier. The three rings on his sleeve denoted his rank as wing commander. He said his name was Douglas Bader, 'pronounced "Bahder", if you please'. He had been transferred from Lübeck. Most of the men had heard of Bader in early 1940, but few had believed the story of the legless flyer. They had found flying demanding enough themselves without any handicaps.

The Germans were delighted to have captured Bader, his fame had spread to the Fatherland and their top airmen wanted to meet him. It was not long before the prisoner-of-war branch of the *Luftwaffe* regretted their capture. Pilot Officer Maurice Butt said of Bader:

'He was a natural goon-baiter, as a prisoner he provoked mischief and fun with the Germans at every opportunity. On parade during counting – particularly after an escape – he would stand on his pins swaying slightly to maintain stability and when a German officer or NCO came within range he would manage to fall all over him, much to the glee of all except the Germans. After two successful pull-downs the Germans insisted on his having a chair to sit out the count and whenever they spotted him about the camp they would hurriedly steer clear.'

Bader became prime material for being moved away along with other trouble makers.

The legless airman's presence in the camp did not receive an unalloyed welcome from all. His imperious manner, unreasoned and frequently unreasonable efforts at escape, without thought for the consequences for others, did not endear him to those who had spent a couple of years in careful planning, or even to those who believed that attempting escape was a game for idiots. Bader's persistent goon-baiting and opportunist but hopeless efforts would bring searches, restrictions and loss of privileges to hundreds or even thousands of prisoners. It is also true that Bader could get away with things which other prisoners would find impossible. To the Germans he was a distinguished captive and they would look after him, but there was never any doubting the man's personal courage or resolution.

A 'Latrinogram' rumour said that there was to be a purge of some of the RAF to a new 'super camp' in the east. Exaggerated hints from the Germans meant that the Kriegies knew it sardonically as 'Hermann Göring's Holiday Camp' before any had seen it. It had been especially built for RAF prisoners, and where all the bad eggs were to be retained in one basket.

In early May 1942, 80 RAF officers were destined for Stalag Luft 3 at Sagan in Silesia. At *Appell* on the morning before their departure they were told that anyone who felt they were disabled and unable to walk the two miles to the station, should report to the German Medical Officer after the *Appell*. Maurice Butt immediately thought the Germans were providing alternative transport, clearly with Bader in mind. Butt had previously experienced trouble with his left leg so he dashed back to his hut as soon as the roll call was over and, grabbing a scrubbing brush, he abraded the skin of his leg to simulate inflamed flesh. A glance at Butt's medical record and the glowing skin was enough to convince the *Artz*.

Derisive calls from the marchers greeted the pony and trap carrying Bader and three other prisoners as it passed the main column. Butt was amazed to find that they had been allocated a plush first class carriage, quite different from the wooden-slatted seats, known to all as travelling 'hard-bottomed'. The Kriegies deduced the hand of Hermann Göring and his keen sense of chivalry from the Great War. To him Bader was an 'equivalent' man.

Before the journey started the usual warnings and threats were made by a German officer. 'You will not attempt to escape otherwise you will be shot without warning. You will not stand up in the compartment. If you wish to go to the *Abort* make a request to the guard. Do not approach the window or you will be shot.' There were six prisoners in the compartment and a guard in the corridor to watch two compartments. By a careful series of questions the Kriegies discovered the destination of the train, and a diagrammatic map above the seats enabled the train's progress to be charted. Bader kept them up to date with a review of the war so far.

After two days' travelling the six Kriegies, unwashed, unshaven and bottom-sore from sitting, were feeling jaded and weary when the train was shunted off at a junction and coupled to a steam engine prior to the last leg of the journey. Suddenly Bader stood up. Holding on to the luggage rack he looked at the weary five and said, 'How about a cup of tea chaps?' The five stared in amazement and concern as Bader reached for his kitbag and dug out a teapot, followed by a two-ounce packet of Red Cross tea. He put the kitbag back on the rack and to the horror of the others he turned to the window, opened it wide and waved the teapot about outside. So far he could have been shot three times.

Guards erupted into activity, shouting and in a state of almost hysterical agitation rifles were unslung and cocked. An *Unteroffizier* ran up, followed by a *Feldwebel* and then a *Hauptmann*. Pistols were being waved around wildly and several guards in the marshalling yard were pointing rifles at the open window. Calmly Bader explained that he wanted a brew of tea and wished someone to take the teapot to the engine driver in order to have the necessary hot water added from the engine.

The *Hauptmann* saw sense. He did not fancy a posting to the Eastern Front just because his distinguished guest might cause a major incident. The order was given and the tea pot taken to the engine by a guard who was as amazed as the Kriegies. Bader's nerve and the sheer magic of the man had worked again.

At the entry search at Sagan Bader, as usual, had the searchers in a turmoil. '*Herr Hauptmann*,' he called provocatively, 'make sure you look inside my tin legs – they are full of contraband.' The guards froze but the *Hauptmann* in charge had already suffered loss of face from the tea on the train incident. He waved Bader through into the East compound of Stalag Luft 3, complete with his tin legs stuffed with contraband.

Bader was such a nuisance to the Germans at Stalag Luft 3 that they determined to get rid of him. Using the pretence of sending him to a hospital camp where he would receive better treatment for his stumps, they ordered him to get ready to move next morning. Bader simply said, 'Bugger off, I'm not going,' and refused, apart from swearing at them, to carry on the conversation.

*Hauptmann* Pieber was at first taken aback, although he had not really expected his best-known prisoner to go quietly. On another occasion Bader threatened to jump into the fire pool and defy all attempts to get him out.

On Friday morning, 10 July 1942, Pieber thought he had solved his problem by arriving with 50 armed men with several more officers hovering in the background. The watching Kriegies were then the ones to be astounded. Squadron Leader Ken Campbell and others were struck by the ludicrous situation of 50 armed men and a posse of German officers arriving like a royal guard to escort one legless prisoner from the camp. The Kriegies let the Germans know their views with loud, ribald catcalls, pithy comments and derisive laughter.

The Germans were being made to look fools; they did not like it and tempers were rising. Bader, warned by the SBO that someone other than he might be shot, reluctantly decided to accept the inevitable. He jauntily swaggered through the compound gate, his square jaw held high, majestic in his jerky gait and appearing to inspect on parade his lined-up escort. Cheers and cries of 'Cheerio Doug' echoed across the camp as every Kriegie in the compound turned out to say goodbye.

Although forced to accept their orders Bader had won yet another victory: he had made the Germans look ridiculous again in front of their own staff and the Kriegies. Bader was destined for Stalag 8B Lamsdorf and it is certain that *Kommandant Oberst* von Lindeiner was heartily glad to see him go; the arch goon-baiter was no longer his problem.

At Lamsdorf Bader still appeared to have little consideration for other prisoners and was rarely able to understand their viewpoint, especially those who had been prisoners longer than he. He felt that some had lost their push and drive, their very Britishness. Bader questioned a sergeant pilot on the reason why he had never attempted to escape. The sergeant took a deep breath and replied: 'There is less chance of a well-known person like Wing Commander Bader being shot than unknown Sergeant Smith.'

On another occasion, Bader, due to move, took food and hid in the rafters of a hut in an empty compound while the rest of the men in the RAF compound stood 'on parade' for several weary hours, with the Germans asking the whereabouts of Wing Commander Bader. One Kriegie said that all the RAF men knew where the 'bloody exhibitionist' was, but out of loyalty they remained silent.

## THE TREMBLING TRIGGER FINGER

Paul Hilton was disappointed when he missed the second 1,000-bomber raid. Flight Sergeant McKay had detected a whiff of glycol from a leak and aborted the take-off. Hilton thought that 'Chiefy' had probably saved the crew's lives and determined to buy him a drink in the Mess on his return.

Hilton had his trip to Essen later, on 2 June. The night was clear with a bright moon, the attacking aircraft were plainly visible and fighters were expected. Hilton's Halifax was jumped by three Junkers Ju88s but the attack had been inexplicably broken off. Perhaps it had been Hilton's violent evasive action, or the Halifax gunners' spirited fight and accuracy with their .303in 'rifle' bullets had been sufficient to deter the nightfighters – anyway they had left. Now it was up to Hilton to nurse the Halibag home on its two outer engines but when the starboard outer developed an internal glycol leak it was bale-out time.

By the time the crew had jumped and it was Hilton's turn to go, the aircraft was too low. Ditching in what appeared to be a patch of swamp seemed his best chance. Laboriously bringing the sinking Halifax round he realised too late that ground mist had obscured a row of trees and some houses. On the point of a stall the Halifax's starboard wing crashed into a house and was torn off, the remainder of the aircraft slewed round in a 180-degree flat cartwheel.

Paul Hilton was unconscious for a few seconds but opened his eyes in time to see the port engine blazing. Struggling out of his seat and climbing through a reluctantly opening overhead hatch, he crawled on to the top of the fuselage. Sliding on to the port wing Hilton could see that the dinghy was inflating and he grabbed the iron rations as he passed.

The instinctive reaction of an airman escaping from burning wreckage is to put as much distance as possible between him and the conflagration; the tanks still held several hundred gallons of high octane fuel. Hilton ran as fast as his long legs would carry him towards the nearby trees until a scream of *'Halt!'* and a vicious prod in the back from a rifle muzzle jerked him to a panting standstill.

The lone German sentry wielding the rifle was hysterical with fear. He had narrowly escaped the crashing Halifax and the sight of the running airman had reduced him to a quivering jelly. Hilton wondered fearfully if the sentry's finger was trembling on the trigger, certainly the safety catch would be off. Anything could happen now. The German was in a highly excitable state and both he and Hilton were still very near the frizzling heat which was about to explode into something like a volcanic eruption. Even a minor explosion would make the man jump and pull the trigger. As the cold sweat ran down Hilton's back, the thought raced through his mind that the sentry might even shoot on purpose. Perhaps his family had been bombed in Cologne a few nights ago. 'The English-man started to run,' the German might say, and who would disbelieve him?

Still, the sentry screamed and prodded with his rifle and when a small explosion in the burning outer port wing tank made the German jump, Hilton was sure that his last moment had come. Fear overwhelmed him, he felt helpless and out of control of this deadly situation. It could not go on much longer. Hilton could only hope that the end would be swift and painless.

A torch shone in the distance, there was shouting and another torch flashed. Slowly the tension diminished as the sentry saw others coming to his aid. It seemed an eternity before Hilton was surrounded and taken to a safer distance from the roaring flames. Passing Hilton over to others, the sentry melted away into the darkness, relating his exciting story as he went. As he left, the main wing tanks exploded with a muffled roar enveloping them all in a momentary blanket of suffocating heat.

Captors and captive watched the remains of the Halifax burning furiously for a while and then Hilton was led away to the local barracks. Here he saw for the first time the standard German army double-tier bunk, complete with the wood-wool filled palliasse. Paul Hilton lay down, exhausted by the fight, the struggle with the crippled Halifax, the crash and the total shock of the night's events. He was now a prisoner of the enemy and too late to find that moment to talk to the CO and too late to buy Chiefy a thank-you drink in the Mess, but in that bare half an hour he had survived by a succession of miracles. Seconds later he was asleep.

### 'WO IST DER TOMMY?'

The crew of Wellington K-Katie numbered this operation to Duisburg their 11th trip. Had they counted the two operational North Sea sweeps it would have been their 13th but RAF aircrew, like most men engaged in dangerous work, are riddled with superstition.

The crew room was crowded and hot. Navigator Sergeant Don Bruce fingered the lucky blue top he always carried when flying and thought about the ugly, dustbin-shaped 4,000lb bomb that K-Katie would be carrying to drop on Duisburg. The lightly cased 'Cookie', dangerous even for the armourers to transport on the ground, was studded with detonators. It had a protruding rim to prevent it penetrating too deeply into the ground before exploding, so achieving maximum blast effect. Bruce ruefully considered the implications of this hazardous cargo. Even with the bomb-doors removed to accommodate the 'Cookie' the barrel-like shape protruded below the fuselage, and with all its modifications the Wellington would not fly on one engine. Neither would she float if they were forced to ditch. The whole crew hated this bomb. The one consolation was that the Germans' hate would be even greater.

The 'Cookie' was to be dropped late in the raid so 'Katie' was scheduled to be one of the last aircraft over the target, due to arrive during the lull after the Main Force had dropped their load and left. It was reasoned that the Germans would assume the raid finished and their rescue services would be in full swing when 'Katie's' maximum blast bomb dropped among them.

It was 13 July and really their 13th trip. Don Bruce felt that he ought to have bad feelings about it. The outward flight was uneventful. The crew of 'Katie' were battle-hardened and just a bit blasé but as they neared the target the pilot, Del Mooney, was cautious. Flying round the perimeter of Duisburg at 13,000ft he saw a Wellington 500ft below. As the other aircraft was attracting the flak 'Katie' flew over unmolested but the action was getting too hot for the Wellington beneath and it dived away.

'Katie' was now directly over the target so Mooney ordered the release of their 4,000-pounder and then banked the Wellington sharply away, but the defences had locked on. A blue beamed searchlight snapped on to the aircraft and all the beams clustered around it followed swiftly to cone 'Katie'. Her pilot was blinded by the dazzling light and Bruce knew it would be only be seconds before the aircraft's height and course was predicted by the gunners below. With a noise like a stick being run along corrugated iron the flak found them, striking the port engine.

Flak had injured rear gunner Ron Esling before and, not relishing a repeat performance, he shouted for the pilot to get the aircraft out of the beams. In desperation Mooney pulled the aircraft's nose up and up. The crew felt that hanging, inert, sensation before a stall, then the Wellington was swinging over and diving in the opposite direction. As 'Katie' plunged some 5,000ft the crew floated in space inside the fuselage, only the navigation table held Bruce down where it pinned his knees.

The searchlights lost them but the Wellington was in danger of being torn to pieces. Loose objects were floating past Bruce's face. Accumulators, maps, pencils, nuts and bolts, cruised past but his eyes were fixed on the navigator's air speed indicator where the needle had turned on to the inner circle, moving up to 320, 330, 340, 350mph. Flashing in his mind was the red warning plate on the pilot's control panel which stated: 'THIS AIRCRAFT MUST NOT BE DIVED AT SPEEDS IN EXCESS OF 350 MPH.'

Gravitational force pressed the crew down into their seats. Eyelids began to close involuntarily. Through the intercom Bruce could hear Mooney panting with exertion as he hauled the Wellington out of the dive. Every rivet in the plane seemed to be screaming. As suddenly as it had begun, the aircraft steadied to straight and level. The crew began to breathe more easily and Bruce looked around him. Debris littered the navigation table and the floor. The ops ration case had burst open and the table had been showered with raisins. In the dim cabin light Bruce could see an earwig emerging from the sticky heap.

Quickly Bruce took stock, gathering his maps from the floor near the bed before flashing a look at the pilot. Mooney was desperately try-ing to keep the port wing with its dead engine on an even keel. Pulling the Wellington back he gained 500 feet and almost immediately dropped the same amount as the starboard engine overheated. Height was being lost rapidly. They were not going to reach the coast. After a hurried consul-tation between the pilot and observer, 'Jump, jump, rear gunner,' was shouted over the intercom but Esling had heard the hurried talk, jetti-soned his turret doors and dived out. The front gunner found his para-chute pack which had been dislodged from its stowage during the stall turn, he clipped it to his harness and jumped through the hatch. The wireless operator was unaccountably looking for his gloves under his table. Bruce jerked free his intercom plug, remembering the instruction that the leads could strangle a jumper if caught up by the opening para-chute. He loosened his tie, rammed the pack to his harness, kicked the wireless operator to attract his attention and pointed forward. The oper-ator motioned him past. Racing forward Bruce glanced at Delmar Mooney who smiled and gave a thumbs up. Then he was at the open hatch. Four thousand feet below, the ground appeared to move slowly past, dull, grey and uninviting.

As he hesitated at the gaping opening, Don Bruce could hear the instructor's words at OTU: 'When you have to go you should dive out head first, but if you have time you will probably lower yourself by your hands.' Bruce decided that was the way he would go. Facing the rear of the aircraft with his hands on either side of the hatch, he gingerly low-ered his feet and legs into the slipstream. The pressure whipped them away and like a straw he was swept along the underside of the fuselage, his parachute pack jammed against the edge of the hatch. Struggling hard to free himself Bruce eased his shoulders out into the clutching slip-stream. The wind wrenched him into the night.

When his parachute opened Bruce's descent was quiet until the whining, roaring scream of the dying Wellington plunging to earth ripped the air. Then the exploding, spreading blossom of fire as the plane crashed and gouts of petrol from the shattered tanks spread in flowing, glowing rivers was beneath him. The oxygen bottles detonated with brilliant blue flashes and ammunition crackled like a huge, angry, log fire as it spat indiscriminately. Alert again Bruce peered downward. Slowly, dim shapes began to appear. He was heading straight for trees, quickly he moved his legs into a sitting position. The parachute, trailing ahead in a slight breeze, snagged on a tree and Bruce swung into soft earth.

Getting to his feet and rubbing a grazed elbow, Bruce looked around. Just ahead was a farmhouse with people standing in a group outside watching the fire. He should be in Holland, he thought, perhaps there was help ahead. He called out a loud 'Hello'. It was greeted by a woman's piercing scream and everyone disappeared. Bruce realised his descent was silent and unseen. The people were startled and scared. So was he, standing alone in the darkness in a strange country.

In the farmhouse the van Dijk family peered through a window at the strange apparition. They watched the airman take off his Mae West life jacket and then disappear down the road. Was it a German plane that had crashed in flames, was the man a Nazi, one of those who imposed the strict curfew on them in Nijnsel? The van Dijk family was frightened, the flyer may well come back.

A sudden hammering at the door set them trembling. Mr van Dijk opened the front door to a steel helmeted German patrol. They had found the parachute and assumed that the RAF man was in the house. *'Wo ist der Tommy?'* they shouted, roughly elbowing their way into the hallway.

Mr van Dijk declared that the airman was not in the house, while secretly fearing that he may have sneaked indoors for shelter. The Germans disbelieved him. Determined to find the airman and posting a man with a loaded rifle pointing at the van Dijks, they searched every room and the hay loft, poking their bayonets and digging forks deep into the hay.

Down the road Bruce threw his helmet into a hedge and strode quickly away to get clear of the area. As he was in a friendly country he asked a man wheeling a bicycle for help. The man led Bruce to a cottage but the door was slammed in his face. The locals were scared. He walked on until daylight. A knock on the door of a Presbytery was unanswered. In a village where people were coming from the church he asked for help, whereupon Bruce was taken to a local baker who asked if he would like to meet a friend. Rear gunner Bill Margerison was ushered into the room. Each felt the overwhelming relief of no longer being alone yet they were uneasy. When a smiling Dutch policeman arrived and arrested them their worst fears were confirmed.

Bill Margerison's pockets seemed to be full. Bruce was worried. Margerison was happily showing family photographs to a young girl from the next house. Bruce leaned over and asked: 'Have you got your identity card in with that stuff?'. The reply made Bruce answer urgently, 'You had better get out to the bog sharpish, tear it up and drop it down the pan. Ask this Dutch goon if you can go outside.'

The Dutch policeman had been smiling pleasantly, but when he was going to accompany Margerison he suddenly produced a pistol and waved at Bruce to go with them. The smile had been false, the Dutchman was pro-German.

When the *Feldgendarmerie* arrived, Margerison attempted to give his Irvin jacket to the young man who had helped and shown him kindness but the German policeman snatched it and threw it in the back of the car. Later they stopped and Ron Fermor was brought from a house. He walked dejectedly to the car, his Sidcot suit slung over his shoulder, but his expression lit up like a Christmas tree when he saw Bruce and Margerison. Del Mooney and Pilot Officer Bill Hancock, the wireless operator, joined them later. The crew was complete. After Dulag the NCOs were sent to the RAF compound at Lamsdorf. Sagan, was full.

### SAGAN ELECTRIFIED

Throughout the summer of 1942 the NCOs' compound at Sagan had filled and prisoners from Dulag had been sent to the inferior, three-tier bunk huts in the RAF compound at Lamsdorf, Stalag 8B. Sagan must have seemed more comfortable than Lamsdorf yet the camp had been short of Red Cross supplies. Wagons for the camps were packed in Switzerland, according to the number of inmates in the camp to which they were assigned. The complement of Sagan had been continually increasing and the Red Cross supply was always in arrears. Soon 1,400 RAF NCO airmen crowded into the centre compound and the last two fenced-off huts, which had been used as a reception area, were incorporated into the living area. With so many in the camp the theatre had to put on each show for several nights to accommodate everyone.

A *Luftwaffe* corporal electrician duly arrived to supervise the wiring of the huts for the lavatories and emergency lights. Language differences were no barrier: wiring diagrams are a universal language. In two weeks the job was completed, a red light on a small mast was fitted outside the main entrance controlled by a switch in the vestibule, the rooms had separate switches and the Kriegie store of wire, screws and various electrical sundries was considerably enlarged.

Ten of the 11 block conversions had been carried out in accordance with the prescribed scheme, but in Bristow's block there were minor but important differences. Behind two wooden clothes pegs two unofficial sockets had been fitted and invisibly wired behind the cavity of the partition. In future the radio men would be spared the inconvenience of removing lamps and screwing adaptors made from bulb caps into the sockets.

The radio now had its own power supply in the kitchen of the hut and news operations could be resumed. Every night the set was manned by Bristow and Stubbs to receive the midnight news from London. Stubbs still insisted on transcribing his shorthand immediately the news broadcast had finished, and as the news did not begin until 1.00am local time he had to make up for lost sleep during the afternoons.

The radio receiver was still mounted in the end of the accordion and the valves stored in their dried milk tins. The earphone was safe in a small tin buried in a container of soft soap for cleaning the cooker. The mains unit was the converted gramophone, the electric shaver smoothing choke had been camouflaged inside the hull of a model sailing ship which had long stood on the top of a locker in the kitchen. Connections were taken from the deck rails. The whole apparatus including the large smoothing condenser, still took far too long to assemble and then dismantle to pack away. Commercial components were needed to enable both weight and bulk to be reduced. More pounding of the compound circuits were scheduled for discussion of the problems.

In early autumn a telephone was borrowed from the Germans as a stage prop and the radio constructors thought they had better have a look inside. To their surprise they found in the base a block condenser of 3 microfarads and another of 2 microfarads. Bristow swiftly nipped them out. The working voltage of 200 volts was a bit low but the trio crossed their fingers and hoped for the best.

There were certain to be reprisals if the theft was detected so the condensers were quickly built into a model Boulton Paul Defiant aeroplane which hung innocently from the kitchen ceiling. Connections were taken to the four guns protruding from the leading edge of the wings. Reprisals there were, the theatre was closed for a fortnight but the Firm hung on to their loot.

*Feldwebel* Heinze was new at Sagan. He was a keen Nazi, a fluent English speaker and heartily disliked by the Kriegies, particularly those who had something to hide from the ferrets. Bristow had just finished working on a wooden clock and decided to tighten the tuning condenser which had a habit of drifting off frequency when in use. It was usually a fairly safe hour but suddenly, without warning, Heinze burst into the room. He knew immediately what Bristow was holding and grabbed it with triumph.

The Kriegies were not surprised when a massive search took place early the next morning. Plans for such an event had been well rehearsed. The ferrets found nothing but paid a great deal of attention to Bristow's heavy wooden clock and its pendulum. Bristow put the whole episode down to Heinze's vindictiveness and told him so. When he looked Heinze in the eye and called him, among other epithets, a 'square-headed bastard' everyone knew the certainty of having to say goodbye to 'Curly' for a while. Retribution was swift, Bristow was whisked away to the *Arrestlok* for 10 days' solitary.

When the charge sheet arrived in 'Dixie' Deans' office, Stubbs and Young were relieved to see that it merely accused Bristow of 'addressing a German *Feldwebel* in a highly arrogant and cheeky manner'. They thought that one of the year's understatements, but happily there was no mention of 'being in possession of forbidden articles' such as radio sets and no mention of espionage. They had wondered – often.

Although few components had been lost, the most serious aspect of the incident was that from now on the radio trio would be constantly under suspicion. It was therefore important to start immediately on the construction of a second radio. Out came the Admiralty Handbook again. A coil was made on the base of a Gibbs' solid dentifrice case and a small coil for reaction fitted into the space where the dentifrice had been. For adjustment the box was hinged at the edge. They made a paper dielectric tuning condenser similar to the old one. A utility version of the rubber valve socket was fashioned from plywood and brass, and the whole compact set was fitted to the hexagonal base end of a concertina. They were banking on the double bluff that the Germans would credit them with more sense than to use the same kind of hiding place twice. By the time Bristow had completed his term of solitary in the Cooler, the Firm was back in business.

Grimm was a *Dolmetscher*, an interpreter who often dropped in for a chat and a coffee. Such men were useful and often let drop valuable nuggets of information, some by accident and others by design. Grimm mentioned that there was consternation among the *Abwehr* staff that no headphone had been found and they were determined to search it out. It was strange that the *Abwehr* were so concerned about a headphone because there also had to be a valve and some kind of power supply, but that did not seem to worry them, it was the headphone they wanted.

The radio men had never been happy with their 60-Ohm mis-matching ex-post office home-made substitute, and they and Grimm seemed to arrive at the simple solution simultaneously. He, Grimm, would supply them with a proper pair of headphones and when they had proved them to their satisfaction they, the radio men, would plant their home-made product in a block at the other end of the compound. By strange chance Grimm would see an odd-looking tooth dentifrice box with holes in the lid and some wires in it and report the discovery to his superiors.

Everything worked like a charm. The Kriegies watched a detachment of ferrets march resolutely to a distant barrack and return bearing their loot and wreathed in smug smiles. The conspirators looked distressed whilst inwardly gloating about their splendid pair of ex-*Kriegsmarine* Telefunken headphones.

A few days later Grimm sought out Bristow and Co. He was greatly pleased at being highly commended for his diligence and powers of observation. With his pat-on-the-back went some special leave which he intended to spend in Berlin. Some coffee, he suggested, would make his leave even more acceptable and fruitful. Grimm went, never to return. His nefarious dealings and his running with the hare and the hounds caught up with him. His fate was unknown but the usual punishment after a spell in a penal camp was a posting to the dreaded *Ostfront.*

The news service was resumed. The smaller coil in the new set was probably less efficient than the old one wound with the Barth corridor wire, but any loss was more than compensated for by the new headphones. The trio still wanted to rid themselves of the heavy, cumbersome and difficult to hide mains transformer. They cast querying and covetous eyes at the two loudspeakers fixed high on the outsides of the two cookhouses. They knew that each loudspeaker was fitted with a transformer to match it to the line, but there was no way of knowing the impedance involved. Carefully, Bristow made a visually accurate replica from wood and tinplate. At a suitable time and with lookouts posted, Bristow replaced the loudspeaker transformer with the replica, re-connected the voice coil to the line with a pencil lead resistor of unknown value, and waited for the next announcement.

The *Deutschlandsender* radio voice came through, not loud or particularly clear, but it was acceptable and the resistor did not seem to affect the other loudspeakers on the system. Although the Kriegies had no voltmeter, they had accumulated a number of torch bulbs of various ratings and were able to assess the output of the transformer when its primary was connected to the mains. As far as they could judge it was about four volts and would serve their purpose admirably.

Another replica was made and the second transformer purloined at the first opportunity. The trouble was that both speakers were now practically inaudible, but the arrangement was at least symmetrical and the Germans were now having less to shout about. *Sondermeldungen* were less frequent and a disparity in phraseology was becoming apparent. A German 'evacuation according to plan', 'a straightening of the line' and 'a strategic withdrawal' signalled an advance by the Allies.

The Heinze incident caused Bristow and Co. to tighten general security, and casting around they fastened on a small white First Aid cupboard with a red cross on the door. It was screwed to the wall of the kitchen near to the modified clothes pegs and contained a couple of bandages, a small bottle of iodine and some aspirins. They modified the cupboard so that the left side was hinged to the wall, the receiver components were mounted on its back and a hole was cut in the wall to house them. When rock wool insulation was removed there was room for the headphones to hang down inside the wall when not in use and remain connected to the set. When swung back against the wall, the cupboard was secured by a single screw which was hidden by the shelf which had to be raised half an inch to uncover the screw.

Another gramophone was converted into a mains unit, using the two loudspeaker transformers. This time it was possible not only to leave the motor in position but also to maintain normal gramophone operation. The internal horn was modified by using a bent piece of plywood which was placed under the base of the tone arm and a vertical partition screened off the motor compartment. These modifications replaced the internal horn assembly which originally encircled the motor in order to increase its length and enhance the bass response. It was still necessary to lift off the turntable to plug in the rectifier and connectors, but these could be removed and the turntable replaced very rapidly. A small adjustment enabled the minimum speed setting to stop the motor so it was possible to leave it already wound and to have a record playing in a matter of seconds. The whole lot was joined together by a connecting harness encased in rubber tubing supplied by sick quarters. This too was stored in the wall cavity behind the small First Aid cabinet.

The mains connector was separate and connected by the clothes pegs to the gramophone. The aerial was a clothes line left permanently in position as at Barth. The emergency concertina had served its purpose well but was no longer needed. It was restored to working order and returned to its owner.

It eventually became common knowledge that some form of radio receiver existed in the camp, so there was less inhibition encountered in trying to buy components from the Germans. Methods of trading with the enemy outside the wire had become more controlled during the summer. Individual direct negotiating was replaced by a committee which did the deal if possible, paying from a communal cigarette fund. Apart from the radio men, others carried on a brisk tailoring industry making civilian clothes, and forgers were hard at work copying passes and other documents for would-be escapers.

### 'SECOND FRONT NOW!'
'War hath no fury like a non-combatant.'
— *C. E. Montague*

On the night of 18/19 August 1942, 5,000 Canadian and 1,000 British soldiers sailed across the English Channel on Operation 'Jubilee'. The operation was loosely termed a 'Reconnaissance in Force', although no-one seemed to know quite what that meant. It seemed that the laudable objects were to harry the enemy and to test the German defences of a Channel port with a view to learning valuable lessons for an eventual landing and invasion. Dieppe, surely one of the most easily defended ports, was chosen. There was talk that the Canadian troops in Britain were restless due to forced inactivity since their Atlantic crossing. There was pressure, too, from the Russians for a second front and an ill-judged, ill-informed outcry in Britain to hit back now at the Germans in that way. A more difficult target could hardly have been chosen. Whatever the reasons for the raid on Dieppe the planning was poorly conceived and carried out, with abysmal intelligence about the area's defences and the difficulties to be encountered by those about to set foot on the shore.

Corporal Herbert Noy was the Engineer-Fitter on a 63ft 'Whaleback' RAF power boat, one of several that left Dover to take part in the action that morning. They were Air/Sea Rescue (ASR) units and their part in the operation was clear – they were always at sea during air and naval activity.

Above the launch in one of the Spitfires providing as much fighter cover as possible for the raid, was Pilot Officer Donald Morrison, RCAF. Morrison had previously been awarded a DFM as a sergeant in June and on the morning of the Dieppe raid he had flown top cover for USAAF Flying Fortresses who were staging a diversionary raid on the airfield at Abbeville. Now he was in the thick of a dogfight with Focke-Wulf Fw190s above Dieppe. As he twisted and turned Morrison held a 190 in his sights long enough to get in a good shot and saw the German go down a 'flamer', but his plane had been hit. By then he had tumbled down near the sea and while fighting his way up again Morrison's Merlin coughed and died. Rapidly jumping out, his parachute barely opening before he was in the water, Morrison inflated his dinghy and climbed in. He was floating around for some 15 minutes before he was pulled aboard an ASR launch and changing into dry clothes.

But on the beach at Dieppe there was slaughter. The Churchill tanks landed could make very little headway across the shingle and over the sea wall. The ships and support craft offshore were harassed, shelled from the land and continuously attacked from the air.

Corporal Noy's 'Whaleback' was attacked by Fw190s and within seconds the engine room was blazing fiercely. Noy struggled to the deck and found chaos as the surviving crew abandoned ship. Quickly he released a Carly Float, leapt overboard and drifted away from the burning vessel.

The launch on which Pilot Officer Don Morrison had been dragged from the sea now moved further in towards the shore and picked up other downed pilots and naval men in the sea. Noy's launch nearby was on fire and all around ships were burning with Carly Floats bobbing in the sea beside them. A second launch went in to help and was itself attacked and burst into raging flame. German bombers were adding to the carnage and Don Morrison watched with frustrated anger as wounded men in the sea, screaming in agony, were methodically machine-gunned. The single Lewis machine gun armament of the boat was useless against the diving 190s. The six Focke-Wulfs attacked Morrison's boat as he dived overboard to rescue one of the ASR crew. A destroyer which had been called in to help drove off the attackers with its Oerlikons. Turning back towards England with its cargo of wounded air and seamen, the boat successfully ran the gauntlet to Dover.

Noy however found himself drifting away from the centre of the battle but inexorably towards the French coast. Two days later he was washed ashore to a reception by members of a German regiment waiting to take the exhausted man prisoner. Within a week he was at Dulag.

Don Morrison, promoted to flight lieutenant and awarded the DFC, did not have long to wait before he too joined the Kriegies, but he was to spend a lengthy spell in hospital. On 8 November 1942 he led his section of Spitfires to Lille, covering for bombers, when he was shot down near

St Malo. Severely wounded, his left leg severed near the hip, Morrison was the leading fighter pilot of the RCAF when captured.

The Kriegies were shocked by the apparent failure of the Dieppe raid and the Germans made much of this 'attempted invasion'. This was, they claimed, the ultimate failure of the Allies. *Festung Europa* had withstood, with ease, the most powerful force that could have been thrown against its defences. What remained of the attackers had been forced to withdraw licking their wounds. The propaganda newspaper *The Camp* gloatingly printed photographs of lines of prisoners, wounded and dejected, being marched away; but it was the pictures of the wrecked landing craft, the beach littered with distorted bodies and burning tanks which brought the matter painfully home.

The hearts of the Kriegies went out to the gallant men who had fought so hard against impossible odds and a well prepared foe. Deeds of outstanding heroism were committed that day by Canadians and Britons, but of the 6,000 soldiers who went to Dieppe only some 2,000 returned and all the equipment that had been landed – tanks, landing craft, guns – were lost. Despite the whitewash excuses, 'Jubilee' was a disaster

The commanders asserted that many valuable lessons were learned for a subsequent invasion of the Continent but by far the most valuable was negative: how *not* to mount an invasion. A frontal attack on a well-defended port was prohibitively costly in men and material. The idea of 'Mulberry' was born.

### FRIENDLY ENEMIES

In German-occupied Crete an RAF flyer was learning a strange lesson in wartime friendliness of the enemy. The Germans had recently placed three RDF stations on Crete which, on 22 September 1942, gave them advance warning of the approach of Les Ford's PRU Spitfire. Two Bf109s shattered the side of his Spitfire while he was flying straight and level on a photographic run. After several weeks in a Cretan hospital, Ford, an injured foot still painful, was collected for his move to Dulag Luft by two escorting German officers travelling on leave from North Africa. A Junkers Ju52 flew them to Athens but there was no train that night for an onward journey.

While one of the Germans negotiated for a three-bed hotel room, Ford stood on one leg in the crowded street with the other officer. Six boys ran towards them, dodging in and out among the pedestrians. One ran straight into Les Ford, nearly bowling him over and causing him to grasp the wall for support. When he recovered his balance Ford found notes to the value of one thousand Greek Drachma in his hand.

Les Ford was by this time on reasonably friendly terms with his generally inebriated escorts. He was taken into the hotel and allotted one of three beds in a room. Ford was glad to settle down but his escorts seemed restless. After several searches through their kitbags and calls for the housemaid it became apparent to Ford that the currency being used in a transaction was British Bully Beef, and the product desired was the voluptuous girl herself.

When the second officer had returned to the bedroom and after an appropriate interval, the Germans clubbed together and offered the remaining tin of Bully Beef to Ford for him to pay for a similar service. Les Ford thought he was beginning to appreciate the comradeship of war and hoped that his refusal was accepted with the warmth and generosity with which it was offered.

His journey to Dulag Luft began next day from Athens with the officers in a first class compartment to themselves. As the journey progressed Ford's comfort gradually depreciated until he joined 30 POWs in a cattle truck.

*'... I'm sorry, dear, but I love a soldier.*
*I know you'll understand...'*

# PART 4
# 1943

## EMERGENCY EXIT

For the RAF the year 1943 began well. In January permission was given for the use of H2S on operations, the first Target Indicators were dropped and No 8 (Pathfinder) Group was formed, commanded by Don Bennett. Bomber Command was moving into a higher gear.

An experimental raid by 20 Lancasters was mounted on a particular target to be pinpointed by three Pathfinder Mosquitoes using H2S and Oboe, and centred on the industrial city of Essen. The Met forecast for the night of 3/4 January was eight-tenths cloud over the target, giving the crews hope that they might gain relief from the great mass of searchlights encircling the city. But the skies over Essen were almost cloudless. Despite this, most of the bombers successfully aimed their loads at the Pathfinder flares. Five had already turned for home due to icing and the remaining Lancasters were heading for the feared German nightfighter belt across Holland. At briefing the crews had been told that the Germans were using ground radar to vector their nightfighters on to the bombers and that if the bombers lost height of at least 5,000 feet at a time, they would drop from the *Luftwaffe* radar screens and make it necessary for them to reset their radar equipment. As it was a clear night without moonlight the chances of seeing approaching nightfighters was remote.

Just as wireless operator/air gunner Sergeant John Banfield in the front turret advised the pilot to begin a 5,000-foot drop, their Lancaster was attacked from below. Cannon shells struck the main batteries amidships, pierced the starboard inboard petrol tank and destroyed the intercom. Seconds later Banfield felt the navigator tugging at his trouser leg and yelling: 'Bale out, bale out!"

Ramming his parachute into the harness clips Banfield dashed to the forward escape hatch in the fuselage floor. It was jammed shut. Turning swiftly Banfield was surprised to see the navigator disappear through a gaping hole where the starboard perspex blister had been. The inboard airscrew came within a foot of the fuselage at that point, but because of the blazing petrol tank behind it the flight engineer had feathered the motor. As Banfield climbed out of the plane the slipstream ripped the parachute from his chest and blew it inside the aircraft. Holding the shattered fuselage with one hand Banfield reached inside, drew the parachute out, held it to his chest and released his grip. His last memory before losing consciousness was of falling under the mainplane and the Lancaster roaring away in flames.

He awoke hanging in his harness in a tree some 20 feet from the ground. Banfield could not move, his body ached with the pain of having struck either a part of the aircraft or a branch of the tree into which he had fallen. There was nothing for it but to shout for help. His cries were heard by a party of Dutch crop watchers and two *Luftwaffe* men. Four months later Sergeant Banfield was transferred in quick succession from an Amsterdam Hospital to Dulag and Stalag 8B at Lamsdorf.

## TREADING THE BOARDS

Theatrical activity was at its height during the winter; pantomimes, plays and orchestral concerts conducted by New Zealander violinist Frank Hunt filled the theatre in Sagan's NCO compound. In the officers' compound the Germans had allowed them to remove partitions from a hut so that a theatre could be constructed. Great use was made of the thin plywood boxes in which Canadian Red Cross parcels were transported. Practically nothing was used that did not come into the camp for other purposes.

Ken Campbell's room which he shared with eight other officers, was next to the newly constructed theatre. The stage backed on to their room wall. During rehearsals for *Treasure Island* it was found that there was insufficient room for people to squeeze behind the moving backcloth, so permission was obtained for a trap door to be cut in the right side of the stage into Campbell's room. During a show the cast moved through the room continuously.

It was not long before the possibilities of the trap-door as an escape cover was seen. The trap opened on to Campbell's bunk and because of his serious leg wounds Campbell was allowed to stay in the room during roll-call.

When a Kriegie succeeded in getting beyond the wire his absence was covered for as long as was practicable before the alarm was raised. He needed time to get clear of the camp area, so a prisoner would report sick in a room at the other end of the block. Immediately after reporting his name to the German guard he would dash through the theatre, jump through the trap door which Campbell had opened in readiness, and quickly hide under the blankets of another bunk. The guard who had meanwhile been checking in other rooms appeared at the door and Campbell would report himself and the other man who could obviously be seen beneath the bedclothes. In that way three men would be counted as being present in the block instead of two. The information regarding the trap-door had not been passed down from the German *Abwehr* to the ordinary guard who did the counting.

## SAGAN GALVANISED

When Sergeant George Grimson was taken prisoner in July 1940 he immediately determined to escape from the restrictions of rifles, machine guns, savage dogs and a few hundred yards of tangled barbed wire. It was a common reaction for men newly taken. After a few weeks the urge to face the enormous dangers dimmed and the desire to survive took over. But Grimson was one of the most persistent of 'Wings' Day's estimate of five per cent of prisoners who would devote every activity to the planning and attempting of escape. Without delay he started to learn German in preparation for the day when he would use his knowledge outside the wire.

Many prisoners thought Grimson withdrawn and uncommunicative, or even a little crazy. But the mantle of a prisoner did not settle comfortably on the broad shoulders of this young man of 25 who, although born and raised in the London suburb of Putney, knew it as an area of wide-open spaces that he enjoyed. Most importantly, the Thames, an oarsman's paradise beside and on which George spent much of his time, flowed within yards of his home.

He had about him what 'Jock' Alexander called a kind of unsettling tension, he was stifled by the restriction, he had to get out. The rumour of a move in the spring of prisoners from Sagan had spurred George Grimson into speeding up his latest plan. By now he had worked so hard at mastering German that he had a convincing colloquial fluency. He was ready. Friends and members of 'Tally Ho' had expertly worked on the civilian clothes and equipment he would need. A belted, boiler-suit type overall, covered his smart breeches and jacket. A *Luftwaffe* side-cap, an impressive pseudo-ammeter/voltmeter with a large dial and electrical leads, a few tools in a bag and a ladder completed Grimson's disguise as a *Luftwaffe* electrician. Even more necessary was the cool courage with which he went about the attempt.

Stooges made sure that the compound was free of ferrets before Grimson collected the ladder from the camp theatre and walked steadily up to the warning wire. There he called up to the guard in the *Posten* box to ensure that he, as a *Luftwaffe* electrician, would be clear to cross the wire. The guard agreed and then telephoned to the guard in the high box at the next corner of the perimeter wire to warn him that the electrician would be working within the area prohibited to prisoners. So far so good.

Grimson's heart must have been thumping as he stepped over the warning wire, leaned the ladder against the high perimeter wire and climbed to the top. It was the moment when a staccato roar of machine gun fire could so easily have cut him down. Kriegies watching from safe, hidden positions, were breathless with fear for this apparently fearless man.

Grimson carried on with his pretence of testing bulbs and electrical wiring with his meter near the top of the inner tall stand of barbed wire, successfully satisfying a couple of inquisitive patrolling guards outside. Then he placed a short plank across the inner and outer stands of barbed wire. Beneath him were the massed coils of twisted barbs, meant to inexorably trap anyone foolhardy enough to become entangled. Had Grimson fallen the 10 feet into the interlaced wire and been unmasked, he would undoubtedly have been shot. Guards did not question a Kriegie in that position, they fired and happily accepted their customary week's leave for shooting an escaper.

Climbing on to the plank Grimson carried on his 'testing' until he 'accidentally' dropped his ammeter. It fell, as he planned, just inside the outer wire. Volubly cursing, Grimson called to the guard in the *Posten* box for permission to climb down to retrieve the meter. Permission was given and Grimson climbed down, picked up the ammeter, complained that it was broken and that he would have to go back to the stores for another. He grumbled that he would be stopped pay for the broken ammeter, placed the plank on the ground outside the wire as a kind of afterthought as if to prevent it falling into an errant Kriegies' hands, then he strolled away – complaining. It was an exploit worthy of the highest awards for sheer courage and an acting performance worthy of the highest awards for acting, but every move and word had been rehearsed and carried out in deadly earnest. A word mispronounced or a move out of character and the principal player would have died, not in the actor's sense, but in reality.

It would have been gratifying had Grimson's enormous efforts and matchless courage been successful but five days later he was recaptured, until then the Germans did not know he had gone, so well was his escape covered. Neither did they know how he had escaped. Kriegies had persuaded a friendly guard that a ferret had left a ladder against the wire and it belonged to the camp theatre. Could they have it back please? He was happy to oblige.

The rumours of a move for the NCOs were confirmed in early May. Sagan was to be enlarged by the additional compound and only officers were to be imprisoned there. The NCOs were to transfer to a camp at a place called Heydekrug in Memel, hard by the Lithuanian border. The radio was secreted by Bristow, Stubbs and Young in tins and packets and the modified gramophone was placed with records to be transported with office equipment.

## 'CLARKIE, I'LL SHOOT YOU MYSELF!'

From his capture Joe 'Nobby' Clark, an orderly in the officers' compound, had been up to his neck in escape activities. One summer morning in 1943 a flying officer came to his room with an imperious summons. 'Clark come with me,' he ordered, 'you're wanted by Big X.' Wondering what crime he had committed, Clark was marched to Roger Bushell's room. The room was packed with officers 'wearing rings up to their elbows'. He had rarely seen so many group captains, wing commanders and other senior officers in one place.

'Christ, I'm right in it this time,' Clark worried as, dazzled by the display of rank, he took an indicated seat. But Bushell smiled and handed him a cigarette. In a corner of the room stood a blackboard scrawled with chalked mathematical equations, but with the 'all clear' from a duty stooge the board was reversed revealing an escape plan. It was obvious that Clark was to take a major part.

At set intervals parties of 25 officers accompanied by a guard were allowed out of the compound to go to the shower block. This time the guard was to be a German-speaking Kriegie in *Luftwaffe* uniform, complete with a dummy pistol and forged passes. Once past the two gates the shower party would turn right past the Guard Room and out of sight of the guards, except for the one in the *Posten* box on the corner of the compound, who could see straight down the road. The plan was for 'Nobby' Clark to go near this box and distract the guard's attention from that area. Once the party had turned down the road he was to allow 30 seconds to pass and then give a blast on a trumpet as a signal for them to scatter.

Roger Bushell lectured and instructed Clark in his best court-room manner, following it up with:

'If you bugger this up Clarkie I'll shoot you myself!'.

'Well, don't bother to get your gun,' rejoined Clark as he was handed a watch synchronised with the others.

At the appointed time Clark began scraping the soil in front of the *Posten* who apparently thought he was probing for a tunnel air vent. Keeping the bogus shower party in view Clark was aware that the guard in the box was ignoring the shower party and watching him very closely. Carrying their blankets for delousing, the party of Kriegies passed through the gate to the *Vorlager* and the outer gate under the escort of the pistol armed *Unteroffizier*, but this guard was a German-uniformed Kriegie. Clark watched them turn down the road and pass out of sight. He waited as the long 30 seconds ticked by, then raising the trumpet to his lips he gave a loud blast, the signal for the Kriegies to scatter.

A diversion of six senior officers was escorted by another disguised Kriegie with a supposed permit to see the *Kommandant*. At the second gate the bogus guard was recognised as a Kriegie. There was uproar but when the chief German security officer arrived he was smiling broadly and highly elated. 'Hard luck chaps,' he said in his usual patronising best English, 'better luck next time.'

Ten minutes later his smile had turned to anguished threats and pleadings when it was discovered that 26 Kriegies were out on the supposed shower party. Almost frothing at the mouth he begged, then demanded, the names. His temper was not improved by the quiet smiles on the faces of the six senior officers.

It was unfortunate that a member of the German camp staff had been in Sagan town longer than intended during his lunch break. To make up time he had taken a short cut through the woods and stumbled over a bundle of clothes. Looking about him he saw more bundles and gave the alarm.

All the escapers were quickly recaptured near Sagan station but the Germans were astounded by the quality of the forged passes and copies of uniforms and equipment. The *Gestapo* descended on the camp, searches were made but, as always, they found little and the Kriegies' escape stock was increased by a trilby hat and a powerful torch. Later Bushell called on Clark.

'Thank you very much for what you did,' he said. 'Christ, I think I was more scared than you and I shall see that you get promoted for this.' But Clark never did know of any change of his rank from leading aircraftman until he came home and found himself, like many captured aircrew, to be a warrant officer.

### ALARM AT ALMELO

One of more than 400 aircraft that took off on 13 May 1943 was a Halifax of 51 Squadron from RAF Snaith in Yorkshire. Because of the heavy bombload the pilot, Flying Officer G. Byres, gave the Halifax a long run to lift it off at the end of the runway. Hanging beneath the crew in the bomb bay of the Halifax were three high explosive bombs of about 1,000lb each, and 1,000 small 5lb incendiary bombs. A similar load was being carried by most of the other aircraft in this large raid on the Ruhr town of Bochum.

Bomber aircraft from airfields in Yorkshire, Lincolnshire and East Anglia were to meet over the Channel to form a stream. Flying Officer 'Bobby' Stark navigated the Halifax to Bochum and Sergeant Dennis Emes, the bomb-aimer, directed the Halifax precisely over the target area. Refusing to be distracted by the heavy anti-aircraft fire, Emes pressed the button at exactly the right moment and with his calm announcement of, 'Bombs away!', Byres again took command, turned the aircraft and started to climb back to 20,000 feet to rejoin the stream as quickly as possible. He was anxious to regain height lost during evasive action.

A nightfighter's attack was so unexpected that the air gunners were unable to fire a single round. Within seconds a red glow lit the interior of the Halifax and three of the four engines were burning. To Byre's anxious enquiries the crew reported no casualties, so he followed with an order to prepare to abandon aircraft. Navigator Stark clipped on his parachute, opened the first hatch and stood by for further instructions. The fires from the engines were spreading and were far too intense for the automatic fire extinguishers to be effective. Height was being lost rapidly and every second of delay would be fatal. Byres gave the order, 'Abandon aircraft!'.

It was a fine warm night in the Dutch town of Almelo. At number 9 Asterstraat, the family of Johannes Burgers had gone to bed and were asleep by 11.00pm. Within an hour the family were wakened by the throbbing noise of hundreds of RAF bombers passing overhead. Beneath the deep, continuous roaring could be heard the faster more urgent sound of the German nightfighters from nearby Twente airfield. Mrs Burgers was frightened, she feared that the bombers when attacked by the fighters might jettison their bombs, or that one of the loaded aircraft would crash nearby. The Burgers decided to go downstairs taking their two sons, Heert aged three and Wibo aged 10. They sat in the living room until the bomber stream had passed over. The family was exhausted: this procedure had taken place night after night. As the sound of the aircraft moved to the east at about 2.00am, they decided to go back to bed, hoping to rest for the remainder of the night.

It seemed a short while before the Burgers were awakened by a scraping and clanking against the roof tiles followed immediately by a heavy thud. Mr Burgers leapt out of bed and wrenched back the bedroom curtains. He could hear his neighbour calling him whilst a screeching, screaming noise, the death cry of an aeroplane, came from above, terrifying the family. Burgers was unable to see through the window into his garden because it was screened by a yellow wall. Fearing that some kind of time bomb had crashed into their garden Mr and Mrs Burgers ran to the children's bedroom to carry them away. As they ran downstairs Burgers called to his wife:

'You take care of the children, I'll see what I can do outside.'

As he opened the kitchen door his neighbour, 'with eyes like dishes' shouted to him: 'He is as dead as a door-nail.'

Burgers, confused and heavy with lack of sleep asked, 'What on earth has happened? Dead? Who?'

His neighbour said that a man on a parachute had dropped on to the roof of his garage. He pointed upwards to a great piece of yellow silk covering most of the roof of Burgers' house and the tangled lines that led to the flat roof below. Mr Burgers realised that it was the silk that was hanging over his bedroom window.

Burgers did not feel much like going up on the roof. The sight of blood sickened him and he pictured a bleeding mutilated body lying there. He and the neighbour decided it was better to telephone the police, advise them to bring a stretcher and take the corpse away. Burgers quickly ran across the street to a telephone.

After making the call he ran back to the house but was surprised and puzzled to find more than a dozen of his neighbours, most in their nightclothes, crowded around a uniformed man who was enjoying a cup of tea. The neighbours, excited and full of enthusiasm, convinced him that this was the man who had come down by parachute and that apart from a few scratches on his nose he appeared to be unhurt. Quickly resigned to the fact that the police had been told, Stark knew that more important to him at that moment was that he was alive. Mr Burgers knew that too many people had seen the flyer for it not to get back to the German authorities. The *Feldgendarmerie*, or 'Green Police', would have known of Stark's arrival from their headquarters in a nearby school.

To the Dutch, Stark was, as Burgers expressed it, 'An oasis in the desert. He came from a free country.' They could not take their eyes from him. When the Dutch Police arrived they were surprised that their 'corpse' was in such good health. As Stark was led away he shook hands with everyone and thanked them for their hearty welcome. To Mrs Burgers he gave the signal whistle on his uniform as a souvenir.

Bomb-aimer Sergeant Dennis Emes followed Stark through the Halifax hatch. During his parachute descent he had anxious moments when a Fieseler Storch reconnaissance plane flew very close. Emes could see the pilot inside the cockpit and was convinced that the German had spotted him in the moonlight, but the plane flew on. Emes listened intently for its return but the sound of the engine faded in the distance. He landed unhurt and in his struggle to escape from the area he twice fell into water-filled ditches. Shortly afterwards, while still soaked, he came face to face with a German patrol. The command: *'Hé Sie dort... Stehen bleiben!'* and the click of a rifle bolt told him he was a prisoner. Shortly afterwards Sergeant

Emes was taken to Almelo and locked in the same room as Bobby Stark. It was, despite the circumstances, a happy reunion.

## BETRAYAL IN PARIS

When Sergeant Bill Garfield was told to go back to find out why the rear gunner had not answered an intercom call, he found the turret riddled 'like a colander'. Struggling forward again he was shaken to find the rest of the Wellington's crew had gone. Grabbing a parachute he clipped it to his harness, kicked out the side emergency hatch and jumped. Flames from a burning wing streamed past him lighting the black night, but the aircraft soon disappeared taking its roaring noise into the darkness. His soft landing in a field took Garfield by surprise. During his parachute descent he had been engrossed in destroying the contents of his wallet. He was uncertain into which country he had tumbled: was it Germany or Holland? The difference was almost that of freedom and indefinite imprisonment, or perhaps life and death, but he was in Holland.

Garfield was lucky at first, a farmer took him to a Father Gerard who traced an escape route on a Mobiloil map across Holland, Belgium and France to Spain. After sleep in a straw loft, Garfield was taken to a market and introduced to a farmer and his daughter. Travelling on a horse and cart through Roermond they passed a long line of 10- to 14-year-old girls of the *Nationale Jeugstorm*, marching four-abreast, all dressed in black skirts and white blouses and carrying sheaves of grasses.

Led by a young boy and girl and dodging German dog patrols, Garfield was soon in Belgium and meeting with another airman named Coventry. Journeys by cycle and train followed. It was not long before Garfield and Coventry were with a party in Paris after a nervous passage through border customs posts. There was no bother, no suspicious looks, it all seemed casual and easy.

In the Metro, waiting for a train to central Paris, they were suddenly surrounded by *Gestapo* and police agents, handcuffed in pairs, taken to the street and driven off to *Gestapo* Headquarters. The driver of the car ignored other traffic. He zig-zagged madly from side to side, thumping a cycle taxi without stopping.

Their next journey was in a kind of Black Maria van across Paris. The van was equipped with tiny individual cells with a sloping seat so that the pressure was on one's legs. From a small slit in the side Garfield saw German soldiers on the steps of the Opera House talking to women. He and his friends had been betrayed by French or Belgian traitors and felt despondent that there were so many.

Soon the van passed through a large gateway, then along a tunnel into a large, vaulted room. The prisoners were in the *Gestapo* prison at Fresnes. Each man was taken upstairs to the rows of cells. Garfield was pushed into a cell in which he was to stay, in solitary misery, for 76 days.

When the French Government decided to build a new prison seven miles from Paris near the village of Fresnes-les-Rungis, it was to be the most modern of penal establishments. It opened for its first inmates in August 1898 and was held to be a model for other prisons. The prison had a central section containing kitchens, a bakery, a laundry, clothing and other stores. There was also a chapel and hospital section, but what was important to those imprisoned by the Germans in the 1940s were the four storeys of cells on either side of the main prison entrance. Each cell was four metres long, two and a half metres wide and three metres high.

The cell galleries on each side stretched into the distance, the closed steel cell doors lay flush with the wall so that a prisoner felt he was stepping in to be immured. The thickness of the cell walls prevented sound from passing through. The window opposite the door was of hardened, frosted glass, casting a dim light on the few spartan furnishings of a small table hinged to the wall, a thin mattress on an iron framed bed hinged to the opposite wall, and a lavatory basin with a tap above in a corner near the door. Two small shelves and a stool completed the equipment.

This was the extent of Garfield's world. Hunger was a constant companion, it woke him at dawn. As he looked at the ceiling and remembered where he was he wondered what would happen to him if the Germans won the war. Perhaps he would still be in this cell in 20 years' time, or perhaps Hitler would decide to shoot all RAF men in retaliation for the bombing of Germany. All speculation was a torment.

His morning drink was brought by another prisoner accompanied by a guard. The rattle of the trolley and the key in the lock announced their visit and his bowl was filled with tasteless, pale brown liquid made from ground, roasted acorns and hot water. At noon the key would rattle again in the door and a cupful of soup would be handed in. It was pale green water with scraps of cabbage leaves floating on the surface accompanied by some bloated green caterpillars. In the afternoon at 4.00pm, food for the day ended with a small slice of bread and a spoonful of ersatz jam. Garfield saved half of his slice for breakfast.

Then it was time to talk to the cockney in the cell above. The Londoner was shut in with three Frenchmen and liked to hear a little English occasionally. This afternoon Garfield stood on the chair and removed the already loosened ventilator grille and whispered, 'Hello up there'. The cockney answered almost at once.

'Hello Bill, there's a guard snooping around, be careful.'

'Any news?' Garfield asked.

'The Allies have invaded according to a French newspaper but I don't believe a word of it,' said the voice from above.

'Won't be long anyway,' said Garfield, replacing the grille as footsteps sounded outside.

One evening he decided to swap books with the man above by tying a string to the books and lowering or raising them via the ventilator shaft. Garfield collected his book safely but the cockney's replacement jammed in the shaft, tore loose from the string and plummeted to the basement. Garfield decided to give the cockney his book back but then heard the trolley scraping along the corridor. He was forced to hand the book over to the guard who thumbed through the pages and suddenly stopped. Eyes bulging he started shouting and thrust a page at Garfield. The page was scribbled over with lewdly explicit and suggestive drawings. Drawing his pistol the guard beat Garfield on the head with the butt. The German was very short and had difficulty in reaching the top of Garfield's skull so he received only a few bruises. When later he found a small pencil in a cavity, Garfield disposed of it as quickly as possible before the guard could find it. He preferred not to think of the consequences of its discovery

Each lonely, frightening day was very much like any other in the grim misery of Fresnes. Garfield found that he could open the frosted glass window with the handle of a spoon and every morning voices could be heard calling out in a variety of languages. Then there would be silence again as the guards began their rounds. Staring at the wall, hungry, frightened and bored, Garfield was jerked alert by the sound of Morse code being tapped along the pipes as prisoners talked to each other.

The view from the opened window was of squares of grass surrounded by high walls. Then came the main wall and beyond that a view of grassy slopes. The squares of grass were used by the prisoners, who were allowed to tramp around them once a week in a silent single file.

To obtain some relief from the monotony Garfield would save a slice of bread every day and at the end of the week have a feast. The sound of machine guns could be heard outside the prison and Bill Garfield knew that prisoners were being executed. He started to save bread again but then put it in the cell of a Frenchman as he passed his door. He had heard that the Frenchman was soon to be shot.

At the beginning of August Garfield was taken back to *Gestapo* Headquarters for further interrogation, but the passage of time had rendered useless any information he may have had, although an interrogator was so incensed at Garfield's name, rank and number reply it threw him into a tantrum. 'You have had your last chance. Stay here and rot!' he shouted. That worried Garfield; he knew that some Britishers had been incarcerated in Fresnes since taken at Dunkirk, but on 20 August 1943 he was lined up with other RAF men. When the names were read out he was told that he was the only man there to have withheld his date of birth. Garfield gave it. He knew when he was beaten and did not want to go back to that cell.

At the railway station French civilians were driven out of the railway carriage at bayonet point and the Kriegies, three with two guards, entrained for Dulag. The new *Luftwaffe* guards were friendly and chatted about the air-raid damage in the Ruhr Valley through which the train was passing. As the guards were armed with sub-machine guns the RAF men thought it best to keep quiet about their exploits.

The train passed through the beautiful Rhine Valley, with woods stretching for miles, hills with castles on their summits, bare hillsides used for the growing of vines, and fruit trees planted alongside the railway track, so that it seemed as if they were travelling through an endless orchard. 'Why,' Garfield wondered, 'should men living here want to conquer other countries? Perhaps beauty is not enough.'

The *Luft* camps were so full that after a brief stay at Dulag, where Garfield envied the comforts and food of the 'permanent' staff, he was shunted away with a party of 40 RAF men on a shock cattle truck journey. With no room to lie down, cramp soon set in, so that their eventual arrival at Stalag 4B Mühlberg was a leg-stretching relief.

Stalag 4B was a rectangle of electrified and barbed wire with a road running through the centre of the long axis. At the ends of the road were the main gates and guard rooms. Along each side of the road were compounds containing huts, divided laterally into two large rooms filled with three-tier bunks with palliasses for 200 men. At each end of the hut there was a primitive, foul-smelling, grub ridden, indoor lavatory, the only 'convenience' after lock-up. 4B was awful but to Bill Garfield it was infinitely preferable to the torture of 'solitary'.

## HEYDEKRUG

From 10 June 1943, the 1,700 NCO population of Sagan began the move to a new camp at Heydekrug near Memel, on the borders of Lithuania and East Prussia. Heydekrug was to be designated Stalag Luft 6. Sagan was to be populated entirely by officers of the RAF and USAAF.

Their conveyance was the usual box-car with a sliding central door, but this time some dozen Kriegies occupied about a third of the space in each truck at one end behind a barbed wire barrier. A low, barbed wire gate, reminiscent of that in a rabbit hutch, was the only entrance and exit.

Four guards occupied the remaining two-thirds which included the centre section with the sliding door. The doors were left open during the journey allowing a breeze into the truck to cool the June air.

The train rattled and clanked its way through Glogau, Posen, Thorn, Deutsche Eylau, Ostrode, Allenstein, Insterberg and Tilsit. There the train stopped for the whole afternoon in a siding. Throughout the journey there was an impression that time was regressing. The scenery changed, the farms became smaller, the roads narrower and road traffic almost non-existent. A look of poverty encompassed the area and people.

During the stop in a siding the guards manned the embankment while the Kriegies were allowed out to relieve themselves and stretch their legs beside the railway track. Climbing down they saw that behind their train another train of box-cars had halted. From these cars women helped each other down to the trackside. It was difficult not to stare. The women were dressed in long, white, cowled habits resembling nuns. Armed, laughing guards watched as the women stood astride to urinate. The Kriegies turned away to avoid embarrassment to the women and themselves. The disgust they felt showed in their shouts and comments to the guards.

*'... now I wonder if I packed my toothbrush?'*

They had learnt several derogatory epithets and insults from the guards and now these were hurled back at them. There was much discussion afterwards about the clothing; were the women members of some religious order or was it a form of local peasant costume? No-one knew.

After Tilsit the train left the main line. The engine struggled; it chugged and puffed at a decreasing rate until grinding to a squealing halt. The locomotive, the Kriegies were told, had run out of steam. A few men nevertheless managed to obtain some boiling water from the engine, rewarding the driver with a cup of tea.

On a hot June day, the long trek to the camp from the station with all their goods and clothing was exhausting. Although it was always a joy to be outside the eternal barbed wire, the Kriegies were thankful when the *Posten* towers came into view.

The camp at Heydekrug was the usual clearing in a pine forest but it had differences. Four long, single-storey buildings, crudely built of brick and concrete blocks, were divided into nine separate rooms each with a door to the compound and each room accommodating 60 men. Eight wooden huts placed across the line of the dormitory blocks were to serve for administration and there was at least a view across the flat, featureless countryside to where, a mile away, an occasional steam train puffed. There was nothing else. The camp was so far away from any fighting and beyond the current limit of air activity that the Germans did not consider a blackout necessary. There were no means for individually cooking the Red Cross food or the little issued by the Germans, so all food was pooled and issued from a communal cookhouse. From time to time this resulted in some strange mixtures or 'glops', an expressive term describing any liquefied mixture of any ingredients, sweet or savoury.

Exploration of 'A' *Lager* disclosed no easy escape routes, but Sergeant Gammon found a rare and exciting place to spend a while away from the ubiquitous sand dust. Running through the compound on one side was a tiny, trickling stream and in its small pools there was frogspawn. Along the miniature banks there was just a two-foot width of grass where ants worked mightily carrying their huge loads. Studying the creatures in this small world Vic Gammon would lose himself for a brief spell, forgetting his surroundings and the uncertain future. As always, the grass was not to last very long beneath the soles of caged men circuiting the compound, like frustrated animals continually searching for an exit.

The NCOs from Stalag Luft 1 Barth were the next to move into Heydekrug, occupying 'K' *Lager* in October 1943. They were followed by the USAAF NCOs who moved into 'E' *Lager* in February 1944. Heydekrug was now filling up.

In 'A' *Lager*, the radio team had managed to stay together but their difficulties had greatly increased. Heydekrug was much further from any BBC transmitter and the open shutters at night and lack of black-out meant that they were always likely to be watched. Their unlawful activities were to be severely curtailed. Heinze and other keen members of the *Abwehr* staff had accompanied the Kriegies from Sagan. It was clear that Bristow, suspect number one, would have to dissociate himself from the operation of the radio receiver.

It was necessary to contrive a simple arrangement in a single unit, which could be operated by a member of the headquarters staff who were moderately secure in their own private room in the wooden office hut. The partitions were movable within limits so it was arranged that the bedroom would be accessible by the most labyrinthine route possible. Then the radio team started to design their new set.

Now that they had an increased stock of proper components, there was no reason why the whole receiver should not be built into the gramophone containing the mains unit. The added weight and extra space taken was minimal. The tuning and reaction controls, operated by easily removable toothbrush handles, were to protrude through the motor board under the turntable. Because of the obvious limit to the length of clothes-line that one might expect to see in the Camp Leader's bedroom, the signal effectiveness would be reduced from the more distant transmitter. They decided to add a stage of low frequency amplification to increase the volume. With the addition of one valve, one coupling condenser and two resisters there was still room inside the gramophone.

The radio men instructed Ron Mogg, an ex-journalist and shorthand writer, in its use. After several rehearsals they were confident that the gramophone could now be playing a record in less time than a visitor would need to reach the inner sanctum from the main door of the hut. All that was necessary now was to hide the headphones, unplug the leads, adjust the governor and replace the turntable. The valves remained *in situ*. The modification was a success.

Every night in the comparative security of the headquarters hut, Mogg would take down and transcribe the bulletin. It was then copied, lookouts posted and the news read by an army of readers in every room the following lunch-time. As the news was now generally favourable to the Allies, morale in the camp rose.

Meanwhile Mogg made the acquaintance of *Gefreite* Adolf Munkert and quickly concluded that Munkert was anti-Nazi, a practising Christian and, from the Kriegies' ruthless viewpoint, probably corruptible. It was cruel but the Kriegies desperately needed a reliable contact on the other side of the wire. Nat Leaman, whose job it was to investigate every possible German who might be a weak chink in the camp-staff armour, was told to work on Munkert and report back to 'Tally Ho', the Escape Committee.

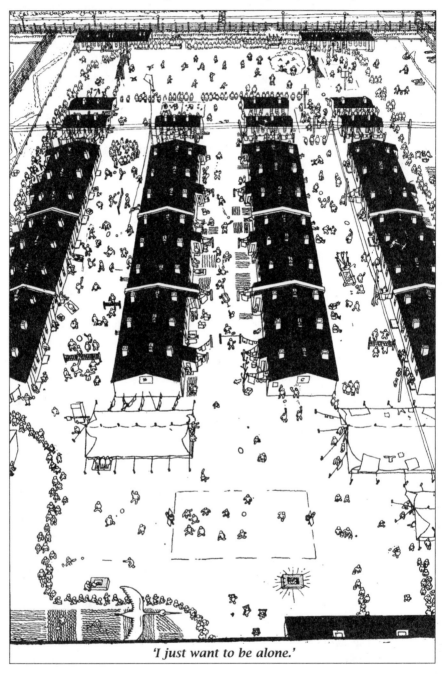

*'I just want to be alone.'*

Eventually Munkert was found to be completely reliable for the Kriegies' purposes and was promised that at the end of the war he would be protected and rewarded by the British Government – but he was not to survive. Neither was *Gefreite* Sommers, the camp photographer, a Pole who had passed himself off as a man of German and Polish parents but who secretly supported the Polish Home Army.

Dave Young felt cheated. The acquisition over the years of so many proper components and valves had removed the challenge, and the radio job was becoming a routine chore. Now it was just a matter of keeping the receiver working and hidden from Heinze's prying eyes. To allay any lingering suspicions the *Abwehr* might have, Bristow's steam-boat was fitted with a new tie rod and used from time to time on the short navigable stretch of the little stream.

Bristow had to find something else to occupy his mechanically minded self and it was, again, a clock. He used a gramophone motor as the basis and cut the escape wheel and hour-hand reduction gear by hand. Unfortunately this motor had helical gears designed to produce an upward thrust to partially offset the weight of the turntable. Used vertically the thrust caused the centre shaft to jam in its bearing. The solution was to reverse the direction and thus came about the only anti-clockwise clock that anyone had seen. Visitors from other rooms would infer that Bristow and his friends were all slightly mad. Dave Young thought it surprising how quickly one got used to it and no longer needed a mirror to tell the time. To Germans coming into the hut it was just one more pointer to the fact that all Englishmen were mad.

The school really got underway for the NCOs at Heydekrug. The *Kommandant, Oberst* Hermann von Hoerback was a typically straight-backed Prussian-type officer, strict but fair, who allowed such activities as would keep the prisoners occupied and divert them, he thought, from devising means of escape.

Food was no longer the chief preoccupation so nourishment for the mind assumed prominence. Classes held by competent Kriegies were available upon most subjects, some so obscure that the Germans were frequently baffled. *Lager* Officer *Major* Peschell, entering a classroom with a party of visiting German officers, asked Sergeant Harvey, the instructor, what subject they were studying.

'The Theory and Practice of Forward Exchange to Foreign Currencies,' he was told. Peschell turned his eyes to the ceiling and hurriedly said: 'I think we will go elsewhere.'

Passing to the next room he saw that Sergeant Griffiths was lecturing on Elizabethan history. Written on a blackboard were the words 'The Balance of Power 1588'. Peschell studied the inscription, slowly turned to his companions and said, 'The Balance of Power 1588, and after 350 years they (the British) are still at it.'

Although space was very limited at Heydekrug there were still plenty of activities in which a Kriegie could participate. There was football, rugby (with due care for tackles on the rough surface), basketball, baseball, plays, orchestral works, choral works and, above all, education in the 'Barbed Wire University'. Stalag Luft 6 became probably the best organised of prisoner-of-war camps.

Kriegie 'Batch' Batchelder had feared that with so many men squeezed into a relatively small area there could have been immense problems of discipline and personality clashes. It did not happen. In Batchelder's words: 'The vast range of abilities, knowledge and technical skills seemed to blend and become a community in which the "thinkers and doers" formed a well-ordered homogenous society, all prepared to work for each other.' The inspiration for the atmosphere in Luft 6 was undoubtedly due to the men's unquestioning loyalty to and respect for 'Dixie' Deans. Deans led by force of his exceptional personality and example.

The comparatively comfortable surroundings (despite huge, red, viciously biting sand fleas in the palliasse straw) did not result in complacency among the inveterate escapers. The Escape Committee tended to concentrate on supporting escape attempts by small groups of two or three men, which were considered more effective and enabled their absence to be more efficiently concealed. It was essential that those on the run should get as far away from the camp as possible before any hue and cry. So a 'hole-in-the-wall' method was devised similar to that in the officers' compound at Sagan.

Bricks were carefully removed from an area about two feet square in the dividing wall between two rooms, and similar sized squares cut from the plywood sides of Canadian Red Cross boxes were carefully covered with plaster 'borrowed' from the sick quarters. The plaster was then scored and coloured to simulate the brickwork. The plastered boards concealed and effectively blocked off the hole.

A few Kriegies were permitted to stay in their rooms during *Appell*, providing they were really ill and had a suitable certificate from the camp doctor. Compact Batchelder was the right size for a 'cover' job so during the twice-daily *Appells* it was arranged that he, armed with a forged 'sick' certificate, should stay in his bunk, fully dressed but under a blanket, and be counted by the patrolling guard. In the few seconds it took the guard to walk from that room to the room next door Batchelder had to climb from his bunk, uncover the hole, crawl through to the adjoining room, cover the hole on that side and be there, composed and ready to be counted again. For more than an unbelievable six months Batchelder maintained this deception, always keeping the numbers close to those that the Germans wanted. Keeping a low profile meant that Batchelder was himself unable to take part in any escape attempts.

A serious crisis with possible grave consequences occurred during a *Gestapo* search when Batchelder had his fingerprints checked and verified. It seemed that the deception was about to be uncovered but the disturbance of a diversionary 'fight' among his room-mates was enough to allow Batchelder to slip through the hole where he was merely counted again.

Every new camp was quickly and thoroughly investigated by the Kriegies for means of escape. The first few weeks of settling in were crucial to those intending to get outside the wire. Even though experienced German staff were transferred with the prisoners they also had to discover the snags affecting security in a new camp. Any slips and the Kriegies would exploit them to the full. Some strong-stomached men had already started a tunnel from one of the latrines, when Australian Ron Damman and others saw the possibilities of a boiler in the wash-house. By passing two rods through some catches in its side, the boiler could be removed even when its burning base was alight and so a tunnel entry beneath there would be virtually undetectable. This was a chance for a mass exodus not to be missed.

With the full co-operation of the Escape Committee some 20 diggers went ahead while other Kriegies were seconded to the making of clothes, forging and the manufacture of replica rifles and small arms. Bob 'Smudge' Coles, when he was not taking photographs for forged identity cards with the 'Tally Ho' secret camera, busied himself making dummy heads to be used to represent sick men confined to bed, thus making up the number that should be in camp and covering for escapers.

To pass under a ditch circling the outside of the compound and to avoid triggering buried seismograph alarms, the shaft went down 30ft before heading towards the wire and a planned exit in a wooded area. Electricity lit the tunnel and sand and soil were drawn back from the face in a trolley on runners. Despite a shortage of bed-boards for shoring and several roof falls, the tunnel was driven ahead.

When the tunnellers calculated that they were beyond the wire a narrow shaft was dug up to the surface. To the horror of the look-out the signalling stick appeared between the warning wire and the main wire entanglement. Hurriedly disguising the exit hole the diggers carried on. It was proving extremely difficult to judge the length and gradient of a tunnel. As they burrowed onward a chance was taken to make a few more holes to improve the air supply. Soon the tunnel was 150ft long from the base and well outside the wire.

Excitement was mounting. Many tunnels had been dug but few reached the stage of breaking ground outside the wire. It was decided that 50 Kriegies should go out every night until the inevitable discovery of the tunnel. Ron Damman was to be the 24th to leave in order to travel with his friend Mike Roberts with whom he was teamed.

After a roll-call, 50 men did not return to their barracks, instead they made circuitous journeys to the wash-house to be ushered by the controller down the shaft. With three feet space each, kneeling nose to tail in the stifling air were businessmen, *Gestapo* agents, young ladies with their boyfriends and a chimney sweep complete with his usual top hat. Each man carried an absolute minimum of luggage.

At last, when the tension was rising and a trace of claustrophobic panic appearing, the face of the tunnel was broken open and fresh, cold air rushed in to revive flagging spirits. One by one the leaders left for the exit in the wood and those behind crawled forward. The 13th man was unlucky, an unusually alert sentry detected a movement and the alarm was raised.

Shouting guards came running from all directions, a shot was fired down into the tunnel exit. The men in the tunnel tried to back-up until there was no space and there they had to wait until the Germans had been led to the tunnel entrance. They had been unable to find it unaided. The Kriegies were forced from the tunnel entrance with much rifle and pistol brandishing and shouting of *'Los, Schnell!'*.

The Germans were staggered as 37 Kriegies climbed out of the tunnel entrance. Hiding their identity papers in the tunnel, the men were met in the compound by a horde of cat o' nine tails-wielding guards and fierce Alsatian dogs. Neither the 'cat' or dogs were used but the threat was clear. Kriegies knew this kind of tense situation, one inflammatory word or incautious movement could start bullets flying and rifle butts crashing down. It was a time for sensible but proud submission. Hands on heads they were made to march to the *Vorlager* but Mike Roberts' waistband loosened and his trousers began to slide down over his hips. Not being allowed to lower his hands Roberts continued to shuffle forward with his ankles spread. Even in such an explosive situation it created some mirth.

Twelve got away from the camp temporarily, two even succeeding in commandeering a sailing boat for a trip to Sweden but they grounded on a sandbank and were returned to Heydekrug. Bill Garrioch, the pilot who had brought his blazing Wellington down on the thin Zuider Zee ice, escaped from the camp area and had reached the suburbs of Vilno when the Germans made a round-up of partisans and he was caught in the net. For his 18 days of freedom, Garrioch spent a similar time in the *Arrestlok* and thought it a fair exchange. There were too many to go into the Cooler so the escapers had to take their punishment in turn. Many thousands of Germans were employed rounding up the runaway Kriegies so the attempt was far from being a complete failure.

### THE SHEEP PEN

The roll-calls at Heydekrug were becoming lengthier and more tedious, particularly for the Germans. The escapes and attempted escapes continually upset the count although the Kriegies did their best to make sure that the numbers counted equalled the numbers the Germans thought they should hold. Kriegies were assembled on the sports field-cum-*Appell* ground and made to stand with those in their individual rooms and lined up in rows of five. Any number that was not divisible by five threw the count into instant confusion. The prisoners did not make it easy for the Germans. Men in the back rows slipped from one block of prisoners to another so altering the numbers; others supposedly sick inside the block quickly slipped through holes in the partition wall to be counted twice. By these means the strength of the camp was adjusted to conform to what the Kriegies believed the Germans wanted it to be, but for some weeks the *Kommandant* had been forced to admit to his higher authority that he really did not know how

*'I've been searching Barrack B35 – couldn't find a thing.*
*Well, what are you all staring at??'*

many of the prisoners in his charge had succeeded in escaping from his 'escape-proof' establishment. Something had to be done.

Early one morning guards and blue-overalled ferrets poured into the camp and turned the prisoners out into the compound. At first there was utter confusion with Kriegies milling around, apparently aimlessly but being deliberately obtuse and awkward. Paul Hilton found himself beside a table which had been laid out with hammers, crowbars, jemmies, saws, screwdrivers and a large pair of pliers. Hilton quickly slipped the pliers into his trouser pocket. Unfortunately they were open as he snatched them and they clicked shut. A ferret heard, looked round and asked his friends if they had picked up his pliers. Hilton decided it was the moment to disappear into the crowd and unload the pliers on to another Kriegie. He began to saunter away but had walked only a dozen paces when he was roughly grabbed from behind and frogmarched to *Major* Peschell, who looked at him and growled, 'Cooler'.

Carefully searching each room to make sure that everyone was out-side, the Germans laid ladders horizontally across boxes in a 'V' shape, over a section of the compound between two long huts. Herding the Krie-gies to one end of the compound the guards then drove them towards the wide end of the 'V' and then singly through the gap at the narrow point of the 'V'. Loud cries of 'Baa, Baa, Baa,' arose from the Kriegies who saw the likeness to a sheep check. The count and identification from record cards containing photographs and fingerprints worked well until it was discov-ered that some Kriegies had appeared in the queue twice. The Germans had neglected to block off one side of the huts properly so the prisoners were going round again, bypassing a guard who was easily distracted. The count was hopelessly out.

There were threats, an unsheathing of bayonets and hysterical shouting from the German officers. In the ensuing chaos a box of record cards disappeared into the depths of the foul pit beneath the latrines. The count was abandoned for that day.

The next morning the performance was repeated with the lengthy addition of photographs and fingerprints being taken to make a fresh set of record cards. With the pretence of admiring the Leica camera used for taking the identity photographs, Reg Cleaver contrived to stick a piece of paper to the camera lens which remained unnoticed throughout the exposing of several films.

Their cursory search of the huts had not produced any contraband, radio or escape apparatus. The security officers were unhappy with the results obtained and decided that they must call in the local *Gestapo* to carry out a thorough search. The camp guards resented the slur on their competence so they passed a warning to the Kriegies in advance. The gramophone/radio was spirited away to the sick quarters, tools and other contraband were buried under piles of tins in the incinerator. The Kriegies sat tight to await events.

One morning, at 4 o'clock, a motley collection of civilians wearing swastika armbands arrived. The Kriegies were expecting them. Turned out into the compound by guards, the prisoners studied the *Gestapo* men who were trying to be officious. They were a weedy looking, middle-aged lot led by one hard faced and probably genuine *Gestapo* officer. The red armband carrying a black swastika failed to give the rest of them any air of authority. Nevertheless, the Kriegies played a dangerous game when they proceeded to catcall and harass the *Gestapo* men.

When one Kriegie was called over and told to strip to be thoroughly searched, he undressed slowly as the other prisoners moved closer and closer despite a guard's protests. Soon Kriegies were standing in a tight circle around the *Gestapo* man who suddenly felt menaced and separated from the guard. With the abuse he was receiving and men breathing down his neck he decided that he would not be a hero that day. The Kriegie who had been standing naked before him looked the *Gestapo* man straight in the eye with a shaming dignity and contempt which added to the civilian's discomfort. The Kriegie was hurriedly dismissed and within seconds he had been absorbed into the crowd which closed around him. The *Gestapo* man was last seen searching for the gloves he had carelessly left protruding from his pocket. The crowd melted away to harass another of the visitors.

The compound searches now rarely caused the Kriegies anything more than discomfort and nuisance. They were driven from their rooms which were then enthusiastically rather than conscientiously searched, leaving an appalling mess. Vital equipment was able to be hidden or even taken from the compound and returned after the search. After the invasion of the compound, the man with the pulled-down hat brim and black ankle-length leather coat led away his band of nondescripts, little of significance had been lost. Gains to the Kriegies from the recent search were two pork pie hats, a torch, various tools, a pair of gloves and, extraordinarily, a pair of trousers. The searchers had not yet learned that to put an item down for even a second whilst looking away, meant it was lost forever.

### 'NO-ONE LAUGHS THERE ANY MORE'

Reports came into the camps of the devastation done to Hamburg by the raids and the firestorm. The city was no longer recognisable, no vehicles travelled through the blocked, rubble strewn streets, thousands of people had fled to the countryside and those remaining led a troglodyte-like

existence in the ruins, the cellars and the scarce homes usable on the outskirts of the city. Few had any water supply. Every family was mourning
the loss of members. Suicides among young and old were commonplace.
Some of the sadness rubbed off on Kriegies when a gentle, older guard,
recently returned from where his home in Hamburg had been, said quietly, 'No-one laughs there any more'.

### 'SOLD LIKE A SACK OF SPUDS'

Six hundred and fifty Pathfinder-led bombers successfully attacked
Nuremberg on the night of 10/11 August. A Stirling lost on its homeward
flight was from 15 Squadron stationed at RAF Mildenhall. When crossing
the French/Belgian border an unseen Bf110 poured tracer and cannon
shells into its nose and starboard wing. The Stirling flared up so furiously
that Sergeant John 'Chip' Sparrow in the mid-upper turret distinctly saw
the attacking Messerschmitt brilliantly illuminated by the flames of his
own aircraft. As the fighter approached for a second attack Sparrow and
the rear gunner shot it down.

The fire had gained an unshakeable hold and the crew were ordered
to bale out. Sparrow clambered out of his turret, grabbed his parachute and
raced to the rear escape hatch. The navigator and wireless operator dived
through the front hatch. The inside of the fuselage was a raging furnace as
Sparrow jumped. He was closely followed by the flight engineer who was
to die as he leapt from the inferno without his parachute.

Sparrow's smooth descent ended suddenly when he crashed
painfully into bramble bushes. He struggled frantically but unsuccessfully to free himself until exhausted, he wrapped his parachute canopy
around him and slept.

It was not until dawn that Sparrow broke free, buried his parachute
and made his way westward towards the Meuse. He was concerned to find
that the river was more than 100 yards wide and fast flowing. To Sparrow,
a non-swimmer, it was an impassable barrier. While searching for a boat
he came to a busy public ferry. From his escape kit he took a 1,000 French
Franc note and offered it unobtrusively to the ferryman – but this was Belgium. The ferryman eyed the note and Sparrow carefully, then called a colleague to tell him that he was going for change and to take his place.
Signalling Sparrow to follow he led the way to a nearby estaminet.

Sparrow was astonished by his reception. A priest and his friends in
the estaminet recognised his uniform and immediately bottles of wine
were uncorked in his honour. Such was the joyful celebration that 'Chip'
Sparrow remembered little of the subsequent events until he was put to
bed that evening.

The following morning he was taken to the end of a long garden to receive instruction from an English-speaking 12-year-old girl on how to say in French, 'I don't understand, I am Flemish'. Following different people, sometimes on foot, sometimes on a bicycle but always staying at 100m distance, he arrived at Haybes where he met again with Sergeant Cave, the wireless operator on his Stirling. For several days they lived above a hairdresser's, staying silent and unseen as *Wehrmacht* men came and went.

Spirited across the French border to Rienne, Sparrow and Cave stayed with a Belgian Resistance worker codenamed 'Arsen'. The airmen seemed to be in secure hands and a swift journey home was in prospect.

September 2nd was Sparrow's 21st birthday. The French and Belgians were always quick to grasp any reason for a party so a celebration was arranged at a local café. The meal of venison steaks and potato chips was washed down with a drink they called *Alcool*. *Alcool* was distilled from fruit and the only way in which it could be drunk safely was to place cubes of sugar on a saucer which was then filled with *Alcool*. The sugar cubes were then ignited and after they had dissolved into a syrup a small spoon was used to take up the mixture. It was said that three saucers full was more than enough to make one very drunk. At the café, 75 bottles of *Alcool* were hidden away – ready for *La Libération*.

Two more airmen were brought in at Rienne and 'Arsen' arranged for a party to leave disguised as patients in an ambulance. One, a fluent French speaker, had faked injuries to a leg; the others, including Sparrow, were supposed to have head injuries which required a swathing of bandages which effectively prevented them speaking. Sparrow's identity card named him as Johanne Romane Jules, a Flemish farm worker. In Brussels Sparrow, now joined by 10 other aircrew escapers and evaders and two French Resistance men, were hidden in a flat until the whole party was assembled and put on a train to Paris. There they were led the 200m from the Gare du Nord to the Hotel Brussels.

Sparrow felt uneasy the instant he walked into the foyer. The party hesitated as their guide crossed to the reception desk. Sparrow was looking around cautiously when tough, determined-looking men appeared with drawn pistols at the doorways and at the foot of the staircases. Someone muttered, 'Sold like a sack of spuds,' as the disguised *SS* men closed in. Sparrow smiled wryly and then staggered backward as a fist slammed into his face.

A bus drew up outside the hotel and the now handcuffed prisoners were bundled aboard. The next stop was Fresnes Prison. It was evident that treatment there was to be harsh. Sparrow was sickened as a large SS man kicked a Frenchman very hard in the small of his back. The Frenchman fell and remained still. Sparrow was sure that the man's back must be broken after such a heavy blow.

Fresnes has been described as the *Gestapo* slaughterhouse. Many prisoners had written their names on the cell walls, followed by the words *Condamné a la mort*. Sparrow added his name and address and fervently hoped that the other words would not be added. Pushed into a basement cell with four others he found that the walls were covered with green slime and his mattress crawled with bed bugs. Then his boot laces, belt, braces and tie were taken away. The Germans wanted him alive until they had finished with him. Taken next to a solitary confinement cell he was held for seven agonising days while he was slapped and punched by a questioning *Gestapo* man. Soon his face was so swollen that he was almost unable to see.

Sparrow's next interrogator was a *Luftwaffe* officer who politely called him sergeant. When to his probing questions about his aircraft and squadron Sparrow said, 'As an officer and a gentleman you could not expect me to answer,' the German merely threatened that Sparrow would be shot as a spy. Sparrow had already considered that possibility. From the information he had gleaned, the general atmosphere of the place and the harsh treatment already meted out to him, he knew that he was completely powerless. In Fresnes Prison the *SS* and *Gestapo* could do just as they wished. Sparrow became resigned to his fate and was unperturbed by this latest threat.

Two days later the guards took him from his cell. In complete silence they marched him along a corridor to what he could see was the open air. Was this the end? Was he for the gallows or for the firing squad? The guards remained silent. The walk ended in the exercise yard but Sparrow's first few circuits at a trot were anything but athletic – he was mentally and physically drained.

Without warning, in early October, Sparrow was taken from Fresnes and with others he left by troop train for Frankfurt. The city was still burning from recent air-raids. When the train arrived the prisoners' *Wehrmacht* escort was ordered to fix bayonets and the lorries in which they were to travel to Dulag were covered with sheets of tarpaulin to hide them from the vengeful, lynch-inclined populace. When Sparrow found himself again in solitary confinement it was a rest compared to Fresnes and the distant sound of English voices gave him new heart.

### CHAINS AND SLAVES

The bomb-aimer had just announced the welcome words 'Bombs gone' when Squadron Leader John Mahoney's aircraft staggered and shook. A fierce fire was roaring through the bomb-bay. When he had made as certain as possible that the crew had left, Mahoney forced his way through the smoke to the escape hatch and jumped. Landing near houses he saw that he had crashed down close to a high spiked fence. He was a few feet from being impaled.

Mahoney attempted to bury his parachute in a shallow drain but heard footsteps coming towards him. He stretched out on the ground, hoping not to be seen but the footsteps stopped a few feet away and a torch beam settled on his face. Mahoney climbed to his feet and walked towards the light with his hands up. The German spoke and Mahoney could see a pistol coolly levelled at him. He thought it better say something before the gun went off.

'English', he gulped.

'Komm hier', said the German and Mahoney realised that he had already learned some of the language.

He was driven towards the city centre of Berlin as dawn lightened the eastern sky and was awestruck by huge mountains of billowing grey smoke rising above the bombed area. The faces of the Germans in the car were tense with anxiety as they stared at the havoc. As they travelled down the *Unter den Linden*, Mahoney noticed the feeble attempts at camouflage with netting.

During the day, five of his crew arrived with other airmen who had been shot down in the raid. At dawn next day they were driven to Potsdam Station to wait for a train to Frankfurt and Dulag. At the station a column of chained slave workers, old men and young girls, were marched off in single file. They were dressed in rags and were clearly starving. Their heads and shoulders bent forwards, and their weary, hopeless eyes and features, brought to the Kriegies a searing picture of the meaning of the horrors of Nazism.

As the train drew out of Berlin the airmen stared at row upon row of burnt out houses, only the walls standing. Destruction appeared complete over an area of some 10 square miles, but Mahoney felt little compassion for the German populace after seeing the despairing hollow eyes and despondency of the chained slaves.

Escape was in the forefront of the minds of the new Kriegies during the journey. While still outside they were just watched by armed soldiers, inside the compound they would be confined and watched for 24 hours every day. But their escort never relaxed their vigilance. Dulag Luft was already known by reputation to aircrew in Britain and to the men on their way there. The prospect was not pleasant, but after the usual Red Cross ploy and interrogation Mahoney was happily surprised to find food plentiful and good in the main camp.

A warning and exhortation to march with dignity and quiet from the *Kommandant* preceded their next journey to the station for the rail trip to Stalag Luft 3. 'You are British officers and gentlemen,' he reminded them. 'Remember that so you will not stir the wrath of the civilian population who will see you.' But the civilians that Mahoney saw had sallow, pasty complexions with unsmiling, sullen expressions.

At the station the RAF officers were herded into box-cars with straw-covered floors. They protested but the German officer in charge said that ordinary coaches were being used to evacuate women and children from heavily bombed cities. That made them feel better. The cramped and uncomfortable journey to Sagan ended on 2 September 1943.

Kriegies arriving at Stalag Luft 3 at this time found a camp that was highly organised and comparatively comfortable. When Mahoney entered the North compound he found the camp had a canteen from which tooth powder, brushes, stationery, shoe polish, pots and pans and various odds and ends were distributed. There was a barber shop manned by other ranks who had volunteered to work in the camp. A good reference and fiction library had been established. There was a fire pool which was sometimes used for a dip, a shower room which Squadron Leader Ken Campbell had organised, and a fine theatre with a raked auditorium. All the conversions of ordinary bare huts had been carried out by the Kriegies to make the confined life more tolerable. The showers had been erected and plumbed by their labour and the seating and stage of the theatre had been constructed from Canadian Red Cross boxes. Almost all work within the compound had to be done by the Kriegies, the Germans often supplying materials but claiming lack of manpower for labour shortages.

The old wind-up gramophone was a popular pastime. Records received through the Red Cross included classical and dance music. Among the dance music was a record which became the theme song of the camp. It was entitled *Don't Get Around Much Any More.*

### A VISIT TO THE OPERA

It was during a 'flat-out' period that 19-year-old gunner Flight Sergeant Harold 'Mac' McLean's Halifax of 427 Squadron attacked the BMW factory at Munich. McLean had flown 24 operational trips, 15 with his present crew. They had recently carried out five raids in seven days and on this September evening they were briefed for their second consecutive operation over Germany. They were very tired. Mannheim had been the target on the previous night, a loud groan greeted the news that they were destined for another heavily defended target – Munich. On this night too, the bomber stream was directed to fly over London on the outward journey so

116

that Londoners might hear the powerful, throbbing sound that was soon to be heard in the dark sky over Germany.

A nightfighter closed in and fired his first burst of tracer. It was so far wide that McLean could hardly believe it was meant for them, but he called to the captain to corkscrew so that he could see the fighter. Mac knew they were on a bombing run and that the skipper was unlikely to deviate from his run-up to the target. The fighter pilot knew it too. The delay in jinking was fatal and gave the fighter his chance. The next burst riddled the Halifax. It was time to bale out.

McLean jumped into the silk and fell smoothly until briefly caught in the branches of a tree. He then crashed heavily to the ground and lay wracked with the pain of a broken spine. Eventually he struggled to his feet and hobbled into a farmyard. Dogs alerted a farming couple who treated the injured man with kindness until the police arrived. McLean knew that he was badly hurt and needed medical attention.

A month later he had improved but was still hobbling round Stalag 4B Mühlberg when a call came for him to go to the main gate. He thought perhaps a parcel had arrived for him but when he reached the gate he found 21 other Kriegies waiting there. It dawned on them gradually that they had all been taken prisoner the same night during the raid on Munich. The significance was worrying. They were sent back to their huts uneasy and wondering.

A few days later a *Luftwaffe Hauptmann*, a *Feldwebel* and several *Soldaten* gathered the same men together, marched them to the station and entrained for Munich. They were taken to *Fuerstenfeldbruck* aero-drome and lodged in a barrack block. Despite their situation and destination the Kriegies had established good relations with their guards. For a week they stayed at the aerodrome, eating in the NCOs' Mess where some of the men liberated a few useful pieces of cutlery.

During the week they tried to make sense of the guard's mutterings. The words *'Opern Haus'* frequently occurred in the Germans' conversations and the Kriegies feared that they were to be exhibited to the inhabitants of Munich on the Opera House stage as *Terrorfliegers*. It was not a pleasant prospect.

Eight more Kriegies joined them from Dulag Luft, making a total of 30 survivors of the Munich raid. The Dulag Kriegies were distinctive, their hair was uncut, so unlike the closely shorn men from Stalag 4B. The morning came when they were lined up outside and surrounded by 50 guards armed with machine pistols. A *Luftwaffe* officer read out a long statement in English in which the words 'an eye for an eye' came across very clearly and ominously to McLean. As they were herded on to a bus and trailer, each Kriegie was accompanied by an English-speaking *Luftwaffe* or *Wehrmacht* officer.

Touring round Munich the airmen were shown a brewery, a football stadium and a maternity hospital, all of which had been damaged. McLean was asked, 'What were you bombing? Munich is an unarmed city.' McLean pointed to some tall chimneys and was told they were part of the power station. That seemed a reasonable explanation.

Soon the cordoned-off Opera House square was reached and the Kriegies were ordered off the bus. McLean was apprehensive. He could see that the others felt the same when their eyes met. But as soon as they walked into the Opera House they could tell it was empty, there was no warm hubbub of voices from within. They were not going to be exhibited. McLean was strangely comforted by a bust of Shakespeare on the staircase up from the foyer. As the party walked into the rear of the circle, the Kriegies could see the sky through the hole made by a bomb which had fallen through the centre of the roof.

The Kriegies were even more surprised when they were joined by some English-speaking German generals. It seemed a pointless exercise on the Germans' part, but at least one advantage was gained by the Kriegies. A general asked why their hair was shorn like the Russians and did they like it? When told it was compulsory at Stalag 4B, possibly for health reasons, the general said he would have it stopped. No more hair was cut off from Kriegies when entering Mühlberg.

Back at Mühlberg camp, parted from the friendly guards, McLean puzzled over the strange business but then its possible purpose became clear in a flash. A fortnight before the attack on Munich, Peenemünde had been raided and the rocket research plant badly damaged. Were not the rockets made and assembled at Munich? Were the Germans anxious to know how much the Allies knew of their activities? If that was so they could have gained little knowledge from their prisoners.

### REPATRIATION '43

In early October 1943 the rumours of repatriation for the severely wounded were circulating again, raising the hopes of those who so desperately wanted and needed the comfort of their loved ones, the hospitals and recuperative treatments at home.

Back in October 1941 the severely wounded were sure that they were going home. They had travelled as far as the racecourse in Rouen en route to Marseilles, only to be told that owing to some technicality the repatriation had fallen through. The disappointment for Bence and the others was crushing. Now, two years later the 'Repat' was on again and

Ron Bence, Bill Legg and other wounded who were considered to qualify for repatriation were warned to get ready.

By the 13th the Repats, packed and ready to leave, were trying to relax. Excited, muted chatter continued into the early hours until they drifted into a drowsy half-sleep, their excitement tempered by fears that the repatriation process could stall again. It needed only a minor incident for the Germans to call off the whole exchange. Some of the Repats felt that a further breakdown of the procedure would be the last straw. The depth of disappointment would test their sanity.

At Lamsdorf the Kriegies crowded to cheer the Repats as they assembled to leave for the station. Some were on crutches, others were carried out on stretchers and just a few appeared physically healthy. Their wounds were not those which could be seen at a glance, the damage had been to their inner selves and would probably take much longer to repair. Helped into lorries, they left with the cries of 'good luck' ringing in their ears. Many had messages for relatives of those staying behind.

As the Repats left a strange dichotomy was felt among the Kriegies remaining in the camps. Few would wish to have received the injuries which would qualify them for the party that was leaving – but – they were envied for going home. They would soon see their loved ones, would eat good food and, above all, they would be free.

The Repats boarded a train on 14 October and started on a roundabout journey through Thorn, Danzig, Stargard, Stettin and Swinemünde to Rügen, where they were taken on board a German ship which arrived at Gothenburg in Sweden on the 18th. When they saw that the Germans had mounted an armed guard to prevent anyone leaving the ship all their old anxieties returned. This was not going to be an easy transfer. A ray of hope appeared when the Swedes objected to the armed guards and they were removed. Those who could manage it were allowed ashore where they were well treated by the Swedish people.

On the morning of the next day three hospital ships arrived loaded with the German wounded who were to be exchanged. The procedure did not go smoothly, several times the Germans threatened to call off the exchange, alleging that they were two German Repats short. Finally they were satisfied and Legg, Bence and the others were on the *Atlantis*. Still more were on the *Empress of Russia* and the *Drotningholm*, a Swedish hospital ship. The three ships left harbour on 21 October preceded by a Swedish destroyer.

At 7 o'clock on the morning of 26 October the ships sailed into Liverpool Bay. The wounded men looked at the welcoming crowds on the Lancashire shore with tear-filled eyes. They were home.

# PART 5
# 1944

### IMPERMANENT STAFF

Flight Sergeant Syd Murrell was the wireless operator on a 35 Squadron Halifax from RAF Graveley. On the night of 21 January 1944 the Halifax was Pathfinding for a raid on Magdeburg when it was attacked by a fighter. Or was it flak? No-one was certain, but it was time to jump out.

On 10 September 1943, the Dulag Luft transit centre had moved from Oberursel to Palmengarten, a park in a residential part of the city of Frankfurt less than a mile from the main railway station. The Germans knew this was a target area as was proved by their systematic evacuation of civilians. The moving of the prisoners to the park was a flagrant violation of Article 9 of the Geneva Convention, but Generals Jodl and Keitel had agreed to a plan to place prisoners-of-war in the centre of a town likely to be bombed.

Senior NCO at the Palmengarten Dulag was 'Buck' Taylor who asked Syd Murrell and Bill Lawes, bomb-aimer on the same crew, if they would like to take the place of two Kriegies on the Red Cross staff who wished to move to a permanent camp. Murrell and Lawes agreed.

The location of the camp ensured that there were many air-raid alarms during which the Kriegies were shepherded into underground shelters, but on the night of 18/19 March a full-scale attack by over 800 aircraft of Bomber Command devastated Frankfurt. The area shook with enormous blasts and earth-shaking vibrations, but the sturdy air-raid shelter withstood the assault. Murrell and Lawes were shaken by the intensity of the raid but considered it poetic justice. They had taken part in two raids on the city themselves. One tremendous explosion brought down a beam across the entrance shelter which fell on a Kriegies' head and killed him. The shelterers climbed out to find the ruined huts still burning. A clothing store and some German quarters had survived the onslaught but the Palmengarten Dulag was effectively destroyed.

Frankfurt's main railway station had been put out of action and it took time to make arrangements to move the 40 Dulag Kriegies to another camp. They were very much on edge, the area in which they were confined had unexploded bombs. The *Feldwebel* in charge was sympathetic to the Kriegies' plight. Alcohol had loosened his tongue and he was

120

critical of Hitler whom he blamed for everything. Murrell wondered what the *Feldwebel*'s end would be.

At four in the afternoon the Kriegies were led from the remains of the camp and through the ruins of Frankfurt. Hostile crowds lined some streets but vigilant guards prevented any attacks. One elderly man leapt at the group with a knife but he was disarmed by a *Gefreite*. Seeing the devastation the raid had caused, Murrell was not surprised at the people's anger. After a two-hour walk they were put into a passenger coach for the seven-day journey to Heydekrug. Finally a trudge through the snow brought them a welcome from the Luft 6 Kriegies and a hot meal.

The Palmengarten Dulag was no more. The Germans constructed a new transit camp two miles north-west of Wetzlar, some 30 miles north of Frankfurt.

### JOURNEY OF PAIN

Journeys across Europe by the usual means of Kriegie transport of railway horse-boxes or cattle trucks, were always uncomfortable, miserably confined, and claustrophobic. Starvation, thirst and filth were thrown in for good measure. It was hard to imagine anything worse, but for men who had been seriously wounded such mid-winter journeys were unmitigated torture. A three day and night, freight train journey across Eastern Germany, Poland and East Prussia, was suffered by Sergeant Bill Bloxham and seven companions. All had spent a lengthy stay in German hospitals and were still in agony from severe wounds sustained during their clash with the enemy.

It was 31 January when they left the hospital, a converted factory near Obermassfeld close to the Czechoslovakian border, their wagon was hitched to a series of freight trains and shunted and shaken through days and nights of the mid-European continental winter. The train passed through the seemingly endless Leuna petrochemical complex near Leipzig, arriving at Cottbus south-east of Berlin where the train stopped and thin *ersatz* soup was issued. Temporarily out of the trucks the men were unable to get any rest in the bitterly freezing weather. The only warmth was in the anger directed at them by the passing civilians.

In the early hours the wagon was hitched to a goods train and it continued its rattling, clattering, journey through thick snow to Thorn in Poland. At a brief halt beside a *Wehrmacht* training camp the wounded captives were treated to what Bill Bloxham described as, 'the sorry sight of ill-clad Cossacks who had been won over and were now in training for service in German mounted battalions. On whichever side these men fought they were almost certain to die.'

At the end of the third day, the refrigerator-like wagon was shunted into a siding at Insterberg, a major East Prussian staging post for the northern sector of the Russian Front close to Hitler's command headquarters. All the prisoners were now suffering severely from raw wound and post-operative pain, dysentery and despair. The depth of their misery was aggravated by a forced, staggering struggle on sticks and crutches in complete darkness, through the deep and blowing snow to an unheated hut where they were to spend the night. Stumbling about in the pitch darkness they found three-high wooden bunks and were given a bowl of the tasteless, watery soup which did nothing to ease their gnawing hunger. Despite the cold, each of the men tried to rest but sleep was impossible. Their body warmth brought lice emerging quickly from the bags of wood shavings which served as mattresses. The incessantly biting lice and biting cold made sure that there would be no rest.

Breakfast next morning consisted of a slice of the sawdusty black bread and a cup of ground acorn coffee, then it was back to the sticks and crutches for another agonising mile back to the railway wagon. That wagon had assumed the image of a torture chamber with its jerking and crashing wheels adding to the purgatory of pain. The prisoners dreaded the rest of the journey.

Eight hours later the train slowed after a run along the marshes bordering the coast of the Baltic Sea. Flocks of storks rose, flapping their huge wings then gliding gracefully above. The last stage of the journey was in a horse-drawn wagon through the sandy floored forest to Stalag Luft 6 Heydekrug. The pain wracked, bedraggled, evil-smelling, tired and starving group found relief and comparative warmth in the crowded prison camp. There among 2,000 RAF men, the eight wounded were relieved to be among their own. Here was warmth, food and rest – it was the easing of one nightmare.

As the year progressed losses in Bomber Command and the numbers of RAF men killed and taken prisoner increased alarmingly. The Germans were overcoming 'Oboe'.

### THE HUT BEYOND THE WIRE

Wilfred 'Peachy' Harrison had what Kriegies regarded as a 'cushy number' at Heydekrug. He controlled the meagre store of items that the *Reich* deigned to hand out to the prisoners, a few bowls, knives, spoons, mugs and cleaning materials. Those drawing supplies stood at a counter behind which were visible racks of equipment. On the right was a floor-to-ceiling partition in which was a glassless window through which Harrison's office could be seen. The spaciousness invited comment when many were having to live in tents. The muslin curtain over the front window and the armchairs made from Canadian Red Cross cases frequently led to cries of 'rackets', but few knew that the partition was double sided. Removing a panel would reveal shelves containing cameras, forged papers and photographic negatives of various documents and passes which 'tame' guards had loaned for payment. There were larger pieces of German equipment under the floor. Harrison was sitting on dynamite.

George Grimson intended going out dressed in German uniform and visited Harrison to say goodbye. Grimson planned to mingle with the guards and then dispose of his dummy rifle and uniform in a latrine near the main gate. The Escape Committee were unhappy about the loss of this valuable gear, but Grimson did not fancy being in civilian clothes so near to the camp. The problem seemed insoluble when Harrison remembered a shed about a mile from the camp which held the overflow of Kriegies' personal possessions. The Germans had claimed that there was too much held in the barrack rooms and extra goods were placed in named Red Cross boxes in the hut. Harrison held the only key and when there was a sufficient number to make up a party of Kriegies wishing to collect something, a visit, under guard, would be arranged.

The scheme had done little to clear the huts, mainly junk had been taken but it needed about a dozen people to pull the handcart to and from the hut. It made a pleasant outing, so several unnecessary trips were made to keep the scheme going. Behind it all was the possibility that one day it might be used to facilitate an escape.

Harrison suggested to Grimson that he might change in the hut but the rifle would still have to go into the latrine: off-duty guards did not walk around near the camp armed in that manner. Grimson welcomed the idea, he would feel less conspicuous near the camp in uniform and did not relish the idea of entering the latrine in uniform and emerging in civvies.

But Grimson had never been to the shed. It was not visible from the camp and there was only one key. Harrison drew a map of the area and gave Grimson the key with instructions where to hide it outside the shed. For an hour Grimson committed the instructions to his extraordinary memory and then on 21 January he strode from the camp perfectly equipped, mentally and physically – as a German guard. Grimson's absence was covered by another man lying in his bed, muffled under a blanket pretending to be sick. George Grimson had made his last escape from a prisoner-of-war camp.

The next day Harrison took a dozen Kriegies and a guard to the shed. At the hut door he pretended to drop the key, swore, found it and opened the door. The guard was happy to smoke a cigarette outside which gave Harrison the opportunity to hide the uniform at the bottom of a packing case with Red Cross boxes on top. He then lifted it on to the cart, locked the shed and with the dozen men pushed the handcart back to the camp outer main gate. However, the guard at the gate was unsure.

'Will you give me your word as an Englishman that there is no contraband in the cart?' he asked. It was a tricky moment. Harrison thought quickly.

'I can't do that,' he replied. 'I have no idea what people have in their boxes. If you are not satisfied you had better search the lot. We,' indicating the Kriegie cart party, 'are in no hurry to get back into the bloody camp.'

The German still hesitated but he was tired and hot. The task of searching such a large load did not appeal to him. He shrugged, pushed the gate open and waved the party through into the compound.

Grimson was 'out' and establishing his escape line that Harrison was due to follow after Nat Leaman. To aid in Harrison's disguise, Sergeant Le Voi had tailored a sports jacket expertly converted from an Italian uniform tunic. The beautiful jacket was hanging on the inside of the cupboard where the rest of the trading goods were stored when without warning the *Gestapo* descended on the camp.

Harrison decided that the best way to cope with the *Gestapo* man who walked in was to be nice to him, to humour him with the offer of a cup of coffee, a cigarette and a chat. Momentarily forgetting, Harrison opened the cupboard door and there the jacket hung resplendent in all its glory. The *Gestapo* man spotted it, felt the texture and asked, *'Uniform?'*, to which Harrison replied *'Ja,'* proffering a cigarette. The *Gestapo* man accepted and Harrison breathed easier as they chatted for a while until the German left, refusing cigarettes for himself or chocolate for his *Kinder*.

Not long after that Nat Leaman made his escape from the camp. His absence was covered for a while but he was recaptured and brought back to Heydekrug. The Germans were furious and as Harrison said, 'appeared ready to tear down the entire camp to find escape equipment'.

A large *Unteroffizier* and two ferrets armed with crowbars thrust their way into Harrison's office, announcing that they were about to rip up the floorboards. This time there had been a tip-off and the goods removed, but the storage places were intact and, though empty, their purpose would have been obvious.

'Go ahead,' Harrison said, standing back. 'But first you will have to take down the partition wall and then re-erect it. You can see by the floorboard cracks that the partition has been added over the floor and it will be impossible to lift any board without its removal.'

After discussion between themselves the Germans concluded that Harrison was right, it would obviously be too much trouble, so gathering up their tools they left. Harrison relaxed, he had avoided another lengthy spell in the Cooler. Had the Germans known, the sliding up and outwards of one of the wall beadings would have revealed that the whole wall could be opened on hinges, exposing a handle to lift up an entire section of floor.

Despite the icy weather there had been another escape from Heydekrug. 'Paddy' Flockhart had walked from the compound, perfectly disguised as a surveyor. His upper middle-class clothing, tailored from Italian uniforms, probably prevented his too close questioning. On his hazardous struggle against the elements and the ever-present and suspicious *Gestapo*, Flockhart was helped by the indefatigable Grimson who guided him, found him temporary resting places, told of the location of a gap in the dock fence and the whereabouts of Swedish ships in the docks and Danzig. Grimson also obtained overalls and a cap for Flockhart's final disguise as a Swedish seaman. After several narrow escapes Flockhart successfully stowed away until the Swedish ship in which he was hiding was in its home waters. He was soon back in Britain.

### AN UNCONQUERABLE WILL

A few weeks before the 'Transients' arrived at Heydekrug, 'Jock' Callender slipped out of the camp. He had been itching to escape from Heydekrug and in early March 1944 he saw his chance. A tame guard had told him that a new drainage system was to be installed and a compound wash-house would be fenced off during the work. Callender reasoned that there would have to be an exit in the perimeter fence on the opposite side from the compound through which workmen would pass. If he could hide in the wash-house until the temporary fence was erected and the opening made, he would have a good chance of getting out as a workman. 'Tally Ho' agreed and Callender, equipped with civilian clothes, *Ausweis*, travel permits and food, climbed into an emptied water tank on the evening before the fencing was to begin. For more than two days he lay there tense and silent, until the new surrounding fence was built and an exit made. Then, convincingly acting the role of a senior workman, Callender walked out of the wash-house and the camp. Although there were rumours later that 'Jock' Callender had been in touch with some French prisoners, he was never seen again except by the *Gestapo* – who shot him.

## RUSSIAN RESISTANCE

Russian prisoners were not all starved and cowed. The Germans had need of workers so those capable after their long march from the Eastern Front were given the bare minimum of food to keep them alive. But the Russians were also expert at doing the minimum amount of work. Their faces expressionless, they could reduce the overseeing Germans to a state of frantic frustration. Flying Officer Bill Rolfe witnessed such an exhibition in Sagan's North compound.

To strengthen the protection of a coal dump the Germans brought in three Russian prisoners laden with rolls of barbed wire, cutters, staples and hammers, and put them to work under the watchful eye of a guard in the *Posten* box above. A few hundred interested Kriegies gathered on the other side of the wire to watch. They soon became enthralled at what they saw.

The first Russian slowly unrolled the wire and laid it in position. The second tapped in the staples with incredibly light hammer blows which barely held them in place. The third cut the wire and then proceeded to snip off all the barbs from each strand. Eventually the guard up in the box saw what the Russians were doing and began to scream threats and abuse, but the poker-faced Russian continued with his barb snipping. The guard jumped up and down with rage and still screaming he swivelled his machine gun round on its mounting and levelled it at the Russian. It was time for the RAF Kriegies to take a hand.

It needs a considerable degree of insensible callousness to commit murder under the steady gaze of 200 pairs of unblinking eyes. The Kriegies crowded their side of the wire and stared at the guard. It was a risky ploy they had used before with 'nutty' guards. This one could not take it, he cocked the machine gun as a final threat but resumed his screaming. The Russian finished his de-barbing, then with hands on hips, he turned and stared at the guard for a full minute before deliberately spitting in his direction. After that, he surveyed the naked strands of wire to ensure that no barbs had been left then delicately dropped the cutters from his outstretched hand.

Watching admiringly, Kriegie Bill Rolfe fervently hoped that those courageously unbowed men would survive the war – but he had his doubts.

## NOT ANY OLD TOM, DICK OR HARRY

'Tom', 'Dick' and 'Harry', the tunnels in the North compound at Sagan had taken the time, energy and ingenuity of hundreds of officer Kriegies. They were efficiently constructed under the experienced eye of Canadian mining engineer Wally Floody, although he confessed that the drilling he had done through rock was rather different from burrowing through the soft sand of Silesia. Nevertheless it was Floody's expertise, hard digging and common sense which drove 'Tom', 'Dick' and 'Harry' straight and level with less danger of roof falls than in previous tunnels, which Roger Bushell had described graphically as resembling 'the work of some weary badger'.

Bushell was more than just the organiser of escape activities: he was the inspiration, the driving force whose dedication to confounding the Germans and freeing as many airmen as possible was his continuing priority. Maurice Butt declared, 'Bushell seeded the will to make a professional approach to a mass escape, hence the simultaneous digging of "Tom", "Dick" and "Harry".'

As a cover Bushell took up acting in the camp theatre but as 'Big X' he headed the escape organisation. In each barrack block of some 120 prisoners there was a 'Little X' who liaised with the others and Bushell, and from which spine of control a multitude of escape activities was co-ordinated. 'X', the unknown factor, was intended to be baffling for the sake of security, not drama. For the same reason the word tunnel was banned from conversations and the tunnels given names meaningless to the Germans.

Rolfe had police experience so on his arrival at Sagan he was immediately roped in with George Harsh for security work. The tunnel was nearing completion and suppressed excitement was felt throughout the camp, but Rolfe was uneasy. He had strong premonitions, more like prophesies, when caught in raids on London's dock area. As he stood holding a backcloth for photographs for forged papers, he had the same kind of premonition. Turning to 'Wings' Day he remarked quietly, 'this is going to be a disaster, deep down I am certain of it'.

'Perhaps,' 'Wings' replied positively, 'but it is going to be done.'

Shortly after morning *Appell* selected men were sent down the shaft of one of the tunnels and the trap closed. The manual pump impelled air towards the man working at the face, but the sooty smoke from the melted-margarine oil lamps quickly made the atmosphere hot and stuffy. When electric lighting was extended along the tunnel the digger became a little more comfortable, although body temperature continued to be increased by the 'Long John' underpants and vests worn to keep the working Kriegies reasonably clean should they have to emerge in a hurry.

Pilot Officer Geoff Fletcher was employed as a carpenter at the base of the shaft, fashioning the hundreds of supporting timber frames that prevented the soft sand from burying the diggers. Fletcher knew conditions were worse for the man at the face of the tunnel, lying on his side, scraping away at the sand and passing it back to be loaded into the small wooden trolleys. There was also the ever-present danger of the roof falling in before the wooden frames could be rammed into place. Wally Floody had already been buried by a roof collapse and dragged out semi-conscious.

Before the NCOs were moved from Sagan in the summer of 1943 bed boards for the tunnels were running short. 'Dixie' Deans was asked if the men in the NCOs' compound could help. Although short of boards because of their own tunnelling activities, the NCOs found the appeal irresistible when a hint was given that a tunnel was near completion. The hundreds of boards smuggled to the North compound were received with delight.

The officers in the North compound were shocked when Glemnitz and his ferrets discovered tunnel 'Tom' on 11 March and blew it up. 'Dick' was unusable as a new compound was being built where it was to have exited, so Roger Bushell decided that the digging of 'Harry' was to be continued until such time as the weather was suitable for his proposed mass escape. But the Germans were still suspicious. Glemnitz and the ferrets prowled around continuously; they sensed the expectant atmosphere and were certain to intensify their investigations after the discovery of 'Tom'.

Despite the cold and snow at Sagan it was decided to go ahead with the break-out on the night of 24/25 March during the first moonless period. Most of the compound's inmates had been involved in the preparations for the escape or in the digging of the tunnel. The first places were allocated by the SBO and then those who had worked on the project had their names drawn from a hat. Five out of every 40 were allotted to outstanding workers who had been unlucky in the draw. Ken Campbell noted that 240 men were equipped for escaping, all having maps, compasses and items of clothing which they had organised themselves. A dietician in the organisation had prepared a special concentrated food.

The first 10 men scheduled to leave the tunnel were equipped with all the necessary passes and papers that would enable them to travel by train. They would have the best chance for a home-run. The remaining 230 escapers would, as Campbell put it, work out their own salvation, spreading over the *Reich* in their own way and creating a multitude of red-herrings for the pursuers to follow.

Geoff Fletcher was picked as number 117 to go down the tunnel. Every man's feelings were a mix of excitement and fear. The thought of attempting to cover hundreds of miles through hostile country was exhil-

**Right:** A typical prisoner-of-war registration card. That illustrated is the card for Squadron Leader Roger Bushell, 'Big X', murdered in 1944 after the mass escape.

**Right:** A Posten tower at Stalag Luft 1 with the searchlight clearly visible. To the left can be seen the Marienkirche at Barth.

**Right:** Prior to the funeral of Sergeant Johnny Shaw his body lay under honour guard in the small chapel built by the prisoners at the end of a cookhouse. Shaw was afforded full military honours by the Germans. (See The Hatching of a 'Canary'.)

**Left:** The brutal and detested *Unteroffizier* Küssel – 'Ukrainian Joe'. (See 'Poles Apart'.)

**Below:** The memorial erected to the murdered 'Fifty' by the prisoners at Sagan after the great escape.

IN MEMORY OF THE OFFICERS WHO GAVE THEIR LIVES. SAGAN MARCH 1944.

**Right:** The prisoner's memorial to those who died at Stalag Luft 3. They were unable to complete the inscription in 1945 because of their sudden departure. (See 'Goodbye to Sagan'.)

ERECTED BY THE
PRISONERS OF WAR
OF THE ALLIED AIR
FORCES IN HONOURED
MEMORY OF THEIR
COMRADES WHO DIED
AT STALAG-LUFT 3
DURING THE WAR
A.D. 1939 – 194
PER ARDUA AD ASTRA

**Below:** The courtyard of Spangenberg Castle in 1939. Left to right: Bach-Griffiths, RM, MacLachan, Bewley, Heaton-Nichols, Baughan, Thurstan, RN; seated: Casey, Tilsley, Murray, Harry 'Wings' Day, Thompson, Edwards; front: Coste.

**Left:** The exit of the great escape tunnel at Sagan in March 1944.

**Below:** Sergeant George Booth, AC2 Larry Slattery and Pilot Officer Laurie Edwards interviewed at the Wesermünde Hospital by German radio. (See 'Flying Start'.)

**Bottom:** An earphone made from the author's plastic tooth powder box.

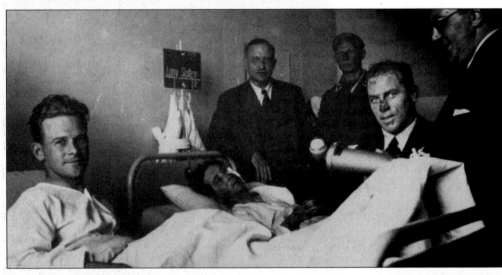

**Right:** The discovery of a tunnel entrance at Stalag Luft 3 Sagan.

**Right:** Blessed release in the spring of 1945 for Jack Casselden and Len Clarke.

**Above:** A view of Dulag Luft transit camp at Oberursel.

**Left:** Wing Commander Harry 'Wings' Day, arch escaper.

**Left:** James 'Dixie' Deans on parade at Sagan. 'Dixie' Deans was the highly respected leader of most of the RAF NCO prisoners throughout their captivity. (See 'Man of Confidence'.)

**Above and right:** Two views of the 'forty-holer' at Lamsdorf.

**Right:** A horse-drawn latrine suction tank at Lamsdorf.

**Left:** *Major* Simoleit checking prisoners leaving for Schubin; 'Wings' Day with hands in pockets.

**Left:** *Feldwebel* Glemnitz leading the prisoner party leaving for Schubin.

**Left:** *General* Wolff inspecting the guard at Stalag Luft 1. At the far left is *Major* Burchardt, the *Kommandant* at Barth.

**Above and below:** Severly wounded navigator Bill Legg successfully crashedlanded this Wellington 1c while fire raged in the vicinity of the main spar. (See 'Unrehearsed Solo'.)

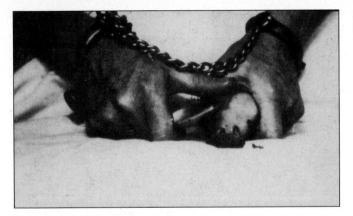

**Left:** Manacled hands could still be put to work.

**Left:** A RAF sergeant at Stalag 8B Lamsdorf.

**Left:** Frugal prisoner-of-war life and cooking facilities at Lamsdorf.

**Right:** Humour prevailed, as evidenced by this Christmas menu from 1941.

J. Houston  
'Wally' Barber  
Lefty Vol  
Jimmy Fisk  
J. Gilmour  
[signature]  
L. Busby.  
Robt. J. Beidley  
[signature]  
Lel Garrioch  
Stew 'Brooks.  
'Ben' Blown  
[signature]  

[signature]  
W. H. Jordan  
[signature]  
"Horloger - Dodie"  
[signature]  
"Transport & Dick"  
L. Boulons

# X M A S

Sgt. J. Houston  
"Haggis"

Stalag

Luft

1941  
AND  
A BRIGHTER NEW YEAR

## — TOASTS

**THE KING**  
SGT. G. BUSBY.

**ROOM SIX**  
SGT. J. WHALLEY

**WIVES AND SWEETHEARTS**  
SGT. W. H. JORDAN.

**ABSENT FRIENDS**  
SGT. D.L. DICK

**W./CDR. DAY AND OFFICERS**  
SGT. M.A. OLIVER.

## — MENU —

HORS D'OEUVRES

POTAGE AUX LÉGUMES  
(MIT CURRY)

POMMES EN PURÉE

JAMBON FRITE

CHOUX À LA LUFT.

XMAS PUD

BISCUITS ~ FROMAGE

CAFÉ

CIGARETTES

HAGGIS (BY SPECIAL REQUEST)

GOD SAVE THE KING

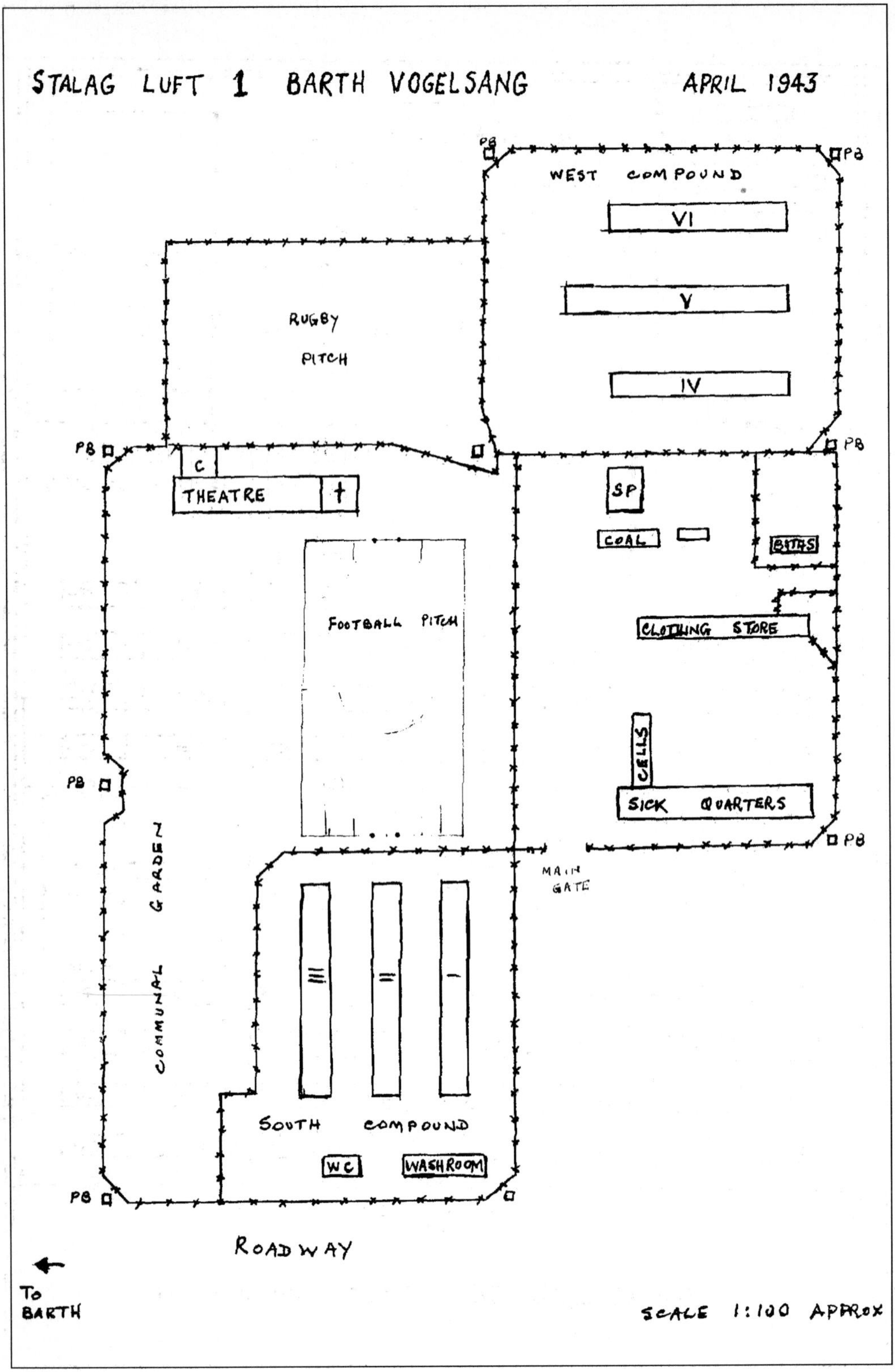

STALAG LUFT 1 BARTH VOGELSANG          APRIL 1943

WEST COMPOUND

VI

V

IV

RUGBY PITCH

PB

PB

THEATRE    C    †

FOOTBALL PITCH

SP

COAL

BATHS

CLOTHING STORE

CELLS

SICK QUARTERS

PB

MAIN GATE

COMMUNAL GARDEN

SOUTH COMPOUND

WC    WASHROOM

PB

ROADWAY

To BARTH

SCALE 1:100 APPROX

A sketch map of Stalag Luft 1 Barth Vogelsang.

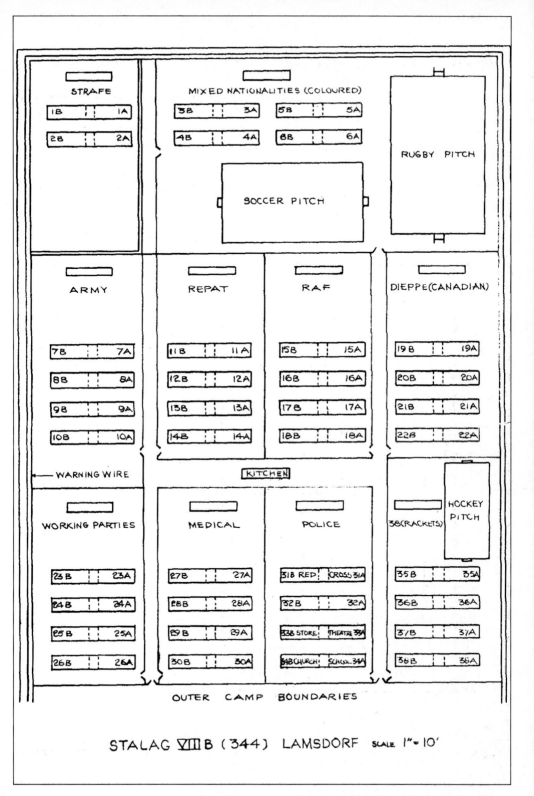

An amazingly precise plan of Lamsdorf based on one drawn by Ernest Winfield and Tom Hedley, both of whom 'resided' in 17B. A successful tunnel was dug under the outer wire from the Dieppe compound to the woods beyond.

**Left:** 'Wings' Day and officers waiting to leave Stalag Luft 1. In the background can be seen the *Arrestlok* or 'Cooler'.

**Left:** *Feldwebel* Glemnitz leading 'Wings' Day and the column of officer prisoners from Stalag Luft 1.

**Left:** Glemnitz leading the column past the town gate of Barth.

# To all Prisoners of War!

## The escape from prison camps is no longer a sport!

Germany has always kept to the Hague Convention and only punished recaptured prisoners of war with minor disciplinary punishment.

Germany will still maintain these principles of international law.

But England has besides fighting at the front in an honest manner instituted an illegal warfare in non combat zones in the form of gangster commandos, terror bandits and sabotage troops even up to the frontiers of Germany.

They say in a captured secret and confidential English military pamphlet,

## THE HANDBOOK OF MODERN IRREGULAR WARFARE:

". . . the days when we could practise the rules of sportsmanship are over. For the time being, every soldier must be a potential gangster and must be prepared to adopt their methods whenever necessary."

"The sphere of operations should always include the enemy's own country, any occupied territory, and in certain circumstances, such neutral countries as he is using as a source of supply."

*England has with these instructions opened up a non military form of gangster war!*

Germany is determined to safeguard her homeland, and especially her war industry and provisional centres for the fighting fronts. Therefore it has become necessary to create strictly forbidden zones, called death zones, in which all unauthorised trespassers will be immediately shot on sight.

Escaping prisoners of war, entering such death zones, will certainly lose their lives. They are therefore in constant danger of being mistaken for enemy agents or sabotage groups.

<u>Urgent warning is given against making future escapes!</u>

In plain English: Stay in the camp where you will be safe! Breaking out of it is now a damned dangerous act.

<u>The chances of preserving your life are almost nil!</u>

All police and military guards have been given the most strict orders to shoot on sight all suspected persons.

*Escaping from prison camps has ceased to be a sport!*

German warning to would-be escapers. To escape was never considered a sport, particularly after the shooting of Johnny Shaw.

**Above:** The shaft entrance to tunnel 'Harry'. The fixed ladder and shoring was formed from bed-boards.

**Right:** A mock certificate for the apathetic fire-fighting skills of Sergeant 'Jock' Houston.

# DIPLOMA

ISSUED BY THE "KREIGY SOCIETY FOR THE PREVENTION OF FIRE" TO = Sgt. "Jock" Houston.

FOR BRAVELY AND WITH NO REGARD TO HIS PERSONAL DANGER, EXTINGUISHING A RAGING FURNACE in ROOM 7 WITH THE MAXIMUM OF DELAY.

SIGNED :-

SECRETARY

HON TREASURER

CHIEF FIRE MAKER.

arating and terrifying. On Fletcher's previous escape he had been recaptured within 24 hours. He was teamed to travel with Peter Waddington, a stocky navigator with a large, bushy moustache who smoked a pipe continuously. They were to pass as foreign workers. Forged papers had been prepared for them; clothing to fit the characters was much harder to produce, but others willingly helped who had been unlucky in the draw.

After evening *Appell* darkness covered the huts, the compound lit only by the perimeter floodlights and the occasional sweeping searchlight flashing across the roofs and *Appell* area. Inside the huts men were dressed for their parts beneath their outer clothing.

One by one those to go were ticked off as their numbers were reached. Slipping on their overcoats they crept by predetermined routes to Hut 104. There they were checked and allocated to a room where they were made to lie on a bunk and stay silent. Fletcher lay tense and nervous while Waddington puffed away furiously at his pipe, the usual occupants ignored them. A gramophone played, meals were eaten, card games were dealt and men tramped up and down the blocks to the toilets.

Ken Campbell was still limping badly. In the snowy, bitterly cold weather he stood no chance of escape; it was as well that he was unlucky in the draw. Instead he was allocated the job of marshal to Hut 103. His job and that of the marshals of the other huts, was to ensure that each selected man would leave the hut at specified intervals, see that they carried only the authorised equipment, and that their escape clothing was well camouflaged for passing through the compound. The marshalling went well. Completely unsuspected by the Germans the men passed wraith-like from hut to hut. The slightest detected movement would have been like an alarm signal.

Still Fletcher and Waddington waited in Hut 104 for the word to pass on. In the other huts there was little sleep to be had, whispered conversations carried on throughout the night. Just before dawn a rifle shot echoed over the huts. Everyone leaped from their palliasses. Sudden shouts from the tunnel entrance room at the end of the corridor warned Fletcher of trouble. The outer end of the tunnel had been spotted. Ford and others stayed in their rooms watching the would-be escapers stream back from the danger area.

In the corridor outside the room there was breathless chaos as those in the tunnel tried to back up and those next in line raced back into the rooms. Some determined Kriegies jumped from the windows and tore across to other blocks before the guards outside the camp realised what was happening, chancing a spraying of machine gun bullets across the compound. Fletcher saw the danger and stayed put.

129

Squads of armed guards ran into the compound, shouting and brandishing rifles, bayonets and sub-machine guns. They roughly ordered everyone out into the compound where they could be seen. The area was flooded with light, every *Posten*'s searchlight centred on the *Appell* ground. Fletcher turned to Waddington with a few words of commiseration and was immediately marched under guard to the *Arrestlok*.

Bob McBride arrived at the exit hole to see a rifle-aiming German shining a torch down into the tunnel and shaking his head in disbelief. Seventy-six Kriegies were out and running hard through the snow.

The Kriegies stood shivering for hours on *Appell* while the Germans checked and re-checked their numbers and identities. *Major* Simoleit trembled with fear for his bleak future. He believed that the Germans would probably execute him as a traitor, or the Allies as a war criminal. *Major* Broili trembled with suppressed rage and seemed about to explode. *Hauptmann* Pieber was regretful and sad, as if the escapers had let him down. At first *Oberst* von Lindeiner was red-faced with temper but quickly regained his composure and became pale, straight-faced and correct. He had no illusions about his perilous situation.

A writ from *Luftgau Kommando III* was handed to von Lindeiner on 26 March, informing him that he was relieved of his duty as *Kommandant* of the prisoner-of-war camp and was to stay there until the beginning of court-martial proceedings. Three days later he collapsed with a heart attack and was taken to his estate Jeschkendorf Manor near Sagan to recuperate. His place as *Kommandant* was taken by *Oberstleutnant* Cordes who in turn gave way to *Oberst* Braune. Braune was a tall man, not unlike 'Wings' Day in appearance, with a similar lined face and balding head. Braune knew that he was taking on an exacting task, bristling with unseen difficulties.

The German staff at Sagan were tense. They feared punishment. Retribution for such dereliction of duty as failing to forestall a mass escape was fierce and spread through the ranks from the top to bottom. There were reports reaching the prisoners of vicious beatings.

Henry Söderberg, on his usual YMCA visit to Sagan, was met by *Major* Simoleit who warned him for safety's sake to stay away. He told Söderberg that von Lindeiner had been taken away and no-one knew what had happened. There was confusion and a desire by German staff to dissociate themselves from von Lindeiner and to wriggle out from any blame for the escape. Simoleit was a worrier in any case. A Nazi party member, one time flak commander and a professor of geography, ethnology and history in civilian life, Simoleit had been with the prisoners since the early days at Barth and was avoided by most Kriegies who thought him sly and dangerous, constantly looking after his own skin. His worry over possible discrepancies in the twice-daily count caused him sleepless nights unless well calmed with sleeping pills.

In the odd way of *Kriegsgefangenschaft* Geoff Fletcher was lucky. Apart from the boredom he found his days in the Cooler restful and food had been sent in from the compound to supplement the usual meagre German rations. When he returned to the compound he was given a food parcel to make up for one he had missed. His spell in the cells also allowed him to miss the interminable searches and headcounts that continued until the Germans were convinced that they had lost 80 prisoners. The totals were wrong, as usual, but no Kriegie was going to spoonfeed the 'goons'. Instead every possible impediment and stumbling block was laid in the tellers' paths to prevent them arriving at the correct figure.

Early on 1 April at RAF Benson, Flying Officer G. 'Bill' Newby, navigator of a sky-blue Mosquito, was briefed to fly to a small, barely discernible, pinpoint map reference near Görlitz named Sagan. The orders to Newby and his pilot were to photograph as wide an area as possible and stay at high level as long as they dared. Then they were to make a fast low level run below 5,000 feet and then head for home. Newby's idea of 'below 5,000 feet' was to knock off two noughts. The 50 feet burst over the area must have heartened some of the Luft 3 Kriegies.

When the news of the mass escape broke in Britain a few days later, Newby realised that he and his pilot had been photographing the camp area and 'showing the flag'. He hoped it had cheered the men in the camp. The low level beat-up caused the crew of the Mossie some problems on the homeward run: it had used up extra fuel on what was already a long trip, but they made it back. They were not so lucky on a later flight, after which they joined their friends in Sagan.

On 6 April, Group Captain Massey was asked to see the *Kommandant, Oberst* Braune, who told him that 41 of those who had climbed from the tunnel had been shot whilst attempting to escape again. Massey was staggered, standing rigidly with his stick supporting his injured leg, he asked: 'How many were wounded?'

'None were wounded, all were killed.'

The reply convinced the group captain that he was being told of a premeditated execution. When he asked to see the bodies Massey was told that they had already been cremated. He demanded that the ashes be handed over to him and turning his back he stiffly left the embarrassed Germans and crossed to the compound to tell the sorry news to the Kriegies.

Group Captain Massey walked on to the stage of the theatre in the North compound and unhesitatingly spoke directly to the assembled Kriegies:

'Gentlemen, I have some tragic news to impart to you. The *Kommandant* has received a statement from the German High Command to the effect that 41 of the officers who escaped have been killed. They state that these men were shot while attempting to resist arrest or to re-escape after being arrested. Obviously this is the work of the *Gestapo*. A *Luftwaffe* officer told me personally that he deeply regretted the affair and assured me that it had been taken out of their hands. In closing I ask you not to display a spiteful or vindictive attitude to the Germans. Let us show them we are men of discipline.'

But when a list of those shot was pinned to the notice board there were 47 names. On 25 May a notice on the bulletin board announced the deaths of three more of the escapers, bringing the round total to 50 which number was, in itself, enough to arouse suspicious anger. The prisoners knew very well that Kriegies who had been recaptured, had their escape equipment, food and civilian clothing confiscated, would never have tried again immediately.

Compounding the Kriegies' grief was an intense unease about the remaining escapers. Massey demanded from the Germans that those escapers caught should be immediately returned to the camp where they would be under the jurisdiction of the *Luftwaffe* and among their fellow Kriegies. There was a fear that they might be in the hands of the *Gestapo* or the *SS*. Massey was simply told that they were being held by a higher authority.

Hugh Collins looked round his Sagan room with a deep sense of loss. Of the six men who had occupied this room there were now two and four empty bunks.

Memorial services were held at Sagan and other camps on 6 April, dye was concocted and used on any available material to make black mourning diamonds or armbands which were sewn on every Luft 3 Kriegies' left sleeve as a mark of respect, and to show the Germans solidarity with their murdered friends.

German reprisals, usual after any attempted escape, were remarkably few. The *Luftwaffe* men were shocked and shamed by the calculatedly murderous and uncivilised actions of the *Gestapo*. The theatre was closed for a few weeks and there were other minor irritations to which the Kriegies had become accustomed, but apart from a kind of homily that 'escaping is no longer a sport' the Germans preferred to let things simmer down.

Surprisingly, they allowed the SBO to join the Repats. He left for home on 11 April with the whole sorry story fresh in his mind.

Fifty were dead and 15 had been returned to the camp, where were the other 11? Eventually letters arrived in the camp with obviously false names. Three had escaped to Britain. Two had been hidden by Swedish sailors and taken to Stockholm and the third, Dutchman Bob Van Der Stok, had been passed through tortuous and dangerous escape lines to Spain. Now there were eight unaccounted for. It was not until after the war that it was found that three were, until then, in concentration camps in Czechoslovakia.

'Wings' Day and Pawel Tobolski were betrayed and captured in Berlin where they were separated. 'Wings' did not see Tobolski again. Both had been told by *General* Nebe, Head of the *Kriminalpolizei*, that they would be sent where they would cause no further trouble. Tobolski was shot and 'Wings' was despatched to Sachsenhausen concentration camp where, behind the high stone walls in a small wired compound he found his old friend 'The Dodger', Major Dodge.

Later they were joined by Sidney Dowse and 'Jimmy' James. The last pair made the list of those who had crawled from the tunnel complete. Two other prisoners were a SOE member, Peter Churchill (who had been saved by his name and the remote possibility that some day he might reveal the secrets of the SOE), and the unrelated Lieutenant-Colonel 'Mad Jack' Churchill of the Commandos. The name Churchill caused the Germans to believe that they might have captured a relative of Winston.

## A TOUR OF DÜSSELDORF

Düsseldorf, the great Rhine river port and industrial centre, was the target for nearly 600 bomber aircraft on the night of 22/23 April 1944. Mid-upper gunner, Sergeant George Woodhead, thought the operation was going well until the Lancaster overshot their last turning point and slipped out of the bomber stream. The Lancaster was then in that position aircrews dreaded, flying through the heavily defended Ruhr Valley alone. The crew could see the raid taking place behind them. Searchlight beams probed around them and they were not surprised when the cold blue beam of a radar-predicted light fastened onto their aircraft. Blinded by the coning searchlights and with flak bursting all around, the captain would not dive because he was on a bombing run, and continued to fly straight and level.

The terrific explosion of a flak shell in the rear fuselage shook the aircraft and within seconds the whole tail unit and turret were engulfed in flames. There was no answer from Woodhead's anxious intercom call to the rear gunner. He reported to the skipper who ordered, 'Bomb doors open'.

Woodhead fired at a Bf110 which was ignoring the flak and coming from behind. As the Messerschmitt dived away, more flak set fire to the Lancaster's starboard wing. Now directly over the target, it was still in the grip of blinding light. At the bale-out order Woodhead clipped on his parachute pack and turned to spurt for the rear exit, but his way was blocked by fire which had now reached as far as the mid-upper turret. He turned, climbed up the bomb-bay steps and along the fuselage floor, struggling against the G-force of the dive. Momentarily losing consciousness due to the violent exertion and lack of oxygen, Woodhead dragged himself over the main spar at last reaching the cabin, brightly lit by the wing fire – and deserted. Woodhead had no time for correct procedures, he was hot. He plunged feet first through the escape hatch.

As he floated gently down he looked up at his parachute canopy, pink-coloured against the dark sky. Peering downwards he saw the reason – he was dropping into a sea of flame and billowing black smoke. He had escaped from a blast-furnace type fire and now seemed likely to land in an incinerator. He pulled the rigging lines of the parachute to escape the glowing mass below, then he was suddenly in the smoke cloud, retching with nausea and unable to see.

Woodhead opened his smarting eyes to find he was through the smoke and drifting away from the fires. Trees and buildings came into view, he seemed to be heading for the roof of a cottage. At the last moment he swung away and landed heavily. Releasing his parachute Woodhead tried to stand but searing pain in his ankle sent him tumbling to earth. As shouting voices came near he knew that his descent had been seen. There was no escape. He had landed on a road with houses on either side. The darkness of the night emphasized the glow of fire at Düsseldorf which lit the whole area. The shouting and footsteps neared. A torch stuffed into his flying boots had switched on, showing the way for his hunters. Soon he was surrounded by a crowd of excited Germans. An elderly man came to his side. He had been a prisoner in the Great War and said in English, the unoriginal 'For you the war is over'.

Woodhead was searched in a house nearby and then made to remove his flying suit. All around people were pointing at him and chattering. Feeling in his pocket he found chocolate and sweets from his flying rations. Knowing that they would be taken from him he threw them to the youngsters gathered around him. He was then allowed to sit and given a cigarette from his own full case. The remainder along with his loose change, was spirited away.

An hour later a commotion at the door signalled the arrival of an armed soldier. Told he would be handed into the soldier's care, Woodhead was warned that if he attempted to escape he would be shot. As he could scarcely stand there was little chance of that. Seated with a soldier in the back seat of a car Woodhead was driven towards the fires.

It seemed impossible to find a way through. Row upon row of firefighting vehicles lined the road on either side, trying to enter the outskirts of Düsseldorf. The car drove through the city at a walking pace, threading through streets littered with debris. Fires roaring on both sides threatened to merge, the heat hurting Woodhead's eyes. Repeatedly streets were blocked and the driver was forced to stop and find another route. There were great gaps which Woodhead guessed were caused by the explosion of a 'Cookie'. As they drove on into the city the fires around increased in number and ferocity. The air was chokingly thick with dust and smoke, the heat searing.

At a city centre crossroads Woodhead saw one of the awesome effects of the raid. A large hotel on a corner had received a direct hit and was blazing furiously. Crowds of rescue workers rushed into the building and brought out the injured and dead. The bodies were simply laid on the pavement. Woodhead saw no ambulances or medical attention and no attempt to tackle the fire.

The driver then followed a road that ran beside a railway line until the car screeched to a sudden stop. A steam locomotive lay on its side in the road. Blast had thrown the engine down from the embankment above. Taking another detour, threading his way carefully the driver gradually left the area of heavy damage but the scene was still brilliantly lit from the fires behind. This road was lined with large houses with steps up to the doors. On the other side of the road was a park surrounded by railings.

Taken inside a house, Woodhead was escorted to the basement which had been converted into a police control room. On one side girls were manning telephones and on the other uniformed police were giving instructions. Woodhead was made to stand at one of the tables, he guessed that the man seated behind it was in charge. People constantly dashed in and out and suddenly a man, covered in dust and blood, saw Woodhead and jerked to a halt. Then, shouting and waving his arms, the enraged man threw himself at him, knocked him to the ground gripping his throat tightly. The officer at the table leapt up and pulled the attacker away who was then led from the room still struggling and shouting. Woodhead began to understand just how lucky he was. He had escaped with his life several times that night.

Locked in a small upstairs room and exhausted by the events of the night, George Woodhead still could not rest. At daylight he could see from the window at the back of the house, huge clouds of smoke still rising above the roofs. He was handed back his flying boots at mid-day and given into the charge of an English-speaking *Luftwaffe* officer. Driven through the rubble covered streets he saw that while fires were still burning and the fire service was battling to put them out, a way through the streets was being cleared. Many of the fine houses in the area were damaged and as the car gradually pulled up, the escorting officer pointed to a house across the road. It was his home he said. A tarpaulin sheet covered the roof and the windows were boarded up. The journey continued to an airfield outside Düsseldorf where Woodhead was pushed into a cell already occupied by another airman, his wireless operator.

During the next four days the pair were joined by six other aircrew. All were given a bowl of evil smelling soup and coffee made from acorns, before being ordered into a covered lorry with more guards than prisoners. Driven into Düsseldorf again they saw the effects of the raid in every road. The lorry drove slowly through cleared streets to the damaged railway station which had been repaired and made serviceable.

As the prisoners climbed down from the lorry they were immediately surrounded by guards and taken through a propped-up tunnel entrance to the platform above. A hostile crowd hemmed them in as they emerged from the tunnel on to the platform. Abuse was shouted and one man fought hard to get at the prisoners but the guards remained in control and held the angry people at bay. The airmen were fully aware of their dangerous situation and of the hatred and bitterness of the population. They were relieved when they were hustled aboard and the train started its journey to Dulag Luft.

### THE THREAT

On the night of 12 May 1944 more than 200 aircraft were sent to bomb a German military camp at Bourg-Léopold. Haze covered the target area and because of the danger of causing casualties to nearby civilian housing, the Master Bomber ordered the attack abandoned after half of the force had bombed. But five Lancasters were lost. The flight engineer on one of these was 21-year-old Devonian, Sergeant Roy Witham. Shortly afterwards he was in the hands of the *Gestapo* in a Brussels prison. Time after time he was questioned until one of his interrogators said:

'We are not going to be bothered in taking you back to a prisoner-of-war camp, we have got enough prisoners and we would have to send guards back with you to Germany. Frankly we just can't be bothered. We are going to take you out tomorrow morning and execute you.'

That Witham's face had suddenly drained to an ashen grey colour did not concern his Oxford-accented interrogator. He had asked about a particular bomb the Lancaster was supposed to be carrying and when again Witham denied knowing anything about it, he said:

'You lie! Ah well, the execution will take place tomorrow at 8 o'clock.'

Throughout the night Witham stared at the hands of his watch. He was sure that death was near. At 8.10am the cell door opened and the same German officer stood outside. To shouts of *'Raus, Raus, Raus!'* Witham was marched through long corridors and past electronically operated doors to a yard.

The yard wall once had three inches of concrete facing but now it was covered with great gouges and ugly brown patches. It had evidently been used for shootings and executions. Mustering his courage, Witham straightened and prayed. At 8.15am the interrogating officer accompanied by a high ranking brass-hat walked over to him saying:

'Now, regarding this aircraft and its special equipment, what are you going to tell me about it?' Witham looked at the wall, he was already at the rough and pitted end.

'I know nothing,' he answered quietly. Resignedly the officer asked:

'Do you want a blindfold young man?' Witham thought of his father, a captain in the Army and holder of the Military Cross. How would he judge his son?

'No,' Witham said, 'I will close my eyes.'

A shouted order and Roy Witham collapsed, a crumpled heap.

The limp form was dragged away and thrown into a cell. The bomb-aimer, the only other survivor of the crew, was stunned and horrified – but Witham was not dead. The mock execution had been a cruel exercise in torture. It was not long before he opened unseeing eyes to stare at a blank wall. Deprived of speech by shock, Roy Witham sat silent and immobile for three blank days.

When he recovered Witham thought about the hours he had sat looking at his watch believing that every second was a second nearer death. Prisoners' watches were frequently confiscated. He believed that the *Gestapo* had left him his watch to increase the torment of waiting.

## THE BREACHING OF *'FESTUNG EUROPA'*

At Heydekrug, 6 June dawned bright and unseasonably chilly. At *Appell* dust devils were whipped up by a cold early summer wind. The NCOs were feeling disappointed about the miners' strike and the lack of push by the Allies. The war seemed to have come to a halt. But one Kriegie was excited. Walking swiftly into the camp office John Bristow blurted out to 'Dixie' Deans and Ron Mogg:

'I've just been testing the canary and I think something's happened. There was someone talking German and going on about *"Festung Europa"*. I don't know German well enough to get the message but it sounded important.'

Deans looked at his watch.

'Can we get the BBC in an hour's time?' he asked Bristow. Then, his head bowed in thought he spoke as if to himself.

'This might be *it*, but it might just as easily be the Jerries trying to pull a fast one on us. Even if it is true we will have to be careful how we break the news.' Straightening, he ordered:

'Call all the news readers in and warn them to be ready, but no-one is to pass the word until I say so. If the camp breaks out cheering the Germans will know for sure that we have a radio.'

Mogg circuited the compound trying to hide his excitement, wanting to tell everyone that he thought something big was about to break but not daring to say a word – except to Cyril Aynsley, his fellow journalist with whom he shared the duty of taking down the news in shorthand.

Back in the office, the radio, concealed in the wind-up gramophone, was assembled ready to take down the noon bulletin. By then Mogg was excited and his hands shaking so much that he had to ask Aynsley to take down the news. It was *it*!

John 'Hank' Heape and Mogg 'bashed out' the report on the old upright typewriter provided for camp administration. Peter Thomas and Ken Griffiths assembled the news readers who were then briefed on the security measures. They were to forbid any outburst of cheering or audible emotion that could tip-off the Germans that the Kriegies were aware that the invasion had taken place.

The news-readers slipped away. Deans and Mogg watched as they entered the barracks. The camp was silent, discipline seemed to have prevailed. Suddenly a burst of cheering from Room A1 quickly spread along the whole of A Block. Deans and Mogg looked at each other, worried and frowning until Griffiths dashed in and said:

'It's alright, one of the Goons is going round telling everyone the invasion has started – it is on the German news.' Shortly after, the same German arrived to tell Deans and Mogg.

'You have invaded Europe,' he told them confidently, 'soon we shall push you back into the sea and England and the Americans will want peace, the war will end and you can all go back to help us to fight Russia.' Without waiting for their reaction he dashed off to spread his news.

That night Mogg took down the midnight news. Afterwards, overwhelmed by the day's events he slipped into his bunk, mentally exhausted. Just before settling down he sleepily said to Deans:

'Do you know, it's my girl friend's birthday June the 6th – what a day!'

At Sagan most compounds had some form of radio receiver and although it was suspected or even known by the *Abwehr* there was little point in advertising the fact. Also it had been gleaned from 'tame Germans' that the guards' orders were to open fire into the compounds should any mass demonstration occur. The SBO ordered that in the event of any important news such as an Allied landing on the French coast, it should be taken calmly with no show of jubilation.

In the early afternoon Les Ford was sitting at a window watching people gather round the fire pool when he saw a Kriegie dash towards them from the kitchen where the German radio loudspeaker was fitted. As he spoke a sudden silence descended over the whole camp and then the group scattered quickly in different directions. Ford was convinced the 1,500 Kriegies knew of the Allied landing within minutes.

Squadron Leader Ken Campbell noticed a sudden change in the usual compound noises. The shouts of the basketball players outside his hut window, the shuffling of feet round the circuit of the sandy compound had all ceased. Campbell, suddenly aware of the unusual, complete silence, put down his book. Then came a sound of rapidly pounding feet and a flushed face appeared at the window. Quickly scanning the room to see if there were any strangers the man hoarsely whispered, 'It's happened!' then ran to other huts. The silence continued for another two minutes and then the normal background noise resumed.

John Mahoney was standing in a queue for tickets for a forthcoming theatre production when he saw people running madly from the canteen. Kriegies in the queue looked on in amazement thinking the place on fire. Then Mahoney remembered the German loudspeaker was in the canteen.

At that moment a Kriegie raced past crying out, 'The invasion's come!' Faces lit up immediately. Mahoney had seldom seen such a mass transformation. In the rooms there was excited chatter, everyone talking at once, all happily optimistic in their prophesies of an early end to the war.

The first announcement by the Germans was brief but the BBC news that evening was reassuring. The 6th of June was a day of joyful celebration in the prison camps. Sing-songs rang out until the early hours. The invasion was a major milestone in Kriegie life, giving them hope, strength and courage to face the months ahead. Those months were bound to be difficult and, most probably, dangerous.

Most Kriegies heard the thrilling words read to them by selected news-readers:

'Under the command of General Eisenhower, Allied naval forces supported by strong air forces began landing Allied armies this morning on the northern coast of France.'

This was what they had been praying to hear. For the first years of 'Kriegiedom' a landing on the Continent had seemed impossible, but from the end of 1942 to the middle of 1943 when the tide had turned against Germany at Stalingrad and El Alamein and landings had taken place in North Africa and Sicily, hope had changed to trembling anticipation of an Allied rush across Europe. Freedom, many thought, was just around the corner, at the most no more than six months away. But there were older, wiser heads, particularly among those who had been prisoners in France, Germany, Lithuania and Poland for a long time and for whom disappointment and disillusionment were part of daily life. Unless there was a sudden change in control in Germany, the iron fist of the *SS* and *Gestapo*, both in the armed forces and civilian life, would ensure that power remained in their ruthless hands.

When the landings in France became common knowledge the Kriegies intensified their pastime of 'goon baiting', telling the guards and ferrets that this was the beginning of the end for Germany. Where Germans would discuss the landings they remained unconvinced. This, they averred, was the chance for them to destroy the Western Allies. They would push the armies into the sea and the West would never be able to mount such an action again. The Allies would sue for peace and Germany would then be able to turn her complete attention to the destruction of Russia.

At Belaria, Typhoon pilot Squadron Leader Frank Jensen successfully wagered that his date for the invasion would be the nearest. He was right and Canadian Flight Lieutenant Brown was the loser. Brown's penalty was to carry out 'The Belaria Crawl'. He must circuit the compound crawling on his hands and knees. As this was a 'solemn wager' the preliminaries were carried out with ceremony more appropriate to a medieval challenge. A Master Buckler was appointed to buckle on Montescue Brown's tin kneepads. Further appointments were made of a Master Herald, a Master at Arms, an Envoy Plenipotentiary, the Fourth Estate, a Master Starter, Victuallers, a Tinsmith at Large who supplied the Bucklers and Gentlemen of the Bodyguard to accompany the 'crawler'. 'The Belaria Crawl' was carried out under the watchful eyes of the highly suspicious Germans who believed the performance a diversion for a massive escape plan. When it was over and there was no 'break', the Germans reverted to their first conviction that all the 'English' were mad.

### FIRE RAISER

Just before midnight on 12 June the Kriegies at Heydekrug heard a commotion outside in the compound. German voices shouted raucous and unintelligible instructions. Running hard between the huts, a crew of four *Luftwaffe* firefighters towed and pushed a two-wheeled hose-trolley, unreeling the hose as they ran. The theatre block was burning. Quickly the fire crew connected the hose to the water outlet, turned the tap and directed the nozzle towards the fire. A trickle of water dribbled out only to be lost in the dusty earth.

Although shut in their rooms the Kriegies soon realised that their theatre was alight and if the adjoining wooden huts, including the library, were to be saved it would be up to them to do it. The Germans welcomed the help. The doors were opened and once outside the Kriegies swiftly formed a bucket chain. Buckets of water were heaved up to men who threw the water on the fire from adjoining roofs, but the theatre was soon past saving so water was then dashed down the steaming walls of the huts nearby to prevent the conflagration spreading.

Hours later when the fire had been damped down and the Kriegies returned to their huts, John Bristow, Dave Young and Peter Stubbs figuratively rubbed their hands with satisfaction. The amplifying equipment that had been on loan and held 'on parole' for theatre use could not be easily removed without causing immense trouble, unwanted searches and severe repercussions. Their untraceable loss in such a fierce fire would be credible and difficult to prove otherwise. The radio makers, with the ready connivance of Camp Leader 'Dixie' Deans, now had some vital components for a transmitter and Bristow had a new attribute, he was an accomplished arsonist with an ability for constructing efficient incendiary devices. It may be apocryphal, but Ron Mogg claimed that of the few warped records dragged from the fire the top one was of Vera Lynn singing *I don't want to set the World on Fire.*

A week later rumours abounded about a move from Heydekrug. The fire-raising had been just in time. No-one knew what the future of prisoners would be, particularly if the *Gestapo* or the *SS* took over. The shooting of the 'Fifty' was proof of their unpredictable behaviour and in a desperate situation a transmitter could well be the only method that the Kriegies might have to reach the outside world.

### HOSPITAL 'SNATCH'

When more than 360 aircraft of Bomber Command attacked Mailly-le-Camp in France on 3 May 1944, the target was accurately marked but there had been a delay in getting the Main Force in to bomb. *Luftwaffe* fighters arrived in time to tear into the bombers and a fierce aerial battle raged over the area of the vast camp. Forty-two Lancasters were lost.

Flight engineer Jack Marsden was one of the airmen forced to bale out. Falling swiftly with just one harness webbing attached to his main parachute strap, Marsden was lucky when a tall bare tree caught his canopy and he hung there hardly daring to move until daybreak. With his first attempt to reach the ground he fell 30 feet, but again a branch held him although this time he was within jumping distance. Tearing skin and clothes Marsden at last reached solid earth. He could see the still burning wreck of the Lancaster and walked instinctively towards the flames. Villagers were already there so he turned back into the forest where he met a woodman. Together they tried to retrieve his parachute but it was out of reach. At nightfall the woodman took Marsden to his home.

Marsden was eventually passed over to some *Maquisards* who planned to spirit him across the border to Spain, but the occupying Germans got wind of their presence and attacked through the wood, driving the Resistance men into the open. There were casualties on both sides. Jack Marsden was captured and taken to Sens Hospital with severe head wounds where the Germans took away his uniform and identity discs.

But the resourceful *Maquisards* had no intention of allowing the Germans to keep Marsden. With the co-operation of French surgeons and nurses of the male surgical ward they planned a daring rescue. Speed was essential, the Germans had already said that they would remove Marsden to a prison camp as soon as possible.

At 11.45am on 19 June six determined men cycled to the hospital entrance. Four stayed outside with a spare bicycle, the other two resolutely made their way to the room in which Jack Marsden was held. A policeman stationed at the door decided that discretion in the face of such determination would save his life so he allowed the *Maquisards* to disarm him. He could not know that the rescuers had orders not to use any weapon against the police or hospital personnel.

Marsden was snatched from his bed, a blanket thrown over his pyjamas and, supporting him on each side, the two men swiftly marched him down the corridors to the exit. Brushing past a group of scared nuns they halted briefly at the porter's lodge to hand in the policeman's pistol and pass on a warning not to raise the alarm for 10 minutes. The warning was unnecessary – the shocked porter had collapsed.

Now wearing a raincoat and cap, Marsden cycled groggily away from the hospital entrance surrounded by his group of 'protectors'. The operation had lasted eight minutes.

The D-Day landings meant that French police were guarding all main roads to keep them clear for the free passage of *SS* troops towards the battle front. This caused detours which tired the wounded man. He was exhausted when he arrived 25 minutes later at the safe house of Father Camus' farm.

That evening the *SS* arrived in force and occupied every farm in the area except the small, remote farm of Father Camus. Immediately the Resistance men began to organise an evacuation. Speed was again necessary. Marsden was buried under straw and manure on a cart and taken to a rendezvous arranged on a rough dirt track. There he was transferred to a car, finally arriving near Sens as an air-raid warning sounded and ack-ack opened fire. The railway was bombed and as the local petrol depot went up in flames Marsden had to be moved to another group of Resistants. He was finally entrusted to the care of a family who treated him like a son. More than 50 people had been concerned with the escape. Three weeks later American troops arrived and liberated the village.

Marsden, still unable to speak, could only gesture when questioned by American officers. They were convinced that he was a German trying to fool them. Marsden had no identification papers and was unable to explain. The Americans sent him to a prisoner-of-war camp for captured *Wehrmacht*. Fortunately one of the men who had been concerned with snatching Marsden recognised him and he was moved back again to Sens Hospital from where he was sent home to England.

Nineteen-year-old Jack Marsden, although a prisoner of the Germans for a short while, never went to a prisoner-of-war camp – except one for captured Germans.

## THE HIGH PRICE OF FREEDOM

The near success of the Heydekrug 'A' compound tunnel had severely shaken the camp Germans. They would have been in serious trouble had all the 50 prisoners in the tunnel escaped. As it was there were courts-martial in the offing. Their efforts to count those in the camp and the subsequent searches had been a fiasco. The Germans were determined to come down hard on the perpetrators of their troubles and take every means to prevent further escapes. As far as 'Tally-Ho', the Escape Committee, was concerned the first half of 1944 had been marked by the brilliant success of the April home-runs of Flockhart and Gilbert, but the consequences were terrible.

Outside the camp the *Gestapo* had clamped down with its customary brutal efficiency. The king of escapers George Grimson had been caught and shot as had Townsend-Coles, Callender and Lewis. Little Munkert, the German democrat who had done so much liaison and smuggling work for the escape committee was also to face a firing squad. Sommers the Polish/German camp photographer who had experienced *Gestapo* methods, was under suspicion. Denied poison or pistol by the escape committee and unable to be certain of his ability to withstand torture, Sommers hung himself in his cell. Everyone from the German side of the wire who had been useful to the Kriegies was never seen again. With the savage clamp-down, the rumours of a move away from the advancing Russians and the prospect of an early end to the war, all large scale escape attempts were shelved.

## 'DRAUSSEN WEHT EIN KALTER WIND'

The Red Army was grinding ahead menacingly and nearing Heydekrug. The Germans would have to decide what to do with their prisoners in the east. Should they leave them behind, murder them or move them away from the fighting? The first option meant losing their bargaining powers; the second option, favoured by some of the hierarchy and *SS*, meant the certainty of fierce retribution which many felt was coming anyway; the third option retained the prisoners as hostages and might even make it easier for some of the Germans to hand over the prisoners and themselves to the Allies with dignity. The Kriegies weighed all their captors' options and decided that being left behind was unlikely, so had to face the possibility of the second or third options being chosen.

Fear of the Russians dominated the populations in the east of Germany and the occupied territories, and feeling against Allied airmen throughout Germany was growing. The people of Germany were at bay and felt that any action against their enemies was justified. There had been many stories among the RAF men of lynchings by angry mobs in bombed cities. Escaping was not a way out for Kriegies now, their best hope was planning, discipline and where possible, the internal organisation of self-defence and vigilance within the camps. 'Dixie' Deans, Vic Clarke – senior man of 'K' *Lager* Heydekrug – and most of the Kriegies, had long foreseen the perilous position in which they were likely to be placed during the closing stages of this vicious, bitter struggle. Clarke and Deans saw that if there was to be a move from eastern camps such as Heydekrug, a journey to western Germany was certain to run into some nightmarish hazards. A few words from the *Kommandant* confirmed the view when, in July just prior to announcing an evacuation of the camp, he said to them, 'There is a cold wind blowing outside'.

The American NCOs at Heydekrug had received a visit from the *SS* and *Gestapo* telling them of the shooting of the 50 escapers at Stalag Luft 3. It put a stop to their escape activities. During the second week of July 1944 the American prisoners were told that the camp was to be evacuated. The evacuation was to take place in several phases, 1,600 USAAF men and 900 RAF NCOs were taken by rail to the Baltic port of Memel. The main group of Americans left the camp in the late afternoon of Friday 14 July with their senior man, Frank Paules. This group boarded a vessel named the *Masuren*. The second group of mainly English NCOs and less than 100 Americans left the following day. The last group to leave was an almost all-British contingent from 'A' *Lager*. Apart from three would-be escapers hidden under the floor of the wash-house, 3,000 went by train from Heydekrug to Thorn in Poland.

The leading group of Americans and a few British from 'E' *Lager* marched the two miles to the railway station and were hustled into rail box-cars. The box-cars were each packed with more than 50 men. Most had fashioned some kind of haversack which was now filled with clothes and food. With another Canadian Red Cross parcel handed to them as they left the camp gate they were heavily loaded with all their worldly possessions. Because of the crowding in the cattle trucks they were forced to stand crushed together for the half-day ride to Memel.

The *Masuren* was a rusty collier captured from the Russians and still bearing the hammer and sickle emblem on the funnel. The Americans were the first of the Allied airmen to have their bags and packs taken from them and thrown in to the hold. They were then told to follow their goods down the single ladder into the unbearable heat and darkness below. Hyman Hatton felt that they were physically stuffed into the hold like sardines into a tin. Some men with the party were ill and one in particular was mentally unstable. On the first day out when they had been able to ascend the ladder to the deck to relieve themselves and get some air, that disturbed man, when he finally reached the deck, could stand it no longer and jumped overboard. The MO's frantic shouts of, 'He's *krank! Krank! Krank!*' were of no avail. The guards shot the deranged man as he floundered in the water.

There was a touch of panic among the battened down men. It was dark below the water line and the only opening was where the ladder went up to the hatch cover on deck. An RAF man among them claimed that he had sown mines in the area to which the ship was heading. There were hundreds of them around he said. They had all seen the mine-sweeping assemblies on the sides of the ship but occasionally they could hear something clang against the hull and scrape along the ship's side. Now they were all suffering from intense heat, fear and crippling cramp in their legs and bowels. At 6.00am on Monday 17 July, the *Masuren* docked at Swinemünde.

In Heydekrug's 'K' Lager those men who had passed the recent repatria-tion board were told to parade near the main gate with their belongings. John Dennis had reduced his load to a minimum. Walking was going to be hard enough for him without carrying any kind of load, but at the gate there was a two-horse wagon to take them to the station. There they were loaded on to a Red Cross train with carriages, not the usual box-cars. The train was frequently shunted into sidings while troops and tanks went speeding by to face the oncoming Russians, but after four days the train arrived at Annaberg Castle near Dresden. The castle, once the home of Queen Anne of Saxony, had been converted into a hospital especially for repatriates. Run by British orderlies it was spotlessly clean and restful after the chaos of Heydekrug, and food was plentiful. John Dennis went to bed that night with a full stomach.

Sergeant Joe Stule in 'K' Lager could hear the distant rumble of artillery. At first it was like a muttering in the air and could be felt rather than heard, but now the Red Army was nearer. Stule knew that American and some RAF prisoners had already been evacuated by train from East Prussia to a camp close to his home-town of Thorn. The 'Ivans' must surely be in Poland soon, he thought, a transfer there gave a hope of 'safe houses' and hiding places until the Red Army's arrival. Max Rech, a pilot from Posen and another man from 300 (Polish) Squadron had similar ideas but when the harsh order to be ready for an immediate move was made, the destination of the 'K' Lager men remained a Teu-tonic secret.

'Thank God it's July,' said a prisoner feelingly, 'at least we'll not be dragging through the snow.' There was general murmured agreement, the men knew the cruel bite of winter on the flat lands near the Baltic. But this was the summer of 1944, Allied troops had captured Caen and Cherbourg, Rome had fallen and the Russians were in Vilno, Lithuania, so very close to the camp. Perhaps this coming winter was to be their last in German hands.

'You can take only what you can carry,' the Germans had ordered and it needed careful thought. Just recently life had been comparatively easy at Heydekrug. Many of the RAF men had been prisoners for several years and had amassed a considerable amount of personal belongings; Red Cross food and cigarette parcels had been arriving regularly at Heydekrug, so by the standards of most prisoners-of-war they had been well supplied. Now that there was to be a move away from the Russian steamroller advance an agonising decision had to be made – what to abandon?

Giant bonfires raged all the day and through the night on 14 July as the Kriegies burned rations and cigarettes. They were loath to leave anything for the Germans. The guards did not intervene.

Vic Clarke was another of those men who, like James Deans, was thrust by extraordinary circumstances into a position of leadership, trust and danger, and who acquitted himself in such a way that thousands of prisoners-of-war were to remain indebted to him for the rest of their lives. Clarke had worked in the import/export business and his German was word perfect. Archie King said of Clarke: 'He never lost his temper or allowed the Germans to get away with anything and always carried himself with dignity; he was a wonderful chap, a first class fellow in every way.' Now Clarke's leadership and his contact with the Germans was about to be tested to the extreme.

By a judicious wager on the date of the landings in France and many sharp hands of poker, Sergeant Dougie Waters had accumulated more than 7,000 cigarettes – he was rich with the wartime currency and felt that he must find room in a kitbag for the cigarettes, some food, a blanket and necessary clothing. Throughout the camp men were manufacturing haversacks by attaching strips of cloth as webbing straps to any container that would leave their hands free. No-one knew how far he would have to march. Despite the July weather, farseeing Vic Clarke had advised every man to retain his winter clothing and greatcoat and finally, to carry drinking water. They were going to need it.

The second party, mainly British with a few Americans, marched out of Heydekrug camp in two groups on the warm July afternoon of Saturday the 15th. As they left, Germans, first the *Luftwaffe* guards and then the *Wehrmacht* guards from a nearby camp, poured into the compounds. Like scavengers they ransacked the rooms for anything the prisoners had left. Stan Hurrell watched in disgust as Germans swarmed in but his temper was soothed by seeing guards leave clutching half-filled Klim powdered milk tins. They were not to know that the powdered milk had been well laced with quicklime especially for them.

Long, straggling columns marched dustily out of the main gate, each sweating prisoner carrying every item he possessed plus provisions for the unpredictable journey. Wary, armed *Luftwaffe* guards walked along each side of the column as it wound down the road towards the village. They passed a funeral with elderly, much bemedalled mourners in top hats and frock-coats. Archie King ruefully said later that had he known what lay ahead he might have jumped into the coffin with the corpse.

Funerals and marriages, the most common of wartime ceremonies, go on as usual, even with the enemy hammering at the gates. As the head of the column turned into the approach to Heydekrug Station a wedding party emerged from a nearby church, the 'groom a burly *Luftwaffe* corporal. But it was the expression of sad and bewildered dismay on the face of the slip-of-a-girl bride that haunted Sergeant 'Tommy' Tomkins. The girl watched the westward-trudging old people and children showing all the evidence of civilian panic evacuation, their valuables piled high on handcarts and prams or strung from bicycles. This and the prisoners on the move could only mean to her that the area was to be abandoned to the Russians with all the unimaginable, horrific consequences.

The railway sidings held the usual forbidding row of dark and dirty box-cars bearing the stencilled markings of '*40 Hommes ou 8 Chevaux*'. The prisoners had come to know these filthy wagons as their normal means of transport other than their feet, and it was here that the harsh *Abwehr* control of the transportation of prisoners, ordered after the escape from Sagan, became obvious. One end of the interior of each truck was quickly crammed with the men and their kit, hemmed in behind a roof-to-floor partition fashioned from birch branches nailed together and laced with barbed wire. A few guards occupied the rest of the space. The clanking and desperately uncomfortable journey was mercifully short and the train was soon passing through the main station of the port of Memel. Here lines of apprehensive and unhappy looking *Todt Organisation* labour corps troops and *Volkssturm* home guards stood on the platform, armed with spades. With nightfall the long train screeched and jangled to a halt on a railway line running parallel to Memel dockside. Shouting guards ordered the prisoners out and then hustled the long column of laden men along the shadowy quay, past the huge, dark bulk of a whaling factory ship to a smaller vessel, visible only in the odd pools of light from overhead gantries.

To Desmond Dunphy the sombre scene had an atmosphere of eerie menace to which the prisoners, accustomed though they were to living on the knife-edge of German irrational behaviour and intolerance, felt exposed and vulnerable. They were outside the strangely protective barbed wire and whatever was going to happen, Dunphy thought, was certain to be dangerous and unpleasant. The ascent of a ship's gangplank was a wearisome shuffle despite the harrying by the guards' shouted orders and threatening gestures. The reason for the slow progress became clear when arriving on the deck, each prisoner was ordered to a small hatch, forced to leave most of his possessions piled on the deck and then compelled to make a slow descent down a long vertical steel ladder into a dimly lit hold. There were protests and some defiance which was quickly overcome by the threat of the use of fire hoses, and in one case of steam hoses, being turned on those who resisted, while machine guns mounted in the ship's superstructure were loudly cocked.

The ship was a collier with two holds, one hold, it was said, already contained prisoners and the RAF men were directed into the after hold which slowly filled so that eventually there were some 900 men crammed below the water line with no room to sit and little on which to stand. Bill Baird compared them to packed herrings in a barrel; to Ron Akerman the atmosphere was grim and frightening. Men were clinging halfway up the inner slope of the hull and continually sliding down. The light was so dim that no more than 30 or so rows of men could be seen, all with their knees tucked up under their chins. Dunphy thought the scene must have resembled Dante's vision of Purgatory.

The hold was cold at first with only the damp steel shell of the hull between the crowded prisoners and the sea, but as more men came down the ladder, the crowding, lack of air and the accumulated body heat became acutely distressing. 'Tommy' Tomkins, one of the last on board, stared in disbelief when ordered down the ladder. It seemed impossible that even one more body could possibly squeeze into the hold but a roaring, raving German Major waving a sub machine-gun, forced him to descend the ladder. Doug Fry found there was no room on the bottom of the hold and perched himself on a foot-wide girder where he stayed throughout the voyage. Dougie Waters tied a belt around his waist and an iron stanchion and spent his voyage half sitting and half standing, only releasing himself to use the communal bucket.

When the last man was in the hold and the hatch was battened down there was no possible way out and the claustrophobic atmosphere became unbearable. Only the glimmer from a weak, hanging lightbulb illumined the middle of the compressed crowd in the black hole. It was not until the early hours of Sunday 16 July that the *Insterburg* weighed anchor but there was no relief for those packed beneath the deck. Vic Clarke, the prisoners' leader and spokesman, cooled tempers and calmed the atmosphere by persuading the guards to open the hatch and allow a few men up to the deck in rotation to relieve themselves over the ship's side and greedily gasp for fresh air. A bucket lowered on a rope was the only other means of sanitation provided by the Germans. The same bucket was believed by the prisoners to be used during daylight to occasionally lower drinking water.

After protest the genuinely sick and a few stretcher cases were allowed to stay on deck and be spared the ordeal below. Ron Akerman felt deeply sympathetic when he saw that some of the young, newly captured American prisoners among them were crying. They were clearly more emotional and overwhelmed by the bestial treatment. He reckoned that the RAF men who had been prisoners for three or more years were hardened by experience to some Germans' lack of humanity and scruples.

It was believed the *Insterburg* had also been captured from the Russians, some of the crew being retained to run the ship. These men were sympathetic to the prisoners but there was little they could do other than to maintain the water supply. Some of the guards, *Luftwaffe* men and others more easily 'trained' according to Archie King, were disgusted but powerless.

Morale sank among those below as the temperature rose with the sun and the hot steel decking turned the dark, packed hold into a humid oven. Archie King's spirits were briefly lifted by a courageous American who climbed up the sloping side of the hold shouting, 'Don't let the bastards get us down'. Then, taking full advantage of the hold's natural acoustics, the American began to sing. In a rich baritone voice *My Wild Irish Rose* echoed through the gloom. Archie's spirits sank again. His young wife and two babies were at home in Dublin – he wondered if he would ever see them again. The lump in his throat and the tears in his eyes stayed with him for the rest of the day.

Vic Clarke had been busy. While encouraging the men who made the long climb to the deck for their brief visit to the upper world, he had discovered the destination of the *Insterburg* and was also able to pass on snippets of news gleaned from the Germans. Few of the guards realised that Clarke was fluent in German and understood their conversations. In his dealings with the Germans Clarke was firm, calm, dignified and unrelenting in his struggle on the prisoners' behalf. The men had absolute confidence in him.

There had been a belief among some prisoners that the Germans meant to scuttle the ship as the easiest way to rid themselves of their troublesome charges, but Bill Baird knew that Vic Clarke had convinced the captain that the British Secret Service knew him and every one of his German crew by name. If anything happened to any of the prisoners, Clarke warned, the captain and his crew would hang. It was a superb bluff in a desperate situation.

Down in the hold the men, hearing the water rushing past the sides of the ship, took stock of the situation. Supposing the ship was torpedoed or struck a mine? Jack Paul reasoned that the 10 or so prisoners on deck at the time might have a slim possibility of survival, but those in the holds would have no chance at all. There were rumours that the ship was passing through a minefield. The men held their breath, their hearts racing as metallic scratching sounds ran along the length of the hull.

Des Dunphy, a German speaker, persuaded the guards to allow a few more of the prisoners on deck during the night when conditions below were rapidly deteriorating. Jack Paul, in his capacity as a barrack room leader, took his turn in regulating the daytime ladder climbers and could see that the long wait and slow progress up and down the ladder meant that some of the men were unable to restrain themselves. Ken Goodchild was very aware that a corner of the hold had been set aside for use as an unofficial latrine. As the heat increased so did the smell. The Baltic was comparatively calm so there were few cases of seasickness but the continuous vibration of the central propeller shaft tunnel added to the burden of misery.

During the second day out, as Arthur Minnitt was finishing his long climb up the ladder he was startled by the sight of shouting guards in lifejackets, rushing about the deck in apparent confusion. Fascinated, he watched a submarine surfacing nearby. There was panic among the ship's crew until they were sure that it was a U-boat, Minnitt was also relieved that this time it was 'one of theirs'.

On the second night out from Memel the guards were persuaded to allow a few more men to take a turn in the fresh air on deck and there was a continuous stream up and down the ladder. Dunphy felt that there was some strange communication between the guards and the prisoners. Certainly the Germans were edgy, they knew that the war was lost but far from finished. As Dunphy was sitting on a deck life-raft with a row of prisoners someone unseen thrust a rifle onto his lap. It was a nerve-wracking situation, was there 'one up the spout', was it a trap, what was happening?

Dunphy held the rifle, looked around and saw a German peering at him from behind a large ventilator as if waiting for him to move. Did the Germans want them to attempt to take over the ship or was it just a move with an empty rifle so that the prisoners could be slaughtered with what the Germans would call a 'just' excuse? Dunphy looked at the open hatch, at the many hand grenades possessed by the guards, at the pairs of men patrolling with machine pistols and quickly decided that any such move would be to invite annihilation. He told the men near him about the rifle, placed it in the scuppers while they all rose and walked away.

That night those on deck saw light from a city reflected in the northern sky and concluded that it must have been from Sweden. They were so near civilisation yet, as far as the prisoners were concerned it could have been a thousand miles away.

When the *Insterburg* docked at Swinemünde on 18 July the prisoners were ordered up from the hold. It was as slow as the embarkation. Few had eaten or drunk since they descended into the hold at Memel. They emerged slowly, one by one, dirty, exhausted and blinking at the dazzling brightness of the midday sun. They had a fleeting glimpse of warships at the quays before being shackled in pairs, made to remove their boots and herded once more to a train of box-cars for an unknown destination. Bill Baird heard that, because they were *Terrorfliegers*, the *SS* would be waiting to march the prisoners, naked and handcuffed, through the streets of Stettin. It seemed their ill-treatment, misery, and degradation was not even nearing the end.

When the guards threw back the central truck doors it was as if the cover of a blast furnace had been raised. Goaded by bayonet points to help each other up into the trucks, the Kriegies were now trapped inside another dark, cramped and stifling prison. The fierce sunshine had transformed the truck interiors into torrid ovens. The prisoners' only moment for breathing freely had been during the rushed, bayonet jabbing, transfer from the hold to the box-cars. Now they were in hell again, without water to drink or to wash their soiled bodies, and with no way of helping the majority who were suffering from severe dysentery. They had been manacled in pairs with three feet of chain between them and the heat, the all-pervading smell of ordure, urine and sweat, the raging thirst and fear of what was to come, prolonged the nightmare.

Vic Clarke, alert as ever to avoid helping the enemy, had asked Jack Paul and some other former barrack room leaders to hang back during the disembarkation to ensure the destruction of any goods or equipment abandoned by the prisoners. They were consequently some of the last to leave the hold, by which time the guards had run out of patience, handcuffs and shackles and were anxious to get the last load of prisoners safely shut away in the trucks, particularly as a distant air-raid warning siren had just started to wail.

Archie King thought he heard the whoosh of falling bombs. So did an elderly, dignified and immaculate *Luftwaffe* officer in a white summer uniform who provided some light relief to the grim situation by throwing himself full-length into the combined sludge of oil and coal-dust which smothered the quay side. In King's opinion, the resultant cheer from the watching Kriegies was of Cup Tie proportions.

The siren's sound signalled the approach of Flying Fortresses. Jack Paul noted the anxious looks of the guards as they rammed on their steel helmets. A smoke screen was formed by dripping oil on gas heated sheet steel plates. Enormous clouds of boiling smoke rapidly covered everyone and everything, including the *Lützow* (the renamed Deutschland) berthed nearby. In their haste to get away from an obvious target, the panicking guards bundled the remaining men into the box-cars and locked the doors. To add to the misery of the Kriegies the anti-aircraft guns of the battlecruiser roared deafeningly and rocked the train.

Despite the danger, the Kriegies maintained the pretence of being happy about witnessing an air-raid on the Third Reich until, as 'Tommy' Tomkins said, a low-flying aircraft was heard and bombs were falling near. The combined noise of the guns from the battlecruiser and nearby flak guns was thunderous and stunning. The Kriegies threw themselves to the floor as the trucks shook and swayed as if in an earthquake. Tomkins watched the roof of his wagon split as massive vibrations rocked the train. No man moved until the bombers had passed. To their relief an attack on Swinemünde had not developed and they reckoned that a straggler aircraft in trouble had jettisoned his bomb-load.

The guards, who had disappeared during the attack, returned to the wagons. Four or five guards at one end manning a machine gun on a tripod pointed at the Kriegies and the Kriegies, some 24 of them, behind a fence of birch branches and barbed wire at the other. These guards were older, *Luftwaffe* men. Archie King thought that despite the rigours of the journey they were still 'tameable'. King was interested to see that Paddy Leach, a small, tough, wiry Ulsterman, had unlocked his manacles within an hour, using a piece of wire with the manipulative skill of a lock-smith.

With a succession of jolts and resounding clangs the train jerked away from the dock area and some air filtered through the stifling boxes. During the last stage of the journey the train shuddered to a halt and the guards climbed out. To the surprise and alarm of the Kriegies the guards were replaced by *Kriegsmarine* youths dressed in light summer uniforms. It was clear that these new guards were conditioned by their training with loyalty to Hitler and the *Nazi* regime. Hate sparked in their eyes and their aggressive gestures with unsheathed bayonets was a show of open hostility towards the prisoners. That night the journey ended but the trucks stayed locked and barred on the outside. The Kriegies spent another sweltering, odorous night in the closed wagons, gasping for air and water.

During the night some Kriegies in the wagons heard parties of the young *Nazi*s outside, laughing and noisily sharpening bayonets on grinding wheels. It seemed over-dramatic but it was ominous and frightening. Bill Baird had determined that the Kriegies were on a propaganda journey to annihilation.

It was afternoon before the Kriegies were shouted out of the sweltering box-cars and made to line up beside the track. They were then marched out beyond the station in columns seven or eight deep and stood, most still manacled in pairs, carrying what possessions they had retained and wondering what the next torture was to be. Spread along the road ahead in the distance were two lines of the *Kriegsmarine* youths through which the prisoners were to pass. Behind and between the youths were *Luftwaffe* men with machine guns levelled at the prisoners. It looked as though this was going to be some brutal version of running the gauntlet. The helpless Kriegies thought the sentence of death was about to be carried out.

Vic Clarke rode the length of the lines of 900 men in a bullock cart. Accompanying him were the ever-elegant Army medical officer and Padre 'Jacko' Jackson. All were in sombre mood.

'I am afraid we are in for trouble,' Clarke warned. 'I ask you now to restrain your impulse to run as much as possible; don't give them,' he said, nodding towards the machine gun troops, 'any excuse to open up.'

The Kriegies were lined up into five columns of 150 to 200 men. Bill Baird in the second group saw that they were being filmed. At the head of the first column was an extremely tall German officer who was to lead it from the front. Baird thought him the biggest man he had ever seen, close to seven feet tall.

No-one was allowed to rest or take the pack from his shoulders. Sweat poured from every man soaking his clothing. Backs and shoulders ached as though on fire, there was no relief. 'Tommy' Tomkins was surprised by the number of guards when he considered Germany's desperate need of men. One guard for every two prisoners, all heavily armed, was unusual. Ginger-haired German Major Pickhardt arrived to take over command. His orders to the guards, staccato and *guttural*, were brief and to the point. There would be no rest for the *Terrorfliegers*, commands to them were not to be given by word, only by weapons. The bayonet and gun were to speak for the guards. Kriegies who came near Pickhardt were repelled by the heavy perfume in which he seemed to have bathed. He was quickly summed up as a sexually perverted sadist.

As the first column moved off they were ordered to keep up with the tall German at the head but he had such a long stride that the prisoners had to run to stay near him. A gap was allowed to develop between the first and second columns and then the second column was told to catch up with the first. Soft, deep sand, the stifling heat, the worsening thirst and the fear of what was going to happen made the dragging slog a terrifying agony.

The track wound slightly uphill through a large pine wood. Arthur Minnitt, near the rear of the column saw the German officer shouting at his men who in turn shouted at the Kriegies to increase tempo. Des Dunphy saw Major Pickhardt, his face purple with rage, waving a pistol, screaming invective and urging the guards to keep the Kriegies running as he rode up and down the column on the running board of a Mercedes. After haranguing the guards he fired his pistol into the air. The shot was a starting signal for the *Kriegsmarine* youths to begin lashing out at the Kriegies with their rifle butts and stabbing them with their bayonets. With each blow or stab they shouted, 'That's for Cologne – that's for Hamburg, – that's for Berlin,' listing the bombed cities. Clarke's warning and advice had to be ignored. It was then that Minnitt realised that the head of the column had started running. This created a kind of concertina effect. The rear men had to run fast, catch up and then had to virtually stop as the ranks closed. The Germans were shouting at them throughout, using their rifle butts and bayonets to drive the prisoners onward.

Breathless and soaked with sweat, Ron Akerman was startled to see an older, English-speaking *Feldwebel* running alongside him.

'For God's sake stay by me,' the *Feldwebel* gasped, 'I was a prisoner in the last war and I don't agree with this. I'm not going to have it – you stay by me and I'll see you all right but throw away your stuff, you have got to go in with nothing.' Akerman tossed away his last remaining bag of cigarettes.

The entire column of Kriegies was now running. The front of the line moved faster, abandoning their possessions as they ran. Those coming behind fell over the bags in their mad scramble. Dust from the dry track rose in clouds. Archie King whose wounded legs made him one of the first to fall, saw only chaos all around. Men were collapsing in crumpled heaps as the rifle butts and bayonets hammered and stabbed. King tried to rise but an Alsatian dog was biting fiercely at his left ankle. As he fell again two *Kriegsmarine* youths rained blows on his back and head. Through a mist of pain King felt this was the end for them all.

Archie King could not understand why a *Luftwaffe* officer intervened, ordering the *Kriegsmarine* youths to leave him, telling King to sit against a tree and putting one of his own men on guard. The British Army medical officer ran along and took charge. Helping the shaken King to his feet he walked him along the road while encouraging other Kriegies around to go ahead as quickly as they could.

The guards, who had been running with the Kriegies moved in on an order and began to cut the packs from the Kriegies' backs with their sharpened bayonets. Blood was drawn turning the accompanying Alsatians ferociously savage. As one of the berserk dogs was shot the Kriegies thought the bullet had been for one of them. Bill Baird described the panic as unbelievable, no-one knew where they were heading but believed it was for certain death.

The run became a grotesque two-and-a-half kilometre obstacle race, sweating and bloody men crying out in pain, leaping over bodies and bags, falling and picking themselves up and stumbling on only to fall again and become another obstacle for those following. Any prisoner still holding a bag became a special target for the guards. Razor sharp bayonets flashed to the carrying straps, cutting indiscriminately the man and the webbing. Here and there a man would stop to help another who had collapsed, then half carrying, half dragging his comrade he staggered on, dodging blows and bayonet thrusts. Men who had been stabbed and clubbed fell, dragging their shackled partners to a stumbling halt. The sight of men lying on the ground with their chained friends standing over them seemed to provoke some of the more vicious guards into frenzied attacks.

Canadian J. Sheridan, a 'great bear' of a man, had a rifle butt smashed on the back of his head. The butt snapped off leaving the brutal and surprised German with just the broken barrel in his hand. With blood flooding down his neck and staining the collar and back of his coat Sheridan shook his head and staggered on.

The heat, the dust hidden men, the cries of the injured, the yells of the guards and the snarling, barking dogs was a vision of a harrowing Hell.

Bill Baird had somehow slipped from his shackles and moved up near the leaders. Turning a bend the column stopped. One hundred and fifty yards away was the barbed wire and *Posten* boxes of a prisoner-of-war camp, but between the Kriegies and the gate was another tunnel of guards wielding rifle butts. A further gauntlet run awaited them.

The men, wounded and shaken as they were, struggled to their feet and, helping one another, staggered on through the rain of blows, the medical officer encouraging them to move as fast as possible. Stopping himself just long enough to help a Pole who seemed to be having a heart attack, Archie King and the medical officer half carried and half dragged him to the outer fence of the camp and collapsed.

As the Kriegies stood gasping and apprehensive outside the camp a horse-drawn wagon passed into the main gates loaded with injured prisoners from the road, then came the final gauntlet stagger into the camp through the narrow lines of clubbing and stabbing guards. The shocked men stumbled into the *Vorlager* and collapsed on the ground. Ahead were tents where USAAF aircrews, who had arrived earlier, lay quiet and subdued. The Germans told the prisoners that they were entering a *Gestapo* camp of which the Red Cross had no knowledge and consequently any rules of the Geneva Convention would not apply. No-one would be allowed to speak. Prisoners here would have no rights whatsoever. The outlook was grim.

The pitiable line of exhausted and wounded men lay stretched out on the grass. A few were almost hysterical, all were at least badly bruised, cut, utterly drained and desperately dry. The only water was the drainings in a few tins or bottles that had survived the run. The guards were jubilant and triumphant at their easy victory, displaying the cigarettes they had looted from dropped packets. Tomkins heard the guards carefully point out that the Americans, who had 'run the gauntlet' previously, had done the run in one minute less.

Des Dunphy, panting on the ground, heard the guard who had broken his rifle on Sheridan's head talking to a *Feldwebel*. Snapping to attention the guard lifted up the two parts of his rifle held together only by the sling, and replied to the *Feldwebel's* question: '*Aber wir haben viel von solchem Holz in Deutschland!*'

To a German doctor the 'run' was a huge joke. Refusing first-aid to anyone, he walked among the wounded, smiling and chuckling, '*gut, gut*'.

Vic Clarke went among the prisoners telling those who had head wounds, cut and stab wounds or dog bites to fall out and move to the end of the line. Ron Akerman thought the call to 'Fall out the wounded' a grim irony. Almost every man was injured in some way and blood covered everything. Of his group 186 were bleeding from serious cuts and slashes. It is a number burnt into Akerman's memory.

Civilian spectators of the torment, mainly local women and young girls, had arrived to watch the sport. The casualties were told to line up in front of them and remove their trousers. *Luftwaffe* orderlies went down the line of injured Kriegies who were ordered to bend over. A blunt-needled hypodermic was plunged to the hilt into their buttocks, it was said, to prevent tetanus. The female spectators hooted with laughter at the men's naked misery. Archie King straightened up and looked at the women in pity. Perhaps, he thought, the display of virile if bloody, British masculinity stimulated the emotional starvation of the Prussian females.

Doug Fry was in the last party to move up the road from the Keifheide railway siding towards the camp. He was astounded by the sight of kit and Kriegie belongings strewn along the whole length of the road. The skulking machine gun-armed guards could be seen in the woods each side. The situation was still very dangerous, yet the last column was not to be subjected to the same treatment. Although relieved, Doug Fry could never understand why. Had the Germans run out of manacles? They obviously preferred to mistreat prisoners who were securely pinioned.

Many of the Kriegies had spent that night lying on the ground. Then the violent searches began. Corporal Jimmy Jordan, a little Lancastrian medical orderly taken at Dunkirk, was standing next to Archie King when they reached the search table. They were faced by a short, fat, middle-aged *Gestapo* thug. The Kriegies were already stripped down to their underpants and carrying their clothing but Jimmy had a gold crucifix on a chain around his neck. The *Gestapo* man ripped it off and threw it to the ground. Feeling around the waistband of Jordan's underpants the *Gestapo* man found a pound note that had been sewn in and which Jordan had carried with him since 1940. In a paroxysm of rage, the thug whipped back his fist and hit the defenceless and naked Jordan a full punch to the jaw which floored him. To fight back was certain death.

But the *Gestapo* brute had not finished with Corporal Jordan. In a wallet he found a photograph of Jordan's mother and sister. By now he was frothing at the mouth with rage. Taking the photograph he tore it into shreds and then, ripping open his trouser fly he rubbed the shredded picture around his genitals. King watched in disbelieving horror at this exhibition of Hitlerian *Kultur*. Bill Baird watched similar exhibitions when photographs precious to the Kriegies were torn up by the searchers who then urinated upon the fragments.

Naked and desperately shaken, Jordan walked away helped by King. Once inside the compound King gave Jordan a vest to keep off the summer sun and organised a whip-round from other Kriegies for clothes.

Canadian Mo Vineberg was Jewish. The German searching Vineberg's wallet found a family photograph. Here was a fine chance for the searcher to demonstrate his racial superiority and contempt for the Jews. Taking the photograph he screwed it up and rubbed it between his buttocks as if using it as toilet paper while simultaneously snarling, 'Scheisse'. Jack Paul watched helplessly, thanking God that such specimens of humanity had not overrun his homeland.

As the searches ended the RAF men were pushed at bayonet point into the *Vorlager* of Stalag Luft 4 Gross Tychow. There they were ordered to lie prone on the dusty earth and forbidden to talk. But the German 'silence and no communication' order was almost impossible to maintain as the flaps of the tents into which the Americans were crammed had been rolled up to ease the torture of the intense heat. Also Americans from a completed compound were helping to distribute water from their meagre ration. There was no water tap in the *Vorlager*, all drinking water had to be brought in from another compound in a small bowser-like tank. Thirst had plagued the men since they left Heydekrug. The Americans bringing round water advised the Kriegies to lie still and not to provoke the patrolling armed guards.

Before the British arrived the Germans had made a start on searching the Americans. The search had been stopped and the Americans pushed to one side. Orders were given that the British should pass through and be admitted to the compound first. It was patently done in an effort to create friction between the Allies but the motive was seen and its purpose frustrated. Instead a splendid spirit of friendship, cooperation and alliance blossomed between the men who had similarly suffered. The scarce food and essentials were frequently shared with typical American generosity. Their 'run' said the Americans, had not been so brutal as that of the RAF men, they had been through one and seen the results of the other.

Despite threats not to recognise him as the prisoners' leader, Vic Clarke persuaded the Germans to provide extra tents for the last arrivals and the British MO insisted on transferring the worst cases to a temporary sick-bay in an internal compound. A team of orderlies worked until after dark, patching up the wounded as best they could.

On the next day conditions improved slightly and efforts were made to bring order from the chaos. Hut and tent leaders were appointed and the Camp Leaders pestered the Germans until a minimum of food was supplied. Mint tea was brought into the *Vorlager* with a small amount of Red Cross food but water was still short. Baking under the blazing sun Tomkins and Bob Hart watched with fascination as more fortunate prisoners in the compound collected buckets of water. It looked beautiful, they watched and swore that at the first opportunity they would connect themselves to the pump and drink and drink.

The overflow of the Kriegies was eventually housed in what they described as 'dog kennels'. Windowless and little larger than a small garden shed the only furnishing, if one was lucky, was the usual straw palliasse. The Kriegies were to crawl into and live in them for many weeks until proper huts were completed. The kennel was entered through an aperture similar to that used by a dog. Once inside there was only room for some 10 men to lie down squeezed together. Jack Paul described the eventual move into the 'normal' grim barrack blocks as relative bliss.

The Kriegies had left Heydekrug in parties of approaching 1,000. The first parties were those that travelled by train and then by boat across the Baltic. The rest, the bulk of the prisoners, were transported to Thorn by rail freight trucks. Stalag Luft 6 was no more. At first the destination of both parties was a mystery despite their constant questioning of the guards.

Rest was impossible on the two-day train journey. It was an agony of heat and crushing conditions with little chance for relief, and no room to sit or lie. Soon too there was the now familiar stench of urine and ordure, the usual stomach ailments taking their toll. It was only by persuading the three guards in each truck who occupied two-thirds of the space, that eventually the sliding central doors were opened during daylight to allow fresh air into the trucks.

The train passed through Poland and slowed on a section of the line near a labour camp. Kriegies could see what conditions in such a place were like. Fifty feet away from the railway line, below the embankment, skeleton-like figures toiled in the open under the eyes of a huge jackbooted guard. One inmate recklessly lifted his head as the prisoners in the wagons yelled their encouragement to a fellow prisoner and vilified the guard. The Kriegies immediately regretted their action; the guard swung round to see the callers and with one movement he swung back bringing round a whip across the face and body of the man who had dared to look up. The whipped man collapsed. The Kriegies were momentarily shaken and hushed but then could not help erupting into an outcry of boos and shouts from their comparative safety inside the horse-boxes.

As the guard threateningly shook his whip at them the Kriegies called in German that he would be hanged after the war and cries of 'You square-headed bastard!' and 'Deutschland Kaputt!' echoed across the Polish plain as the train rolled again. It was a foolish risk for all but it must have been strange for the sadistic bully to hear such vociferous sentiments when he was used to a beaten and cowed populace who dared not answer back.

At Posen station the train halted opposite a platform where people were waiting for a passenger train. There were men and women dressed comparatively smartly and, above all, there were some young girls. Many of the Kriegies had not seen a woman for up to four years. The effect was startling. As the train was in a station with the sliding doors open, the guards in the trucks were on the alert. The Kriegies were staring. Then a few cautious calls and wolf-whistles sounded, mainly from the men at the rear of the crush against the barbed wire divider. A pretty girl smiled, she had probably recognised a call from one of the Polish Kriegies. When the train started off again the men could not settle, she had stimulated further the overwhelming desire of the young men to be free but the guards were trigger-happy and sensitive to the mood swings of their charges.

The train clanged noisily into a siding near Thorn from where the Kriegies were marched to a nearby prisoner-of-war camp for British Army men. The RAF men were astonished at the vast area of the camp. The perimeter was miles round and there were even parts where the barbed wire was out of sight. Conditions at Thorn were as poor as ever. The primitive plumbing was constructed of wood, the only metal the nails that held the whole thing together. A wooden pump raised water from a well and filled a wooden cistern. Through a series of wooden ducts the water flowed by gravity to two troughs into which half-inch holes had been drilled. The Kriegies washed as well as they could under the trickles flowing from these holes and began to smell sweeter.

### 'RAUS! RAUS! SCHNELL!'

When Flying Officer Ken Chapman landed on French soil in the early hours of 8 June and was quickly followed by his skipper, Squadron Leader Phil Lamason, they were lucky in finding several French families who were in contact with the Resistance. Chapman and Lamason hoped it would not be long before they were returned to Blighty. But after being passed down an escape line they were betrayed by their last two French contacts. Driven into a guarded barracks in Paris they were suddenly handcuffed and roughly searched. The airmen were in the hands of the *Gestapo.*

Chapman and Lamason were shaken; disappointment and apprehension left them exhausted and in deep despair. Handcuffed together they were put into a cell crowded with terrified French men and women and two American airmen. A suspicion of what was in store came when a young Jewess who had been tortured was left in the cell with a water-distended stomach. Crying in pain, she banged in vain on the cell door for someone to allow her out to go to a lavatory. To her distress and that of the others who could do nothing to help her, she was forced to relieve herself in a corner of the cell. The woman's handcuffed brother was later thrown into the cell. He had been beaten so badly that he could not sit, his back a crimson mass of weals.

At 5.00pm the prisoners were taken down to a prison van, the handcuffs removed and each man placed in one of the tiny, dark cells on either side of the van. The women travelled on the floor of the middle corridor. After 20 minutes the van drove into a small courtyard where the prisoners were counted. Their ties, belts and shoelaces were taken from them and each person was thrust alone into a bare cell with a high, small barred window. Chapman was in a turmoil of despair as he looked at the bare walls. His wretchedness brought pictures of his wife Muriel to his tormented mind. She was expecting their first baby. Would he ever see her again, would he ever see the baby? There seemed little hope. Eventually Ken Chapman reached the limit of endurance and despite the horror and misery of Fresnes and the constant attention of a multitude of viciously biting fleas, he fell into an exhausted sleep on the filthy mattress.

As the cell door was opened the clanging rattle wrenched Chapman awake to the claustrophobic stone walls. A guard brought him a bowl of odious *ersatz* coffee and then he was escorted down to the basement of the prison. Deep in the lower bowels, seemingly cut off from all contact with the living world outside, the prisoners were assembled and then in threes squeezed into tiny three-foot square, wire-roofed box-cells. Chapman heard that the Germans had called all those they had sent to the lower cells 'saboteurs'. They were positive they were all to be executed. Already, the firing squad had been heard at their murderous work. Chapman wondered how he would behave if he had to face them and prayed for strength.

The prisoners were alarmed when they were taken up to the third floor. Pushed into Cell 311, Chapman was pleased though to find himself with an American whom he knew and a Frenchman, Jean, who had been there for two months. The typical cell was furnished with one bed, a small table, a few utensils and a lavatory unit. The window was permanently closed.

The days were long. To pass the time between the two *ersatz* coffees, the 10-minute exercise period in the small walled yard and the bowl of soup, they played patience with a handmade set of cards or Chapman read the only book they possessed, a New Testament in French. Some of the prisoners in other cells had managed to open their windows and news was being shouted from window to window. The optimistic French exaggerated the advances of the Allies. When he heard English voices singing, Chapman realised that there were Britons in the prison including Dick and Jack, two friends he had met on his journey to Paris. Communication was established with them by shouting up the lavatory drain pipe.

Having worn the same clothes for weeks on end, the prisoners were continually attacked by an army of fleas which made the nights particularly hard to bear, and their bodies were covered with furiously itching bites. Searching their clothes and destroying as many fleas as they could find made little difference. Once a week Chapman and his companions shaved with a razor blade blunted from continual use.

On 12 August they were moved to an even filthier cell and the Frenchman taken away. That night three more Frenchmen and an Englishman from Jersey were roughly pushed into the cell. Between them they succeeded in opening the window sufficiently to enable them to join in the shouted conversations that echoed around the prison. Resourceful Americans in the cell next door passed cigarettes to them using the pole from the middle of a blackout blind.

Just when it seemed that only death would make any change to the hell of the awful routine, the whole of the prison population, numbering about 2,000 captives including RAF and American airmen, Allied soldiers and men and women of the Resistance, were assembled on the ground floor, hustled into buses and driven through Paris to the Gare de l'Est. There they were suffocatingly packed, 80 to 90 people to a box-car on what was to be the last train out of Paris. Allied troops were nearing the city and the Germans did not want to lose any of their captives.

Sergeant Ian Robb, one of the airmen imprisoned in Fresnes, described the following six days as harrowing. Eighty or more squeezed into a sealed box-car left no room to sit, no means of relieving oneself, no view of the outside world, little food and water and always the homogenous mass unable to move apart. The thick, foul air made breathing difficult and sleep impossible, only a kind of stupor was induced by total exhaustion.

The coming of daylight brought a hope of relief but the train entered a tunnel and stayed in the oppressive blackness for two hours, shunting back at last because of a blockage caused by an Allied air attack. The prisoners were ordered out of the trucks and made to walk five miles to the far end of the tunnel. The freedom to breathe was welcome. Villagers gave them potatoes and bread as the staggering column passed and the French Red Cross handed them welcome milk for their parched throats. For once the guards did not interfere.

Then it was back into the foetid trucks. Near Nancy the train stopped for the prisoners to relieve themselves outside and for their sanitary buckets to be emptied. Chapman was disgusted by the guards and town civilians watching the French women prisoners, one of them heavily pregnant, being forced to use the railway embankment for what should have been their most private functions.

During the second night of the train journey a 17-year-old French youth put his hand on the barbed wire across the tiny window. It was excuse enough for a guard to shoot him through the hand. Immediately the boy was taken out of the truck and shot again. Dick Rowe and Ken Chapman were called out of the truck. They scrambled down, believing their moment to face a row of rifles had come but Chapman was ordered back. Rowe and a Belgian were put to work burying the boy's body.

Six Frenchmen and an American succeeded in tearing up a board and escaping. The guards were furious and ordered the remaining prisoners in the truck to remove all their clothes which were taken away for 36 hours. Little could be done for a British prisoner who had a violent epileptic fit. He was refused medical aid. The rest of the prisoners, naked and terror stricken, were squeezed into the tiny space of part of the truck.

The tormenting journey ended outside the city of Weimar deep in the Thuringian Forest. The haggard men and women almost fell from the train as it stopped. Within moments they were being kicked, beaten and driven by *SS* men towards the huge outer iron gate of a camp in a vast forest clearing. Over the gate was the inscription in German, 'Every Man the Same'. Behind the gate was a square building with a tower. The prisoners' first and abiding feeling was of horror, just to look at the place was a terrifying nightmare like an unearthed cemetery.

Low hutments were enclosed within a high electrified fence with tall watchtowers at regular intervals. Patrolling inside and outside the wire were uniformed *SS* men looking as vicious as the dogs they led. Even more horrifying was the appearance of the inmates. There were shuffling thousands, all looking alike with shaven heads, emaciated bodies and tattered, striped pyjama-like clothes. Over the whole camp hung the sickly stench issuing from the continuously smoking chimney of the crematorium. This was *Konzentrationslager* Buchenwald.

Even after the terrors of Fresnes and the agonies of the packed truck journey the realisation that they were to become one of these skeleton-like half-alive figures filled the prisoners with cold dread. Shaven heads with sunken eyes stared in mute curiosity as they passed the wooden huts. After a three-hour wait the men had to go through the de-lousing process. They were taken out in groups, the Frenchmen first. Then the RAF and US airmen were ushered into a room where their clothes were taken from them. Russian, French and Polish prisoners working there, busily shaved every hair from the heads and bodies of those to be de-loused. Then it was into a shower room where the filth of ages and of living day and night in lice-ridden rags was removed.

In a clothing store each man was given a cap, a striped cotton shirt, a thin jacket and trousers. They were then marched barefoot through barbed wire gates from compound to compound, each gate guarded by German political prisoners on the camp staff. They were pushed into the grim quarantine area known as the 'Little Camp'. This section contained two large tents and a number of windowless hutments in which 6,000 unfortunates had to find shelter. It had an evil and frightening reputation because of its proximity to the Medical Experimentation block.

The thin, grotesque clothing was all the men were to have to keep them warm. Just before nightfall they were given an issue of soup but with the night came the cold. There was no shelter so with folded arms and shivering bodies they huddled together to try to keep warm. Even the stars above seemed cold. On the second night Chapman crawled into the lavatory capable of holding a thousand people 'at one sitting'. Despite the nauseating smell of the place there was some warmth inside and it was preferable to being so chilled. The first of several lengthy roll calls at 4.30am made the days seem unending. Food was only *ersatz* coffee, thin soup and a small piece of bread each day with potatoes every third day. On that day the soup portion was halved.

After the months in Fresnes and Buchenwald where one day was the same as another the airmen lost all sense of time. There were no newspapers or radios. Apart from immediate friends or crew members the prisoners existed only by their registration numbers. All were dressed alike in the same striped prison garb and lived in a block of some 850 inmates. Twice-daily *Appells* meant every prisoner was absorbed in a scrambling crowd, each inmate fighting to avoid being in the front row. That usually incurred a punch in the groin or head as the counting *SS* NCO passed. Everyone wanted to be faceless, anonymous – invisible.

The RAF men realised from the outset of their incarceration in Buchenwald that their survival depended as much on morale and disci-pline as on the starvation rations, so the men organised themselves into Flights under Squadron Leader Lamason. Lamason protested at their treatment and was told that the aircrew were designated *Terrorfliegers* and subject to summary execution. The airmen of course did not wish to be associated with the Terrorflieger image that prevailed whenever they grouped together, but they were all of a similar age and by comparison with the thousands of human scarecrows that surrounded them, were obviously more fit, still carrying their military bearing and composure. But keeping one's head down was the way to survive in Buchenwald. Despite this, the bearing and fortitude of the airmen rapidly earned the respect of other prisoners and even, eventually, some of the Germans in charge.

It took six minutes on the morning of 24 August for two waves of Flying Fortresses to reduce to a fiery rubble the *SS* barrack area and the Gustloff Armaments factory adjoining Buchenwald. Hundreds of prisoner workers, *SS* guards and their families were killed. The bombing was accurate but shrapnel flew across into the airmen's compound and some received minor wounds in their buttocks, the only part of their anatomies exposed as they strived to burrow into the ground.

Deafened by the explosions and trembling with shock and fear, the RAF and USAAF men were called out by the guards. Again they were sure they were to be shot as *Terrorfliegers* in reprisal for the bombing. To their relief they were sent clearing rubble in the factory area and fighting fires which had spread to the compound.

During heavy rain the prisoners were made to stand for hours which ensured they would spend the night in soaking clothes. Medical attention was practically non-existent and because of bad water, dysentery was endemic and uncontrolled. Many of the airmen were very ill. Finally they were issued with a blanket each and moved into barrack Number 58 in which young gypsy boys aged from seven to 16 years were housed. With the 168 airmen there were now 765 cramped bodies in that barrack. Thirty-five of the airmen were ill enough, many with suppurating sores, to be kept in a hospital barrack. Sleeping was almost impossible. The gypsies were filthy and their accumulated smell equalled that of the malodorous lavatories. There were no washing facilities. An RAF man and an American flyer died in the so-called hospital. Barrack lights were put out at 8.00pm, cards and games were forbidden so the nights became as long as the days. It was a wearing existence which weakened men until the inevitable end.

Various nationalities gave the airmen *Lagergeld* with which they could buy up to 25 of the poor quality cigarettes per week, and there was the incongruous event of the occasional film show and orchestral concert put on by the inmates. Within the camp was a brothel containing 17 girls which was open to prisoners of six months' standing. They would have had to have been extraordinarily strong or privileged to have lasted six months.

Most of the prisoners went out on working parties (*Arbeitskommando*) dressed in the usual striped pyjama-like clothes. They were mercilessly bullied and beaten by the *SS* guards. It was unsurprising that at the end of each day many had died.

Four days before the arrival of the airmen from Fresnes a party of 37 SOE men, including Wing Commander F. F. E. Yeo-Thomas, had been brought into Buchenwald and put in the main camp in Hut 17. On 9 September, 16 of the SOE men were told to report to the square building with a tower. On either side of the tower were the punishment cells. It was a lovely summer morning but Yeo-Thomas was chilled when told by a block leader that no-one ever came back from the tower. Two days later he was told that SOE men had been executed, hung from hooks on a wall and slowly strangled. The crematorium chimney belched smoke all night. Later another 15 SOE men were ruthlessly and coldly murdered in the same way.

Although the airmen were not officially permitted to go into the main camp, from time to time they received visits from some SOE officers in Block 17, including Wing Commander Yeo-Thomas. Yeo-Thomas, an RAF officer who had become an SOE specialist organising Resistance movements on the Continent, was betrayed by a subordinate and had been arrested near the Passy Metro station in Paris. He had also broken his own cardinal rule not to wait for a contact who was late for an appointment.

Yeo-Thomas and Squadron Leader Lamason became friends. Yeo-Thomas had some influence with certain of the camp authorities, claiming that he was an *Oberst* which impressed the rank conscious Germans. He also said that he had already sent a list of names of guilty guards back to Britain. It was a ploy that Vic Clarke used on the *Insterburg*. Yeo-Thomas in effect blackmailed the *SS* doctor in organising his escape and that of Captain Burney with two others. He also arranged for the smuggling out of a nominal roll of the RAF and USAAF 'political prisoners' and its sending to a nearby *Luftwaffe* station. Late in October the *Luftwaffe* managed to gain access to the camp and sent in a team of 'Interrogators' who were content merely to obtain the airmen's service details. A ray of hope appeared when an interrogator said they were to be moved within 10 days to a prisoner-of-war camp. For the airmen, 21 October was a glorious day – they left Buchenwald for Stalag Luft 3. Behind their happiness was the realization that few inmates ever leave a concentration camp, except up the chimney of the crematorium.

Neither do prisoners normally enter a prisoner-of-war camp with joy but to the men from Buchenwald, Stalag Luft 3 was Heaven, particularly in the officers' compound. Here were clean clothes, food, a rough bunk to themselves, order within the compound maintained by the prisoners and above all the companionship of their own kind. Their stay in Fresnes and Buchenwald as *Terrorfliegers* and saboteurs had been a close brush with death. It was a nightmarishly unforgettable experience.

Ken Chapman found the East compound an unbelievable change. It was wonderful to eat a good meal of soup, meat, potatoes and a dessert in a civilised manner with a knife, fork and spoon. To talk with friends in their own small room and, as he was so tired, to go to sleep in the first reasonable bed he had known for many months. Pyjamas, sheets and blankets were an almost unimaginable luxury.

Chapman's shaven head amused the men in his room. As he told them his story he knew it must have sounded pitiful and gruesome but they were kind, giving him useful articles of clothing and a free hand to their communal cigarette stock of which they had the astonishing store of 20,000.

## SPLASHING OUT

Generally, the army prisoners at Thorn were quite pleased to see the first party of RAF NCOs from Heydekrug move out again on 8 August. The journey from Thorn to Stalag 357 near Fallingbostel took place mainly at night. This time three armed guards occupied the centre of the box-cars, whilst 24 Kriegies occupied each end behind a screen of barbed wire spread over wooden frames reaching from floor to ceiling. A tiny gate was cut in the wire which was only opened during infrequent stops deep in the countryside, where small batches of Kriegies were permitted to jump down beside the track to relieve themselves. During daylight hours when the interval between stops became too long for comfort, the Kriegies were allowed through the tiny gate, one at a time. They would then hang on grimly to a vertical rail at the side of the wagon door and urinate as the train thundered through the countryside.

Paul Hilton had joined a vociferous queue of Kriegies anxiously awaiting their turn at the box-car door. When it was his turn to go through the small gate he dashed to the door, feverishly ripped open his remaining metal buttons and clung on to the side rail. The train had started to slow down but Hilton was in full flow when he saw that they were approaching a level crossing. Some 30 Germans were standing patiently at the level crossing gate waiting to pass over the line. Hilton passed slowly by, just out of their reach and still in full spate.

Any embarrassment soon passed for Hilton and as he had seen no reaction from the group he assumed that they were used to being so treated by their captives. At the same moment he had an almost uncontrollable urge to give a *Nazi* salute, he felt it would have completed the performance but his right hand was fully occupied in holding on to the rail.

## HUNGRY AGAIN

This time some of the army prisoners at Thorn followed the RAF to Fallingbostel. The Russians were getting close to the Polish camps. Stalag 357 was a mess, there was no light or heating but it was summer and the weather was generally fine. Cooking, such as it was, was done on blowers – Kriegie-built, fan-assisted forced-flame cookers operated by turning a handle geared to a rotary fan. The fan forced air underneath any burnable material and a blower would burn almost anything. A 'brew' or a quick 'glop' was made from the burning of coal-dust, twigs or wood chippings, even rags.

Stalag 357 was a sprawling, roughly built collection of brick and concrete single-storey barracks, and some dozen wooden huts. It seemed to have been thrown together for the smallest cost and with the minimum of facilities for the more than 7,000 men caged there. During September electricity for some lighting was installed, and wood collecting parties were allowed out of the camp so that heating could be arranged for the bitter continental winter to come. Despite the grim surroundings the Kriegies were not slow in organising themselves. Two football pitches were levelled and marked out but almost as games began so were they halted. The supply of Red Cross parcels ceased and simple survival assumed priority.

Physical games needed energy and sustenance and without food there was neither. Prisoners were back to where small cuts immediately festered and blood poisoning was frequent. Although there were army medical officers in the camp, they had practically no equipment or supplies. The MOs had to work in conditions of gross overcrowding with patients suffering from chronic malnutrition, and where there was a lack of water and drugs. German medical supplies seldom exceeded a smear of Gentian Violet, their panacea ointment. It was not until the middle of November that Red Cross parcels began to arrive again at Stalag 357. There was an immediate revival of interest in, at least, intellectual activities. Interest was again centred on the camp theatre and a production got underway.

## 'GET THROUGH AT ALL COSTS'

In Warsaw the Polish Resistance was fighting a desperate battle. A 178 Squadron Liberator from Foggia was to drop canisters of arms and ammunition to the beleaguered Poles. The importance of the drop had been emphasized by the Polish airmen at the base. Patriots within the city were fighting for their lives and short of arms of all kinds. The Liberator's mission was to 'get through at all costs'. Bomb-aimer, Sergeant Lloyd Lyne, determined to drop the arms in the right place.

Taking off on 13 August in the evening sunshine, the route took the Liberator over great stretches of sea before the crew needed to worry about enemy fighters. Five long hours passed before moonlight was seen shining on the Vistula. A dense pall of smoke hung over Warsaw. As the Liberator was brought down to 400ft, Sergeant Lyne saw the grey ghost-like appearance of the once beautiful city flashing past beneath. At that moment Lloyd Lyne had the feeling that this was to be their last flight.

During briefing the crew had been told they would run into the thick of the defences if they left the course of the river, but all too soon they could see an archway of light flak hose-piping up from both banks. It was going to be a dicey approach and Lyne was not surprised to hear the skipper call him to man a beam position .5in machine gun. The move was to save his life. Shells were smashing through the bottom of the aircraft and out through the top, looking like great, fiery red cricket balls. Gunners in all positions were told that they would have to shoot their way through and to keep up a heavy fire on the ground flak positions. The hail of light flak was terrifying. Even as Lyne sprayed the flak points, the aircraft was peppered with hundreds of holes. Within seconds flames leapt from the engines and enveloped the wings. The Liberator dived, screaming towards the ground. Lyne remembered nothing more.

When he opened his eyes the early dawn lit a dismal scene. Twenty yards away lay the blazing remains of the Liberator. Bullets were still whining in all directions from the fire. Everywhere around was so dim that Lyne thought briefly that he was blind. Unable to rise, he could just make out the River Vistula. He was deep among thick undergrowth which had helped to break his fall. He could see that his flying helmet, parachute harness, one flying boot and a leg of his leather Irvin trousers had been ripped off – and every bone in his body felt as if it had been broken.

The only thing he could do was to shout for help. Two elderly men ran to him. He hoped they might be Russian but they were not. Lyne tensed himself for rough treatment but the men picked him up as carefully as a mother would her child. As they carried him to a rowing boat Lyne saw that he was on a small island.

He carried out a sort of injury inventory. Both hands were burned and cut in many places, blood streamed down his face from scalp wounds, a painful leg was bleeding from shrapnel wounds, his hair and eyebrows were burned and he shivered uncontrollably from shock. His eyes worried him most but even as he lay there his vision improved. As the Germans carried him away he saw his flight engineer, who lay nearby with an aircraft engine across the lower part of his body. With a sinking heart Lyne heard that he was the only survivor of the Liberator crew.

Carefully placed on the back seat of a car, Lyne was driven nearer to the heart of Warsaw. The car pulled up in a deserted street, heavy gun-fire rocked the area, masonry fell from the damaged buildings and all around flames roared to the sky. A *Wehrmacht* doctor gave him an injection then he was transferred to a lorry and driven off. Lyne was relieved, the gunfire seemed too close. A second German officer had Lyne carried to a couch in an empty house where his gory clothes were cut off and his wounds dressed. A young German covered him with a blanket to help reduce his shivering and a small mosquito net was produced to keep the flies from his face. When he had been tidied up a mirror was produced for him to see how he looked. He immediately wished they had not been so kind.

Wearing clothes that had been given him to replace those cut off, he was again carried to another car. All those Germans who had treated him with such kindness and consideration turned out to wave him off. As he was driven away Lyne felt that he was leaving old friends.

At the hospital in Modlin, Lyne was treated with meticulous care and attention by the medical staff, and in particular by a German nurse. Polish girls worked in the hospital as cooks and were not permitted to visit him, but at one time as many as eight disobeyed the order and brought him apples, sweets, cider and once, three fried eggs. One girl, startling in her national costume, brought him a silver-backed mirror and a couple of handkerchiefs. She was caught in the room by a German orderly and reprimanded but after the shouting the girl touched her heart, pointed at Lyne and left the room. It was a demonstration of sympathy which touched Lyne deeply and which he has never forgotten.

Dreams tortured him some nights. He would wake half-demented but always found the German MO sitting in the dark by his bedside. Lyne was never sure whether it was an act of kindness or whether the doctor was hoping for information that Lyne might blurt out. Whichever it was, Lyne was comforted and felt that there was someone helping him. He slept soundly after.

*Wehrmacht* men were continuously brought in to the hospital with terrible wounds and burns. It made Lyne ponder the stupidity of war and the awful state of the world. Even when he left the hospital for the railway station it was in an ambulance with three wounded German soldiers and a hospital train full of wounded from the Russian Front, many in an appalling condition. Seated in an ordinary compartment with seven *Wehrmacht* soldiers Lyne found that they soon relaxed and spoke to him. At every stop where food and drink could be bought they made sure that he received exactly the same as they. Throughout the three-day journey to Frankfurt, the nights in cells and the walks between railway stations, Lyne had been treated with friendliness and compassion.

At one station Russian prisoners shovelling coal saw him and were immediately 'all smiles'. When the guard's back was turned they pointed to Lyne and then to the guard, making signs of throat slitting and laughing when Lyne nodded. The final walk from Frankfurt to Oberursel exhausted him. He was glad to see the barbed wire of Dulag Luft.

After the usual de-lousing and bogus Red Cross form Lyne was to spend 11 days in hungry and tormenting solitary confinement. A drop of soup spilled on the floor was rapidly spooned up and eaten and a piece of bread that had been thrown under a wash bowl Lyne took back to his cell. Food could not be wasted.

To pass the dragging hours Lyne made himself a plan for noughts and crosses from four strips of paper and used rolled up balls for the noughts and flat pieces for the crosses. If an opponent made a slip Lyne worked out a way in which he could never be beaten. For hours he watched a caterpillar, a bee and like Robert the Bruce, a spider.

Lyne's identity discs were taken when he was examined, giving an interrogator the opportunity to accuse him of being a spy and threatening to have him shot. Another interrogator took a different tack asking:

'Were you in Squadrons 148, 31, or 178?' When Lyne would not answer he said,

'You know my dear fellow, this operation is an open book to us, there is nothing about it that we do not know.' Taking up the bogus Red Cross form again the German wrote in pencil '178' and asked,

'There, is that satisfactory?' Lloyd Lyne feared that the flicker of a smile that crossed his face had given him away.

Lyne went back to his cell with the words 'You will be going to a permanent camp soon' ringing in his ears. He could have sung with happiness. Within an hour he was on his way to Dulag Luft at Wetzlar.

Wetzlar was a revelation and very different from the early days at the Oberursel Dulag. New Kriegies had a shower and were issued with new American uniforms. Given a small Red Cross suitcase, they filled it with shirts, woollen vests, a tie, soap, tobacco, a pipe, pipe cleaners, a belt, a holdall with needles and mending materials, a pullover, a brown woollen hat and other small items.

The next call was to the dining room where the walls were decorated with cartoons. Then came a meal for which Lloyd Lyne had waited so anxiously. He had eaten little during the 11 days he was in solitary confinement and was famished. The mainly Red Cross food was delicious and the day ended perfectly when the new prisoners were taken to a room with three-tier bunks in which to sleep.

Strangely, they had the choice of three prisoner-of-war camps to which they could be sent. Lyne and several others elected for Stalag Luft 1 at Barth and four days later they were marched to the station where a special train waited in a siding. Once more Sergeant Lyne started a long journey across Germany, but this time to the Baltic.

## THE HAPPY LIBERATORS

The German guards at the American Military Hospital at Rheims were First World War veterans. They were strict but not unkind, although they told Flight Lieutenant John Grimer with satisfaction that London was being destroyed by V1 flying bombs. The news of the Normandy invasion did not reach the RAF men in the hospital until the end of June.

In the late summer of 1944 the Americans were about to capture Rheims and the hospital. John Grimer was still in great pain from his leg wounds, although the German doctor had worked unceasingly for him and the other wounded. The doctor's care was limited by the lack of drugs and bandages. Once only did Grimer know this dedicated man to lose his temper. During a daylight raid the hospital had been bombed and three nurses killed. The doctor was furious and threatened 'to cut off all your arms and legs'. Such a threat was but a momentary lapse from his professional ethics. When Grimer begged him to amputate a leg that was badly infected with gas gangrene the doctor declined, telling him that if the hospital was liberated by the Americans they would have adequate drugs with which to save his leg.

One morning at the end of August the doctor walked round the ward saying 'Goodbye' and shaking hands with the wounded RAF men. The Americans were near, he told them, then he left with the guards. The prison ward remained unlocked and those of the eight prisoners who could walk pushed the others, in wheelchairs or trolleys, to the *Kommandant*'s suite of rooms. The setting was sumptuous but the only nourishment the near-starving prisoners could find was a supply of Champagne and tomatoes which immediately upset their shrunken stomachs.

Several hours of distant gunfire was followed by uncanny silence. Suddenly the door was thrown open and framed in the doorway stood an huge black US Army master-sergeant levelling a sub-machine gun at the startled prisoners. Hysterically the RAF men identified themselves. The master-sergeant was drunk when he arrived and the plentiful supply of Champagne increased his intoxication. He regaled the prisoners with tales of his wild exploits, punctuating his story with repeated jabs into the highly polished rosewood table with a great Bowie knife. As his wine consumption increased so did his extravagant flourishes with the knife. The prisoners became alarmed for their safety and were relieved when a small American major arrived. At last, thank heavens, they thought, discipline will be restored. But the Americans were old buddies and soon the small major was the more sodden of the two.

An ambulance ride followed through corpse strewn lanes. The stench of death was overpowering. Sometimes bodies and parts of bodies were neatly piled along the hedgerows. As they passed through villages, laughing and cheering girls threw flowers and offered wine. Grimer was filled with admiration for the American troops and their complete informality and compassion. In their striped hospital pyjamas the ex-prisoners were often mistaken for Germans. It made no difference, they received every kindness and consideration. German prisoners lined up with American GIs for 'chow'. Grimer saw precedence for a flight to England given to a badly wounded German private over that of an American general. The German's medical needs were greater. It was a remarkable lesson in humanity.

Because of their emaciated condition the prisoners were soon aboard a Dakota and then quickly comfortable in the American hospital at Taunton, Somerset. Proper drugs, good food and a quart of Guinness daily put Flight Lieutenant John Grimer on the road to recovery. Despite Grimer's protests the Americans gave him a GI uniform, crutches when he could walk, and awarded him a Purple Heart. Two months later the RAF claimed him back and he went to the RAF hospital at Locking near Weston-super-Mare.

### 'ABOUT FACE!'

Early October had seen the Warsaw uprising ruthlessly crushed, box-car trains emptied their pathetic loads of Polish prisoners at concentration camps in Germany. At Stalag 357 Fallingbostel the men who had come from Thorn were surprised to hear from 'tame' guards that the 400 Polish women captured at Warsaw would pass by the camp on their way from de-lousing. The men were told by Germans, who held their cupped hands over their mouths in the manner of a schoolboy telling a smutty joke, that as the women's clothes would be in the de-lousing oven they would be naked as they passed. It was another attempt to humiliate their captives.

The prisoners knew what the Germans wanted. At *Appell* time they were standing around casually but deliberately facing the wire until Deans received the indication that the women were approaching. His voice rang out across the square, 'Parade – Attention! About face!' As one man, the Kriegies turned away from the wire, studiously avoiding any glance towards the women who were walking to the camp a few kilometres along the road near the village of Bergen Belsen. Calls of 'thank you' rang out across the wire from the Polish women.

### 'MUD OR BLOOD?'

Aircrew prisoners were young, intelligent men. The horrors and the tragedy of war had been thrust at them and here, confined in the prison camp, they had time to think. Area bombing was anathema to the Christian ethic and the Germans published incessant propaganda photographs of dead and injured children, victims of the *Terrorfliegers*. Equally repugnant were the *Nazi* doctrine, the occupation of defenceless countries, the concentration camps, the killings, the deliberate murder of 'the Fifty', the deportations, the tortures and beatings that had always been the methods of totalitarianism. Most prisoners could and did push any turmoil in their minds to the rear of their consciousness, concentrating only upon the present and upon survival. For a few it was not that easy.

Flight Lieutenant George Atkinson was shot down on a raid on Münchengladbach at the end of August 1943. The Germans sent him to the North compound at Sagan. There he joined in the compound activities, the theatre evenings when they dressed to go 100 yards as if visiting the West End of London; the swimming in the fire pool until the October chill froze them out; the always anti-clockwise (RAF-style) 'pound round the compound'; the meetings with Bushell and Day; the long winter evenings when they were locked in the huts; the sense of shock that fell over the camp like a black cloud when the mass escape turned to tragedy; the dedication of the memorial and the repatriation of Group Captain Massey.

Atkinson had been absorbed into Kriegie life but now in mid-1944 he turned inward upon himself. The utter futility and the increasingly sad tragedy of total war appalled him, turning his mind into a whirling turmoil of conflicting thought, sapping his mental and physical strength. He sought aid from the Anglican and Roman Catholic chaplains but they were unable to help. Inevitably, he collapsed with a nervous breakdown.

Desperately thin, weak and now completely apathetic, George Atkinson was sent to a mental home in Lublin where he endured the misery of drug and electric shock treatment.

The memory of those days was to remain as if etched in his mind. The procession that entered the ward headed by the white-coated German doctor carrying the small silver box of fearsome tricks; the terminals fixed to his temples; the stick placed between his teeth; the sudden twist of his legs which was succeeded by a gradual return to awareness; his mind a blank. Then a splitting headache was followed by strange illusions and a slow return to normal. George Atkinson hated the whole miserable torment – but it worked. Soon he was out in the hospital yard working with others unloading logs and timber in the hard, sunny Polish winter, all working with a mutually agreed slowness born of the doubtful conviction that working too fast might assist the German war effort.

Atkinson and several others were sent back to Lamsdorf and just after Christmas 1944 rumours flared up again about the repatriation of the severely disabled. This was always a harassing torment for them but suddenly they were on a hospital train. When the train reached Oppeln later that day, the Kriegies, by peeping under the carriage blinds, saw trainloads of tanks heading east. As their train passed over the Danube at Vienna and the shadow of the great Ring*strasse* wheel fell across them, a huge locomotive passed with the slogan 'Räder Müssen Rollen für den Sieg' emblazoned on its flanks. In the streets below the occasional car passed with a huge gas bag on its roof, and to the south-west of the city skiers could be seen on the mountain slopes. The Alps and Ulm with its towering cathedral were passed and as dusk fell the Kriegies were beside the grey waters of Lake Constance. Switzerland was near.

Hearts were beating fast, things could so easily go wrong. Ordered down from the train the Kriegies were escorted across the frontier, passing the Germans for whom they were being exchanged on the way. Freedom! Even the air of Switzerland was different: pure, fresh, wholesome. Now they really were free. On board a luxurious Swiss train they were welcomed by the British Consul who walked along the corridor passing on Royal greetings.

At 8.00pm that evening the train pulled out. It was hard for the men to wrest their eyes from the lights of the passing towns and villages. Later, transferring to a French hospital train with drawn blinds, they once more crossed a frontier. Now in France, the train slid down the Rhône Valley to Marseilles.

176

Roy Hale, suffering from tuberculosis, was struck by the considerate treatment he received from the German orderlies and nurses on the 'rough and ready' German hospital train and the contrast with the opulent luxury of the Swiss train at Geneva. His transfer was organised by a stalwart *Feldwebel* who carried him bodily from one train to the other. Hale was put on an American ship in the harbour at Marseilles to await the Canadian ship that was to take the Repats to England. The Americans treated them as VIPs although the nursing orderlies' pre-breakfast questioning cry of – 'Mud or blood? Mud or blood?' perplexed him until it was translated as 'Do you require coffee or tomato juice with your breakfast?'.

The Americans had been ordered to destroy the clothing of all prisoners-of-war so an orderly asked Hale:

'What rank are you soldier?'

'I am a warrant officer of the Royal Air Force.'

That posed a problem for the orderly but he eventually returned with an American uniform complete with stripes and brevet and the information that 'You're a "Top Kick"'.

Pilot Officer 'Johnnie' Johnston was on his way home for treatment by the great surgeon Archibald McIndoe. Johnston, a one-time special duties man based at Tempsford, was severely injured when he was shot down. His right leg was destroyed, his right arm badly fractured in three places and his body covered with gashes and abrasions. Despite all this Johnston was a happy man, he had been taken prisoner just before the day that had been planned for his wedding. Now he was going home where his fiancée Ruth was waiting impatiently for him to fix another day.

George Atkinson needed the eight-day voyage to Liverpool on the Canadian ship Letitia to adjust to the food and freedom. The docking at Merseyside was a happy blur of Mayor's welcoming speeches, bands and flags. Then it was into coaches for the RAF hospital near Blackpool. A few days later George Atkinson stepped off a train at Paragon Station, Hull, walked to the concourse to meet his father and broke down in tears. He was home and free and the battle to recover his health completely was about to begin.

Although a German offensive with 21 mixed divisions had punched a gap in the American lines in the Ardennes on 16 December, there was, throughout all prisoner-of-war camps, a realisation that this would almost certainly be their last Christmas as prisoners. They had put away their home-made Armistice Day poppies and prepared themselves for the best and the worst. Every Kriegie knew that the end of this bloody war would be violent and perhaps after all they had been through, they may well feature on the casualty lists again. The future was clouded but exciting, at least the flyers would not have another year of deadening confinement. No-one knew what would happen in the next few months, no-one knew where the flailing, last convulsions of the doomed *Nazis* would strike. Helpless captives had frequently been the targets of the beaten bully, but the Kriegies looked forward to the coming year with courage and more hope than they had felt since they had literally fallen into enemy hands.

Major Simoleit did his best to dash their hopes by telling them that the German attack through the Ardennes would cut the Allied forces into two easily defeated sections, and the war in the West would be over. Germany could then devote its whole effort to pushing the savages back to the east.

By Christmas day the *Wehrmacht*'s Ardennes offensive had been halted. As the turkey sandwiches were being passed forward to the men at the front, General Patton looked at the clear sunny morning and wrote in his diary that it was 'lovely weather for killing Germans, although the thought seems somewhat at variance with the spirit of the day'.

*'Life seems full of Ups and Downs.'*

# PART 6
# 1945

## CHETNIKS AND COCKROACHES

The 148 (Special Duties) Squadron Halifax had just made its supply drop to Tito's partisans in Croatia and turned back to Brindisi, when a heavy machine gun scored a hit. Flight Sergeant Roy 'Lofty' Bromley watched with rapt fascination as a sudden line of holes ran along the floor of the aircraft, making little dust puffs as they went. Smoke appeared, then fire and then the order came to abandon aircraft. Groping forward to the parachute stowage Bromley felt his foot crash through the floor and a searing pain shoot up his body. Pulling his leg free Bromley grasped the parachute, clipped it on and jumped through the escape hatch.

Soon he was hanging motionless below his parachute which was snagged on a tree. He dropped the 10 feet to the snow-covered ground. Touching his legs gingerly, Bromley could feel that they were burned, the right worse than the left but flying boots had saved them from really serious damage. Because he could hardly move he was quickly discovered by Mihailovic's pro-Axis Chetnik partisans and taken to a local village where his burns were dressed.

A few hours later he was taken down to the yard and shown a cart. Lying there on a bed of straw were the bodies of three of his crew, his close friends. Gordon Walker the skipper had gone down with the plane, navigator Australian Wally Lyon had been killed by the machine gun burst, and Australian George Lowe the bomb-aimer had baled out but had been shot on his way down. The shock was worse to Bromley than his own shooting down. That short action had killed almost half his crew. He returned to the room, closed the door and burst into tears.

Two days later Bromley was collected by a German escort and spent the night in a cell. There he found cockroaches and to pass the time he rolled back the palliasse, put a few crumbs of bread at one end of the bunk, lined up the cockroaches and held a kind of Cockroach Derby. The evening passed quickly but the January night was cold. Next morning Bromley was taken out and helped into a lorry and there, holding crutches, was wireless operator Bill Rowe. It was a happy meeting. Rowe was suffering from frostbite after falling into a freezing stream. Bromley told him of the deaths of the three whose bodies he had seen on the cart.

On their way to Dulag they stopped at Zagreb. Near them was a column of manacled young women partisans, one of whom turned towards him and whispered, 'Thank you for your help'. Bromley was saddened. He could only guess what was to be the fate of the women.

## THE SCRAMBLE FROM THE EAST

At the start of winter 1944/45, RAF men and officer prisoners were distributed all over Germany and Poland. Most were in Stalag Luft 3 at Sagan, Stalag Luft 1 at Barth, Stalag Luft 4 at Gross Tychow, Stalag Luft 7 at Bankau, Stalag 8B at Lamsdorf and Stalag 4B at Mühlberg. Others were at Nuremberg, Eichstätt, Moosburg, Colditz, Bad Sulza, Kirchain, and a few in the Army NCOs' camp at Hohenfels. From the German viewpoint the camps were being menaced from both directions but particularly from the east.

The Red Army poured like a tidal wave into East Prussia and ahead of it rushed a torrent of horrifying accounts of rape, torture, murder, robbery and destruction. The German people were terrified. Families of young and old took to the roads westward by any transport they could find or by foot. Pushing perambulators, pulling carts or sledges, often carrying children, they painfully staggered and lurched through the snow as though the devil was at their heels. Many were led and protected by French prisoners who had been working on farms and factories, and were the only able-bodied men in East Prussia. Soon the Kriegies, unwillingly, were to join this struggling throng.

Roadsides became strewn with grotesquely shaped snow-covered mounds disguising those who, reaching the limit of their endurance, had collapsed and been frozen to death where they lay. Directly in the Russians' path were camps containing over 100,000 soldiers of the British and Commonwealth Forces, and nearly 10,000 RAF men, mostly aircrew. American aircrew were in large numbers at Barth, Sagan and Gross Tychow. These were the constituents of a powerful force that the *Oberkommando des Heeres* had no intention of allowing to be freed to join the fight against the retreating *Wehrmacht*. In the third week of January 1945, the German High Command ordered the evacuation of the camps in the east. Stalag Luft 6 at Heydekrug, the most easterly of the camps for airmen, had already been hastily abandoned in the summer and the prisoners distributed between Stalag Luft 4 at Gross Tychow and Stalag 357 at Fallingbostel.

Stalag Luft 7 at Bankau in Silesia was the first of the RAF camps to be called to move out for a winter march. At 11.00am on 17 January the Kriegies at Bankau were given one hour to be ready. Ober*Feldwebel*

Frank ominously snarled that for every man who fell out of the column on the march, five would be shot. The Germans were in a frenzy of fear, the Red Army had broken through on a wide front 40 miles east of Bankau and was heading straight for Breslau. Kriegie kit was hurriedly packed with bare essentials when the news came that the order was 'scrubbed'.

The Kriegies sat in tense readiness. It was not until 3.30am on 19 January that, what Albert Bracegirdle called 'The Retreat from Bankau', began. The next day, 20 January, the march out of the huge camp for Army prisoners-of-war at Lamsdorf began. The RAF compound at Stalag 8B had been a kind of enclave of NCOs who, by the rules of the Geneva Convention, did not have to work. It was surrounded by compounds of Army men who laboured unwillingly for the Germans on farms, in factories, quarries and mines.

Next camp to move out was Stalag Luft 3 Sagan and its satellite, Belaria. The Americans of the West and South compounds were the first on to the icy road on 27 January, followed by the North compound and Belaria. By the morning of Sunday the 28th the East compound was cleared. During the march the column from Sagan split, some being crushed into box-cars at Spremburg, the others turning north to Luckenwalde Stalag 3A.

At Stalag Luft 4 Gross Tychow, the USAAF and RAF men did not receive their orders to move until 6 February. None of the Kriegies knew their proposed route or destination. It would obviously be westward but even if the German officers in charge or the guards knew, they were not going to tell.

The situation at Stalag Luft 1 Barth was quickly resolved by the Senior American Officer and the SBO flatly refusing to allow their men to leave the camp. They had correctly judged the *Kommandant* as being a humane and just man and did not believe he would use force to evacuate the camp.

From prisoner-of-war camps, internment camps, forced labour camps and some concentration camps in the east, huge columns of mixed nationalities from every continent were on the move, trudging westward in sub-zero temperatures and blinding snow. With them, often inextricably mixed, were thousands of German civilian refugees, mostly women, children and elderly men fleeing ahead of the terror from the east.

Although they did not know it the men from Luft 7 at Bankau were also to finish their winter journey at Stalag 3A Luckenwalde, and those from Luft 4 Gross Tychow were to meet with the column from Stalag 8B

Lamsdorf and finish their trek at Fallingbostel. Most of the officers from Sagan were to end this journey at a naval prisoner-of-war camp at Westertimke in north-west Germany. Others joined the NCOs at Luckenwalde. So now most, but by no means all, the main groups of RAF men were to be finally assembled in four camps at Barth, Luckenwalde, Fallingbostel and Westertimke. For those in the last two camps it was not to be the end of their forced travels. It is probable that had the two senior officers at Barth not refused to move they too would have been added to the numbers at Fallingbostel.

## THE RETREAT FROM BANKAU

Anarchy reigned throughout the camp at Stalag Luft 7 Bankau. The cookhouse was raided for potatoes, bread and coal, other Kriegies rifled the parcel store taking all the personal goods and cigarettes they could carry. The clothing store was ransacked, the sports store and library were plundered and the theatre wrecked.

Heavy snow was falling as the prisoners trudged out of the compound. The air was so icily cold that breathing was difficult. No transport was to be provided for any sick who might fall out on the march and the only medical supplies were to be carried on their backs by the MO and three Sanitäters.

Most Kriegies had loaded as much of their personal possessions as they could into Red Cross boxes, and fixed straps to their bags so that they could be carried more easily on the shoulders. The 'march' quickly deteriorated into a long uneven, straggling line of struggling men. It was quickly realised that the carrying of items unnecessary to the sustaining of life, was exhausting. The countryside was soon littered with miscellaneous equipment, and abandoned items were searched for food by the refugees, and then left to become more snow-covered mounds.

After ten hours the Kriegie column had plodded through Kronstadt and Kreuzberg before finally halting for the night at the hamlet of Winterfeld where they spread themselves through barns and haylofts, resting as best they could. At 5.00am they were on the icy roads again competing for a place amid crowds of refugees and retreating *Wehrmacht*. Scores of tractors towing carts containing families and all their possessions, passed the Kriegie column. Often a tractor would be towing two lorries similarly loaded. Horses, sweating and bleeding, were being flogged as they were urged on by the blind fear of their owners. Weakened by the chafing of the harness and sheer exhaustion, many horses collapsed and died. Their carcasses, frequently hacked apart for food, were soon a common sight. The remainder, frozen and stiffened into gaunt, grotesque shapes at the side of the road, were swiftly smoothed into rounded, unidentifiable hummocks by the heavy snow. Freezing, strong headwinds drove stinging ice into the faces of the marchers making progress slow and laborious. Where the wind had swept aside the snow a three-inch ice layer made even a small step a dangerous balancing act.

Experience had taught the Kriegies to ration out their food, they knew their survival lay in their own hands and provision had to be made for any eventuality. Soon their pockets were filled with whatever food they had and their cases and bags were abandoned at the roadside, with the dead horses and the dying refugees who had dropped out of the columns. At the roadside too, even in the main streets of towns, men squatted in an agony of twisting stomachs and rectal pain. Diarrhoea and dysentery wracked their bodies adding to the misery of starvation, raw cold and the continuous driving of the Germans.

As the column passed through a village a full milk churn was seen on its collecting platform outside the gate of a farm. Within seconds the churn was on a trolley and the milk passed round among the Kriegies. To Sergeant Phil Potts it was the most satisfying drink of milk ever. Here Potts was forcibly struck by the futility of war. The village, but for the deep snow, looked like any in England and had in its centre a war memorial to those who had died in the Great War. Passing the memorial in deepest misery was the sorry procession of thousands of refugees, displaced persons, foreign slave workers, German soldiers and their prisoners. It was all so insane.

A seven-mile slog brought the main Kriegie column to Karlsruhe where a filthy, abandoned brick factory provided shelter and here some German tried to make amends for the conditions. Two field kitchens, each capable of cooking for 200 men, were provided for the more than 1,500 marchers, although the only warm drink for all was a mug of *ersatz* coffee. The MO was given a horse and cart for the transport of six men only – provided they could sit up.

After a rest of 11 hours the Kriegies were again ordered on to the road. Despite protests from the Camp Leader and the MO, the *Abwehr* officer said it was an order that must be obeyed. The guards told that the bridge across the Oder was to be blown next morning at 8 o'clock. Anyone left on the east side would be left behind. Rapidly the word passed round the Kriegies, 'Go slow!'. Every delaying tactic to the already crawling progress was to be used. The rumble of heavy artillery behind was continuous. If they could hang back, even a little, the Red Army might catch up with them but the Germans were wise to the go-slow.

Once more the bedraggled column set off in a temperature of minus 13 degrees Centigrade. From 8.30pm the prisoners were subjected to a hurried, agonising forced march. The MO's wagon was full before three miles had been travelled. Men were being picked up at the roadsides, exhausted and frozen. Thirty prisoners collapsed and were unable to continue. They were assisted to houses on the route and left for the advancing Russians.

Fog, reducing visibility to 32 yards, blanketed the last few kilometres of the approach to the river and bridge, but it was with enormous relief that, dodging round the huge holes containing the explosive charges, the Kriegies reached the west bank. Sheer willpower and mutual help enabled them to cross the Oder and finish the trek to Schönfeld where they collapsed on the floors of cowsheds and barns at 9.00am on 21 January. A half-cup of coffee and 3 oz of biscuits were issued to the weakened men as their ration.

The Kriegies had been told that no move would now be made for two days. Despite their poor accommodation the rest would be welcome, indeed necessary. It was not to be. At 3.00am on 22 the Germans gave orders to prepare for an immediate resumption of the march. The men had difficulty in finding their few possessions in the dark and there was some delay. It was too much for the patience and rising fear of the Germans who marched into the barns and cowsheds firing their rifles and pistols.

As the Kriegies gathered outside a quick numbers check was made. To their dismay 23 men were missing. It was believed that 31 men had been evacuated to Lamsdorf, nothing further was heard of them. Of the 23 missing men, they may have escaped or been left behind asleep. Most likely they had dropped out from the column, unnoticed in the darkness and falling snow, to die a cold and lonely death by a remote Silesian road. Marching had now become very slow. The road was choked with German mechanised transport and panic-stricken civilians causing the Kriegie column to stretch for almost a mile. Snow drifts reaching a height of almost 10 feet and a stiffening wind meant each man saw only the back of the man in front. They plodded on.

Day and night, with little rest and a minimum of food, the Kriegies from Luft 7 were forced onward. Although the broken promise of transport at Peterwitz was a crushing disappointment there was a day of rest, and from time to time a small ration of bread or oats was issued. The food was insufficient to sustain life in a sedentary and warm state, but for men who were forced to march in such appalling conditions it was killing. A rumour that the Russians had already crossed the Oder to the north of their positions caused sudden terror among the guards. The attempts by a few Kriegies to hide to await the Russian advance were quickly thwarted by shots fired at random. Nevertheless there were many missing when the march resumed, no-one knew if they had escaped or died.

The Kriegies who had managed to hold on to a few belongings now dragged them on makeshift sleds, but Bracegirdle and his 'Oppo' hung their blankets around their shoulders bandolier fashion and took turns to carry their one small case. It was on the tenth day of the march that Bracegirdle felt he had reached the end. Exhausted and aching from head to foot, he had to summon all his willpower to push himself forward. His calf and thigh muscles were centres of excruciating agony. Looking up at a village clock at Stansdorf and seeing it was 12.15pm, he dreamed of his mother cooking the Sunday lunch at home and looked at his present lunch of two thin slices of black bread and a little raw sugar beet. How life had changed!

At the end of the day the usual half-cup of watery soup had to stay them before they burrowed under some straw for warmth. By now the Germans were really hated, the forced march was so obviously futile. No longer were the Kriegies prisoners-of-war, they were hostages. Like so many of the marching men Sergeant Bracegirdle prayed to the Almighty for strength. The now gale-force wind and driving snow had frozen their clothes into ice sheets. After an hour's delay on the march a giant snowplough cleared the road ahead but the Kriegies still had to wade through three feet of snow in Indian file. With his face frozen and set like a mask, Bracegirdle knew they had to continue with this nightmare. To collapse and fall by the roadside meant freezing to death before anyone could find him. The evidence was there in the contorted frozen bodies lying in the drifts.

Several men had fallen out of the column on the night slog through the snow of 29 January and no-one knew what had happened to them. The MO continuously amputated frostbitten toes in his operating theatre in a stable. Peter Thomson, the senior man, told them that Sagan had been evacuated so he did not know their destination. The news that the Kriegies were to march on to the next town was greeted with despair. Bracegirdle was so exhausted that he pulled some straw over him and 'slept like a log'.

The Kriegies awoke next morning to find the temperature had risen. The farmyard was a quagmire. A Polish woman living in the house nearby made hot drinks and soup throughout the day for the constant queue at her door. That afternoon the men were told to be ready to march at 8.00am. The Russians were said to be in Breslau and advancing rapidly in the north near Danzig. This deadly retreat could not go on forever.

At Prausnitz a real break came with a five-day halt, during which the *Kommandant, Oberstleutnant* Behr, visited the farm where the men were lying and read out an incomprehensible and purposeless order from the Oberkommando der *Wehrmacht*. Five men were to be released, the order said, and would be liberated as soon as possible. The Kriegies could only wonder at the idiocy and mentality of their captors.

On 4 February frost hardened the ground again and the Padre held a service in the road, taking as a Lesson the 23rd Psalm. Albert Brace-girdle felt the appropriateness of the solemn, 'The Lord is my shepherd, I shall not want'.

It was 2.30am when the Kriegies were roused by shouting guards. The cries of 'Raus! Raus!' and kicks and bayonet prods forced the men out, but it was not until 6.00am that with an issue of less than one-third of a loaf per man and some tinned meat the Kriegies were marched out of Prausnitz on 5 February, their destination Goldberg, five miles distant.

At Goldberg, in groups averaging between 55 and 63 men, they were forcibly crammed into rail box-cars. Few were allowed out to relieve themselves and they were quickly ordered back into the trucks by shouting guards. Dysentery, frostbite and sickness were rife. The close confinement, the severe malnutrition and the utter fatigue were debilitating; morale and life were approaching their nadir. For three days the men suffered the hell of the train journey, travelling only during the day. The nights were spent in sidings. Only military trains travelled at night and the transporting of Kriegies, as always, had the lowest priority.

It was not until 10.30am on 8 February that the men almost fell from the box-cars. For 21 agonising days they had slogged through the bitterest period of a Continental winter on the absolute minimum of food. Gaunt and wasted they formed up in fives to shuffle through the town of Luckenwalde. Many were past even that activity and had to be carried or dragged along. Visions of food and rest kept the others going forward, thankful to at last see the barbed wire and *Posten* towers of Stalag 3A.

In the second week of February Göbbels proposed that Germany denounce the Geneva Convention and take reprisals against Allied prisoners-of-war. The proposal was leaked to Sweden and then to London where a sharp warning was issued and the proposal dropped. But Göbbels still complained in the privacy of his diary that the USAAF bombed during the day and 'during the night the cursed Englishmen return to Berlin with their Mosquitoes and deprive one of the few hours' sleep which one needs more than ever these days'.

## THE LEAVING OF LAMSDORF

The Kriegies incarcerated in camps in the east had hoped for a rapid Russian advance to release them. Those at Lamsdorf had been confidently saying, 'Moscow next week'. It became a catchword. Hopes were shattered when, on 13 January, a party of RAF prisoners arrived from a camp to the east. These were recent captives owning nothing but the clothes on their backs. They were exhausted. Each table or combine of 10 men 'adopted' one of these unfortunates, supplying him with food, cigarettes and essentials.

It now seemed that a westward march was a distinct possibility. The RAF men had heard stories from the Dunkirk Army men of their problems during the march across Europe to Poland in the summer of 1940. Now they were faced with a march in the opposite direction which would begin in the depths of winter. Rucksacks were fashioned and packed. Food, warm clothing and the best footwear taking priority.

On 20 January the move began and most of the RAF men formed up outside on the road the following day in what they called 'shooting batches' of 100, herded by guards armed with sub-machine guns. As they moved off Corporal Herbert Noy, engineer/fitter of an ASR boat and a prisoner since the Dieppe débâcle, described it more as a shuffle than a march. Prisoners were warned that if anyone attempted to escape the whole group would be shot. The threat was an effective deterrent. Judging by previous experience the Kriegies reckoned they could tell when the Germans were bluffing. This bald statement had an ugly ring of firm intent.

The evacuation of the vast area of Lamsdorf had begun within hours of that of Bankau. The RAF prisoners marched out of Stalag 344 and Stalag 8B on 22 January 1945, a day of clear skies and biting cold. They were destined for an even longer and more terrible march than those from Bankau. Conditions were the same: ice, snow and sub-zero temperatures. Boots were rapidly frozen solid on their feet. The men had received a Red Cross parcel as they left Lamsdorf otherwise they would have quickly succumbed to hunger and cold. Food, frozen solid, did not last beyond Stalag 8A at Görlitz where the Kriegies, who thought they had reached the limit of their endurance, had seven days' rest before resuming their march, but there was worse to come. At Görlitz some Kriegies boarded the usual cattle trucks to Fallingbostel, others marched to Goldberg where they were herded into similar rail wagons and despatched to Stalag 3A at Luckenwalde. In the chaos of rapid retreat some parties were marched away or were entrained for destinations in Bavaria, Austria and Czechoslovakia, but most carried on slogging their way through blinding blizzards to a vague destination in the west. From then on German rations were almost non-existent, just the occasional small piece of bread or a ration of watery soup.

On the march, the column passed another composed of women. All were filthy, dressed in rags and dragging themselves along. The Kriegies, desperately short of food as they were, tried to pass some to the women. In a flash the guards' pistols were brandished and contact forbidden. As the women passed they made a peculiar sighing noise. To Don Bruce all the degradation of *Nazi* Germany was contained in that sighing.

The struggling men found their breath formed solid sheets of ice on their clothing. Balaclavas and coat lapels quickly became hard and unbending. Eyebrows and eyelashes were coated and frozen. Ice and icicles formed around nostrils and lips became cracked. Lungs became sore from the effort of inhaling freezing air. Despite wearing all the underclothing they possessed, the wind whipped through the layers leaving the skin numbed. Frostbite and chilblains added to the agony as each man trudged on, seeing only the snow-covered boots of the man in front, always holding on to the sustaining knowledge that he must keep going, or collapse and die in the snow.

During a pause Don Bruce lay back, resting on his pack in the snow and feeling desperately hungry. He pictured himself at home, they would now be having afternoon tea. It was so cold, he was so tired, perhaps if they just let him sleep for a while... Shouts of 'Raus! Raus! Raus!' brought him staggering to his painfully blistered feet. Then he was shuffling forward again, into the wind-blown snow, head down, eyes fixed on the shuffling feet of the man in front.

The Kriegies covered a distance of nearly 500 miles between Görlitz and Stalag 9A Zeigenheim. For one period of three days even the tiny German rations were not issued. Ron Fermor sold a shirt to a Polish girl in exchange for three slices of bread. To live it was necessary to steal and during the march nine men were shot by the guards for stealing food. But how else could one survive? Fermor ate raw mangel-wurzels, swede, sugar beet, potatoes and wheat and once, stole oats from a horse's manger. Food of any kind was essential. During the march at the end of the trek Sergeant Fermor could hardly walk. He estimated his weight as 7st. Bones were sticking through his flesh and his hands easily encircled his thighs.

As he shuffled through a village, a smell of cooking meat wafted over Ron Esling. For a man on the verge of starvation it was overpowering. Dogs or no dogs, guards or no guards, the rich aroma pulled him unerringly away from the column to the side door of a Gasthaus kitchen and an unattended cauldron of bubbling stew. Frantically he cast around for a container to scoop up some stew. The boots of a guard crunched through the snow towards the door, in panic Esling plunged a hand into the boiling liquid just as a shouting, bayonet-wielding guard appeared. Dejected, Esling was forced to rejoin the tottering column. He looked at his scalded hand and for the first time in his adult life Ron Esling cried, not because of the pain, that was just another agony to pile on to his burden of misery, he cried about the stew which he had seen, smelt and had to leave. The bitter night seemed even colder and his belly emptier.

Sergeant George Rex was exhausted when the column arrived near Meissen on 16 February. He and another had that day supported a third friend who was 'out on his feet'. That evening they took him to the British MO for the sick man to be put on the cart for the next day's march. The man was plainly very ill but the MO also took a closer look at George Rex and decided that the column had better go on without him. Rex had pneumonia and pleurisy and was left in a *Lazarett* on the east bank of the Elbe.

The only treatment that the MO with the party possessed and which had some chance of working, were a few Penicillin tablets which he crushed, made into a solution and injected every six hours. Despite going down from his normal 11st to 6st 4lb, George Rex recovered.

Tall, slim Sergeant Norman Leonard saw his more than 9st frame reduced to nearly 5st. Earlier he had acquired a folding chair from a public hall to use as a sled but now, as he staggered along, his feet bound in sacking, everything was abandoned apart from the clothes in which he stood.

Russian prisoners that the Kriegies passed were suffering from advanced starvation. The skeletal figures were foraging in dustbins where they retrieved potato peelings. Scraping off the covering of ash the peelings were quickly eaten. Kriegies wondered how long it would be before they were in that state. Even now they envied the Russians the peelings.

At one stop some Kriegies were accommodated in the stables of a *Wehrmacht* barracks. There was little warmth on the stone floor but it was at least out of the snow. In his near prostration, Don Bruce found the gushing of horse urine along a channel a few inches from his head only slightly disturbing.

The combination of malnutrition, dysentery and cold was too much for some men. Falling, they lay exhausted until a comrade summoned his own failing strength to drag them to their feet, only to fall again. Then his friend was too weak to help.

Eventually the column from Lamsdorf staggered into Zeigenheim in early March, but others had already joined the column from Bankau and they all finished their trek at Luckenwalde.

It was not only RAF men who were enduring these 'death' marches, British Army men, many of them prisoners since their capture near Dunkirk, were being force-marched westward from camps throughout Germany and Poland under the same appalling conditions. The criminal agonies were inflicted for no reason other than to keep them as hostages. In the end the marches served no purpose at all and for all the hardships and hunger within the camps at Fallingbostel, the men there had a roof over them and were slightly less miserable than their colleagues on the march from the camps in the east.

### GOODBYE TO SAGAN

Most residents of Stalag Luft 3 thought a move unlikely – 'the Jerries haven't enough transport, they can't spare the troops and they haven't got time'. The camp was geared to stay-put, with or without the Germans. As the Russians came nearer one food parcel a week was issued to each man instead of one between two. Now the officers were eating two or three hot meals a day. The bread issue was reduced and potato peelings were once more pressed into service. Boiled, mashed, mixed with almost any other food, the peelings were baked to form a kind of biscuit.

Despite the convictions of many Kriegies, everything pointed to an imminent move. The *Abwehr* gave permission for large packs to be made without the risk of confiscation, but still most Kriegies found it difficult to visualise a mass move involving 10,000 men. Those who remained unconvinced by the prevalent feeling were the men from the Italian camps. They had seen it before and made their preparations.

During the last week in January the previous monastic/university flavour to life changed. Geoff Hobbs described it so:

'With the Russian advance to the Oder within 60 miles of the camp, the sudden increase in front-line aircraft activity, the shuddering rumble of artillery, the bombing from the south and the east and the mushroom growth of rumours, the whole camp became animated, reaching a fever pitch towards the end of the week when the Russians crossed the Oder south of Breslau and commenced the siege of the city itself.'

Ken Chapman was busily sewing braces as straps on his haversack when 'the big flap' began. Morale in Luft 3 and Belaria had been soaring since the Russians' offensive from Baganov had begun. Now at the end of January 1945 the sound of artillery could be clearly heard. Speculation about liberation was rife and as the sound of the guns became louder and the Russians nearer, a move seemed less likely. That made the order at 9.00pm on the evening of Saturday 27 January, to be prepared to move out of Luft 3 and Belaria immediately, a profound shock.

Geoff Fletcher in the North compound had just finished the first rubber of a game of bridge when a Kriegie burst into the room shouting, 'Evacuating the camp in an hour!'. Greeted by cries of disbelief he shouted, 'No! this is gen, Bill Jennens just yelled it out'. Squadron Leader Jennens was the camp adjutant. The order was from the *Kommandant*, *Oberst* Braune. Only portable kit could be taken.

Cards were abandoned, appetites temporarily banished and the room became like a bear garden. Made-up haversacks were packed and re-packed, excess clothes were thrown on the floor. Just as suddenly appetite returned when it was found they had some time to spare. Cakes were made of the flour and packed for easy carrying. Potatoes were cooked and eaten as a last meal before the trek into the unknown. It was no time for hoarding. Thick slices of bread were spread lavishly with jam so that the full flavours could be relished. Food was not to be left behind. What could not be eaten was stuffed into the haversacks. Cigarettes, the international currency, were pushed into every corner or pocket. Someone calculated that a man could only carry 20lb for a considerable time, particularly as the snow was four to six inches deep. Sledges were made from any materials available. One sledge six-feet long, was constructed from the side of a bunk. Furniture was broken up and inside walls of the huts torn down to make others. The Australians, with their experience of humping swag, quickly made blanket/bed rolls.

Hobbs dressed for a winter march of unknown length. He first put on a heavy woollen vest, then a light pair of pants, a pair of pyjamas, three pullovers, a jacket, a pair of trousers, overcoat, gloves, scarf, socks and boots. Others were dressed similarly and most carried a change of everything. Hobbs' greatest regret was that of abandoning valuable books and papers, plus the prospect of leaving a comparatively comfortable 'pit' for some unpredictable resting place.

Hobbs felt the atmosphere of excitement was not unlike that before an operational trip: 'nervousness, elation, a tendency to panic, and over all an effort to keep calm and go about the necessary jobs unhurriedly and methodically'. There was also relief of tension and uncertainty.

False starts irritated and rumours proliferated. It was said that an enormous offensive had started in the west to match that in the east and that Hitler had been offered peace terms. Word came from the SBO, Group Captain Wilson RAAF, that he considered it unwise for anyone to attempt to escape. Another rumour said that *Feldwebel* Glemnitz had mentioned that anyone wishing to stay behind and take their chance with the Russians could do so. When American officer Irving Grosskind decided to try he found Glemnitz waving a sub-machine gun and shouting that there were too many.

It was past midnight when a dejected Grosskind returned to his North compound room. A room-mate remembered it was now Grosskind's birthday and he had a cake secreted away – so they celebrated. Word came from the sick quarters that anyone unfit for marching was to report to the gate immediately.

Touring around the compound, Kriegies found the 'Foodacco' store had been thrown open for anyone to help themselves. Barry Hamblin found a rough sledge which the orderlies had used for the cookhouse rations. Although his group had previously thought of making a sledge to carry all their kit, the notice had been too short. This find was a godsend. Barry and George Woods set to work strengthening and making it suitable for the road. Soon the loaded 'Flagship' – as they dubbed the sledge – was dragged outside by its knotted sheet tow ropes, ready for the off.

Hobbs wandered from room to room. Every one was a shambles of broken shelves, torn down cupboards, the floors covered with broken wood, discarded clothes and Kriegie-made cooking pans. But not everything could be carried. Corporal Fred Turner masquerading as Flight Lieutenant Rex Reynolds, saw hundreds of thousands of cigarettes deliberately ruined by water. As little as possible was to be left for the Germans. In the belief that the Red Army would be in the camp within days, Squadron Leader Donald Waterer tried out his Russian with a chalked message of congratulation on the wall.

Many extra tins of food were thrown over the barbed wire to the Russian prisoners who threw back matches, an essential for Kriegies on the move. *Wehrmacht* and civilians would certainly dash into the camp as the Kriegies left.

After several false starts the men straggled to the main gates, stopping at the parcels store where one or more American Red Cross parcels were handed to each man. Those with sledges took as many as six per man. Geoff Fletcher decided that his one parcel would cause him enough trouble, and that as he would not need to smoke or wash he dumped his cigarettes and soap.

At the main gate, lit by compound perimeter lights, a single file of men streamed into the *Vorlager*. The muffled figures, dressed in great-coats, balaclava helmets, their trousers tucked into their socks, blanket rolls around their shoulders and shapeless packs on their backs, shuf-fled through the gates on to the snow-covered road. Almost every man dragged a sledge of some kind. The crunch and rumble of runners on the snow was punctuated by cries of 'Stop!' or 'Forward!' as these unwieldy vehicles tended to go their own way.

The procession wound in a huge arc through the *Vorlager* of the West compound, disappearing into the darkness beyond the bright lights of the guardhouse. It was 4.00am when the tired men from the last hut in the North compound passed from the camp, collecting their food parcels as they left. Ken Chapman was aggrieved to see the guards also carrying parcels. He calculated that 20,000 Red Cross parcels were left behind.

The West compound and the Americans in the South compound were already on the road ahead when the column from the North com-pound followed, snaking across the snowy countryside. Guards walked at intervals alongside, struggling to maintain some sort of order. The roadsides were already strewn with broken sledges, clothing, food, even a saxophone. Civilians were reaping a rich harvest and the guards picked up and carried what they could despite their load of an enormous pack and rifle.

Most sports gear and musical instruments from the camp were collected by the YMCA. By approximately 11.00pm the Kriegies in the South compound had moved out. By 12.30am the West compound had emptied, by 4.00am the North and by 6.30am the East compound was cleared. In all 9,500 British and American flyer Kriegies marched from Sagan and Belaria on 27/28 January 1945 in bright moonlight alternat-ing with snowstorms. Eight days later 500 sick men were taken by box-cars to a camp near Nuremberg.

The officers at Sagan had previously formed themselves into Messes in their rooms which normally contained about 12 men. Now they formed themselves into more convenient small 'Combines' such as those which had been usual in the large rooms into which the NCOs had been crowded.

Everyone regretted the treasures left behind, particularly the books accumulated over the years. Les Sidwell carefully selected two slim volumes that would fit into his pocket and bring a flavour of England to him no matter where the Kriegies finished up. They were *A Cotswold Village* by J. Arthur Gibbs and *Shakespeare* by Drinkwater.

Spitfire pilot Ken Campbell desperately hoped that his wounded leg would cope with the walk. There were others more severely disabled than he who would have to be transported, but space was always limited. He decided to take his chance and march with the others.

Heroic efforts had been made to escape from Stalag Luft 3 and many of their friends had been killed. As the Kriegies walked from Sagan they left behind their Memorial to 'the Fifty'. As he walked through the main gate for the last time, a suitcase slung on a pole on the shoulders between him and friend 'Max' Bear, Ken Chapman reckoned that with the addition of the issued parcel his pack now weighed 40lb. The line of prisoners ahead and behind him seemed endless. Armed but fewer *Luftwaffe* guards marched alongside, some with vicious appearing Alsatian dogs.

Once on the main road the long column was almost lost among thousands of civilians fleeing to the west. The peasant farmers' carts, lit by the grey dawn, were dragged through the snow by skinny, exhausted horses or oxen. Their column stretched from the eastern horizon to that in the west. They sat grimly guarding their meagre possessions, looking half-frozen in the bitter wind and staring ahead with a look of utter resignation and sorrow. Peter Hewitt was moved by the pitiful sight of the old, the women and the children, and yet he felt that they were only receiving their just reward for all the misery the German nation had brought upon the people of Europe for the past five years.

The desperate fuel shortage was demonstrated by lorries towing one, two or even three others with frequently a staff car tacked on behind. While crossing the main Breslau to Berlin Autobahn, the Kriegies detoured around buses and lorries abandoned, broken-down or out of fuel. Even troops heading for the Eastern Front were travelling in horse-drawn carts. A breakdown of organisation, shortage of war material and sheer panic was apparent.

Opportunities for escape were now more frequent, the guards were too few to effectively watch the Kriegies, and their morale was at its lowest ebb. But most Kriegies were convinced that the end of the war was only a matter of days or, at the most weeks away, that the perils of escape were hardly justified. The risks incurred in breaking away and hiding until the Russians overtook them were great. There was safety in numbers so most were resigned to trudge along to wherever the Germans might be taking the column.

At first the going was comparatively good in four inches of crisp snow. The Kriegies were in good spirits and highly delighted to be outside the 'bloody' wire. When the column turned on to another main road they found large stretches of bare road surface which the wind had swept clear of snow. Many of the sledges were impossible to move and the first of the Red Cross parcel contents were abandoned. The Kriegies took out the cigarettes and chocolate, leaving the remainder by the roadside. Campbell was amused to see the guards sneak up to an abandoned sledge and craftily help themselves to items they fancied, but most was 'won' by wide-awake civilians to whom the jettisoned food must have been a windfall.

Les Sidwell was forced to abandon his precious suitcase after five miles. Gone were extra shirts, pullovers, socks, underwear and papers. The lanes through which the column now passed were remote and quiet, wending only through small hamlets but the news spread quickly about this strange, long procession of men who were throwing away valuable commodities into the snowdrifts. Local people, mostly the young and old, turned out in large numbers to pounce on this unexpected bounty. Flight Lieutenant Frank Phillips remarked to his friend:

'The poor sods will need all they can get with the Ruskies heading for them.'

'Serves the bastards right,' said another Kriegie, 'they grabbed things when they could, now they've got it coming to them!'

Yet there was much kindness handed out from the cottages that the Kriegies passed and the condition of the refugees, many of whom had trudged hundreds of miles, excited the pity of the prisoners. The struggling very young and the old, the pregnant women and the sick made one despairingly angry at the futility of war and the agonies it brought with it. There was no glamour here, nothing but utter misery, degradation and death.

Sidwell spoke to people who had abandoned homesteads at Rawitsch and Lissa. For them it had been a nightmare journey through the worst winter for years. The refugees had little idea of their destination, only that it was in the west and away from the advancing Russians.

The halts were a mixed blessing, the Kriegies, almost dropping with exhaustion and bathed in perspiration, cooled down rapidly, their sweat immediately freezing into a film of ice and clothes stiffening to the hardness of boards. As Flying Officer 'Eddie' Poulter rubbed a strained ligament in his leg he looked up and saw Wing Commander Maling, his squadron CO, passing in the Belaria contingent.

Every hour and a half the column stopped for a 10-minute rest. The guards seemed dispirited and moved into the ranks of the prisoners for protection from the worsening blizzard. That night the exhausted men rested in a school and church in Halbau, not daring to remove their frozen boots. Bartering took place with German civilians and some men obtained that most precious commodity, bread, in exchange for cigarettes and some squares of chocolate.

Peter Hewitt was astounded by the friendliness of the German people and the refugees. No longer were they enemies but human beings who were all suffering the same terrible conditions of fear, cold and hunger. Children wandered into the school, staring at the Kriegies with childish curiosity while trading continued briskly with the older refugees. In the playground outside where Kriegies had started fires to make hot drinks, Hewitt saw several bearded Kriegies, each squatting beside a brazier with a child on each knee, half-perished with cold, feeding them with pieces of chocolate or sugar lumps. The children seemed sweet and innocent to the Kriegies who had not seen their like for so long. Those in the school were apparently without parents or homes and were pitifully thinly clad, but they were clean and nicely dressed in clothing of bright *ersatz* wool. A few slept in the warmth of the school with the Kriegies that night. The thousands of youngsters seemed to the prisoners to be the last tangible asset of the once great German nation.

Squeezed into the school hall, Sidwell saw for the first time the working of their radio (codename 'Jimmy Higgins'). His combine, squeezed into the floor space beneath a baby grand, were further pushed over by Lou Barry, Howard Cundall and Sydney Smith who tuned in to the BBC, the approaches to the hall well covered by 'stooges'.

Pilot Officer Howard Cundall, one of the men operating the radio beneath the grand piano, was not an RAF man at all. He had been shot down in November 1941 on a radar investigation flight over France, and managed to successfully pass himself off as the second pilot of the Wellington. Cundall was a civilian radar expert who had constructed a radio receiver and a transmitter from the odd pieces of junk smuggled into the camp, or illegally bought from 'tame' goons. At one time Cundall had established an almost daily contact with London, sometimes even during the blizzard march from Sagan.

The morning was cold and it was snowing again. At 5.30am the Halbau town square was crowded with refugees and their carts. The Sagan officers set off, Chapman and his friend Max Bear pulling their priceless sledge. Throughout the day endless streams of refugees passed their column but a party of 100 British soldier prisoners passed in the opposite direction. They had been evacuated from a camp near Breslau and were making for, of all places, Sagan. It seemed so senseless.

In one small town where the column stopped to eat their diminishing rations the *Bürgermeister* strongly protested at having the British airmen in his village. The Kriegies swarmed over the town, bartering cigarettes and chocolate for bread and eggs or a bath. A night's lodging was also bartered for a few, but they were not to stay. There were so many prisoners in this small village that although the local people were friendly, the attitude of the *Bürgermeister* and fear of the local *Gestapo* brought orders for them to move on. Geoff Hobbs saw the huge *Unteroffizier* who had kicked up a stink about the unconventional occupation of the town. Surrounded by a small, admiring group of black romper-suited *Hitler Jugend*, he was shouting orders and waving a scatter-gun. There was no point in arguing with the enraged and dangerous man.

The column carried on still accompanied by refugees. After a cold and sleepless night they were off again at 4.30am. Again a milk churn was found and almost emptied before the guards' intervention. In several hamlets some of the villagers passed hot coffee to a few of the nearest men. By now, one or two of the Kriegies were looking wild-eyed, their minds wandering. The slog through the snow and the bitter north-easter were taking their toll.

'Every few minutes,' Alec Burton said, 'I saw a man crack up and topple over, a still figure in the snow. Perhaps a friend would stay beside him but sometimes those close by were too near to the end themselves to notice, or care.'

A few were left behind in a German military hospital, others in houses along the way. No-one could stop with them for long, a bayonet or a threatening sub-machine gun forced others to stagger on. Leaving behind a crew member or friend was a heart rending agony.

Through Priebus and on to Muskau. There Les Sidwell and John Leetham, sheltering in the doorway of a factory, heard music from within. The beautiful slow woodwind movement of Dvorak's *Carnival Overture* momentarily took them away from the ice and snow. Then they moved into a glass factory for the night. In the factory there was no messing about with 'blowers', elbowing the glass blowers aside the Kriegies hung their pots on long poles and, standing well back, dipped the pots briefly in the furnaces. Then they were quickly withdrawn with the contents boiling. Here was comparative luxury. A staff of women in a kitchen worked hard to get water heated for 'brews' and Ken Chapman was able to have a bath in a tub. Fred Turner described it as a Kriegie paradise. Peter Hewitt was delighted that the place was so warm but for Eddie Poulter and his section it was almost too warm and stuffy. They had been put into air-raid shelters directly beneath the furnaces – but who would complain after the freezing horror outside.

Next morning the Kriegies awoke to find the factory in full production. The workers were unconcerned about the hundreds of blanket-swathed prisoners spread over the floor. Women and girls stepped over recumbent bodies as they worked the conveyor belts and ignored them as they tested long lines of bottles for flaws. The prisoners chatted in bad German and French to the girls as they dressed, shaved and ate their breakfast.

The Kriegies could tell that the Germans were a desperately war-weary people who yearned for an end to the long, bitter struggle which had brought them and the rest of the world such bloodshed and misery. Peter Hewitt believed that 'win, draw or lose, they now did not give a damn'. There was no animosity directed at the Kriegies: the women's miseries and war sickness appeared to have left no room for personal hatred.

After a long cold wait in the blacked-out streets Hobbs was one of those directed into a cinema. The seats had been removed and Hobbs described their entry into the auditorium as, 'crowding in like a herd of wild horses'. Wing Commander 'Digger' Larkin tried to keep order in the confusion of 300 to 400 'self-centred Kriegies all endeavouring to occupy twice as much space as they should'. The cinema had several priceless qualities: it was a warm shelter, there was water on tap, it had flush toilets and there was even air conditioning. All these benefits in a place with gaily decorated walls were novelties to the Kriegies. Hobbs found that when settled down, lying shoulder to shoulder, 'and breathing alternately by numbers', they could just manage. With his knees drawn up, his body crushed tightly by others on either side and a Kriegie lying across his feet, Geoff Hobbs slept soundly.

Ken Campbell was in a queue waiting to go into the cinema. It was to be only temporary accommodation for a few. One Kriegie, a fluent German speaker, persuaded an elderly woman in the house next door to allow six of them to sleep in the basement of her house. The Hausfrau was kind, giving them straw to put on the floor and a carpet to lay on top. The Kriegies were pleased and gave the old lady coffee and chocolate which so overjoyed her that she gave them coal to light the boiler in the basement. At last there was the joy of warmth, a hot meal and the luxury of a steaming bath. But informers were at work. A neighbour reported to the police that prisoners were in a private house. They were roughly ordered out by guards. Slowly they packed their kit and moved into the already crowded cinema. The lady was sorry to see them go.

Whilst waiting in the freezing snow Fletcher saw a Kriegie walking up and down the line of immobile men shouting, 'What's the matter with you? Keep your feet moving! Come on, come on!' Fletcher thought it a bit dramatic, but it was shaming enough to get them moving about. Some already knew that frostbite was eating into their toes. Looking back he saw a man standing stock still, swaying as if about to faint. When others reached him they found him frozen like a rigid statue. They dragged him into cover and with continuous massage his circulation was painfully restored.

A guard who had thrown much of his equipment away sank slowly to his knees in the slush. He was helped to his feet, muttering, 'Krieg ist Krieg'. His rifle was loaded onto someone's vehicle. Kriegies and guards helped each other in a situation which was now no longer a war between them but a case of human beings helping each other in their struggle for survival. The outdoor temperature dropped even further and some of the guards who were forced to stay outside were in a worse state, one eventually having both his legs amputated and another his foot.

The next day was spent in rest, drying out and bartering with the German civilians. A thaw rendered sledges useless. Some Kriegies made carts or obtained prams. That night half of the men moved on, the rest waited until the following morning. To their happy surprise half a Red Cross parcel was issued to each man, no-one knew or could guess from where they had come.

At 6.00pm the men from North compound were told that they would entrain for a camp on the north coast near Bremen, and more than 500 men from other compounds were to join them. The following morning they joined forces with officers from Belaria for the last part of their march where they passed German soldiers digging tank traps. Refugee carts and even old Fiacres from the Kaiser's day plodded on in an endless stream as the Kriegies took a rest during an air-raid warning. At Spremburg the column descended a steep hill towards the station. The wheels of two carts became locked together and one overturned throwing the occupants to the cobbles. Kriegies rushed to help but a child was badly hurt.

At the station the Kriegies were ordered into two separate trains of box-cars, one destined for the camp at Luckenwalde, south of Berlin, the other for Marlag-Milag Nord near Tarmstedt Ost, beyond Bremen. A similar train of box-cars ground to a halt alongside that of the Kriegies. It was filled with young girls, refugees from the east. The English of one of the older girls was restricted to 'I love you' and 'How do you do?'. Frank Waddington replied in his best but limited German, 'Ich liebe dich!' and 'Kein Trinkwasser!'.

The journey was tortuous. On the second night the train passed through Brunswick and Magdeburg, but it was not until 8.00am on 4 February that the train reached Hanover and 5.30pm when the Kriegies de-trained at Tarmstedt Ost for the 1-mile walk through the snow to Marlag at Westertimke. Searches and delays kept some outside for up to eight hours. They were wet, freezing cold, thirsty and near starvation, many at the point of complete exhaustion by the time they entered the bare rooms. A wash, a hot brew and straw on the floor was enough to settle them down for the night. All were 'absolutely flaked out' said one who fell into a heap in a corner and slept solidly for a day.

It was to be another sleepless night for the other party of officers from Sagan. Just before dusk the next day their train of box-cars clanked and clanged noisily into Luckenwalde station. In 19 hours it had covered only 56 miles. When the column of Kriegies left the train to march to Luckenwalde camp they sang. It was February, late afternoon, dark and bitterly cold but they sang. The promise of rest, warmth and food lifted their spirits and the old service songs *Tipperary, Keep the Home Fires Burning* and a deeply felt *Take me back to dear old Blighty* rippled down the length of the column. But an air-raid warning with a blackout had left them crowded, hungry and miserably numb. It was to be nearly 12 hours after leaving the train before they were deloused, showered, searched and allowed to enter the camp proper. It was a bitter disappointment: Ken Chapman looked in dismay at the squalid conditions of what he thought the worst hovel imaginable. He, who had known the horrors of Fresnes and Buchenwald, 'could have wept like a child'.

### THE TRUDGE FROM GROSS TYCHOW

To the rumble of Russian artillery on 6 February 1945, a party of Kriegies who had experienced brutality and the worst horrors of the previous sweltering summer were now to be subjected to the misery of a forced winter march. This was to be one of the longest slogging marches on minimal food for any Kriegies.

The inmates of Gross Tychow were warned in the early hours that they would be leaving. At 11.30am parties moved into the *Vorlager* where they were issued with a Red Cross parcel and one-third of a loaf of sawdust bread. It was the first bread they had seen for a month. They passed the unmanned sentry boxes and the sick-bay where 200 of the prisoners were to be left behind to await the arrival of the Russians. Passing the Keifheide road which had been the scene of the brutal blood-letting of the previous summer, they pressed on, fresh and rested and glad to be on the other side of the wire. But the euphoria could not last: after a few miles the ice, snow, slush and mud made progress difficult. The Kriegies were glad to throw themselves down in the straw of a barn. It was here that a rat nipped Cec Room on the cheek after gnawing its way through straw and a blanket.

Each gruelling day was a struggle for the strength to carry on and of haggling with refugees, Poles, Russians and Frenchmen, for anything eatable. Cec Room bought two cattle cakes from a Russian, dabbed on a little jam and found them reasonably palatable. When later he washed in a pig trough he decided that he really was living like an animal.

During the night of 24 February two men were taken out of the barn with stomach pains. They died, bringing the total known deaths since they had left Gross Tychow to nine. When the column went through a village at 9.00am a funeral was in progress. At least, Kriegies thought grimly, he is past caring who wins the war.

Vic Clarke was still using his diplomatic skills as he had during the 'Insterburg' voyage and the Keifheide 'run'. Now he calmed furious farmers whose stock of chickens and milk vanished with the advance of the Kriegie column. He lost count of the times he faced a threatening shotgun.

On 19 March the tattered, tottering, dishevelled and starving column was passed by a similar group of British soldier prisoners. Each column yelled encouragement to the other. Cec Room was reminded of the old Army cry, 'Are we downhearted?' and the certain reply of an emphatic, 'No!'.

It was not until 28 March that the column arrived at Falling-bostel. Many had died on the way but the majority at last reached Ebstorf station after 51 days and 380 miles of frostbite, hunger and exhaustion. There, 80 weary men were packed into each truck and entrained for Stalag 11B. On 29 March they were met at the gate by Sergeant-Major Lord, the highly respected senior NCO of the Army prisoners. To Bill Baird, Lord looked enormous and a much needed, steady rock.

## RED CROSS RESCUE

Stalag 3A at Luckenwalde, although frequently used as a transit camp, was a well established prisoner-of-war camp and contained people of every nation and race enslaved or imprisoned by the Germans. A main street bisected the camp with numerous side roads and compounds on each side. The German quarters were as big as all the prisoners' accommodation at Bankau. Russians, Italians, Frenchmen, Poles, Serbs, American and Commonwealth officer and NCO aircrew lived in separate compounds. The RAF aircrew had the worst quarters except for the USAAF enlisted men who followed them into the camp and were housed in marquees. Accommodated there was a complete battalion of the US Artillery which had been overrun during the Ardennes offensive. The Americans were young, raw troops, shocked and demoralised by the fierceness of the attacks of the battle-hardened *Waffen SS* and their subsequent treatment as prisoners.

Each barrack hut was made up of two large rooms usually containing about 180 men, although many rooms contained nearly twice that number. Three-tier bunks blocked out most of the natural light and the artificial light was sparse. Separating the rooms was the washroom space and the kitchen. There were no cooking utensils and little fuel for the two stoves in each room.

Outside there were the usual insanitary 'multi-holer' lavatories, always occupied with sick and weakened men suffering the agonies of dysentery and diarrhoea. Exercise space was limited by the wire surrounding four barrack blocks, and the bleak and dismal view was that of similar compounds.

Ken Chapman looked with pity and compassion at the condition of the exhausted RAF NCO Kriegies as they arrived from Bankau. Some were close to death from the lack of food and the trials of the journey. Eddie Poulter reckoned that the NCOs looked 'absolutely all in and in terrible shape'. Frustrated at not being able to help them, the officers from Sagan threw cigarettes over the barbed wire as the NCOs dragged themselves towards their barracks.

The daily food for each man was a bowl of dirty, weak soup and one 53-ounce sawdust loaf between seven men. The only warm drink was mint tea which was unacceptable to British stomachs. It is hardly surprising that in their desperation some men succumbed to the temptation to steal bread from their fellows.

Soldier prisoners from an Irish regiment billeted at the opposite end of the hut boiled a large tin of water and Albert Bracegirdle had his first painful shave and wash-down for a month. The weather was so bitterly cold that Bracegirdle was glad to crawl on to his straw-filled palliasse and pull every piece of clothing he possessed over himself. He lay there, shivering and hungry – and thinking of the vast amounts of leftovers in RAF dining halls.

The Germans did their best to restrict contact between the compounds. The RAF NCOs' compound was on the opposite side of the road to that of the officers, and many men recognised members of their crews but the Germans objected, sometimes violently, to contacts. The enormous quantities of barbed wire were extended and the coils between the fences built higher and denser. Hopes that had once been high of release and of going home were crushed by the latest move. Hunger and the fortifying of the barbed wire brought on deep depression that drove some men to the point of suicide. Success was usually prevented by the vigilance of those with steadier minds.

The interminable roll-calls, when the Germans were unable to reconcile the count with their figures, left the men frozen and weak and almost unable to stand. Soon 200 out of 350 men stayed in their barrack rooms when called for Appell because they were unable to crawl to the parade ground. Bob Cutts noted in his diary: 'We all feel very weak and black-out when we stand up suddenly and have been advised to lie still during the day and conserve strength.'

On Saturday 17 February a representative of the Swiss Protecting Power visited the camp and was appalled. He said he would lodge a strong protest with the German camp authorities. It produced no immediate result. The Germans were past caring.

Morale was lifted a little on Sunday 18 February when Church of England Padre Collins held an ecumenical service encouraging the men to hold on. Prayers were answered on Friday 2 March when a delivery of American Red Cross parcels arrived, enough for a parcel shared between two men. It was the first for two months.

Rooms in Luckenwalde were in an uproar as the parcels were opened. Bracegirdle compared it to Christmas as the men shared out tins of cigarettes, peanut butter, Klim dried milk, meat, jam, sardines, salmon, raisins or prunes, chocolate or cocoa. Thereafter there was a deluge of parcels for the Americans, French and Irish and finally there were 126,000 parcels in store. Each man was to receive a parcel every Tuesday until the store was empty.

On 16 March Bob Cutts was surprised to see a remembered face in German officer's uniform. Sauntering into the barrack room was the well-known heavyweight boxer Max Schmeling. Schmeling's instantly recognisable bruiser's features were frequently on the sports pages of

British newspapers before the outbreak of war. Schmeling had been world heavyweight boxing champion for a brief period, scoring his greatest fame knocking out Joe Louis. But now he was anything but aggressive. Carefully evading war subjects he was all smiles and autographs. Schmeling was a *Fallschirmjäger* and his propaganda photograph, supposedly showing him jumping by parachute from a Junkers Ju52 transport aircraft, was featured in *Der Adler*. His presence in the prisoner-of-war camp was puzzling.

The almost daily visits of Fortress and Liberator bombers to the Berlin and Leipzig areas, and the Mosquito raids twice or three times a night to 'The Big City' cheered the Kriegies. Luckenwalde was only 20 miles south of Berlin and now that they had less worry about food the prisoners were an appreciative audience of the brilliant spectacle of the coloured target indicators and the bursting of bombs.

## CONCENTRATION CAMP CAMPAIGN

'Wings' Day and his friends had not been idle despite being in Sachsenhausen concentration camp. 'Jimmy' James and Sydney Dowse had been chief tunnellers, burrowing their way out with 'Wings', Major Dodge and Jack Churchill cooperating in the arrangements and planning. Their freedom was not to last long. Day and Dowse were recaptured together. Seen by an elderly woman who suspected them of being looters, they were arrested and separated. 'Wings' Day had read something of the killing of the Sagan escapers in German newspapers so when he was handcuffed and driven away he wondered if he was to receive the same treatment. His destination, back in Sachsenhausen but this time in the death cells, seemed to confirm his fears. Still handcuffed and with one ankle chained to the floor, he was apprehensive, cold and fully expecting a call from a hangman. He hoped he would be strong.

After two weeks of slogging through bad weather Jack Churchill and 'Jimmy' James were captured by *Volkssturm*, handcuffed and sent back to the cells at Sachsenhausen. Sydney Dowse and Major Dodge were already there.

In this charnel house few survived. Of the population of the cell block of approximately 100, there were but 13 left after an orgy of executions following an order to reduce their numbers. Perhaps the airmen's apparent reprieve was partly due to Dowse's brilliant lie. Like Clarke and Yeo-Thomas, he said he had communicated their conditions and presence in Sachsenhausen to the world outside. He said that he had written and posted letters to the International Red Cross and the *Kommandant* at Sagan detailing their escape and incarceration. It was important that Sagan was a *Luftwaffe* managed camp. Had they been shot the perpetrators would have needed a plausible excuse – not that it would have worried them too much. Later 'Wings' Day, James, Dowse and Dodge were returned to the *Sonderlager*, to the delight of their friends who had not expected to see them again.

### MARLAG

The column of RAF officers from Sagan that eventually arrived at the old Merchant Navy Marlag at Westertimke were those from the North compound, and half of those who had marched out from the East compound. There was a minimum of furnishings and cooking facilities but a roof was a shelter. The interminable searches before entering the compound had taken a toll of the waiting men. Many were ill after their privations and collapsed in the mud outside the gate. When their turn came they had to be carried inside by their comrades.

Although primitive, the conditions gradually improved. Kriegie ingenuity and improvisation made living a little easier. There were still many suffering from stomach disorders and everyone found their stamina had all but disappeared. There was no indoor latrine and the nearest outdoor *Abort* was 50 yards from the huts. On a wintry rainy night, when two or three visits were necessary, it became a torment. But in mid-February everyone believed that the war had a short time to run and they could put up with the hardship.

At Marlag in early April, when the sound of British guns could be heard as they pounded Bremen and air-raids could be seen on Bremen and Hamburg, there was widespread disbelief that the Germans would move the Kriegies again. But the British troops seemed to have come to a halt at the Weser, contenting themselves with a small bridgehead. A special parade was called to pass on orders from the Oberkommando der *Wehrmacht* that the Kriegies were to be moved away from the fighting – for their benefit. It fooled no-one. Their intentions were clear: the prisoners were to be, at best, held as hostages and at worst exterminated. The ruthless *SS* were thought to be between them and the Allies.

The SBO, Group Captain Wray, said he would refuse to allow the men to be moved and although applauding his sentiments the Kriegies knew it would be of little use. The rifles and machine guns were still pointing in their direction. The Kriegies were told to pack up and be ready to move by 6.30pm that evening. Two and a half Red Cross parcels were issued to take up the stock and they left at 10.00am the next morning, 10 April. Two RAF aircraft raked the column with fire on the 12th

**'He's been doing it all day!'**

and two Kriegies were killed. On the 16th the column crossed the Elbe by boat

When the Kriegies arrived at Lübeck on the 23rd they were taken straight to the new artillery barracks, where they found a few of their friends had been for three days already. They had volunteered to travel by box-car and only suffered one rainy night. The accommodation at the barracks was good and there was no barbed wire. The prisoners felt free although the camp became very overcrowded as large parties of all nationalities arrived continuously.

The main party from Marlag were camped in farms around Lübeck, most at Trenthorst. They were happy to stay. The news was that most of Germany was already occupied by the Allies. There was talk that the Germans might ship the Kriegies off to Norway where a last stand was to be made. It seemed unlikely but the suspense and anxiety were unsettling. Allied planes flew over frequently, making the Kriegies nervous about the possibility of being shot-up again. On the parade ground they marked out the letters RAF POW.

On 2 May, a large parade of Germans was addressed by a senior officer who told them that Hitler had fallen at his post in combat with the Russians, but Germans, he said, must remember that the war would go on. They must continue to fight for their country.

Later that day there were loud explosions in the direction of Lübeck and huge columns of smoke were seen above the city. Two hundred yards from the barrack wall a sunken road passed under a road bridge and at 5.00pm a tank and an armoured vehicle halted beneath the bridge. Then more vehicles arrived and stopped behind those below. Mad with excitement, the Kriegies lined the wall of the barrack. The armoured vehicles moved up the road towards them. A few daring spirits jumped over the wall and ran towards the tanks. A continuous stream of armour passed the camp. Minutes later a jeep turned into the main gate followed by two British lorries. The British Army had arrived.

The German guards had been packing all day. They 'fell in' with their luggage and were quietly marched away under the watchful eyes of a couple of British soldiers. The Kriegies at Lübeck were free.

A column had moved out from Marlag on the afternoon of 9 April, the Kriegies using every possible ruse to delay progress. They had not marched far when the *Kommandant* ordered them to turn back. He was worried by a visible air-raid on Kiel and by Mosquito aircraft roaming the skies at will. The Kriegies were worried too, they had left a message by spreading German white-washing powder over the ground spelling out in the brief language that airmen would understand, 'RAF FINGER OUT! MOVING EAST'. The Germans disapproved and raked the message to illegibility in the sandy soil.

That night there was little sleep for the Kriegies. Food was plentiful so they used their fuel on cooking the food they had been forced to leave behind.

At dawn on the 10th they marched off again. The pace, set by Group Captain Wray and the senior officers at the head of the column, was deliberately slow. The *Kommandant* was told that those behind would not be able to keep up a faster step. The dragging feet were covering little more than half a mile an hour. The German camp officers travelled in cars and trucks loaded high with their possessions, food and records. The pace was abysmally slow but the end was near.

The main roads were continually under air attack so the column of prisoners was led through by-roads and tracks. Their home-made carts began to break down on the rough surfaces. As it was impossible to carry more on their loaded backs, the airmen were soon leaving a trail of discarded kit. The slow progress allowed the Kriegies to trade with the local inhabitants. Cigarettes were the valuable commodity which could be exchanged for eggs and bread. Refugees fleeing from the Russians still impeded the column but it was to the Western Allies that they were now nearing.

There was an odd aside to their march. At a brief halt eight small girls appeared and sang to the Kriegies as they lay on the grass banks. As the young voices sang *Kommt ein Vogel* Les Sidwell was touched by the children's innocence and complete lack of fear of the *Terrorfliegers*.

Armed *Wehrmacht* guards still flanked the column as it crawled forward but their control became increasingly nominal as they struggled to keep going beneath their enormous packs. Studying them closely, Geoff Fletcher still had not the slightest doubt that they would have fired at anyone who attempted to escape across the fields.

By early evening the men were told to spread themselves over farm fields and settle for the night. It was no hardship in the perfect weather and a lead was taken by the Australians who possessed camping skills. Turf was cut and soon fires were burning smokily and bargained eggs were poached in sardine tins. Fletcher thought it quite idyllic as they settled down, smoking and chatting on the long, balmy, early summer evening, wrapped in blankets made up Aussie-style into sleeping bags that would not come apart in the night.

Several nights were spent in a similar way. Liberation had to be close but there were ugly rumours among the more pessimistic prisoners that the *Gestapo* or the *SS* would hold them as hostages or shoot them out of hand. The dangers were reinforced when a guard shot two Kriegies dead with little reason and a German officer, *Hauptmann* Deutsche, lost his temper, ordered the guards to 'put one up the spout' and brandished his pistol threateningly while wiping a flume of froth from his lips with his other hand. The Germans were in a desperate situation and they knew it. Some like the *Hauptmann* felt that the end for Germany and themselves was close. Their itching trigger fingers were a constant threat.

Two thousand men spread across several fields had become almost impossible to guard and control. A few prisoners decided to make a break for freedom but the majority felt there was safety in numbers. As the fighting neared there was an increasing danger of the unarmed prisoners becoming actively involved, and there was the ever present danger of air attack from the Typhoons, Mosquitoes and Spitfires searching for targets. Every evening blankets and towels were spread across the fields, the letters RAF and POW shown as plainly as possible. Persuaded by the Kriegies, the Germans displayed large red crosses on the trucks. That seemed to work until a lone, hedge-hopping Typhoon sprayed the trucks with cannon shells, killing a Naval officer who had been involved with the storming of the prison ship Altmark in 1940. Several other Kriegies, who had been sick and carried in the trucks, were wounded.

There had been speculation among the prisoners about Hitler's boasted secret-weapon rocket-projectile which was being fired at London and Amsterdam. The vapour trails of practice rockets had been seen by Kriegies at Thorn in July but now, near to Marlag, the prisoners were to see them in action. Without warning and with little sound, a great rocket with a brilliant orange tail ascended. Slowly at first the V2 rose vertically to a height of several thousand feet where it appeared to hang almost stationary for a few moments as it settled on its westerly heading, then it began to climb. Jack Lyon, wondering about its destination, watched it gather speed and disappear into a clear blue sky.

On 30 April at Trenthorst, a wealthy farming area, the *Kommandant* called a final halt. Their route had been roughly eastward and the *Kommandant* decided that he would rather be overtaken by the British or Americans than by the Russians. The SBO added his weight to the decision to stay where they were. He had heard rumours that so many prisoners had been crammed into Lübeck that they were all suffering from dysentery and typhus, and he refused to take his men any further. Campbell believed the *Kommandant* to be at his wits' end.

The area was rich dairy and beef farming country not far from the Danish border, and the Kriegies made themselves comfortable among the plentiful outhouses well stocked with straw. Kriegies roamed through the woods and some fished in the lake. To Ken Campbell it was a delightful place.

By now, the war front was close on the heels of the wandering officers. On the second morning at the farm the sound of gunfire was much nearer. It was rumoured that a party camped on the far side of the estate had seen a small British recce tank. At 2.00pm on 2 May, just as the Kriegies were debating about what kind of guns were involved, two British light tanks roared across the fields towards them. Swiftly the tank crews reported the Kriegies' position, told them to stay put and fought their way back to their tanks through the milling mass of happy men. They then roared off to carry on fighting.

In another part of the farm, to the surprise of John Mahoney, Ron Gibson and the men around them, a lone armoured scout car drove up. The *Wehrmacht* guards, quick to recognise their enemy, threw up their hands, their rifles clattering to the ground at their sides. Some prisoners stared in dumb disbelief, hardly daring to trust their eyes. Slowly their faces creased into smiles and they let out a yell which brought others running. Then a mighty cheer rang throughout the farm echoing back and forth. Kriegies surrounded the scout car to greet their liberators. The smiling Army lieutenant also radioed back that he had found

2,000 RAF prisoners-of-war and then continued signing autographs for the happy ex-Kriegies.

For many the journey home was protracted. They were taken in lorries to an Army Reception Centre which had already dealt with thousands of Army prisoners. There they were told that there were instructions to take them on to another post at Emsdetton. They were not pleased. When they arrived at Emsdetton on 5 May, the RAF men asked to be taken to an airfield to be flown home but were brusquely told that there were hundreds of soldiers already at the airfield, and the airmen must wait their turn. Some senior officers scrounged a lift to the airfield and a flight home in a Lancaster; other officers decided to make their own way back, leaving in various modes of 'acquired' transport.

Eventually Ken Campbell found himself in charge of a party of 300 RAF Kriegies, all anxious to get back to Britain. At Emsdetton he met a South African major who was also in charge of a party of airmen, and who had managed to get transport for his men to the airfield with the help of Wing Commander Barwell in charge of the Mosquito Wing at Rheine. Campbell quickly made the same arrangement, gave orders to round up all the RAF men in the town within an hour, told the furious lieutenant-colonel in charge of the Holding Depot that he was taking the RAF men from his charge, transported them to the airfield and got 30 home on the last plane out as the South African's final party left.

It was a start, but there was a further confrontation with the Army embarkation officer who said it was unfair to take the RAF men first. His men, he complained, had been waiting for days to fly home. Campbell retorted that had it not been for the Army the RAF would have gone a week previously. Then they reached a typically British compromise and agreed to take each aircraft alternately.

By 10 May all the men in Campbell's party were on their way back. Campbell and Flight Lieutenant Sandy were flown home in the last Lancaster to leave. Seated in the rest area they could see nothing throughout the flight. They were fighter men and this was the first time either had flown in a heavy bomber. Both were scared but their fear was as nothing compared to that of the accompanying Army men. When the aircraft arrived at the RAF airfield after dark the pilot overshot and, with that horrible sinking feeling among his edgy passengers, opened up the throttles to go round again. Everyone knew of the events on the previous day when a Lancaster had swung on landing and burst into flames. They were all glad when they stepped on to the firm earth of England.

For some the transition from prisoners to free men was rapid and bewildering. After spending a night in a hangar some ex-Kriegies were quickly flown back to Britain in Lancasters, but Geoff Fletcher studied the pilot of his Lancaster with some trepidation. He was an Australian with a monumental hangover from celebrating the end of the war, but apart from plomping the plane down for a very bumpy landing he brought them home safely.

Fletcher's Lancaster party were piled into two trucks and driven through the heart of celebrating London. It was VE-Day, 8 May. Whether by accident or design the party found themselves just two trucks behind Winston Churchill's car, crawling in a low gear between cheering crowds, in a stately triumphal procession along Whitehall.

### THE COMING AND GOING AT FALLINGBOSTEL

Disturbing tales from the guards were filtering through to the Kriegies at Fallingbostel. They were told that at nearby Bergen Belsen, a small town a few miles away, there was a camp where thousands were dying daily of starvation and disease. Ron Damman was sure the Germans were trying to intimidate the Kriegies – and succeeding.

The lack of facilities led to frayed tempers. Water, light, fuel and, most of all, food were desperately short. It had been a terrible winter, the lifeline of the Red Cross had been broken and everyone now existed on the bottom ration scale, while deliveries of even that was erratic. Hunger occupied every thought. The stealing of food from one's fellow Kriegies was considered the most heinous crime and punishment was swift and similar to that meted out to a Kriegie for the same offence at Sagan.

Sergeant 'Bas' Downing was horrified to see an airman, who had been caught stealing another's ration, frogmarched to the communal 50-holer latrine and dumped into the stinking, heaving mass beneath. As he tried to climb out he was pushed back with a pole and completely immersed. When he finally emerged, clawing excreta from his face, hair and clothes, all those watching drew away to a discreet distance. The man crawled and then staggered like a drunken man back to his hut only to find his clothes and belongings thrown outside. He was no longer welcome.

Fights, though few, were vicious. Opponents were quickly parted when they were RAF men but there was no-one who could separate two fighting Australian soldiers: their faces were a bloody, unrecognisable, misshapen mess before one of them could no longer lift himself from the dusty ground.

Rumours of a new move from Stalag 357 were persistent, even ousting food as a topic. One rumour stated that the Kriegies were to be marched into a redoubt in Denmark or the Black Forest where they would be held as hostages, and where the Germans would hold out forever. A more likely rumour was that the *SS* would take over the camp as the Allies advanced and then liquidate the prisoners. Stan Reed thought that a chilling probability.

'Dixie' Deans discussed the possibilities with other compound leaders. There was the chance that the *SS* would assemble the Kriegies in the *Appell* ground, take them in manageable groups near to the usual deep ditch and mow them down with machine guns. They knew that had happened in large numbers to the Poles, Russians and Yugoslavs, and were in no doubt that it could happen to them. The *SS* were experienced and proficient executioners.

Another possibility was that the *SS* would post a heavy guard on the huts, bottling up the men securely inside and then take them out, one room at a time, and shoot them. The Kriegies maintained a day and night watch on the main gates. It was planned that the prisoners, although weak, half-starved and unarmed, would rush the gate as soon as the *SS* entered and attempt a mass escape. There was no alternative. It was a forlorn hope but some might make it. The prayer was that Monty and the British First Army would make a sudden thrust and miraculously arrive in the nick of time. 'A bit like the 7th Cavalry at Little Bighorn – but look what happened to Errol Flynn,' someone said glumly.

Deans set out to reassure the men. He told them that a move appeared to be on, but the *Kommandant* had given his word that no harm would befall the Kriegies whilst under his command. The Kriegies half-trusted the *Kommandant* but also knew that if the *SS* arrived he would have no further influence on decisions.

The military 'experts' in Stalag 357 decided that Montgomery, then at Osnabrück, would advance to Hanover then make a pincer movement to capture Hamburg and Bremen. The same experts predicted that the inmates of the camps would be liquidated before Monty's men arrived.

Evacuation of camps around Fallingbostel was haphazard and disorganised. Unlike those winter 'death marches' this began in mild, sunny spring weather but the airmen who had struggled against starvation, illness and cold to cross Germany from Gross Tychow had only 11 hungry days, without treatment, to recover and begin another march. Their principal need was for water, a constant change of socks and food. Food had been very scarce.

Desperately hungry prisoners of all services had poured into the Fallingbostel Stalags throughout the first three months of 1945. Frostbite had damaged some permanently, leaving them in constant pain. On 6 April 'Dixie' Deans, who now also had the confidence of the Army prisoners, relayed the orders of the *Kommandant*. They were to march out of the camp and Deans advised compliance and go-slow tactics. He also recommended that despite the mild weather each man should wear his greatcoat or equivalent, and ensure that footwear was as comfortable and as serviceable as possible. He should take spare socks and a full container of water. Lessons had been learned from earlier marches. The little food owned would not add much weight to their haversacks.

While the Kriegies queued until the dark early hours for their issue of a 1,500-gram sawdust loaf and a small piece of margarine, the area was illuminated by brilliant flares dropped by Mosquito aircraft carrying out local bombing raids. With the arrival of extra guards came the threat that the area outside the camp was under military control. Escaping prisoners would be shot. Dog handlers accompanied by snarling Alsatians were a further inducement for the Kriegies to stay in line. By a calculated 'go-slow' the first party delayed their departure until the evening of Good Friday, 6 April. The air-raids, bread issue and nervous excitement ensured that the remaining Kriegies had little sleep that night. It was Good Friday but nothing indicated that their walk was to be a leisurely Easter stroll.

Gunfire could be heard in the west, not as loud or distinct as the Russians' guns had sounded to the men at Bankau or Heydekrug, but as encouraging. A 'go-slow' march was a must. It would be slow anyway, 10,000 ill-fed men would, at best, shuffle along. The guards looked as washed out and unenthusiastic as their charges. For weeks they had been demoralised by the highly visible and unopposed daylight flights of USAAF armadas. The Kriegies had never missed an opportunity to point skywards and mouth the crushing words, *'Deutschland Kaputt!'*

Mike Ludlow had no intention of marching again. The march out of Gross Tychow had been enough. When the Kriegies assembled, Ludlow and two others mingled with the last crowd and then slipped into an empty hut. The guards appeared to be searching half-heartedly. The three moved from time to time although Ludlow was certain they had been seen dashing into a shed behind one of the main *Abort*s. When they reckoned the coast was clear they transferred to another *Abort* in the evacuated part of the camp. Two others joined them and gradually the sound of the last party leaving died away. They thought their ruse had succeeded.

A sudden commotion near the main gate signalled a round-up of the dodgers. To the prisoners the belief that the *SS* had been brought in was enough to draw most from their hiding places. Men appeared from all corners. Ludlow watched as a few were flushed from their hide-outs high in water tanks, where they had been standing on precarious footholds since before daylight.

The main parties had now left the camp. The hundred who had been hiding were herded into the centre of the compound. They wondered fearfully what was going to happen but eventually they were marched through the gate. Within an hour they came to a halt by the banks of the River Meisse. The party was then near to the concentration camp at Bergen Belsen. It was learned that the bridge they were expecting to cross had been mined. More German guards and camp personnel appeared and began to cross in a couple of small boats after advising the Kriegies to return to the camp and wait. So they turned back to the Stalag. The Kriegies were pleased.

'Jock' Hamilton, John Leakey and Vic Gammon decided to stay together as columns of approximately 500 men left the camp. A heady excitement from being outside the barbed wire filled every man in the RAF column. Few had seen the 'real' world for so long that looking at houses, trees and fields was engrossing. Even the men who had suffered the torment of the snow marches found this journey different. The weather was kind and the end of the war near. There were dangers present and to come but they had faced plenty during the last six years. They were hungry but they were hungry inside the camp; outside there was at least a chance of obtaining some food, any food.

Adding to the excitement was a sense of insecurity. Within the barbed wire there was a comfort in numbers and the knowledge that 'Dixie' Deans was at hand to stand between a threatened Kriegie and the Germans. Here, it was every man for himself.

For three days parties had left the camp, many hanging back in the hope that the battle line would pass over them. It was not to be, but the last party out and those who had been hiding returned to the camp the same day. To their delight any movement to the north-east was impossible, their proposed route was cut.

The countryside was peopled with German infantry, Panzers, *Waffen SS*, flak and artillery batteries, all making a fighting retreat. Amongst them were refugees, escaping prisoners and foreign workers of all races. Above were Liberators and Fortresses making mass attacks on strategic targets while restless Spitfires, Mosquitoes, Thunderbolts and Typhoons roamed the lower skies searching for enemy tanks, trains and troops.

Flight Sergeant Alec Taylor had marched for several days when the Germans returned his party to Fallingbostel. British and Commonwealth servicemen had managed to restore order and create organisation throughout the camp.

Artillery thundered almost incessantly. On 12 April the German staff had decided to throw themselves on the mercy of their charges. They were demoralised by the sound of the guns and BBC reports deliberately leaked to them by prisoners from their radio. A tank battle with salvos of shells screaming over the heads of hundreds of wildly cheering Kriegies perched on the hut roofs convinced the Germans. Enough was enough. Organised parties toured the sentry posts and took machine guns, rifles, pistols and automatics from the white-faced, unprotesting guards and their officers who were then herded under armed guard into what had been the German compound.

Local women arrived to search for their relatives and men friends. Their emotional reunions were greeted with cheers, jeers, catcalls and exaggerated groans from the Kriegies crowding the wire. They had been parted from their own loved ones by those very people for years.

Foraging parties commanded by armed senior NCOs searched the surrounding countryside. They were supplied with specially reserved toilet soap and chocolate biscuits for bartering with the local people. The Germans had been using their gritty *ersatz* soap for years and a tablet of scented toilet soap was bargainable for two chickens.

Throughout, the British prisoners had been scrupulously correct in their dealings with the locals who were encouraged to bring food and goods to the camp for barter. The populace was understandably nervous, particularly as several thousand Russian prisoners, with little reason to love the Germans, were attached to the camp. Reasoning that the Russians were allies, those in an adjacent compound were released. It was a mistake of alarming proportions. Gangs of Russians immediately invaded the local village on a terrifying rampage of arson, looting, assault and rape. No woman of any age was safe.

Around the town of Fallingbostel there was anarchy. Freed Russian prisoners roamed everywhere, liquor stores were raided and marauding bands terrorised the populace. The Russians had suffered terribly at the hands of the Germans and were going wild, intent on grabbing food, drink, women and revenge. Local civilians begged British and American ex-prisoners to protect them. In some cases Kriegies moved into the houses of Germans and were left in peace by the Russians who assumed their motives towards the women were the same as theirs. Sometimes they were.

In a five-storey high warehouse in nearby Oebke the marauding Russians discovered a store of Eau de Cologne, realised that it had an alcoholic content and drank it through broken bottle necks. Bleeding lips and hands on drunken Russians were a common sight. Even more serious for the Russians was their finding of an almost vertical goods chute on the outside of the building, meant for the rapid delivery of cartons to lorry transport in the road. Although the chute ended 14 feet from the road surface, drunken Russians were riding the chute to crash into an horrific, writhing and growing pile of severely maimed bodies. A scouting party of six NCOs discovered the mayhem when they saw streamers made from bandages, cotton wool and sanitary towels fluttering from the upper storey of the warehouse. Armed parties were organised to round up the Russians, and return them to their compound where they were to be held until the arrival of the Allied armies.

Although almost free, few of the thousands of RAF and British Army ex-prisoners had any increase in their food. Only the omnipresent swede was in plentiful supply, so it was with great joy that on 14 April a double ration of sawdust bread and a large bucket of rich meat stew was issued to each room from the cookhouse. Everyone congratulated the cooks and tucked in. Nothing had tasted so good for years. Next morning, when the horse-drawn rubbish cart failed to appear, rumours circulated about the meat content of the stew. The cooks had disappeared, which tended to confirm the consumers' doubts about the tasty meal. The older Kriegies took it calmly, they had eaten unmentionable parts of a horse many times and were glad of it but some of the newer Kriegies were violently sick. Later they searched aggressively and unsuccessfully for the cooks.

On the morning of 16 April a scout car stopped hesitantly near the outer surrounding barbed wire. To Gerry Harris it seemed that the occupants were unsure of the wire's significance, but when it dawned on them that it was a prisoner-of-war camp containing Allied men they were suddenly jubilant, they were an advanced section of the 7th Hussars, 7th Armoured Division of General Dempsey's First Army. Greetings were shouted and after emptying their pockets and handing over cigarettes, food and medical supplies, they roared away to report.

### THE POINTLESS 'PLOD'

It was quickly realised that the trek through the wild lands of Lüneburg Heath was the best chance the marchers from Fallingbostel had of escaping. Some had already slipped away on the first day as the column turned a bend in the country road. Few had maps but the sound of the guns was in the west and that was the direction in which they would be heading.

The column had split into several groups, many losing touch with those in front and even taking different routes. One group passing through the small town of Bergen Belsen was less than a mile from the dying thousands in the concentration camp. 'Dixie' Deans had acquired a bicycle and rode from group to group, advising and encouraging cohesion. 'Together we survive, anybody who slopes off is on his own,' he said. Nobody was told not to attempt to escape. The Germans had accomplished the hardest part for them, they were outside the wire and for many this was too great a chance to be missed.

John Bristow marched out with the Admin party, taking with him a battery operated radio concealed in a billycan. In the recesses of a barn or hayloft Ron Mogg would note important items of news and pass it around by selected men. It was not as efficient or complete as the copies read out in the camps, but at least the Kriegies were keeping up with events.

The move out of Fallingbostel was slow, the guards were not *Luftwaffe* but older *Wehrmacht* men, well armed but tired and wishing the war finished. As the huge warehouses at Oebke were left behind and the column straggled along country roads, Tom Harvey thought the scenery not unlike Surrey. Lüneburg Heath is deeply wooded yet also possessing wide areas of open land much used for German Army tank training.

One middle-aged guard, distressed by the strain of the march, was sweating profusely. His kit seemed to weigh him down so much that, with other Kriegies surrounding them a prisoner relieved the panting guard of the weight of his rifle for a while, unloading it and slipping the rounds into a ditch as he did so. The guard was so grateful that at the next rest spot he was persuaded to part with a map of the area.

Mosquito intruder aircraft were busy throughout the moonlit night hours, keeping up the pressure on the retreating Germans. In the early hours of Saturday 7 April the Kriegie column was moving on a busy main road. *Wehrmacht* troops were thronging towards the front with armoured vehicles and guns. It was probable that the passing columns would both have preferred to turn around.

It was no surprise, almost a comfort, to hear RAF planes around but when at 2.00am a Mossie flew low over the column from behind, firing tracer over their heads, the Kriegies scattered, throwing themselves into a ditch on their right. The pilot misjudged the height of the tall firs to the left behind the column and the aircraft crashed in a mass of explosive flame. The Kriegies watched, relieved to be alive but shocked and stricken with helpless horror.

After the Mosquito incident the Kriegies became jumpy and when a Tiger tank engine was started nearby its staccato backfiring roar was enough to make them plunge headlong again into a ditch. Such was the number of Allied aircraft in the sky causing the Kriegies to dive for cover that the rare sighting of a Messerschmitt brought forth the cry, 'It's alright, it's one of ours'.

Easter Day, the 8th, dawned bright and sunny. The Kriegies on the march were thankful. They had spent the night in various barns, outhouses and in the open, resting fairly comfortably buried in straw. Then the column went through Marbostel. Trading with civilians and even the passing of humanitarian aid to the passing Kriegies was verboten. Those who tried and were seen were attacked with rifle butts. Buckets of water were dashed to the ground as people handed mugs to the dry-throated marchers. A girl of 15 walked alongside Vic Gammon and held out a hidden hand, quickly passing an egg to him. He smiled and gratefully muttered, '*Danke sehr*,' knocked the egg on a fence and swallowed the contents, thankful for the few vitamins and energy.

No provision had been made for accommodation and the only food most Kriegies had that night was stolen rye, leeks and a few potatoes grubbed from a clamp. Shoulders and feet were now aching and hunger pangs hurting. The next day breakfast consisted of a slice of bread, some boiled rye and a few potatoes baked in a fire. Fences were demolished for kindling much to the anger of the residents, but the Kriegies were past caring. It was soon discovered that columns following where others had passed before had little chance to trade. A diversion round a new village untouched by an earlier Kriegie invasion had better prospects.

### TRYST AMONG THE TREES

The guards were disconsolate, they were either middle-aged or partially disabled and had received no rations apart from a few boiled potatoes. Many of them wished that the war was finished, something they would not have dared say earlier. A 20-year-old guard told Sergeant Harvey that he had been wounded on the Russian Front near Minsk and was in constant pain, he had to hobble along with the rest.

Each day saw increasing air activity. Fortresses escorted by twin-boomed Lightnings passed over on their way to an industrial target. Spitfires, Typhoons, Mustangs and Mosquitoes continually sought out and attacked trains and gun emplacements. The *Luftwaffe* was rarely seen. Days and nights were noisy with the sound of machine gun fire, cannon fire, bomb and demolition explosions but generally, when they had space and cover, the Kriegies slept well in their straw despite the din, hunger and mice and rats running over them.

On the fifth day of the march 'Dixie' Deans had a warning for those intending to run for it: 'Don't try it,' he cautioned, 'the SS are around and shooting any escaping prisoner-of-war on sight.' But the occasional roll-call by the Germans must have been a shock to them. Men had left the columns since the first one had left Fallingbostel. The *Appells* cannot have been any more than a gesture, but for the Kriegies the levelled rifles and pistols were not show.

Leakey, Gammon and Hamilton trudged on in the middle of the straggling column. The road had been hard, they were footsore and the guards were being chivvied to keep the Kriegies moving. At every halt there was, according to the Germans, just two kilometres to go.

So far the weather had been warm and dry. Fine for a country stroll but hard when carrying all your worldly goods and wearing all your clothes. Word ran around the columns that the Germans wanted the Kriegies across the Elbe by Tuesday 17 April. The bridge at Lauenburg was then to be blown. It seemed that the final stand was to be there on the east bank of the river. Vic Gammon could see that an escape to the Allied lines had to be attempted before the river crossing. He moved up beside Leakey and said:

'I've had enough, I think we should get off the column at the first chance tomorrow, what do you say?' John Leakey smiled.

'Yep,' he said, 'I had already made up my mind just now.' Moving on to Jock Hamilton the same question was asked.

'Aye,' he said and seemed surprised that they should have needed to ask.

The opportunity came on the morning of 13 April with suddenness and shock. An RAF aircraft flew parallel to the straggling column of marching Kriegies at a height of 200ft and a quarter of a mile over the field away to their right. The pilot tilted his wings to give him and his crew a good chance to see the Kriegies who waved gaily back as he banked and flew away.

'I hope that pilot recognised us,' said one as six Typhoons circled round. When the Typhoons formed up line-astern at the back of the column and then roared low towards it there was panic.

'Run,' shouted Gammon, 'they're coming at us!'
As one, the trio leaped down into the ditch on their left, up the bank, across the open space and hurtled into the wood.

'Not into the trees,' Jock shouted and panted, 'the ricochets will...' He ran on nevertheless.

Without another word the three raced on until they reached the far edge of the small wood, there they threw themselves into a shallow depression to regain their breath. This was the moment they had been waiting for. The thudding of their heartbeats slowly subsided and there was no sound but the shouting guards in the distance. The aircraft had gone, no shooting had been heard and the column was evidently reforming. Looking back towards the road Gammon could see a guard walking cautiously from the road into the wood towards them, his rifle at the ready. Lying quite still Gammon watched as the German looked around him. Suddenly stiffening, the guard saw the three Kriegies and their eyes met. He stared steadily at them for 10 seconds, then slipping his arm through the sling he shouldered the rifle, turned and went back towards the column.

'He's either going to let us go or get help to round us up, in any case we had better push off quickly,' said Gammon, rising to his feet.

With hearts pumping again the three men ran, and keeping to the cover of the trees stealthily slipped to the edge of the field where it adjoined another wood. There they quickly dived into its shadows. As soon as they were safely hidden the airmen checked their supplies. Food totalled a couple of slices each of the dark sawdust bread, a few raw potatoes and a couple of handfuls of millet. John Leakey surveyed the millet glumly.

'With all the bird food we have eaten lately we ought to be able to fly,' he said.

Without map or compass and only the vaguest knowledge of their whereabouts, the trio had no clear aiming point. They knew only that they wanted to travel west. They set off keeping among the trees as much as possible and towards the setting sun.

With nightfall the three were utterly weary. The sparsely wooded area in which they walked was some protection so they decided to rest for a while. The late night air was cold, but huddled together with their greatcoats around them they dozed fitfully.

Gammon awoke with a start. There was a strange luminosity in the frosty wood, the slight mist made the surroundings appear unreal and even though it was near midnight he could see several yards. He whispered a warning.

'Yes, there's somebody coming. Keep quite still,' whispered Leakey. They lay motionless on the leafy ground hardly daring to breathe and covered as much as possible with their dark clothing. Vic Gammon watched with mounting apprehension as two people appeared to be walking straight towards them. As they neared he could see the outline of a man in German officer's uniform with a woman. Every German officer is armed, any move now was tantamount to surrender. Stepping close to the three on the ground the man appeared to stumble. With a muttered curse he straightened, grasped the woman's arm and led her to a grassy patch a few yards away. They sat, talked quietly for a while and then lay together on the ground. To the airmen it seemed impossible that they should not be seen but the German pair were engrossed with each other and their closeness. Forced to lay stock-still, only Gammon could see the couple. An obvious danger point was reached when the pair sat up and began to talk in undertones. The man, now relaxed, lit a cigarette.

After what seemed an eternity the German pair stood, straightened their clothes and brushed away the leaves. Still talking quietly they walked slowly away in the direction they had come, their voices fading as they vanished into the mist. The airmen rose unsteadily to their feet. Leakey was the first to break the silence.

'Christ! that was a close shave,' he breathed, 'we can't hope for such a near thing as that and get away with it again.'

'A near thing?' hissed Hamilton, 'one of them trod on my ankle!' He looked affronted.

'We had better move,' said Gammon, 'this may be some kind of lovers' lane, we don't want any more adventures like that.'

Walking a few hundred yards deeper into the wood and finding a smooth, level spot, they settled down again, hoping to sleep for an hour or two. Gradually the grey dawn filtered between the trees and their surroundings became clear.

'My God!' Gammon exclaimed, 'we are only in someone's front garden!'

Hurriedly the airmen gathered up their few possessions and stealthily crept away, leaving the woodman's cottage in the half-light of morning. Moving off briskly the airmen decided to travel as much as was safe in daylight. Convinced that the front line could not be more than 20 miles away, it was essential to cover as much enemy territory as possible but the danger was always present in every direction, behind every tree and in every open space. Between the trio and their western advance lay a field with no cover between it, and a small wood which they hoped to make their next stopping place. There was nothing for it but to move out from their hiding place, along a rising cart track to the copse atop a hill. Straightening their backs and hoisting their small sacks over their shoulders the airmen stepped out into the open.

They climbed the track, pausing only to take a can of brackish water from a green edged pond, aware that with every step they could be challenged by a shout and a shot. With relief they reached the shelter of the edge of the copse and breathlessly fell to the earth.

'This is a good spot to boil a few potatoes,' said Leakey. 'We'll make a fire.'

'I don't think it's safe,' Gammon countered, 'smoke can be seen for miles above the trees.'

His objection was overruled by the other two and kindling was gathered. The fire had hardly begun to catch before Gammon, who was sitting facing into the wood, saw a figure some 50 yards away standing quietly watching.

'There's someone over there,' he whispered, nodding to the direction behind Leakey. 'He's very cautious, but looks like a Jerry by his overall and side cap.'

'Take no notice,' said Leakey coolly, 'pretend you haven't seen him – pop the potatoes in the tin.'

Always steady in a crisis, Leakey concentrated on his cooking. Gammon could now see that there were two men. They crept to within five yards and stood, silent, apparently trying to pick up words of conversation. Then suddenly the tension dissolved, with arms outstretched the two men dashed forward with cries of 'Tovarich! Tovarich!' They were Russians, prisoners on the run like themselves.

'Tovarich' was the limit of the Britishers' knowledge of Russian, but communication was quickly established with a kind of pidgin German as the common language, accompanied by handshakes and back-slapping. Leakey invited the Russians to join them in a meal but they politely declined, indicating that the fire was a dangerous give-away. Instead they offered some welcome sawdust bread.

A third man joined them. He worked on a nearby farm and supplied the other two with food. Conversation was surprisingly animated. During that day the airmen were shown the well hidden dug-out in the undergrowth where the two Russians spent their nights. Decisions were made about the procedures to be adopted should the six be discovered by Germans. One or two Germans were to be sharply despatched – an effective looking knife was produced. Should there be three or more, especially if the Germans were armed, the prisoners were to surrender quietly and wait for another chance to escape. It seemed a reasonable plan.

The copse was small and thinly wooded. After a night in which the airmen slept fitfully outside near the entrance of the dug-out, it was obvious that there was insufficient cover for six desperate men. It was also unfair to the Russians, so with nightfall the airmen decided to push on. There was plain relief at their decision, the Russians had been torn between their natural hospitality toward fellow escapers and the greatly increased danger. One of them who could write put names and addresses in a booklet and following an exchange of handshakes the RAF men left.

They walked through the dark countryside in silence, aware of every sound and conscious that their progress could be heard for long distances in the still April night. The silence was at last broken by Gammon who said, with a look at the starlit sky:

'I think we are going on a circular course, if we go on we will double back on ourselves.'

A quick check on Polaris showed that they were turning too far south and they corrected their course to the west and down a steep slope.

'This should bring us to a stream,' said Leakey confidently. Their water supply was seriously diminished but they soon heard the gurgling of a fast flowing brook. Although now in the open they could see almost nothing in the pitch darkness. The stream sounded close so Leakey took the three cans and went down the slope. Within minutes he was back, bubbling with as much excitement as the brook. The water he brought was cold, plentiful, a joy to drink and drink again without worrying about wastage. With the cans filled to the brim, the three set off again.

Almost immediately they had to throw themselves into a ditch to dodge a couple of workers who were striding towards the lights of a railway marshalling yard whose clanging, hissing sounds could be heard in the distance. Burying their faces in their arms to hide their pale features the airmen lay face down, holding their breath as the workers' boots stepped within inches of their heads and hands. Starting off again they were stopped by the sound of aircraft and a sudden shower of Pathfinder pyrotechnic red and green markers which fell to the ground just behind them.

'For God's sake let's get away from this lot,' Hamilton said. The last thing they wanted was to be bombed by the RAF. As no bombs were dropped the trio reckoned the brilliantly coloured 'Christmas Trees' were route markers rather than target markers.

The dark journey brought them to a mature pine plantation with a 220-yard wide area cleared as a fire-break. Out of the trees it was a little lighter. In the middle of the open ground stood a tall fire observation tower. As they walked along the edge of the fire-break a sudden shout of 'Halt!' startled the airmen. They had been heard. A shot rang out but in the dark it would be unlikely for them to be hit and the airmen had no intention of waiting to discover the gunman's intentions. Half expecting floodlights to brilliantly illuminate the area, they cut away from the path and ran across the open fire-break. It was a near disaster: the fire-break was spread to knee-depth with dry bracken and twigs which crackled like machine gun volleys with every high stepping jump, the sound echoing back from the trees on either side. More shouts and shots reverberated across the open space but the airmen encouraged each other to keep running. The crackling noise continued until the far side of the fire-break when soft earth was reached, enabling them to run silently out of the wooded area until they felt safe, and when once more they collapsed into breathless heaps.

After a brief rest the tramp westward continued. It was another clear night with the stars plainly visible. The three reckoned the dash from the fire-break had taken them off their route, so it was decided that as the country seemed fairly unpopulated they would carry on for an hour or two during first daylight. Darkness was a cover but a hindrance to fast travel. They wanted to push on.

The sudden ending of the wood was a shock. Before them was a wide concrete road with trees cleared from a broad swathe each side. It was an Autobahn, a barrier which had to be passed to continue travelling west. Looking in both directions the airmen gingerly walked to the edge of the road. They had that feeling of naked vulnerability again, there was almost a certainty of being seen. It was at that moment that Leakey saw the approaching convoy of German military vehicles.

There was no cover, the convoy of open staff cars and lorries interspersed with ambulances was bearing down on them. They must have already been seen by the occupants of the cab of the first lorry. Muttered exclamations were followed by quick decisions, there was no choice but to try to bluff, as if it was normal for three scruffy, unshaven and bedraggled individuals carrying small sacks over their shoulders to be walking beside a motorway-type road in the morning sunshine. Chatting to each other in an attempt to allay suspicion, the airmen looked directly at the men in the convoy.

Almost incredibly the convoy passed with German soldiers gazing fixedly and quizzically at them throughout. It seemed that none of the drivers would stop to question the vagrants for fear of making himself appear foolish and cause the vehicles behind to halt unnecessarily, dangerously exposed. As the end of the convoy disappeared behind them the trio rushed across the road, over the cleared area and into the woods on the far side. Only then did broad grins lighten their faces. A whole contingent of fighting *Wehrmacht* had passed within yards, but their impudent audacity had seen them through. 'Perhaps they had bigger worries than us,' Hamilton chuckled.

Heading into the trees the airmen decided they had had enough adventures and narrow escapes for a while, and settled down to wait for darkness to cloak the countryside before resuming their march towards freedom. In the dark frosty night they set off again, alert for any sound. The road ahead seemed clear and they made good progress until the early hours of the morning when they reached a village, a danger area – houses meant people. Should they go round or through? A hurried discussion and it was decided to attempt a quick march through to the far side of the village. Straightening, they formed an Indian file and stepped off smartly. The street was quiet and the houses shuttered, but no matter how gently the airmen tried to put their boots down on the metalled road the sound echoed crashingly back from the buildings on either side. They had started; there was no going back.

Whispering voices were heard on the opposite side of the road. They marched on. The next voice was loud and imperative, a shout of 'Halt!' accompanied the sound of a rifle bolt being snapped back. The airmen stopped. To their intense disappointment this bluff had failed. Standing before them, barely visible, was an armed *Wehrmacht Unteroffizier* and an older man wearing a close fitting black cap like a woman's cloche hat, and a black cloak reaching almost to the ground. The strange clothing made the old man's face his only visible feature as it floated greyly in the gloom. The airmen answered his questions evasively until Leakey said:

'Keep talking quickly, he won't understand, I am going to tell him we are French workers,' continuously speaking as if addressing the *Unteroffizier*. Summoning up his few German words Leakey said:

'*Wir sind französisch Arbeiter.*' It was enough to puzzle the soldier. He disbelieved, but was in doubt. He asked Leakey where they were going. Leakey was stumped, he had no idea where they were or where they were going.

'*Er – wir gehen zu Bin-er-Bing er...,*' he said hesitatingly, as if searching for a name.

'*Behringen?*' prompted the soldier.

'*Ja, das ist est, Behringen.*' said Leakey confidently. Unconvinced, the soldier stepped behind the airmen.

'*Komm mit*' he ordered, and with a gun levelled at them the three were marched down the road. In answer to the soldier's knock a door was opened and they were ushered into the dimly-lit passageway of a house.

In the weak light Vic Gammon looked at his companions and then at himself. Although they were wearing a conglomeration of clothing it was basically British service uniform and his own greatcoat was RAF issue. There were no badges of rank or insignia but the uniforms were recognisably British. Gammon was thankful for the identity tags which still hung around each man's neck because, he reckoned, this was the moment when they were about to be unmasked.

The *Unteroffizier* was now talking to a strange apparition that had appeared on a gallery at the top of a staircase. The trio could only stare in wonder. A middle-aged man in a long nightshirt and sleeping cap with a drooping tassel, stood holding a guttering candle in a candlestick. He resembled a fairy-tale book illustration of Rip Van Winkle. Despite the seriousness of the airmen's situation Gammon had to suppress a smile.

They were in the local police station and this village constable was incensed at being dragged from his bed in the early hours. The airmen were just able to follow the conversation between the soldier and the policeman. The policeman had asked who the three were and the soldier had answered that although he had doubts they claimed to be French workers. It was enough to give the policeman a lever to get rid of his unwanted intruders; he said with stern authority that if they were French he did not want them at the police station. They should be taken to the French camp, he growled irritably and ushered all five out.

No-one had yet taken a close look at the dishevelled trio and now in the darkness of the blacked-out street it was too late. With a gun in their backs they were marched along the street and into the entrance of a barn. There another soldier was called from his bed and after an acrimonious discussion between the Germans, the airmen were pushed through a door which was locked behind them. They stood motionless in the dark, fearful of stepping forward into the unknown.

'Where the hell are we?' asked John Leakey urgently.

'I don't know,' whispered Gammon, 'but we are not alone, there are people here, I can feel them around.'

There was a murmuring of voices, matches were struck and small oil lamps lit in several parts of what was gradually seen as a large room full of double bunk-beds. Men talking in excited French were climbing from the beds and coming forward to where the three stood at the top of four steps. They quickly knew who their visitors were and were making them welcome, thrusting bread and cheese into their hands and brewing hot drinks. Knowing their guests were exhausted, three

Franco/Belgian prisoners vacated their bunks so they could rest. Very soon after removing their boots the airmen were asleep. The warmth and secure feeling of being among friends was like a cosy blanket.

Their rest was not to last long. Dawn breaks early in northern Germany in mid-April and their hosts had plans for their visitors. Hastily washing, a party of 20 prisoner farm workers left the basement of the barn with the airmen merged in to the middle of the chattering crowd. The German guards took little notice as the party walked to the village square and split into two groups, Leakey with one, Hamilton and Gammon with the other.

At a farm Gammon and Hamilton were introduced by Belgian Sergeant-Major Fernand Duret to the farm owners as two new French workers. Duret, a tall, well-built man, whose broad shoulders seemed made for handling horses and a plough, was on very good terms with the household of two sisters in their thirties and their black-garbed elderly parents. The womens' husbands were fighting on the Eastern Front so the ladies relied on Duret to run the farm and, it would seem, for his comforting strong, male presence.

Three other residents of the farmhouse were a woman and her two small children, Kristina and Peter, evacuated from bombed Hamburg. The four-year-old blonde girl took to Vic Gammon and was soon calling him Onkel Viktor and ran to him at every opportunity.

Although the pretence of being French could not be maintained within the farmhouse, it was necessary to keep up the subterfuge of being POW farm workers, so Hamilton and Gammon took turns to follow a horse pulling a wheel with thick spokes on the outer rim. At specific intervals as the wheel turned, the spokes dug a hole in the ploughed field and into each hole the airmen dropped a seed potato and trod it into the earth. It was an easy outdoor way of avoiding contact with suspicious Germans. Such workers were unlikely to be interrupted.

In the late afternoon sunshine Gammon seated himself on the back doorstep of the farmhouse, wondering how their war would end when he was joined by one of the guards. The German spoke colloquial-transatlantic English and knew well the identity of the airman. Quietly he said:

'I will be glad when it is all over. At the first chance I will go back to Chicago where I had a used car business.' He was immediately mentally dubbed American Joe.

'What made you join the *Wehrmacht*?' Gammon asked.

'I had to,' the German replied. 'I was over here to see my relatives when I was inducted into the army. Had I tried to resist my relatives would have suffered.' The story was one that Vic Gammon and most other Kriegies had heard before, but he commiserated.

Later that day a warning was sent to the house that at 9.00pm the railway bridge outside the village was to be demolished with a heavy explosive charge. As the family, the evacuees, the two Kriegies and Duret assembled in the main room of the farmhouse, everyone watched the wall clock as the hands neared 9.00pm. The two ladies sat impassively with their hands in their laps. The Grossmutter and Grossvater were apprehensive, although the old man was very deaf. The lady from Hamburg worried about her children. Peter the boy sat on his mother's lap but Kristina ran to Onkel Viktor. Climbing on to his lap she pressed her head into his chest. Covering her other ear with his hand Sergeant Gammon watched the clock's minute hand as it turned to the vertical.

Exactly on time a roaring crash shook the building, a brief cry came from the women followed by the clattering sound of stones falling on the roof and in the yard outside, but the opened windows held. Everyone relaxed, the present danger was past. Wishing the others 'Good night', Duret and the airmen returned to the basement of the barn for a night of real rest. John Leakey had spent a similar day but he seemed to be in a worse state with dysentery and unable to retain the food offered. But freedom must be close they reasoned, and that would surely cure all their ills.

Early next morning Gammon and Hamilton left for the farmhouse with Fernand Duret. As he was unwell Leakey stayed behind in the barn. There was an air of expectancy about the day. There had been little to indicate the approach of the Allies except that the defenders had blown the bridge and some distant small-arms fire had been heard. With the situation as touchy as it was, small-arms fire was common. No heavy artillery had been heard for some time. It was almost too quiet.

At the farm Duret took Gammon to see the room in the house in which he often stayed overnight. On the wall above his bed was a framed picture of King Leopold III of the Belgians. Leopold had been thought by the British to have deserted the Allies by seeking an armistice with the Germans at a crucial time, leaving their flanks unprotected. Duret had no such thoughts. Brimming with patriotism and loyalty he donned his neatly pressed uniform tunic, straightened himself to rigid attention and saluted the picture. Proudly turning to Gammon and indicating the picture of Leopold, Duret proclaimed, 'My f.....g King'. Gammon immediately assumed that Duret had learned his few English words from a British squaddie.

Later, Hamilton and Gammon carried on dropping seed potatoes into the holes as Duret managed the horse until, at mid-morning, the sound of rapid machine gun fire ripped across the area. Duret stopped and looked towards the wood from where the sound appeared to be coming. There was nothing to see. Quickly gesturing to the airmen to accompany him, he led the horse back to the farmhouse.

The old couple had been worried by the machine gun fire. *'Die Tommies kommen,.'* they said anxiously, their old faces creased with fear. Should they go into the cellar, they asked? Gammon doubted if that was a good idea unless there was heavy artillery fire. He was concerned that if the approaching troops thought there might be *Wehrmacht* hiding in the cellar they may toss in a couple of grenades first. The Hamburg woman was frantically worried about her boy and girl.

'Will the Tommies kill my children, will they, will they?' she asked tearfully. Vic Gammon tried to reassure her.

'Do you think I would hurt your children?' he asked. The woman shook her head, she had seen that the children had taken to the two airmen but her eyes were filled with fear and tears.

'Look,' she said, handing Gammon a double-page spread she had torn from a magazine centrefold. A lurid artist's impression pictured British soldiers with simian expressions sitting round a camp fire. They were laughing as they roasted a naked baby speared on a bayonet. Gammon knew well the horrors of war but was appalled at this crude propaganda, and that people believed it. Taking the picture from her he tore it into pieces.

'That is disgusting Göbbels' propaganda. British soldiers are just like Jock and me, they love children. Believe me the Tommies are more likely to give them chocolate and sweets, they will never willingly harm a child.'

A woodshed next to the farmhouse gave a good view of the road. Taking it in turns to peer through a knot hole, Hamilton and Gammon watched the procession of German soldiers. Making their way west towards the fighting were youths with Panzerfaust anti-tank weapons tied to cycle crossbars. Moving away from the fighting were older men, wounded and staggering, bloodstained bandages crudely wrapped around their heads and limbs. It was like a scene depicting the tortures of Hell. A man fell to the road, tried to rise, fell again and crawled two yards before collapsing, his blood staining the dust. The temptation to run out to help was almost overwhelming but the airmen knew it could be suicidal.

As the soldier outside was helped away by another wounded man Duret reckoned the time was right to dash for the barn. He believed they would all be safer together and was sure those on other farms would have made their way back. The airmen and Duret walked swiftly back through the village towards the barn. Soldiers making their individual way to and from the fighting front paid them little attention.

Pent-up expectancy swamped the French and Belgian prisoners at the barn. Everyone felt this the most important day of the war since their captivity. Barring the danger of being in the firing line when the fighting front passed, or some form of atrocity by the Germans, freedom was near. The two German guards had not been seen but were known to be still in their room at the barn entrance.

All seemed quiet outside and the prisoners in the barn were beginning to feel a slight sense of let-down when the door, four steps up from the basement floor, crashed open. Standing on the top step was a young, grime-smeared British Army lieutenant, purposefully grasping a pistol. He was flanked by two sub-machine gun-wielding privates. All trigger fingers were crooked. The lieutenant summed up the situation.

'Any Englishmen here?' he rapped. When the airmen leapt to their feet the business-like lieutenant said:

'You've got two minutes to get ready – we are 20 miles ahead of the troops.' The airmen were ready, eager to go.

'Any Germans here? Where are they? Are they armed?'
His questions came in rapid succession. When the door of the room where the two guards lived was pointed out, he just nodded. The privates smashed open the door and standing there was a sight to gladden the heart of anyone who had suffered at the hands of the Germans.

Looking unlike the vaunted conquering race the two *Wehrmacht* guards stood inside, their jellied legs hardly able to prop them upright. They trembled uncontrollably from head to foot, their arms and hands raised above their heads in abject surrender shook so violently that it seemed to be purposely exaggerated. Their ashen grey faces were rigid with fear and shock. Although the machine guns remained trained on the Germans the lieutenant realised that no-one had anything to fear from this terror-stricken pair. He beckoned them to come down the steps and to avoid their complete collapse they were assisted by French and Belgian prisoners. Vic Gammon had never seen men so petrified, so scared out of their wits and apparently certain that their last moments had come. He felt strangely sorry for them. As the Germans were escorted to a scout car outside, the prisoners, British, Belgian and French suddenly realised that they were free.

The guards' room was an arsenal. A rack of rifles was ordered to be brought outside and smashed, a process led enthusiastically by a revived John Leakey. The French and Belgian were concerned that they would have nothing with which to defend themselves but the orders of the British officer were clear. The destruction went ahead.

Help would soon be arriving to take them home, the French and Belgian men were told, so the three airmen said an emotional goodbye to their new friends. Names and addresses were exchanged, hands shaken and *'Bonne Chances'* shouted as the airmen climbed into scout cars and jeeps. Their journey was short. When the lieutenant was told of the railway bridge that had been blown the previous night he was immediately interested and suspected that the road might well be booby trapped at another spot near the bridge. That was a common *Wehrmacht* ploy.

The scout cars swung round along the road to the east and seconds later, as they rounded a bend, the blown bridge came into view. The left end of the bridge had fallen onto the road beneath and crazily tilted on the remains was a locomotive. Twisted rails projected into the road and sky. Stopping the small convoy 50 yards from the shattered bridge the lieutenant leapt from the scout car. Carefully examining the road ahead, his sudden triumphant shout of 'Here it is!' brought soldiers running with spades and pickaxes. A small bridge over a stream had been well mined with explosive. Seated in one of the scout cars, Gammon was interested to see that a crowd of curious, elderly men, women and children gathered to watch the clearance, unaware of any danger.

'You hungry mate?' a concerned cockney soldier asked Gammon. Not waiting for a reply he apologetically said, 'I've only got bread and bully beef,' at the same time handing him a knife and lifting from a box a freshly baked, crusty white loaf, a good pound of corned beef, a basin full of butter and a bottle of brown sauce. Such luxury was overwhelming and irresistible.

'Want a cuppa?' the soldier went on. Again not waiting for an answer he leaned from the scout car to speak to an interpreter with a 'Netherlands' shoulder flash on his British Army battledress. The interpreter brusquely turned to the crowd of onlookers and told one of the old men to boil some water. When hot – not boiling – water was brought, there was a fierce shouting harangue at the shaken old man until a pot of tea, satisfactory to the interpreter, was brewed. It was the first time the bitter, smouldering hatred held by some Dutch for the Germans was apparent to Gammon. It was not to be the last.

As the soldier was talking Gammon studied the insignia on the soldier's sleeve for the first time. The badge pictured a jerboa. These men were part of the famous 'Desert Rats', who had defeated Rommel.

Sergeant Gammon repeated the name to himself, 'The 11th Hussars, 7th Armoured Division'. He knew these men were part of a fighting force that he would never forget.

'Enough there to blow up the whole village' said the lieutenant, as with the satisfaction of a job well done the excavating and defusing party climbed back into the vehicles. The convoy of light tanks, jeeps and scout cars turned and sped off to the comparative safety of a small occupied village.

'Here,' said the sergeant-major, a tough veteran, 'why don't you have a good night's kip in a real bed? This is the *Bürgermeister*'s house with a nice soft mattress. Nobody will bother you here. I am afraid you will have to come forward with us in the morning, we can't send you back until the supply echelon comes up about 1.00pm.'

Gammon did not care, although he did not relish advancing with the troops and would rather have got out of the war altogether, tomorrow was a long way off, the bed looked comfortable and he was exhausted by the wonderful events of the day. He removed his boots and battledress blouse, crawled under the counterpane and a few minutes later was asleep.

The explosion that jerked Gammon awake and reverberated throughout the house left his ears ringing. Shattered window glass fell noisily into the room and flames roared upward outside the window blocking all else from view. Swiftly he jumped from the bed, snatched up his boots and ran outside.

'What happened?' he breathlessly asked the sergeant-major.

'Some bugger put a bazooka into the fuel tank,' he replied, indicating a blazing light tank. 'We think it is a Hitler Youth in that house over there. Some of the lads have gone after him.' A rattle of machine gun fire sounded across the small village square. The soldiers had found their quarry. Gammon went back into the *Bürgermeister*'s house, crawled under the bedclothes and was soon asleep once more.

With dawn Gammon was awakened by the feverish activity outside. Throwing back the counterpane he pulled on his boots and went out. The sergeant-major, who never seemed to sleep, called to him and said, 'We got another one last night,' pointing to a youth standing a few yards away with his hands clasped on his head. 'These little sods are worse trouble than the army. Soldiers know when they are beaten and give up but these youngsters are full of the *Nazi* spirit and want to die for Hitler.' Jerking his thumb towards the youth he said, 'He'll probably get his wish'.

Later, walking over to a trestle table and chair the sergeant-major invited Sergeant Gammon to take a seat and asked:

'What would you like for breakfast, eggs and bacon?' Gammon nodded in agreement and then gasped in wonderment as a plate of such richness was placed before him with piles of bread and butter at the side. The outdoor picnic-type meal was exciting and he had just started to enjoy it when the sergeant-major placed a .45 pistol beside his plate and said:

'I've put that young bastard facing the wall over there. He's a killer. I've put him near the end of the wall and I think he'll try to run.' Pushing the pistol nearer he said, 'If he does – shoot him.'

Vic Gammon suddenly lost his appetite. He nibbled at the meal and then pushed the rest to one side. The sergeant-major seemed disappointed but Gammon just wanted to get away. He could not have shot anyone in cold blood, and in any case the boy had aroused his grudging admiration when he had withstood a beating with courage and dignity at the hands of the Dutch interpreter. The interrogation had proceeded with an alternate full-blooded punch and a question. The young man's photographs had been torn into pieces and ground under a heel into the mud before him. Gammon did not like it but who was he to interfere? The interpreter had lost his parents, they had been murdered by the Germans and hate filled his soul. Many of the soldiers around him had been at El Alamein, taken part in the Normandy invasion and fought a bitter struggle across Europe. They had endured much that had hardened and toughened them. And they needed information from this Hitler Youth member that could be the saving of more soldiers' lives.

Gammon's liberators assumed that because he had been a prisoner of the Germans for nearly five years he would hate every one of them. It was not so, he had not learned to hate but had realised that there was good and wickedness in many men. Above all he had learned that brutality bred brutality – but how could he protest in this situation with fighting men who had been through so much, even to the point of his own liberation?

The advance that morning began with the three ex-Kriegies allocated to different vehicles, each in the charge of an NCO. Gammon rode with a tough, hard-bitten sergeant who was as caring as a nanny. After a run of 20 minutes the convoy was halted by machine gun fire from woods at the side of the road. Quickly men dropped off the convoy, purposefully carrying machine guns and flame-throwers. The skirmish was brief. *Wehrmacht* men began to run from the trees, their arms held high. They were disarmed and told to walk back along the road to where the bulk of the British troops were coming. As the convoy moved again more German soldiers appeared in ones and twos. They had no wish to take any further part in already lost battles and were desperate to be taken prisoner. Most were pathetically frightened and heartily relieved when captured. All were given the same message of 'walk westward'.

Gammon was shaken when the jeep in which he was travelling screeched to a halt. Expecting a sudden spray of machine gun fire he was ready to duck but the Army sergeant was cool. In reply to Gammon's urgent 'What's up?', his calm reply was one word: 'Elevenses'. A portable gas cooker was brought from the back of the jeep and water quickly boiled for tea, then a side of bacon was lifted out and with a flourish of a razor sharp bayonet the Army sergeant asked, 'One rasher or two?'.

While the thick slices of bacon were sizzling in the pan and the white bread and butter being prepared, Gammon kept an apprehensive eye on the wooded roadside. Although the war had to stop for the tea break and the Army men obviously thought themselves safe, it was not a feeling that Vic Gammon shared.

At midday the convoy drew into the square of a small town. One side of the square was packed with German prisoners herded into a tight group under the guns of British soldiers. Among them Gammon was surprised to see 'American Joe' with whom he had talked on the back doorstep of the farm and who was captured at the barn. The *Wehrmacht* men were being packed into large pantechnicon-type removal lorries. If they were slow in climbing over the tailboard, a British soldier's heavy boot helped them on their way. From across the square Gammon saw that 'American Joe' had recovered from his shock enough to collect the case and belongings he had selected to take into captivity. As 'Joe' reached the back of the lorry, clutching his small case with new boots tied to its handle, he was roughly pushed forward, the case torn from his hand and thrown into the ditch. Soon the ditch was full of the small personal possessions of the prisoners. Gammon watched from the opposite side of the square, saddened that he was unable to help his friendly enemy of a few days who had wanted only peace and a return to Chicago.

Slowly the huge covered lorries loaded with prisoners drew on to the road heading for the prisoner-of-war holding areas. The pantechnicons were crammed so tightly that some of the prisoners were told to climb on to the roofs. Gammon, a passenger in a following jeep, wondered how the men in the front part could possibly breathe in the crush, then he saw that the prisoners on the flat roofs of the tall vans were having difficulty in holding on. As the lorries swerved and swayed the men's bodies swung dangerously from side to side as they clutched at any handhold. The Army driver beside Sergeant Gammon said with a smile:

'D'you see what the drivers in front are doing? They're trying to knock them off by the branches as they swing under the trees.' It was true, but they did not succeed. Gammon was relieved when the journey ended at a large field that had been turned into a massive barbed wire cage.

The travelling and dislocation of war had meant that, except for brief moments, the three RAF friends had been separated. Now, outside the prisoner-of-war cage, Vic Gammon found himself resting on straw in a barn in the company of half a dozen British Army ex-prisoners. His stomach was still churning and the small amount of rich food that he had been able to retain in the last two days made an urgent call to the canvas screened latrine pit a desperate necessity. Running quickly outside he was halted by a screaming shout in a foreign tongue. Standing in front of him with his finger trembling on the trigger of a sub-machine gun inches from Gammon's stomach was a wild looking character in British army battledress. Gammon stood stock still, throwing up his hands. Still the man shouted at him but Gammon saw an army corporal and called to him.

'For God's sake tell this man I'm British.' The corporal, laughing, ambled over. He thought it a huge joke.

'It's all right Popski,' he said to the Pole, 'this bloke is one of us.' With the explanation the Pole lowered his gun and was profusely apologetic.

'He's a Polish prisoner we picked up on the way through' the corporal explained. 'He interrogates the Poles and Russians for us and tells us if they're good or bad.'

*'Would you mind repeating those last instructions?'*

'What happens if he decides that they are bad?' asked Gammon as he calmed down. The corporal smiled and drew his forefinger across his throat in the expressive gesture that Gammon was beginning to know well.

He made an even more hurried dash to the pit, realising that his worn RAF uniform was unknown to the Pole and looked similar to *Luftwaffe* grey-blue. He realised that although free, none of the ex-prisoners were yet out of danger. Later, with his heartbeat slowing to near normal, Gammon went back towards the barn. He waved and gave a wan smile to the laughing Pole and then dived to the ground as a screaming, roaring sound rent the air above. Looking up he was just in time to see a Messerschmitt Me262 soar back into the low clouds. Gammon got up, dusted himself down and was glad to see that although the Messerschmitt had not dropped bombs or fired guns, the Germans in the prisoner cage were all flat down, their faces buried in the dirt with their hands clasped behind their necks and heads. It was probably the first jet plane any of them had encountered. Vic Gammon hurriedly turned back to the canvas screens.

### 'MADE IT, AT LAST'

Veteran escaper Stan Croft, his friends 'Slim' Somerville, Tommy Thompson and Jimmy Abernethy had been marching for weeks, first in the snow blizzards from Gross Tychow and now in the spring rain. They were hungry, foot-sore and suffering from dysentery. They felt the time to break away had arrived again.

Their previous attempt had failed when they had slipped away from the column but being notorious 'bad lads', inveterate escapers, they had been quickly missed. Search parties had been sent out and they were discovered in a farm by an ex-Hitler Youth guard, noted for his indoctrinated mind and hatred for the British.

The guard quickly lined the four up against a farmhouse wall, raised his machine pistol and was preparing as Croft said, 'to dispatch them with the usual German efficiency'. Croft was convinced that they were to be shot there and then and said to Somerville, 'Well I guess we've asked for it'.

Croft and the German had reckoned without the farmer's wife, a compassionate woman, who came running out to tell the guard that if he wanted to shoot them he had better find another farmyard. When she saw the bad shape that Thompson and Abernethy were in she took pity on them, led them into the farmhouse while her husband remarked to the guard, 'If they are going to be shot they are at least entitled to a last meal'.

Food was hastily prepared and the guard ate with them, during which time his temper cooled and he eventually agreed to march the Kriegies off to rejoin the column. That had been Stan Croft's fifth escape attempt. Now, Croft and Somerville lay in the straw, awake and listening to the sound of gunfire echoing across the still night air.

'It's not that far away,' whispered Somerville. There was the sound of freedom in the gunfire.

'How about it? Let's beat it in the early morning,' breathed Croft.

When away from the column again, Somerville and Croft became parted when Croft stole a bicycle which was leaning against a wall. Pedalling furiously towards a wood he was startled by close machine gun fire. He rode the bicycle to the muddy bottom of a ditch. Slowly he crawled back to a farm he had just passed and took cover behind a wood pile. Peering from behind the pile Croft watched as an armoured car drove towards him, stopping 50 yards distant. Not knowing what to make of it he called, 'Who's there?' in German. When a soldier stood up in the armoured car he was wearing the black beret of the Tank Regiment. Croft now stood up and shouted in English, 'Don't shoot!'. The tank man spoke sharply to his companion, then to Croft he called:

'Stand in the middle of the road and identify yourself.'

Relief flooded over Stan Croft as he walked to the crown of the road. He had made six determined attempts at escape and now, on 17 April 1945, when the war could surely have only a few weeks to go, he was free. Every effort over the years had been worth that glorious moment.

## A STUMBLING, SHAMBLING PROCESSION

The men of the straggling Kriegie columns felt that they had been well observed by Allied aircraft throughout the day. They fervently hoped they had been recognised by a Spitfire pilot who 'buzzed' them as some of them filed into an enormous hay-lofted and galleried barn that was to be that night's accommodation. One hundred and fifty Kriegies were ordered into that and a similar barn next door. Exhausted and weary they settled down for the night as guards locked the doors and the remainder of the column moved on to other accommodation.

It was in the early hours that wailing sirens, ground fire and the sound of Mosquito engines roughly shook the Kriegies awake. Two explosions were heard and the aircraft turned away, the sound fading. The ominous sound of a low-level return of the Mosquito was more alarming, the pilot was intent on strafing the barns. There was nothing the Kriegies could do but wrap their arms around their heads and pray.

Incendiary cannon shells crashed through the roof, tearing holes in the thatch which burst into rapidly spreading flames. Flight was urgent, blazing clumps of burning thatch were already falling when men shouted and hammered on the doors for the guards to unlock them. The guards refused, so casting around, Ken Goodchild and others grabbed pieces of timber to use as battering rams. They smashed the doors open just as the guards started firing indiscriminately. The frightened guards were brusquely brushed aside and left in no doubt that if they did not move they would join those inside the barn. Kriegies poured through the door gasping for air, some throwing off clothing on which burning clumps of thatch had fallen. The men at the door then turned back to help bring out the injured and the dead.

Arthur Minnitt and Wally Lowery were showered with bricks and dust as shells smashed and exploded through the wall above their heads as the Mosquito roared away. Lowery thought he had been hit. The pair bent double and dashed through the smoke and burning straw as the doors crashed open. Goodchild saw that an airman who had been lying next to him had been hit during the attack. He rapidly stood astride the man, but while grasping him beneath the armpits to lift him he saw that a bullet had smashed into the man's forehead. The lolling head rattled. Goodchild, horrified, dropped the body on to the floor and scrambled outside gasping for breath.

Hal Croxson and his combine saw the roof was well alight. Throwing their possessions into a blanket they pulled the four corners together to form a bag and ran out into the road. Bill Baird put out his hand to shake and hurry his Scots friend laying by his side. There was no movement. Baird felt only a pulpy, bloody mess. He pulled a blanket round his friend's body and dragged it out.

Dougie Waters thought Reg Brown was in a heavy sleep of exhaustion. He shouted loudly, 'Come on Reg, get up!' and turned on his elbow to rouse him. Waters thrust his hand under Brown to lift him. Ron Akerman on the other side of Brown called out to him to hurry, but Waters' withdrawn hand contained only blood and brains. Brown had not murmured during the attack but his friends could see that one side of his head had been neatly sliced off. Straw was spreading the blaze rapidly throughout the barn: it was becoming an inferno, they had taken too long and had to get out. Akerman and Waters pulled a blanket over Brown's head and ran.

Doug Fry had looked through a three-foot square hole high in the wall opposite and seen the flash of guns and the stream of tracer coming straight towards the barn. Throwing himself face down on the floor he huddled amid the crash of exploding cannon shells. Burning straw was roaring out of control. A whiplash across his back told him that he had been hit although it did not feel serious. Next to him lay 'Joe' Boyle, badly wounded in the neck and leg.

The Kriegies were making a rapid but orderly exit from the blazing barn. When Fry reached the outside he saw Boyle on the ground, crumpled against a wall. As he hobbled towards him Fry realised that he had lost his left boot. Turning back to the roaring flames he saw a boot just inside the barn door. It was not his but the size was the same. It fitted him perfectly. When he turned back Boyle was gone, the casualties had been rushed to a nearby house for treatment.

Fry could feel blood coursing down his back so he joined the casualties for treatment. He did not believe he was badly hurt but his clothing was filthy. It would be as well to have the shell splinter tear attended to. A wounded American was loaded on to the cart with the injured because it was felt that a glimmer of life remained in his body. It was not to be; the top of the American's head had been sheared off. A blanket covering him and the straw on which he was lying was soon drenched with blood. Doug Fry suddenly felt that his minor wound was unimportant.

Ken Goodchild helped to damp down the fire when the worst had subsided. There had been a fear that the fire would serve as a beacon to aircraft looking for a target. Next morning there was little to be seen but the hot, smouldering, blackened beams, but Hal Croxson made use of the embers by cooking a breakfast for his combine. Bill Baird found that the cannon shells had blown open a potato clamp. Finding a jam tin and a water supply meant that they ate boiled potatoes for the rest of the day.

The weary march continued. Hot, dusty days with the men becoming weaker with each step. Dysentery, exhaustion and near starvation were ravaging the columns. Rumour now had it that the destination was Lübeck but no-one could fathom why. The Kriegie columns had to be a great encumbrance to the Germans, frequently clogging roads and making it difficult for the *Wehrmacht* to pass towards the fighting front.

Directly ahead of the Kriegies' line of march a pall of smoke rose from a wood where a flight of Typhoons had roared in, firing rockets and cannon. Next morning, the 15th, the marchers saw the mangled remains of 20 Junkers Ju88s as they passed.

Larry Slattery headed one section of the column, his long experience as a prisoner made him a useful interpreter for the Kriegies but his features, well known to the Germans, meant that he would be quickly missed if he attempted to escape.

When the Lauenburg bridge over the Elbe came into sight and Kriegies saw the Tiger tanks waiting for the Allies on the west bank, the rumours of a German stand at the river with the Kriegies as hostage on the east side assumed a new significance. Alex 'Dusty' Miller was determined not to cross. Feigning a sudden sickness he managed to hang back with three other airmen and two soldiers from the 51st Highland Division. They slipped away in the growing confusion and melted into the countryside.

Heading west with a Polish Army man driving a horse-drawn cart, they were hailed by two guards they recognised from Fallingbostel. The guards said that they had been detailed to take the sick Kriegies to hospital but their intentions were obvious when they joined the Kriegies on the cart and placed their rifles out of the way on the floor. They wanted to avoid any fighting.

Suddenly one of the Highland Division soldiers cocked an ear.

'I can hear tanks coming,' he said. Kneeling, he put his ear to the ground and pronounced with certainty:

'They are Churchills.'

It was the cue for the guards to act as one, throwing their rifles as far into the woods as they could. Minutes later four Churchill tanks, an Army truck with British soldiers, and a German lorry driven by a British soldier containing German prisoners appeared around a bend in the road ahead. They were part of the Guards Armoured Division. After shaking hands and wishing them luck the Kriegies were told to make their way into Lüneburg which was securely in British hands.

Moving off, the Kriegies were joined by other people appearing from the woods around. Their party became a sort of caravan of about 20 Italians, 10 displaced persons and several Germans, two of whom were armed *SS* men from whom the desire to fight had evaporated. They all felt they would be safer if they went into Lüneburg accompanying Britishers, who would say the right things on arrival.

### TRAGEDY AT GRESSE

At 10.00am the Kriegie columns began to cross the railway bridge at Lauenburg. George Woodhead was in one of the last parties to cross. It had been the longest march in any one day and the men were nearing exhaustion. With the Elbe behind them, they were now on the wrong side of the river if the Germans used it as a defence line. The column was slowly trudging through the town when a series of massive explosions shook the area like an earthquake. Whipping round, Woodhead saw the huge steel bridge heave and collapse into the river, a mass of twisted metal.

When they halted for the night at a barn it was already full of German troops. For the Kriegies it meant a night in the open. It started to rain and then turned into a drenching thunderstorm. Eventually Tom Harvey's section was able to shelter in a church. There Tom found a mirror and shaved, his first for many days. He was surprised to see how thin his face had become. His friends at home would never recognise him.

At 5.30am on Thursday 19 April the Kriegies were aroused as usual by shouting guards and soon they had set off again on a colder but fine morning, in conditions better for marching. By 10.30am the column had turned on to a good, made-up road signposted 'Gresse 2km', and when it arrived near the village of Heidekrug the men were told that 'Dixie' Deans had been at work. The Swedish Red Cross was supplying each man with an American Red Cross parcel. A short distance beyond, the column stopped for a rest and parcels were being opened with the almost unbelievable prospect of a real meal at last.

George Woodhead saw the planes coming in the distance but paid little attention, food had priority and previous strikes had been well executed and accurate with the Kriegies watching excitedly.

When Stan Brooks, at the rear of the column, heard a shout of, 'For Christ's sake look out!' he turned to see the Typhoons forming up, line-astern and beginning the dive towards the column strung out along the road. He was one of 12 Kriegies who had been pushing a handtruck, Brooks dropped the Red Cross parcel he was opening, jumped across a grass verge on his left, cleared a four-foot hedge at a bound and, wrapping his arms around his head, threw himself on to ploughed earth.

Jack Broughton in the next party 'walked through' those who had received parcels and was looking forward to receiving his, when six RAF Typhoons roared over his head, line-astern.

Roy Witham had just popped his first piece of chocolate in his mouth when he saw the Typhoons dip low.

George Calvert, hungry and tired, perked up when he saw that men on the long straight road ahead were being ushered in to a large house and then coming out lovingly grasping a Red Cross parcel. He could hardly believe it when he was handed a parcel. Seated against a tree by the side of the road he had just taken out the chocolate when the six aircraft flew past. The black and white stripes on the underside of the wings meant nothing to him. He took little notice, assuming they were German. A mile away he saw them make a low banking turn into line-astern and disappear behind the trees.

Bill Hart threw himself behind a hedge, scattering the contents of his just issued parcel. Kriegies were frantically waving anything white. Hart looked up, the lead Typhoon passed very low above his head, the noise deafening.

Bert Dowty had just collected his food parcel when orders came from the Germans that the column was to move on. He was tying a blanket roll on to Sandy Saunderson's backpack when the roar of low flying aircraft above took him by surprise. There was immediately a second noise of roadside trees splitting as cannon shells struck. Yelling to Saunderson to dive into the ditch Dowty tried to pull a singlet from his great-coat pocket to wave but he seemed to be seized by a paralysis down his right side. He plainly saw two rockets released from beneath the wings of an aircraft. The rockets went past his ears as he looked back for Saunderson. A round, football-size object whistled through the air. Behind him lay a headless body.

Brian Booth had seen the Typhoons turning and diving toward them, putting on speed. He threw himself behind a large tree just as rockets and shells burst about him. With unspeakable horror he saw the legs cut completely from a man who had previously described himself as 'the ugliest man in Scunthorpe'. As Booth ran towards him the man died.

Bill Goodman, his pack still on his back, dived in one move over a fence, into the ditch and crouched behind the bole of a tree. In the same ditch men were throwing themselves down and being struck simultaneously.

Bill Garrioch could see no cover anywhere. As the Typhoons came in low he was one who tried to wave a greatcoat with a red cross on the lining. It did no good so he threw himself down on to the road and prayed. When the attack ended Garrioch scrambled to his feet, relieved to find himself unhurt. Then he saw what had happened to the Canadian who had been walking beside him. The man's legs and lower torso lay in the road beside Garrioch, the upper half of his body was in the branches of a nearby tree. His face looked quite normal. Garrioch was so shocked that he stood rooted to the spot for several minutes, stunned with horror. A perambulator, full with the Combine's few possessions, was splattered with bits of human flesh. Two of the three guards who had thrown themselves into a small depression were dead, their bodies horribly mutilated. Garrioch who had helplessly watched his gunner Taffy sink beneath the icy waters of the Zuider Zee, now saw friends dead or dying all around him.

Australian Johnny Shierlaw and Johnny Gage had dived under the truck. With great composure another Kriegie grabbed and waved his RAF greatcoat, turning it inside out showing its white lining in the hope that it would be recognised by the pilots. Moments later he was dead.

George Calvert had just taken a bite of chocolate when the noise broke around him. Aircraft roared past just overhead, cannon and rocket bursts tossed the men on the road around like rag dolls; then they lay still. Despite his tree cover Calvert bolted into the field. He was one of several running madly when he saw an aircraft coming in low and fast from his right and distinctly saw two puffs of smoke from the leading edges of the wings. Immediately a rocket exploded in front of him, blasting a hot and smoking crater. Calvert tumbled headlong into the crater with two other runners crashing on top of him. There they stayed until the racket subsided.

Cannon shells struck the road and ricocheted, tearing their way through the column of men. Rockets slammed and burst in explosive flame among them, hurtling and scattering parts of bodies in all directions. Deafening detonations mixed with screams, shouts and the noise of aircraft roaring above. Then they were gone, leaving only the cries of the wounded and the stunned Kriegies who gasped and stared in breathless horror at the slaughter and maiming of their friends.

The noise passed and Dowty found his friend Saunderson. Together they went back to where they had been hitching up their packs. The men who had stood on either side of them were dead in the road.

Stan Brooks lay still in the field when the noise had passed. Large pieces of hot shrapnel had torn into his left arm and leg. One hundred yards away the cart was a smoking ruin and popular Australian sportsman Johnny Shierlaw, his friend Johnny Gage and 35 others, including six of the German guards, were dead. Wounded and mutilated lay everywhere, some moaning, some screaming in agony and others ominously quiet and still.

A feeling of utter helplessness came over Arthur Smith, his friends lay dying with no hope of the rapid attention needed to save them. Many of the survivors were so shocked and dazed that they could only ask who had survived, so many of the dead were unrecognisable. Tears of deep sorrow and frustration overcame men hardened to death and war. These were their close friends, they had endured years of captivity and its hardships together. Now, with freedom and a reunion with their loved ones perhaps only days away, they were dead, killed by men of their service.

Ron Buckingham looked up from the road where he had been lying face down. A pair of boots were touching his head. They belonged to the elderly guard who had been walking beside him. Getting to his knees

Buckingham shook the German to bring him round, then with a shudder he saw that the man's head was missing. Within 10 yards of where Buckingham had risen to his feet there were 10 dead men. Others had run into the field on the right waving their arms and coats, but the pilots had seen them as retreating Germans so the Typhoons reformed at high speed into line-abreast firing as they came.

Stan Brooks saw three attacks and so did Tom Harvey. Arthur Smith thought there were four. It was on the third attack that the firing stopped as if the Typhoon pilots had suddenly realised that something was wrong – but it was too late. Terrible destruction had been done although Tom Harvey could hardly believe that he had come through the attack untouched, an incendiary bullet had parted his hair and scorched his sleeve.

Shaken, George Calvert went back. The sickening sight of dead and mutilated friends almost overwhelmed him. Only a few were allowed to aid the wounded or clear away the dead so Calvert returned to where he had left his kit and parcel. The spot had received a direct hit. His wartime log book was sheared in two, all that remained of his kit was a shrapnel-cut sock. Every tin from his Red Cross parcel had been sliced open.

Pulling themselves together Garrioch and others did what they could for the injured before they were marched further up the road for fear of another attack. As Garrioch was leaving the scene he passed a cow in the field a few yards away, it was bleeding profusely from multiple wounds.

Flight Sergeant Freddie Steele, who had so often played a brilliant right wing on the football field, lay unconscious and mortally wounded. Ron Buckingham could not find an identity tag on his friend Duffield's body but Sergeant 'Tod' Slaughter recognised him. Buckingham took a blanket from his pack and tenderly covered the body and then went back to retrieve the rest of his own possessions. His kitbag had been sliced in half, his leather belt and his greatcoat had shrapnel nicks and his tin mug was holed. Buckingham was unscathed.

Dave Young and Peter Stubbs had dived into a ditch. In the midst of the deafening havoc Young shouted:

'How would you like to be an infantryman and do this sort of thing for a living?'

The pair climbed up from the ditch, picked themselves up and extricated what they could from the carnage when Young stopped, rooted to the ground. Before him was a pair of khaki-clad legs ending in a pair of shiny boots. He stared, stunned; there was nothing else.

Spitfire Pilot Bob Morton, veteran of many dogfights, had thrown himself down at the start of the attack. A bullet kicked up the sand just in front of his nose. Now he scrambled to his feet, dusted himself down and decided that he had never been so frightened in his life. He said after:

'The attack was certainly aggressive, I lived more fully during those few minutes than I ever have since.'

Lancaster Pilot Ray Gulliford had become separated from his combine, slipped away from the column, had been recaptured and ended in Stalag 357 again. Had he stayed he might have been beside his fellow crew member Flight Sergeant Mortimer who lay dead on the road at Gresse.

There was sympathy for some of the elderly dead German guards. Many had closed their eyes to prisoners' attempts to escape and some of them, long disillusioned by the *Nazis*, were family men who longed for the end of the fear and slaughter.

Horrified, 'Dixie' Deans hurried back to the scene of the carnage. As always his concern was for the men who had placed such trust in him. He had shepherded them through many trials for more than four years but this was an incident that had been beyond his control. Was there anything he could do to prevent a recurrence? Quickly Deans decided there was, he would go to speak to the nearest Allied commander, tell him what had happened and make certain there was no repetition. The Germans were insistent that the attackers were American but Tom Harvey said to the *Hauptmann* 'we know our own aircraft'.

A sceptical Oberst Ostmann in charge of the column was badgered to write Deans a safe conduct chit to pass through the German lines. Accompanied by *Dolmetscher* 'Charlie' Gumbach, Deans set off on a hazardous bicycle ride westward.

Deryck Polley, Doug Elder, New Zealander Norman Scott, Mike Roberts and a few others carried out the heartbreaking job of clearing up. Stan Brooks, bleeding and shocked, was gently lifted out of the field and placed on the grass verge. Others who could not walk were laid beside him. Some of the injuries were so severe that it was wrenching for the rescuers to realise that many were unlikely to survive. The wounded were gently moved on to carts and taken to the Boizenburg cottage hospital.

They then turned to the frequently difficult job of identifying the dead and taking the bodies to the local cemetery. Identity discs were removed and each body tagged with his name. There in the churchyard at Gresse a German sexton was busy digging a communal grave where the bodies were to be interred. Mike Roberts was appalled to find that a square pit had been dug. Roberts wanted a grave where the men could be laid side by side. This square grave meant that the corpses would have to be laid head to toe and on top of each other. A furious argument between Roberts and the German officer in charge terminated with the officer drawing his pistol and threatening to add another couple of corpses to the grave if they did not get on with the job. Roberts was furious, he told the German that his whereabouts were known and that he had better think seriously about his own future.

When the clearing of the road had finished, the wounded taken away and the dead carried on carts to the graveyard, the weary fatigue party made their way to the barn where the rest of the column was bedded down. Not for the first time the men drew up straw and settled down outside beneath the stars. It had been a physically and mentally exhausting day. Despite the horrors they had seen, the men of the disposal party slept.

Among the dead and wounded, airmen and soldiers, there were Canadians, Australians, New Zealanders, South Africans, Englishmen, Irishmen, Welshmen, Scots and an American. Many were RAF aircrew, others had been taken prisoner at Dieppe or Arnhem or in the hell of the retreat to Dunkirk. They had survived much, only to die when liberation was so close.

Pastor Stuebe of Gresse was no stranger to visions of misery. The conflagration at Lübeck three years earlier could be plainly seen from his parish and the huge firestorm at Hamburg, just 35 miles north-east, was almost on his doorstep. In each case night-time brilliance of flame-coloured skies gave way to the sombre dark of a smoke pall blotting out the daylight. Then there were the refugees; old people, women clutching their children, the injured, the burned, the terrified and the deranged all fleeing from the horror of the stricken city. As ashes settled on his pleasant country village the Pastor, like every other true man of religion in Germany, had to struggle with his Christian conscience. How to reconcile Christian beliefs with the mass killing of people by air-raids and the obscene, cold-blooded excesses of *Nazism*.

Stuebe had no doubts when the dead and wounded of the air attack were brought to his church at Gresse. The mixture of nationalities mattered not to him, they were all human beings. When the wounded had been treated as best possible and sent on to the hospital at Boizenburg, Pastor Stuebe stood beside the graves with an English Padre and conducted a burial service.

On the following morning Pastor Stuebe was alone when he conducted a burial service for the last few to be buried. The English Padre had been forced at gunpoint to move on. By the graveside Stuebe had a large inscribed cross erected and before returning to ministering to his needy flock he planted carnations and roses on the graves.

The calamity at Gresse had deeply shocked the men in the column. From then on an uneasy feeling penetrated every section. The Red Cross parcels had fortified them physically but whenever an aircraft was heard apprehensive eyes would search the sky. So near to the end of their captivity, they had no wish to be victims of another air attack.

As the column moved in a north-easterly direction the farms became larger and more prosperous. In huge cathedral-like barns the men were able to bed down fairly comfortably and with whatever food they could steal, supplemented with sugar, raisins and chocolate, they were feeling much better. Throughout the April trek, until then, the weather had been kind and spring-like with warm sunny days and cool nights. The terrible events of Gresse seemed to mark the end of the pleasant weather. For two nights the 'Pork Butcher', the Kriegies' name for Oberst Ostmann, had let them down, he was unable to find accommodation and during their nights outdoors it rained.

Near the end of April, close to Zarrentin, the columns with the headquarters staff and that with Young and Stubbs were billeted in the same village so Bristow, Young and Stubbs, the old radio campaigners, were able to meet. The radio in the billycan was working well and following the tragedy at Gresse instructions were received on a short-wave frequency that the Kriegies should lay white towels in the form of a cross wherever they camped. By this time the guards were fed up with Hitler, forced marches and the whole 'verflucht' business, and would do or say anything for one Chesterfield cigarette. They were equally enthusiastic that the crossed towels should be laid out at once at every halt.

North of Zarrentin near the Schaal See the column turned northwest towards Ratzeburg. All the night of 30 April they had marched along woodland tracks listening to the sounds of confusion and slow moving traffic. Reaching a main road they found it jammed with retreating military vehicles. Avoiding the town centre and crossing a bridge over the southern end of a lake they settled into a farm which fronted the road on which they had travelled. There was the sound of a fierce battle to the west but the Kriegies were 'whacked' and an issue of Canadian Red Cross parcels helped them to settle down to rest after their long night walk. It was 1 May.

On the afternoon of 2 May a jeep drove up to the barn. A British Army corporal stepped out and asked how many sick there were in the party. Liberation for some was as low-key as that.

Captain O'Regan and a sergeant led a reconnoitring party of half a dozen men of the 6th Airborne Division across the Elbe in a dinghy. Stealthily stealing along a dark village street O'Regan saw a light in a cottage. He badly needed information about the Germans' positions so, as if on an evening stroll, he knocked at the door. When an old lady answered and spoke to the soldiers it was not the presence of German troops that interested them. In her mixture of German and halting English she told them that there were English prisoners in the hospital at Boizenburg.

Stan Brooks was in the first bed of the hospital ward when the men of 6th Airborne walked in. The tough soldiers with their camouflaged uniforms and blackened faces were as caring as nurses, but their solicitude took a fiery turn of indignation. Brooks was ill and looked it, apart from the shrapnel wounds in his arm and leg, shock had induced pneumonia.

'How've they been treating you mate?' asked the sergeant becoming angry. 'If they've been treating you rough we'll take 'em out in the yard and shoot all the bastards.' Brooks was appalled and anxious.

'For God's sake don't do anything to this staff, they have been absolutely wonderful, the German Army doctors have been wonderful too, please don't touch them.'

The sergeant cooled down, mollified until he remembered the *Soldaten* they had taken prisoner outside.

'What about the guards, have they been OK?' asked the sergeant, hitching up his Tommy-gun. 'What about them, it won't take us long, oh yes, no bother at all.'

Stan Brooks' condition deteriorated; his wounds were healing but the pneumonia had a hold. The MO thought it due to the shock of the attack and the subsequent shelling for two days in the vicinity of the hospital. It was decided to move Brooks back to England.

On 2 May Brooks and 26 other stretcher cases were lying on the airfield tarmac waiting for a Dakota air ambulance when a Wing Commander walked up to them.

'Hello,' he said brightly with a transatlantic accent. 'What have you chaps been up to, are you ex-POWs?' A soldier on a stretcher answered:

'Yes, we are POWs but we were shot up by some bastard crowd of half a dozen Tiffies.' The Wing Commander stopped abruptly.

'What did you say?'

'We were shot up a couple of weeks ago by Typhoons,' the soldier said, 'and most of us here are men who were injured. We are on our way back to England.'

'Where did this happen and when?' asked the Wing Commander.

'We are not quite sure where we finished up,' replied another man on a stretcher. 'It was in a little hospital near the Elbe. The shoot-up though was at a place called Gresse on the 19th of April.'

The Wing Commander's face paled.

'My God, I was leading that flight.' There was silence until one of the men on a stretcher said bitterly:

'Yes, and you killed about 30 of our blokes outright. Some of us had done five years and were on the last knockings of getting towards home and this had to happen.' The Wing Commander stood motionless, there were tears on his cheeks, then as he turned away Brooks saw the officer's shoulder flash – it read 'Canada'.

Regimental Policeman Private John Bell was tired. He had been riding to and fro as a despatch rider for countless miles. He and his motorcycle were covered in mud and dust but he had to push ahead and rejoin the 2nd Battalion of the Wiltshires after contacting the rear party. The Intelligence Officer led the way in a jeep until they pulled up in Ratzeburg town square. Jumping from the jeep the officer instructed Bell to stay in the square and control the crowding, curious German civilians. Bell dismounted, put his motorcycle on its rest, then noticed a group of men staring at him. One of the men went up to him and hesitantly asked:

'Are you a British soldier?'

'Yes,' Bell replied, studying the group and realising that his mud and dust covering was a perfect camouflage.

'We are RAF prisoners-of-war and some of these others are French prisoners,' the man said. Bell could see that the speaker and a few others wore vestiges of faded blue RAF uniforms.

'The Jerries have force marched us all over Germany,' said another.

'Have you seen British troops pass through the town?' Bell asked, shaking their hands happily. They had not but were delighted to see him. From his motorcycle pannier he gave the prisoners packets of Woodbines. There was little they could give in return but Bell accepted a cup of their roadside brewed tea and, as he did not wish to offend them, accepted a slice of the sawdust bread they offered.

The Intelligence Officer had disappeared into the Town Hall in search of the *Bürgermeister*. Looking back he saw the crowd and sent his driver back with instructions for Bell to 'get rid of the German civilians in the square'. Bell's German was equal to the task. With a loud, *'Raus! Raus!'* and *'gehen sie nach Haus!'* the square started to clear when a large German policeman joined in the shouting, yelling at the people to go home. Bell assumed that the policeman was trying to help but when he saw the RAF men and Frenchmen walking away he called them back.

'That doesn't mean you, why are you leaving?'

'Well, we are a bit scared of that policeman,' said one of the prisoners.

'Look,' said Bell urgently, 'you are free now. Very soon the Wiltshires will be with you and you'll be sent home.'

Taking the initiative Bell pulled out his pistol, strode over to the large policeman, grabbed him by the scruff of his neck, disarmed him and handed the policeman's pistol to one of the RAF men. Knowing very well that the RAF man would not carry out his order, he said: 'Shoot him!'. Bell had made his point, they were now free and in command of the situation. He had to leave for Lüneburg.

The welcome appearance of despatch rider Bell and the knowledge that they were now free was too much for Flight Sergeant John Pickering and his friends. They immediately cast around for some form of transport, they wanted to get home as quickly as possible but first there was the house of the Ratzeburg *Bürgermeister* to examine. More British soldiers had arrived and Pickering followed one inside. In the first room they found a stack of *Wehrmacht* officers' belts. Wrapping one round his waist, complete with a holstered Luger, Pickering felt ready for anything.

Soldiers pointed out a garage where a large van was ideal for their journey. The German owner nervously handed over the keys at pistol point and the airmen set off, but at Lauenburg the bridge over which they had crossed the Elbe was now in the river. They would find another temporary crossing a mile down river.

The long column of between 10,000 and 12,000 men was now spread over many miles and locations. Despite pressure for him to stay and rest, Sergeant James 'Dixie' Deans, accompanied by his faithful interpreter 'Charlie' Gumbach, had returned from his dangerous double passage through the fluid fighting line and rejoined the marchers at the head of the column. When it had been suggested that he leave Gumbach behind to be put into a prisoner-of-war cage, Deans was equally adamant that Gumbach should go back with him.

The Kriegies were pleased to see Deans' comforting presence and to know that control of the column was back in his hands. He had shown their position on a map to Lieutenant-General Barker, had received assurances that there would be no further air attacks on his men and that preparations would be made for their release.

*Oberst* Ostmann was also pleased to see Deans return. Control of a column of ill-disciplined Kriegies was never easy for him; he knew the German way with the gun and bayonet but realised that it was no longer a viable method. And he had an even greater problem, what to do and where to go next. He felt he had reached a dead-end but news of the death of Adolf Hitler and the certainty that the column would be overrun within days solved Ostmann's problems at a stroke. Now he was no longer bound by his oath to Der Führer and must think of his own clouded future and that of the guards. He must surrender, and surrender to a man who was honourable and honest, and one who may be able to help with a kind word to any military tribunal. With innate dignity he surrendered his pistol and his guards to James Deans who accepted it with equal dignity. Deans' exhausting years of overwhelming responsibility, which would have crushed a lesser man, were nearing an end.

The surrender did not take place simultaneously along the whole of the columns. Many groups were miles apart and liberation came to others in different ways. George Calvert was sitting against a barn door during a rest period when he saw two men coming towards them along the road. They were wearing khaki uniforms, tin helmets and carrying rifles. To him they looked wonderful, as far as he was concerned 'they were the whole British Army'.

Men in Bill Garrioch's section of the column were 'making a brew' outside the barn of their overnight stop when they were startled by the sound of a tank battle five miles away. Then a Spitfire appeared overhead and waggled its wings. 'At least they know we are here,' Garrioch said happily.

Half an hour later a jeep drew up carrying three immaculately smart Military Policeman. With a smile they announced: 'Fellows, you are now free.' Four and a half years of captivity had ended for Bill Garrioch. It was all over, and was almost overwhelming. He looked around him at the smiling faces. Despite their happy expressions and loud cheers, many were wiping their eyes.

The 25 German guards with that section of the column disappeared into the barn, returning minutes later wearing Red Cross armbands. Then they handed over their rifles and surrendered. Four Kriegies armed themselves and started to escort them into the town of Mölln, a few miles away. Overtaken by a British Army motorcycle patrol they were warned to take care as several hundred *SS* troops were still fighting in the wood next to the road. Suddenly scores of *SS* men appeared from the wood and attempted to join the column of German prisoners, but another fierce battle flared up when *SS* gunners attempted to stop them, turning their guns on their own men. But the survivors joined the prisoners and soon the party numbered 400. The escort saw them into the prisoner-of-war cage at Mölln where 'Dixie' Deans, now wearing warrant officer's 'Tate & Lyle' insignia on his sleeves, saluted again and turned over Oberst Ostmann, his officers and guards to the British Army.

### QUICK EXIT FROM MÜHLBERG

As the 1,593 RAF prisoners and the 5,000 Army prisoners at Stalag 4B Mühlberg bedded down for the night on 22 April, they knew the end of their incarceration was near. Excitement was intense but as always, prisoners had little idea of how that end would come, they were still in German hands and maiming or death could so easily be their lot. The news from their clandestine radio (there were four in the camp manufactured by young NCO Eric Gaggini) had told them that the Russians were at Cottbus, 50 miles distant. For many months the prisoners had been well informed by a regularly updated, large wall map of eastern Europe drawn on a wash-house wall. This time the guards had allowed a map to stay and frequently studied it glumly.

Rumours ran rife: 'The Russians were near at hand', 'All resistance in the west has ceased', 'The Yanks should be here tomorrow', 'Ike orders POWs to stay in camp and not to loot'. Orders through their

*'I've just made you a brew on the 'Smokeless Wonder'!'*

senior man gave the impression that the Germans would leave next day. All the Kriegies were hungry, their bread ration had been intercepted and stolen by the Germans although potatoes, issued after dark, gave some relief. There was no electricity so all cooking and eating had to be done by the light of candles.

The BBC news was backed up by news from Moscow which Russian workers in the German staff area had obtained from a German 'one-station' People's Radio which they had 'doctored' to pick-up stations further afield. All the prisoners at Stalag 4B knew far more about the desperate plight of Germany than the Germans themselves.

Harry McLean lay in his bunk listening to distant explosions which he assumed to be the *Wehrmacht* destroying the airfield at Ale Connewitz, 15 miles from Mühlberg. Later the sound of artillery rumbled, followed by sporadic bumps, bangs, machine gun and small arms fire heard from the direction of Mühlberg. Then all became quiet. It was an exciting, frightening and disturbed night.

As the Kriegies prepared for the usual morning *Appell* they were called to order by their senior man Ron Hale who calmly announced:

'We are now under the command of a Russian colonel.'

'How long's he been a prisoner then?' shouted McLean jokingly, not believing the astounding statement. As they were trooping out to their usual place on the parade ground a great cheer rose from a crowd near the main gate. There, a large gathering of Kriegies surrounded four Red Army horsemen and a large Red Flag was being waved. McLean moved closer to see. The Red Army men were a disappointment. Apart from the horses and machine guns they were just as dirty, poorly dressed and indistinguishable from those who had been the Kriegies' fellow prisoners. An RAF man standing next to McLean said quietly:

'Some Russian prisoners found two German camp guards trying to merge with the Kriegies for safety. The Ruskies have just hanged them.' Instant punishment and lynch law had begun. It was 23 April 1945.

There had been no delivery of Red Cross parcels for months at 4B and the prisoners had lived with hunger, but the Russian prisoners tore down barbed wire on the south side of the camp near the potato clamps. There they spent the first day of liberty boiling and eating frost-spoiled potatoes until satiated. Then they decamped for the local villages, throwing away their identity tags as no longer needed now they were free.

Word came from the Red Army that if the Kriegies wanted food they were to 'go out and get it and treat the Germans in the same way they treated you'. Advice from the SBO had been that they should stay put in the camp until definite arrangements had been made for their evacuation.

Instructions from the occupying Russians varied from day to day. 'Go out and find food for yourselves' alternated with 'Anyone leaving the camp will be shot'. With such confusing instructions it was decided that the Kriegies would form a Camp Police. Armed with captured weapons they patrolled the camp and took into custody several German soldiers issuing from the adjacent woods seeking to surrender to the British Army. They were put in the cells for their own protection.

The Kriegies formed themselves into syndicates of half a dozen where three or four went out to forage for whatever was eatable, while the rest stayed behind to guard their belongings and what little food they possessed. The plundering spread to nearby farms. Joints of beef, pork, and mutton and chickens were smuggled into the camp. Some were intercepted by the Camp Police stationed at gaps in the wire. Cattle were led into the camp kitchen, the beef to give body to the thin pea soup. The soup was much improved.

When it came to McLean's turn to go to the village to forage he found that there was nothing. The cupboards were bare but those who had obeyed orders and refrained from scrounging for extra rations, saw those who disobeyed returning loaded with food. Obeying orders meant they were forced to sit by hungry, watching and smelling the cooking of chickens, pork chops and beef steaks.

Outside the camp anarchy was spreading, Russians were killing Germans out of hand and were devastating houses and homes for the sheer pleasure of destruction and their hatred for the Germans. At a house near the camp Vic Munnings saw that despite the presence of a lone woman with six small children, everything had been smashed, even the children's toys.

Enormous waste and unnecessary damage was caused by many looting food and goods for the unprincipled pleasure of taking something for nothing. It saddened Munnings who thought it a terrible business and a heartbreak for the German populace but few prisoners worried about that, remembering well how the Germans had rapaciously and continuously plundered countries, east and west, that they had occupied. Most people were thankful when the Russian prisoners left the camp to rejoin their own forces. It was an odd quirk of war that many civilians came into the camp in the evening for food and shelter among men who had been their prisoners.

The situation at Stalag 4B was becoming desperate. Dysentery was endemic and the Kriegies merely existed from day to day. There were definite orders now that they were not to leave the camp and, with the electricity and water off and no news of going home, life was miserable. Before they left the Germans had installed pumps which provided some water although it was only usable when boiled. The Kriegies were despairing of official help from the Allied Forces and many were making their own way back. The Russian authorities then decided to march them to the local cavalry barracks at Riesa where they said there was better accommodation and they were to be registered. It was getting dark and as they passed a railway yard Harry McLean decided to dodge from the column to see if anything useful could be scrounged. He missed the road back but met a small group of RAF men. By now it was almost dark when a man approached the group who offered them a night's accommodation at his flat. They accepted with alacrity and were entertained by the Donath family in Riesa.

Next morning Harry McLean set off again and passing through Oschatz was recognised as an Engländer. A man whose son was a prisoner-of-war of the British asked Harry to take a letter for him, McLean agreed and the word got around. Soon he had five letters to deliver to England.

McLean was now crossing the no-man's-land which the Americans had taken, but from which they had subsequently withdrawn in accordance with the Yalta agreement. There was no road traffic and all seemed peaceful but the people around were very apprehensive. Helping himself to a drink from a creamery he walked on to Wurzen where he stayed in a house with 15 other Kriegies.

When he set off next morning and reached the railway bridge over the River Mulde, McLean knew he was near the end of his journey. The bridge had been blown but from a small dock it was a simple matter to cross by a lock gate, then clamber up the wreckage of the collapsed bridge until reaching the deck where there was a footpath. McLean and a companion he had met on the road, crossed the river and ran down some steps on the far side. At the foot of the steps sat two chatting GIs.

### A WORD IN THE RIGHT PLACE

On 7 May, Lieutenant-Commander John Casson led a party of RAF who had passed through Lüneburg to Bog Horst near Rheine, where they were housed in an old-fashioned barracks. Casson enquired when they could be repatriated and was brusquely told that it would be a couple of weeks. He was furious, found the RAF liaison officer, borrowed a jeep and drove to Rheine airport where he insisted on seeing the wing commander in charge. To him he blurted out:

'Do you know there's a bloody Pongo major in charge of us 2,000 Royal Air Force prisoners-of-war who says we can't get out for a fortnight?'

'Oh! to hell with that!' retorted the wing commander and immediately contacted Air Chief Marshal Harris. Next morning, Casson said that although it was VE-Day, 'half of Bomber Command flew over to fetch the fellows home'.

## EICHSTÄTT TO MOOSBURG

When the Oflag at Eichstätt was evacuated on 14 April 1945 the officers were destined for Stalag 7A Moosburg. Tom Nelson had the distinct feeling that they were to be held hostage. The tail of the Kriegie column had not left the camp gate when two Mustang aircraft flew overhead and each dropped a single bomb on the bridge 400 yards distant. The Kriegies dropped everything and stood in the road waving, cheering excitedly as the Mustangs flew past at 500ft. They were still waving when the Mustangs turned and flew back down the road towards them, guns blazing. Joy turned to impotent anger as bullets raked the column.

When the planes had gone the Kriegies were turned around and marched back to the camp. Four men had been killed and 30 wounded. One man who had been seriously hurt was a soldier taken at Dunkirk and who had entertained at the piano in the camp theatre. His right arm was severed at the elbow. Henceforth the march to Stalag 7A at Moosburg would be done during darkness.

The American Army was close behind the Kriegies telling them by radio to keep together, not to try to escape and that they would soon be free. After the recent experience the Kriegies did not know whether the Americans could be trusted but eventually, after four nights of marching, they arrived at Moosburg, joining 10,000 others.

On 27 April the Germans departed and the Kriegies took over the camp. The 29th was a beautiful Sunday morning, strangely still, when a US Third Army jeep swept into the camp – General George Patton had made a dramatic and welcome entrance. Not for him the usual dull green helmet, his was a brightly shining four-star general's outfit, his jeep flying his imposing general's flag. It was a surprise when this six-footer grabbed a microphone, pointed to the German flag and coarsely called out in his oddly weak, falsetto voice:

'I want that son-of-a-bitch cut down and the man that cuts it down, I want him to wipe his ass with it!'

The swastika flag was pulled down and 'Old Glory' hauled up the flag staff. Within five minutes an American Red Cross wagon loaded with coffee and doughnuts drove into the camp. Two blonde American girls served the Kriegies.

'Now that's the way to run a war,' mused Tom Nelson. Then he looked for the guards, wondering what had happened to them. The guards were there all right, five times as many as there had been before but now they were Americans. All had their guns pointing into the camp not outwards. They were determined that no-one was going to get out of that place unless they said so.

But everyone was demanding to know when they were to be moved and the American officer in charge resolved the problem with a Solomon-like solution. On a large map of the camp he drew squares dividing the camp into 12 equal sections. Everyone living in the area delineated by the first square pulled out of a hat would be moved next day, those in the second square the following day and so on. Tom Nelson was lucky, he camped in square one and next morning was moved into luxurious apartments in Moosburg. The US commander had previously driven into the town and given the occupants one hour to move out. Nelson felt a trifle guilty about the women and children who had been kicked out of house and home, but that night he slept in a proper bed for the first time in ages.

Next day his party were driven through the town where from every window a white sheet hung down in sad surrender. At the airfield a fleet of Dakotas flew the freed prisoners to Rheims. There that night General Eisenhower took the final surrender of the Germans and Nelson went to the pictures to see Judy Garland in Meet me in St Louis to celebrate.

Flying home on 8 May in a Lancaster, Nelson's fellow passengers were mostly Army officer Kriegies, one of whom used the Elsan chemical toilet and thought he was flushing it when he pulled a cord. He released the dinghy. The dinghy ejected from the wing, crashed into the tailplane and sent the Lancaster into a steep dive from which it pulled out 100ft from oblivion. The dinghy had broken away, the aircraft and crew recovered and Tom Nelson decided that flying was indeed a dangerous pursuit.

Landing at Manston, Nelson was told that he would be sent north for medicals and debriefing, but he had to let his mother know that he was home. She lived in a flat without a telephone and they had not heard from each other for six months. Nelson did not even know whether the flats still existed. Passing through Victoria Station he dashed to a telephone and rang the Savoy Cinema opposite his mother's London flat. He asked the astonished box-office girl:

'Can you see the flats on the opposite side?'

'Yes,' she replied. At least the flats were still there. V-weapons had not smashed them.

'Will you run across there and tell my mother I am back in England, but they are sending me to Yorkshire and I don't know when I am going to get home.' The young lady did as he asked and Nelson's mother knew on VE-Day that he was safe and almost home.

### THE 'STAY PUT' AT BARTH

At Stalag Luft 1 Barth there was tension. The Kriegies, British and American, knew Allied troops were at the Elbe and the Russians in Berlin. Liberation could not be far away but like most Kriegies they wondered if their war was going to end with a whimper or an almighty bang. The Senior American Officer, Colonel Zemke, and Rhodesian Group Captain Grant were told by *Kommandant* Oberst Warnstedt that his orders were to evacuate the camp, marching the Kriegies west. Warnstedt was nonplussed for a moment when the senior officers told him that they had no intention of moving. Eventually Warnstedt said quietly:

'I will not have blood shed in this camp, my men will leave you in charge.' On the afternoon of 30 April, Major Stienhauer left with the last of the guards.

Sergeant George Luke had been one of the first 50 NCOs who had volunteered in December 1944 to go to Barth from Heydekrug to act as orderlies for the RAF officers. As far as Luke knew, none had any intention or were asked to carry out orderly duties but the chance of an escape on the train journey between the camps was a chance not to be missed. Also from that stretch of Baltic coast there was a chance of stowing away on a boat to Sweden. On 31 January 1944 the volunteers were deposited safely at Barth. The Germans were very much alive to their reasons for volunteering and the Kriegie escape plans had been thwarted by tight security. Frustrated, Luke was one of those working on three tunnels and escape attempts which earned him spells in the Cooler.

The shooting of 'The Fifty' at Sagan and threats of similar action by the Germans had made some prospective escapers think more about simply surviving the war. In the early days of 1945 the end seemed near. Rather than attempting to escape the senior officers decided to organise some form of defence by assembling a disciplined force to meet whatever shambles the end may bring. Within the camp were Army glider pilots who had been taken prisoner at Arnhem. They were co-opted as instructors to the newly named 'Fighting Force', contingents of which were raised from the British and American Kriegies. Clandestine lectures on army fighting procedures were arranged and instructions given on the use of *Wehrmacht* weapons and the detecting of booby traps that may be left behind by retreating Germans. Squads and platoons were formed and white armbands printed boldly with the letters 'FF' issued. The secret radio kept the men informed of the advance of the Russians; the FF kept up to date and awaited their call.

Excitement was intensified when for a couple of days near the end of April muffled explosions were heard coming nearer to the camp, eventually reaching the adjacent flak school. Routine within the camp continued unbroken and the guards carried on as normal until the morning of 30 April. When the Kriegies awoke that morning it was to an eerie silence. There was not the usual sound of window shutters being noisily thrown back and no shouts of '*Raus! Raus! Appell, Appell!*' Breaking out of the huts the Kriegies looked around them. Not a sentry in sight, *Posten* boxes empty, all the Germans but one had gone.

Flight Sergeant Archie King worked in the office at Stalag Luft 1 with Group Captain Grant and Colonel Zemke. King was a Dubliner who, like so many Irishmen, had joined the services in Belfast. His legs were seriously hurt during his parachute descent and when the Kriegies were to march out from Gross Tychow in the bitter winter snows he knew that with his wounds he would never be able to keep up. One of the few who managed to successfully hide until the columns had left, King was later transferred to Barth by train. Now the Germans were leaving and the Kriegies were happily looking forward to their freedom when a tall, elegant and impeccably uniformed *Fallschirmjäger Hauptmann* walked into the office. Speaking perfect English the *Hauptmann* said:

'Gentlemen, I want to ask you a very special favour.' Looking at each of them in turn he said, 'Make me your prisoner, disguise me in one or the other of your uniforms and take me back to England with you. My name is Max Schmeling.' When told bluntly to get on his bike and go west Schmeling pleaded.

'Give me an RAF uniform,' he begged Grant. 'The Russians will shoot me.' His answer was a finger pointed at the door,

'Out,' said Grant. Had the Kriegies at Barth known it, Schmeling's visits to the camp at Luckenwalde now became clear. He was scared, preferred the American or British way of life and had been sounding out the possibilities of being transferred safely away from the Russians and war torn Germany.

The Fighting Force had been called out immediately it was found that the guards had left, while the remainder of the Kriegies were confined to the compounds by their officers. George Luke however, was one of those who penetrated the *Vorlager*, the German quarters and the flak school. Using the knowledge gained at lectures they took all precautions to prevent walking into booby traps. On the way they found and kept some rifles, ammunition and machine guns. Suddenly everyone dropped to the floor, hearts pounding as a careless American loosed off a burst of fire. There were no casualties, only curses.

Next morning it was decided to send a detachment of the Fighting Force to the aerodrome to discover if the *Luftwaffe* was still in occupation and then determine if it was possible to take the field. The British detachment of the Fighting Force was selected for the task. Luke wondered who had arrived at that decision. After an apprehensive and furtive approach they found to their relief that the aerodrome had been evacuated. They searched for booby traps. None were found but the airfield was unusable, it was littered with unexploded bombs.

An American officer who could speak Russian and a British officer who could speak German headed out of the camp to meet the Russians, but when they returned that evening they had been unable to make contact. They reported that the town of Barth was deserted of all but old men, women and children. White sheets and towels were appearing at the windows.

On 1 May elements of the Red Army entered the camp and asked why black armbands were not being worn as a mark of respect for the late President Roosevelt. The next day the Russians arrived in force. Mostly of eastern Asiatic appearance and frequently drunk, they discharged their weapons at every opportunity and terrorised the neighbourhood.

A runner breathlessly announced to the airfield detachment that the Russian Army had arrived at the camp. Tanks and armoured columns hardly paused before racing on in pursuit of the Germans. Hiding the arms and ammunition the Kriegies watched as the Russians poured into the camp area. As the days passed there was a dramatic deterioration in the quality of Red Army personnel and material. Eventually they were down to women in horse-drawn carts, poorly equipped troops on foot, on horseback or riding cycles fit only for the scrapheap.

Flight Lieutenant 'Roger' Coverley was proud of the strict discipline maintained by the RAF contingent in the camp between the departure of the German guards and the arrival of the Russians. The 'stay-put' order was followed implicitly but to his dismay some American prisoners abandoned every vestige of discipline and went on the rampage in the surrounding countryside and towns.

Coverley thought the Russians 'a tough but friendly bunch' who did everything they possibly could for the Kriegies. They drove live pigs and cattle into the camp for food but nobody seemed to know how to set about slaughtering them. Despite the enormous distance they were from home the Russians even put on a full 'Ensa'-type show in the camp theatre.

After the senior officers had liaised with the Russians their commander allowed the Fighting Force men to be rearmed and then said:

'As you have men on the aerodrome your men can clear bombs and make the airfield serviceable.' The Fighting Force men were told to remove their white armbands, reverse them, and print the word AMEPNKAHEU, the word for American in Russian. American was chosen simply because no-one knew the Russian for British. Two men with experience as armourers volunteered to defuse the bombs while others made a tractor and trailer serviceable. The hundreds of bombs were gradually moved to the perimeter. The Russians left the force alone while they cleared the field. It was during this work the men heard that it was VE-Day in Britain.

It was decided that the group captain should make his way to the Allied lines to arrange an airlift for the Kriegies. On the 11th a message was received that aircraft would be arriving next day at the local airfield, and the Russians allowed Flying Fortresses to fly in to Barth to take the Kriegies back to France on the first stage of their journey home. The Kriegies were marched down to the airfield where 'Fortresses were dropping out of the sky like autumn leaves'.

The Flying Fortress has a catwalk above the bomb-bay and when the bay is opened there is a raging gale and an open drop, so some bomb-bays were boarded over so that an aircraft could carry 30 men. George Luke smiled wryly as they were detailed off into plane loads – Americans first. He remarked to his pals, 'Look after your own first, eh?' The RAF, who had been the first at Barth, had mounted guard and cleared the aerodrome, were the last to leave. He had to admit, though, that had the RAF been flying them home, their men would probably have been on the first planes.

In batches of 24 to 30 they were flown to Ford in Sussex and by late evening on the 13th every Stalag Luft 1 prisoner had been repatriated. Barth, the first permanent prison camp built for RAF men was left to the Russians.

## THE LONG WAIT AT LUCKENWALDE

March had gone out in a blaze of sunshine, the warmth warming the bones of the men who had suffered in the winter. Now they were returning to health and playing football. Townspeople from Luckenwalde passing on a road outside the camp would stop to watch. German discipline had almost disappeared with the replacement of *Luftwaffe* guards with those of the *Wehrmacht*. The *Luftwaffe* men were off to the Eastern Front. They had not far to go. The Kriegies felt that like the Germans, they were tightly squeezed between the *Amis* and the *Ivans*.

On Thursday 12 April the RAF officers and 400 NCOs left for Moosburg near Munich. On Saturday they were back at Luckenwalde, the evacuation had been too late, the rail link to the south had been cut. While outside the wire they had been in and out of cattle trucks, had traded with the guards and with civilians and heard reports on 20 April that the Russians were just 20 miles away. Two senior officers had been sent on ahead which left Wing Commander Collard in charge of the airmen. Nearly 400 RAF Kriegies had not left the camp, being too sick to travel.

Rumours were ripping around the camp that the German staff were preparing to leave. The 3,000 Russian prisoners were becoming increasingly bold, disregarding German authority and marching in bands along the *Lagerstrasse* singing and shouting 'Deutschland Kaputt!'. The guards looked on apathetically. Excitement throughout prisoners in the camp was intense. Liberation was close.

At midday, guards and *Postens*, marching at first singly and in pairs and then in increasingly large numbers, marched down the road through the camp and out through the main gate. Prisoners lined up along the barbed wire fences cheering the exodus. An hour later the *Kommandant* handed the camp command to the senior British, American and Norwegian officers and then sped through the camp in his car closely followed by his second-in-command on a bicycle. The last few Germans slipped out as quietly as possible. Some left their rifles and other equipment at the gate, where they swiftly changed into civilian clothes already worn beneath their uniforms.

Rumours said that Jüterbog, the important road and rail junction south of Luckenwalde, had fallen to the Russians. Kriegies distinctly heard the rumble of guns and bombs and had seen the glow in the sky.

The pre-arranged Defence Scheme was immediately brought into operation. Tense and excited, the last thing the Kriegies wanted was to be embroiled in a battle but they were ready to do their best to defend themselves if it occurred. The control of the 20,000 mixed nationality prisoners was going to be a problem. Already looting was taking place and growing. Bands of half-starved and ragged Russians were rifling the German clothing store and were running riot in the potato store. No-one could blame them, scores had died every week from starvation. They were allowed to have their heads but the defence organisation did dissuade them from breaking into the *Kommandant*'s and other officers' houses. To their credit the much-abused Russians proved surprisingly amenable.

Some Kriegies were seized with a sense of anti-climax. They had anticipated their freedom for years and now, although freed from German surveillance, they were still not liberated and dare not go beyond the confines of the perimeter wire. The earlier German threat to defend the camp to the last man was now proved to be empty bravado. Those who had administered the camps were not fighting men, they had scuttled away.

A probe into the town reported that shops were distributing available food to civilians. The *Volkssturm* were still in town but a Panzer Jäger Regiment had gone south. A Dutch girl reported the arrival of a Marine Artillery Division at Luckenwalde Station in 25 railway wagons from Berlin. A party of 108 *Wehrmacht* men, led by an *SS* general and including a few *SS* troops called at the camp *Lazarett*. They were desperate and warned that anyone outside after dark would be shot and any overtly hostile acts or asylum given to any of their troops or deserters would bring reprisals. The *SS* general commanding light artillery in the area threatened to open fire unless eight rifles taken from Germans were returned to him immediately. The rifles and ammunition were found. Later some German troops appeared at the main gate surrendering their arms and asking to be taken prisoner. They were put in the Arrestlok.

Contacts outside reported that Russian artillery was shelling Luckenwalde from three miles north-east of the town and at 10.30pm fires were seen to the west. The Kriegies guessed that it was in the town of Treuenbrietzen. It was reported that only 1,000 *Volkssturm* and *Hitler Jugend* armed with sub-machine guns, rifles and Panzerfaust were defending the town.

In the early hours of Sunday morning a delegation headed by the ex-*Bürgermeister* of Luckenwalde arrived at the camp offering to hand over the town to the camp authorities. The members of the delegation were gibbering with fright and terrified of the coming Russian troops. They hoped that by surrendering the town to the British it would become British property and thus avoid it being entered and taken by the Russians. They said that the *Volkssturm* in the town had now been disbanded and no German troops were left in Luckenwalde.

Patrols within the camp discovered several Germans hiding there, hoping to be taken prisoner by the Kriegies. They went straight into the

Arrestlok. Women and children streamed up to the camp's main gate, pleading to be allowed in and given protection. They were turned away. French and Serbs caused trouble by looting and cutting holes in the outer wire through which they smuggled women, giving them a promise of protection as a bribe.

Huge columns of smoke could be seen to the east, north-east and to the south of Luckenwalde camp. The rumble of gunfire was now very close. There was little air activity and few German troops were seen in the vicinity giving rise to the hope that the area might be overrun with little opposition.

It was dusk when three shadowy figures on horseback seemed to emanate from the wood. They were a Russian cavalry scouting patrol on advance reconnaissance. They checked that the Germans had left and said that their advanced tank spearheads were nearing the town. The mounted Russians withdrew as silently as they had come. It was a tremendous thrill for the Kriegies. It was their first contact with the mighty Red Army.

The night passed quietly but the Kriegies were too excited to sleep. In the south and east the rumble of big guns and bombs frequently rose to a crescendo and then subsided to a gentle mutter. The glow of fearsome fires lit the sky but in the immediate vicinity of the camp all was quiet and peaceful.

Despite weariness the Kriegies at Luckenwalde could not rest. A few of those who had seen it all before put their heads down for an hour during the dark of the night, but everybody was awake and lining the wire at 6.00am when an armoured car appeared at the main gate. A Russian lieutenant leapt from the armoured car as Kriegie guards flung open the gates. Calling to them to stay put until the Red Army arrived he ran down the *Lagerstrasse* in pursuit of his armoured car which had driven inside the camp. A wave of ecstatic cheering accompanied him and a burly Australian officer who ran with the lieutenant waving his hat in the air and whooping like a Red Indian.

At the far end of the road a group of Allied senior officers waited to greet the Lieutenant. He happily pumped their hands, finishing with the Senior Allied Officer, Norwegian General Rüge. Indicating that the general, the Senior American Officer and an interpreter should accompany him, the lieutenant leapt into his armoured car and drove off in a cloud of dust. The Senior American Officer and interpreter soon returned to camp after being fired upon.

At 8.15am Russian infantry could be seen from the Norwegian compound. Germans in the nearby woods opened fire with a machine gun but there were no casualties. By mid-morning excitement had risen to a fever pitch. Hundreds of prisoners lined the barbed wire fence on both sides of the camp main road. They had heard a great rumble, rapidly increasing in earth-shaking volume and tempo. Suddenly, round a bend of the road in front of the main gate appeared a gigantic tank, then another and another and another, their caterpillar tracks clangorously thundering on the road. To Kriegie Peter Hewitt they appeared as great slab-sided monsters, each tremendous gun protruding like the proboscis of some roaring primeval beast.

The gate guard leapt to swing open the big double gates to the *Lagerstrasse* but the driver of the T34 was not to be denied the thrill of opening the camp and freeing the prisoners his way. With a splintering crash the gates were brushed aside as if of paper. The victorious Red Army had arrived in force.

To a tornado of cheering the Red Army armoured spearhead rolled majestically down the *Lagerstrasse* while the near hysterically-happy mass of prisoners lined the wire, shrieking, waving and tossing cigarettes to the smiling crews. Hewitt thought the dramatic, triumphal entry was in keeping with all expectations and so was the appearance of the tank crews and mobile infantry. He recalls:

'They were as tough a looking lot of men as you could possibly imagine, all bristling with weapons. Each man seemed to be equipped not only with a rifle but with a pistol and sub-machine gun as well, while arms were strewn indiscriminately around the vehicles. The leading armoured lorries were towing large and wicked looking anti-tank guns while further back others towed mobile flak guns and mortars.

'The soldiers' uniforms were disappointing, field boots, nondescript trousers and grey flock-stuffed cotton jackets similar to those we had seen on so many Russian prisoners. There was not a steel helmet in the whole outfit but what they lacked in clothing they certainly made up for in numbers. The lorries were crammed with troops and they clustered on the backs and sides of the tanks like leeches.'

The Kriegies were interested to see several women in the column. They were told the women were nurses or despatch riders who transported their motorcycles on the lorries. Like the men, all were armed and appeared just as tough. The armoured column continued down the road to the Russian compound where it halted amid tremendous scenes of jubilation as the 4,000 ragged and half-starved men rushed out to greet their comrades. Where they could find room they clambered on to the lorries, while the remainder marched in ragged formation towards the main gate and freedom. Some were carrying bundles of looted clothing and food, and some were already the proud possessors of rifles grabbed from their liberating comrades.

However, the Kriegies were not sorry to see them go. The Russians would have become a serious liability to those trying to keep law and order had they stayed any longer. The inhabitants of the town had already had reason to regret bitterly the liberation of the unruly mob that had been pinned behind wire under dreadful conditions for so long. The Russian prisoners had a great many scores to settle. For four long years they had been the *untermensch,* fit only for slavery and then death when no longer useful. Now, as if with a wave of a magic wand, they suddenly possessed all the despotic power of conquerors and were in no humour to compromise.

The Major in charge of the armoured column was engaged with other flying columns in a vast outflanking movement round the southern and western defences of Berlin. He was anxious to press on and believed that the prisoners should join his troops and the liberated Russians on their final drive to Berlin. When the Kriegies hastily but firmly declined with regrets, the major's face fell. The Kriegies dropped several degrees in his estimation, he could not understand their attitude. The discussion was terminated by an alarm of a German counter-attack from the woods outside the camp.

At this the major, with a bellow to his men, leapt into a tank and spinning in the open space at the end of the road the tank roared down the *Lagerstrasse* to where the front gates had been. As there was insufficient room to pass the moving column of Russian prisoners the tank swerved aside towards the inner boundary fence dividing the British officers from the *strasse.* The fence was lined on both sides with cheering prisoners and it looked as though a terrible slaughter was imminent. The cheering stopped abruptly as the danger was realised and there was a wild scramble for safety. Miraculously, no-one was killed, Kriegies frantically flung themselves clear as the juggernauts roared past, uprooting and snapping the 10-foot high, six-inch thick posts with the barbed wire attached, as if they had been matchsticks. In the wake of the tanks was a mass of splintered wooden posts, tangles of barbed wire and hundreds of white-faced British and American prisoners-of-war. The armoured column left, as it had arrived, a roaring, clanging, clattering procession in a dense cloud of dust.

Luckenwalde town was rapidly and efficiently occupied but most of the Russian troops passed straight through. German civilians began breaking shop windows and looting them of linen goods and footwear. White flags, towels and sheets appeared hanging from the windows throughout the town. The bakery was robbed of all its flour.

Reports confirmed the disciplined behaviour of the Russian occupiers except at night when noisy vodka parties, lasting all hours, were the fashion. German women were then apt to fare badly judging by the many who still came to the camp gates entreating prisoners to go down to live with them and thus protect them from unwelcome attentions.

By 9.00pm an officer returning from Luckenwalde reported everything quiet and orderly in the town, but firing continued around the camp until the early hours. A couple of *Wehrmacht* men surrendered to a patrol from the camp and confirmed that 80 to 100 men from the same unit were in the adjacent woods.

The Russians appointed a liaison officer on 21 April and three lady interpreters visited the camp. Young, smart, attractive and speaking good English, they were dressed in well-fitting, military-style tunics with stand-up close-fitting collars, short pleated skirts, silk stockings and jackboots. Each of the girls wore captain's rank epaulettes. The Norwegians invited one of the interpreters to tea. She told them that she had fixed up a nice little flat in the town. She then electrified them by asking their Roman Catholic padre to come down and spend the night with her. The poor man's embarrassment was extreme, she had asked him in front of the entire company. As he was a giant of a man, more than six feet two and broad in proportion, the Kriegies reckoned it was his size rather than his cloth that attracted her.

A party from the camp searching the houses of the *Kommandant* and other senior officers were interested to find ample evidence from empty tins and cartons that they had not been going short of Red Cross food parcels. They had always been suspected of stealing the Kriegies' parcels. Peter Hewitt thought it little wonder that they always looked so well fed. Now – too late – the Kriegies had proof.

Details were found in the *Kommandant's* safe of an *OKW* order with plans to move the British and American Kriegies on foot to Lüneburg when it was found impossible to send them to Munich. The Kriegies had been saved from a long march by the rapid movement of the Russian spearheads north and south of the camp, making evacuation virtually impossible.

The next day, 23 April, was quieter although mopping up was still proceeding in the area. Russian officers from Konev's army were frequent visitors to the camp. One told that there were still four German divisions in the area, two tank and two infantry, but the tank division had no tanks and the infantry division no boots. A single Russian division was being used to mop up.

Since the arrival of the Russians the food position in the camp had improved rapidly, it was clear that they were doing everything possible to help. One British officer was taken on a food foraging expedition and returned with 12 cows for the camp. Whilst the Russians seemed to do their best for the British and American prisoners, they did not appear to regard the French as allies. It was obvious that they had a low opinion of them.

By 25 April the Kriegies were settling down after several days of mounting excitement. Now they were wondering where the two armies from east and west would meet and when and how they were to go home. Liberation brought a natural desire to be on their way but the anti-climax of liberation without freedom brought with it frustration.

The war had now passed over the camp although large fires could still be seen in the western sky and the impressive drumfire barrage on Berlin could be heard clearly. Ju88s strafed the camp for a couple of nights but there were no casualties. It was a standstill period in the camp during which some Kriegies explored their surroundings.

Some visited the Orthodox Church built by the Russian prisoners in their compound. Peter Hewitt thought it a remarkable work, a triumph of ingenuity and application. Members of a supposedly atheistic society had transformed the squalor of a barrack block into a place of worship. Murals of Biblical scenes covered the walls, one entire end wall depicting scenes from the Last Supper and others of Christ performing the miracles. All were painted in bright colours with perfect detail and proportion. Dyed and stencilled cloth surrounded the altar and before it was a carved and brightly painted wooden screen and reredos. The church had taken six men two years to complete, while the beautiful carving had been worked on a home-made wooden treadmill lathe. The Kriegies looked in wonder at this magnificent conversion and realised that despite the surface adherence to Communism, religious beliefs in Russia were strong and abiding.

The Kriegies noted that there was a high proportion of women among the Russian occupying infantry. They were described as 'husky Amazons with large breasts and larger behinds'. Many wore medals for valour, including much-prized decorations awarded for the bitter fighting around Moscow and at Stalingrad. The women lived, slept and ate with the male soldiers. It was said that pregnancy rendered them liable to the death sentence because it made them unfit for active service and as such it was a crime against the state.

On 27 April the Russians sent 60 German Arbeitsdienst Korps boys to the camp for use as labour. They were underfed and almost paralysed with fright. In their last extremities the *Nazis* had given the boys rifles and told them to go out and shoot Russians. The average age of the labour corps boys was 15. Handing them over, the Russian guard said merely 'We don't fight children'.

A party of Kriegies went out of the camp on the morning of the 28th to visit the scene of the armoured spearhead's last battle before liberating Stalag 3A. No attempt had been made to bury the many dead Russians and the more plentiful Germans. Smashed equipment, four burnt-out tanks, trampled undergrowth and splintered trees made a scene of what one would expect a battle scene to be – but under the bright sunshine, blue sky and against the background of spring foliage with the only sound trilling birdsong, it seemed as unreal and as still as a stage set.

Russian officers were impressed with the discipline and administrative organisation existing within the British and American sections of the camp. Other prisoners liberated had needed Russian administrative staff to run them. The smartness and bearing of these prisoners was also remarked upon by attractive interpreter Sergeant Marja. Other prisoners, she said, had upon liberation, abandoned their camps for luxurious German quarters which they immediately despoiled.

In the town German civilians stopped British and American ex-prisoners, asking when the *Amis* or *Tommies* would arrive. When told that they would probably not come to the area their reaction was dismay followed by tears. Life in the town square was quiet and dull, the people appeared to be staying indoors, venturing out only to hunt for food. They were very frightened for their future under Russian occupation. Demands to Germans for requisitioned items were handed over without hesitation.

Photographic and radio stores had been looted and emptied by the Russians. Other than that, Luckenwalde town had escaped with only some factories and blocks of flats damaged by shell-fire, houses splintered by machine gun-fire and roadside trees uprooted as tanks had crashed past. Despite the looting some Kriegies had obtained radios and relished the pleasure of listening to the BBC.

Trouble was still being caused by Serbian and French prisoners looting in the town and district. Hundreds of men still poured into the camp from *Arbeitskommandos* in the surrounding area, all pushing or pulling carts loaded with loot.

Three Red Army men who had deserted to the Germans arrived at the camp gate and asked for help and civilian clothes in which to escape capture. They were held in the guardroom until a Russian detachment called. A short way down the road three rifle shots closed the incident.

By early May the Kriegies reckoned they had been detained long enough by the Russians. The excuse about registration of the prisoners was seen to be an obvious sham. Some RAF men had left by various ruses and made their way to the American lines. Flight Lieutenant Hugh Collins and two others had walked out behind a party of French workers.

A dangerous situation arose when on 6 May an American officer, despite his credentials from Supreme Allied Headquarters, was refused permission to take more than a few sick American and British prisoners. The following day the American representative returned with a convoy of lorries with which to evacuate the prisoners. He was denied and when he attempted to take some away, Russians raced up on motorcycles, shots were fired over the American convoy and threats were made that if one prisoner-of-war was found on board when the trucks left, all the trucks and their personnel would be interned. The Americans were forced to abandon their task. To complete their abject disappointment the Kriegies dejectedly returned to their rooms to find French and Italian prisoners had ransacked their compound.

Flight Lieutenant de Bounevialle was frustrated when he saw the American trucks sent away empty. He heard that trucks were loading by the sand pits and dashed over there but they had left when he arrived. Walking and running in the direction of Frankenfelde he discovered a line of US trucks and jeeps outside the camp's west gate. Given three minutes to get to the far end of the line he ran and climbed aboard. Three hours later his small convoy of two trucks and nine jeeps crossed the Elbe into the American sector without trouble. Next morning he heard from straggling new arrivals that leaving the Luckenwalde Stalag had become very much harder and that 25 trucks from outside the west gate had been forced by the Russians to drive into the camp, unload the Kriegies and leave.

Tension was rising. The Russians were actively preventing the evacuation of the prisoners despite all their warm assurances. The SBO, Wing Commander Collard, was incensed. He resigned as Allied Senior Officer and demanded that the position be clarified and the repatriation proceeded with immediately. But there were deeper and more sinister reasons for the detention of Allied prisoners. The men themselves saw that they were being held hostage, probably until the return to the Russians of some unwilling repatriates.

Collard issued an order on 8 May that 'No British personnel are to leave the camp except on duty', although Bob Cutts remembers a later order that the men could move within a mile of the camp and the old air-raid siren would be used as a recall signal. The Russians made 9 May their day of victory and they celebrated by firing every available gun. The sky above Berlin was a brilliant display of bursting flak.

Sergeants Jim Palmer and Brian Walley had struggled from Luckenwalde, dodging and avoiding both fleeing Germans and triumphant Russians who wanted to return them to camp. At last, travel worn and exhausted they struck lucky. At Wittenberg an American officer sitting in a jeep, its engine running, called out that he was about to cross the Elbe in the last vehicle to pass over before the sealing of the border between the Americans and Russians. Palmer, Walley and eight other escapers clung to the jeep wherever there was a handhold as it clattered across the swaying, dipping, pontoon bridge to the American occupied area and freedom.

On the 11th a Russian general arrived at Luckenwalde camp. He was incensed that some prisoners had left the camp and warned that if there were any more such 'home-runs' he would intern the SBO. The Russian was also angry about the lack of food for the camp. Captain Medvedev, he threatened, would be court-martialled. The SBO spoke up for the captain and said that in his opinion Medvedev had done his best with the negligible resources at his disposal.

Berlin had suffered continuously from air-raids by Mosquitoes and the camp at Luckenwalde was blacked out every time. Under the cover of darkness Kriegies Jack Boyes and Ron Cartwright managed to creep out of the camp. Each day they hid in woods and ditches and at night they trudged west, hoping to meet Allied forces. At last, hungry, thirsty and dirty they watched a smallholding all day, then, driven by necessity they went to the house and knocked. The owners, a woman and her son, gave them onion soup and then imparted the startling news, '*Der Krieg ist schon drei Tage fertig*'. The Kriegies' skulking in ditches had been unnecessary for the last three days.

Leaving the smallholding the pair walked into the village where they found the manor house deserted. In a drawer they discovered several thousand Reichsmarks in large denomination notes. At a baker's in Raditz they offered a 1,000 Reichsmark note for a loaf. The money was refused but they were given a loaf. The airmen assumed the notes to be useless and burned the remainder. When they met American troops and were taken to Brussels they were asked if they had any German money to change. There was much 'gnashing of teeth' says Jack

Boyes. The woman in the baker's had been trying to tell them that the note offered was too large to change for a loaf. Resignedly Boyes decided that it served them right for helping themselves to other people's property.

On May 18 a dance was held at Luckenwalde for the NCOs in the old German dining quarters. There were now about 500 women in the camp, most of them munitions workers from Berlin. The band was made up from the men from Bankau.

Another Russian general visited the Luckenwalde camp on 19 May and told the Kriegies that they would definitely be on their way homeward the next day. Agreement had been reached on the exchange of prisoners between the Americans, British and Russians by a mixed Repatriation Commission. This was nothing as simple as a handing over of men captured by the Germans. There had to be some hard bargaining.

Next day a huge convoy of 100 Russian-driven three-ton Studebaker trucks drew up at the camp. The staff and the *Lazarett* patients were placed in the first three trucks and the remainder were filled, 25 men to a truck, for the drive to an American transit camp at Halle. Treuenbrietzen was the first town these Kriegies were to see that had been heavily damaged. Burnt-out buildings had been reduced to hollow shells. Bomb craters and debris made the roads nearly impassable. Villages seemed to have suffered the extremes of battle, some destroyed and deserted, others hardly touched.

A fierce rearguard action had been fought along the length of the famous Berlin to Leipzig Autobahn, and there worse troubles began for the convoy. The Russians had not bothered to ascertain whether the road was clear. Every one of the many reinforced concrete bridges crossing the Autobahn had been effectively mined and blown, completely blocking the road. At each demolished bridge hours were spent making detours through woods and fields, chopping down trees and pushing the trucks through ditches.

A bridge once spanning a 200 foot-deep gorge lay a tumbled ruin at the bottom. The trucks had to be driven at dangerous angles down the side of the ravine, through the river and up as steep a slope on the other side. The exhausted Kriegies began to despair of ever reaching the Elbe. The bridge circling performance was repeated several times, the 60-mile journey taking eight hours to complete. Never was there a sign that the Russians had made the slightest effort to remove obstructions which the Kriegies reckoned would, in many cases, have taken Royal Engineers sappers a few hours to clear with some dynamite and bulldozers.

At the Elbe the great three-span steel bridge was lying at drunken angles in the wide river. Girders hung loosely from the piers, the water gurgling through the steel tracery. But American Construction Battalions had thrown an efficient 120 flat-boat pontoon bridge across the river a mile downstream. Every Kriegie was relieved to see American trucks drive over the bridge to collect them.

Albert Bracegirdle noticed that the Russians were forcing the Kriegies to leave all their belongings behind and quickly concealed his diary. The road across the bridge wallowed and swayed as the Kriegie-laden trucks, three on the bridge at a time, crossed to the American Zone of Occupation. Bracegirdle breathed a sigh of satisfaction when his truck ran onto firm earth; he was delighted to be free and equally delighted to be able to enjoy his freedom after that hair-raising crossing.

The Kriegies were immediately struck by the difference in atmosphere. Apart from the absence of German men and the presence of large numbers of American troops, it was as if the war had never been. There was little sign of war damage. Women and girls paraded in their Whit Sunday best and trams, trains and buses ran normally. On the other side of the Elbe there had been ruin and desolation wherever the Kriegies had travelled. Evidence of the last-ditch struggle of the *Wehrmacht* could be seen in the hundreds of fox-holes, slit trenches, felled trees, mine traps and tank traps scattered over the landscape. Members of the American regiment administering the camp told the Kriegies that after crossing the Rhine they had travelled 195 miles without firing a shot, lost only two tanks and that the single regiment had taken the city of Halle. Halle was the beginning of the return to civilisation for the Kriegies from Luckenwalde.

### THE LONGEST MILE
'The longest mile is the last mile home
When you've been away.'
*(Popular song of the 1940s)*

As the pilot of the Dakota Skytrooper looked along the line of scruffy, khaki-clad ex-prisoners-of-war waiting to climb into his aircraft, he noted a man with traces of faded blue in parts of his uniform.

'Are you an RAF man?' he asked. 'You are! OK! Front of the queue.' He positioned his aircraft carefully, there was little space to make a take-off run between the bomb crater to his left and that on the right with another Dakota in it – nose down. With engines roaring the Dakota lifted off on that sunny spring day, its starboard wing skimming inches above the wreck's skyward-pointing tail. The pilot relaxed, this was his third dicey take-off from there that day. The happy duty of bringing home men who had been prisoners of the Germans was more congenial and less dangerous than some of his previous duties, such as towing gliders loaded with airborne troops on D-Day or dropping Paras at Arnhem.

Sergeant Vic Gammon, the lone airman among the score of Army ex-prisoners, turned to take a last look through the Dakota's window. As the plane banked to the west he saw below what had been the neat German town of Rheine. White sheets of surrender draped the windowsills of those houses still standing amid the rubble of war, but the battle front had rolled across Rheine a few days before. For the men flying to England their war really was over.

Gammon noticed that the soldier in the next bucket seat sat with his head buried in his hands. He had not looked up since take-off. The sergeant was surprised by the answer to his gentle enquiry. His voice muffled through cupped hands, the soldier replied, 'I've never been in an aeroplane before, I'm scared'. As the view of the South Coast of England stretched across the aircraft's windows, the airman gently grasped the soldier's arm, wishing to share with him the exhilarating moment.

'Look! Look!' he urged, pointing. 'There are the white cliffs – you are nearly home – after all this time you must look – there's England down there.' The soldier snatched a swift glance and again buried his face in his hands.

Vic Gammon turned to watch the sunlit fields passing beneath the wings of the Dakota. The green land was bathed in the soft sunshine of a perfect April afternoon. The flight had been short. England had seemed so distant during those years in which he had felt every emotion from terrifying fear to unmitigated joy, from abject despair to burning hope. Now, as the aircraft shuddered, the undercarriage and flaps lowered and the engines throttled back for a landing approach, the lost years were being wiped away as a damp duster clears a chalked blackboard.

The Dakota rolled to a stop, the fuselage door opened and the airman looked around at the green hangars and red brick buildings of a typical RAF station; this was familiar ground. At long last he was home.

Two smart, solicitous WAAF girls led Gammon into a hangar and to a chintzy table piled with cakes and pastries. He had been for so long unused to femininity that he found it difficult to answer their gentle questions and their obvious concern confused him. Yes, he was hungry he had said but did not wish to eat now thank you – yes, a cup of tea would be fine.

Looking down at himself, he was acutely conscious of his emaciation and the ragged mixture of grimy clothes in which he had subsisted for months. Most of the water for the few washes he had managed to have during the past weeks had been dredged from the bottom of a green-watered ditch and he was aware that the sweat of the forced marches and the odour of the previous occupants of the sheds, barns and ditches that had been his recent resting places, still clung to him. Experience with the liberating soldiers' rich food had convinced him that to eat a small piece of the offered cake would cause his stomach to cramp and rebel. He would be forced to make a rapid and unceremonious exit. Fingering his stubbled chin he felt like a tramp who had mistakenly wandered into the Ritz.

The de-briefing with an Intelligence Officer was not unlike the first interrogation with the *Luftwaffe* Major at Dulag Luft. It was as if he would try kindness and chummyness first. Gammon almost mistrusted him through habit.

'I say old boy, that's an old number, you're a regular, eh? How long were you in the bag? Four and a half years! Phew! Were you badly treated, any war criminals you can tell me about?'

Gammon thought it hardly politic to mention that the British and Polish troops he had encountered had volunteered to settle any accounts for him 'round the back' without delay, and with finality that would obviate any necessity of a trial.

'I bet you fellows have some stories to tell,' the Intelligence Officer's voice droned on. Vic Gammon considered those words. There would certainly be some extraordinary stories, the actions in which his fellow prisoners had fought had taken place all over Europe, the Middle East and North Africa. There was heroism and hilarity, tragedy and mirth, leaders and loners, brutality and kindness and, most precious of all, companionship and solidarity. Prisoners had been seen at their magnificent best and just a few at their 'there but for the Grace of God go I' worst. They had been close in the way that only those who have been through the hell of war together can know. He was going to miss them; perhaps one day their stories would be told but now he did not want any more talk and strangely, he did not want food. Instead he was going to have the sybaritic luxury of a prolonged soak in a hot bath.

### THE END OF A NIGHTMARE

Roy Witham stirred. He had slept well in a real bed with sheets and blankets. Slowly the realisation that he was waking in a room on an RAF station in Britain sunk into his consciousness. The shooting down of his

Lancaster, the mock execution, the shots fired at him as he ran across the compound, the hunger, the misery of the long march across Lüneburg Heath, the Typhoon attack at Gresse, his release and flight home, had all taken place within a year. Suddenly a voice from the next bed put all his thoughts into a single phrase.

'God! it's good to be home!.' James 'Dixie' Deans was sitting up in bed, looking round with pleasure and profound relief as the responsibilities he had carried so magnificently and for so long, fell from his shoulders.

*Summer Hats (home made).*

# Appendix

**BARTH**

Nothing remains of Stalag Luft 1 or of the adjacent flak school. The area has been levelled.

**BELSEN**

Bergen-Belsen, a few kilometres from Fallingbostel and containing 60,000 prisoners, was overrun by General Dempsey's Second Army on 15 April 1945.

**BRISTOW, John**

On his return to Britain John 'Curly' Bristow, the mechanical and electrical genius, headed his own radio and television business south of London until his death in July 1990.

**BUCHENWALD**

The camp was liberated by American troops on 11 April 1945. Most Jews had been moved to other camps for extermination.

**BURTON, Alec**

On his return from Germany Alec took a degree in biology at St Andrew's University, after which he became biology master at Cheltenham Grammar School. Later he accepted the Biology Chair at Durban University. He died in early 1983.

**CUNDALL, Howard**

The civilian radar expert who constructed a radio receiver and transmitter in the officers' compound of Stalag Luft 3 continued his secret work after the war. He disappeared from a yacht whilst on holiday in 1974 on the Garonne near Bordeaux. His body was found the following day floating in the river.

**DAMMAN, Ron**

Of the 40 Australians sent to the OTU at RAF Bassingbourn in the spring of 1941, only eight survived the war to return home. Ron Damman was one.

### DAY, Group Captain Harry Melville Arbuthnot, GC, DSO, OBE

'Wings' Day was the Senior British Officer at many prisoner-of-war camps and was a prime mover of innumerable escape attempts. He was Vice-President of the Royal Air Forces Ex-Prisoner-of-War Association until his death in 1978.

### DEANS, James Alexander, MBE

Warrant Officer 'Dixie' Deans, revered among airmen prisoners, was the first President of the Royal Air Forces Ex-Prisoner-of-War Association. After the war he became a senior administration officer at The London School of Economics until his retirement in 1977. 'Dixie' died in 1989 from the Multiple Sclerosis which he had fought strenuously since the 1940s.

### DULAG LUFT

Durchgangslager der *Luftwaffe*. Oberursel near Frankfurt-am-Main, close to the foothills of the Taunus mountains. On 10 September 1943 the transit section was moved to Palmengarten in the centre of Frankfurt. It was bombed in March 1944 when it was transferred again 30 miles north to Wetzlar. The original camp site at Oberursel later became Camp King, an American NATO transport depot. The interrogation block was used as an American officers' mess.

### ESCAPES

Only some 30 RAF men are known to have successfully escaped from prisoner-of-war camps and most of those were from army camps such as that at Lamsdorf, Stalag 8B. There they were able to exchange identities

with a soldier prisoner who left the camp daily on a working party among a native population who, although frequently taking serious risks, were sympathetic to the Allied cause. Getting over, under or through the wire of a typical Luft camp was especially difficult where the camp was a simple rectangle surrounded by tangled wire, deep trenches, seismographs, patrolling guards and sentry boxes on stilts with guards armed with machine guns and searchlights.

## GARRIOCH, W.
In 1967 a Dutch farmer uncovered the wreck of 'Bill' Garrioch's Wellington in the mud of the Ijsselmeer (the drained Zuider Zee). In the wreck were the remains of Glynn 'Taffy' Reardon the front gunner. 'Taffy' was buried in the military cemetery at Jonkersbosch.

## GLEMNITZ, Hermann
Was released after a few weeks. He was a natural survivor and had a succession of jobs such as translator, road repairer and metal worker.

## HAMILTON, John 'Jock'
Was driving between his home and work during a storm in 1957 when a tree fell on his car and he was killed.

## JACKSON, Reverend Arthur
After his return from Buchenwald and Dachau, 'Jacko' was ordained and became Vicar of Stone in Staffordshire. He died in 1981.

## JAMES, B. A.
Referred to as 'Jimmy' James, his book Moonless Night covers the whole of the period 1940-1945.

## LYNE, H. Lloyd
In 1988 he attended an unveiling in Warsaw by the Rt Hon Margaret Thatcher MP, of a memorial to the six members of his crew who died during their ill-fated arms drop to the Polish fighters.

## MASSEY, Air Commodore Herbert Martin, CBE, DSO, MC
Senior British Officer at Stalag Luft 3 Sagan, brought back to Britain the earliest first-hand knowledge of the mass escape when he was repatriated with the severely wounded prisoners in April 1944. Air Commodore Massey was Vice-President of the Royal Air Forces Ex-Prisoner-of-War Association until his death in 1976.

## MÜHLBERG

In 1945 when the prisoners had left Stalag 4B, Russian forces found displaced German civilians living in the camp which had electricity and running water. They promptly turned them out and forced the Germans to watch while they blew up the buildings. They then sought out the *Bürgermeister* of Mühlberg, who had sold the land for a prison camp, and executed him.

## NELSON, Thomas

When Nelson joined his surviving crew members at Stalag 4B they told him that their most distressing moment was when they removed the body of their dead pilot, Pilot Officer 'Larry' Cates, which was severely burned all down the left side. When he returned to England after the war Nelson visited 'Larry' Cates' parents to confirm Larry's death and offer condolences. Mrs Cates said: 'But we have known all along that he was dead. On the night you were shot down, I woke up and the clock showed it was 10 minutes past 12. Larry was standing in the bedroom. He was

dressed in his flying clothing and was burned all down his left side. Next morning we received the telegram that we knew would be coming. So you see, we knew we would never see him again.'

## PIEBER, Hans

Lager officer at various times to the NCOs' compound and the east and south officers' compounds at Sagan, Pieber was not transferred after the mass escape. A holder of the 'Blood Ribbon' he was a member of the early *Nazi* Putch. Disillusioned by the *Nazis*' take-over of Austria he refused to wear his 'Blood Ribbon'. After the war Pieber was arrested as a *Nazi* and letters from 'Wings' Day to various authorities helped towards obtaining Pieber's release. He died aged 80 in 1976.

## PLACE NAMES

Due to post-war boundary moves many of the places which have significance for ex-prisoners now have Polish names. Some of the changes are: Bankau to Bakowo, Breslau to Wroclaw, Gross Tychow to Tychowo, Hey-

dekrug to Szylokarczma, Lamsdorf to Lambinowice, Memel to Klajpeda, Posen to Poznan, Sagan to Zagan, Schubin to Szubin, Stettin to Szczecin, Swinemünde to Swinoujscie, Vilno to Vilnius. A Dutch name change is that of Zuider Zee to Ijsselmeer.

## SAGAN

The urns containing the ashes of the 50 officer prisoners-of-war shot in 1944, were removed from the cemetery at Sagan in 1948 and re-interred in the Commonwealth Section of the Old Garrison Cemetery at Poznan. Stalag Luft 3 has been razed and the area overgrown with new pines and firs. The memorial to 'The Fifty' has been maintained by local children.

## SIMOLEIT, Gustav

Simoleit supervised the surrender of German personnel at Stalag 7A. His membership of the *Nazi* Party caused him to remain in abject poverty for some years.

## SCHMELING, Max

He was World Heavyweight Champion 1930-32 when he beat Sharkey on a foul in the 4th round. He lost the return fight. Schmeling noticed a weakness in Joe Louis' defence and knocked him out in 1938, but in the return bout Louis smashed Schmeling in the first round. Schmeling returned to boxing after the war when he was over 40, but was defeated by Walter Neusel after which he retired.

## VON LINDEINER

Brought to London in August 1945, was a prisoner-of-war for two years but was finally exonerated and rejoined his wife in the British Zone of Germany.

# Index

Edwards, L.H., 12, 13
Eisenhower, Gen Dwight
 D., 140, 257
Elbe, 189, 206, 219, 240,
 248-250, 258, 270-273
Elder, D., 245
*Emden*, KMS, 12
Emes, Dennis, 94, 96, 97
*Empress of Russia*, SS, 119
Emsdetton, 210
*Erich Steinbrink*, KMS, 51
Esling, Ronald, 77, 78,
 189
Essen, 66, 75, 89

Fancy, Sgt, 45
Feltwell, 22
Fermor, Ronald, 80, 188,
 189
Filmer, Lt RN, 46, 47
Fletcher, Geoffrey,
 127-131, 191, 193, 199,
 208, 211
Flockhart, C.B., 125, 144
Floody, C.W., 127, 128
Foggia, 169
Ford, Leslie, 87, 88, 129,
 139
Frankenfelde, 270
Frankfurt am Main, 16, 20,
 42, 43, 114, 115, 120,
 121, 172
Fraser, David, 37-40
Fresnes Prison, 98-100,
 113, 114, 162-165, 167,
 168, 200
Freya Radar, 24
Fry, Douglas R., 149, 158,
 238, 239

Gage, John, 242, 243
Gaggini, Eric, 252
Gammon, Victor F., 25-28,
 56, 58, 61, 102, 214,
 218-223, 226-236, 274,
 275
Garfield, William V.,
 97-100
Garrioch, William R.,
 29-33, 59, 109, 242, 244,
 251, 279
Gerard, Father, 97
Gestapo, 34, 94, 97-99,
 107, 108, 110, 111, 114,

124-126, 132, 136, 138,
 140, 142, 144, 145, 157,
 158, 161, 197, 208
Gibraltar, 33, 68
Gibson, Ronald, 209
Gilbanks, A., 48, 49
Gilbert, J., 144
Glemnitz, Hermann, 20,
 21, 45, 46, 128, 192, 279
Glogau, 101
*Gneisenau*, KMS, 48, 50
Göbbels, Joseph, 28, 52,
 186, 187, 229
Goldberg, 186, 188
Goodchild, Kenneth, 151,
 238, 239
Goodman, William, 242
Göring, Hermann, 72, 73
Gothenburg, 119
Grant, Grp Capt, 258, 259
Graveley, 120
Greaves, Stanley, 48, 49
Gresse, 240, 241
 245-247, 249, 276
Griffiths, Kenneth, 106,
 138, 139
Grimer, John, 173, 174
Grimm, Hans, 60, 82, 83
Grimson, George, 91, 92,
 123-125, 144
Grosskind, Irving, 192
Gulliford, Raymond, 245
Gumbach, 'Charlie', 245,
 250
Gunton, A.R., 15, 16
Gustloff Armaments Fac-
 tory, 166

Halbau, 196, 197
Hale, Ronald, 253
Hale, Roy, 177
Hall, E.L.G., 23, 44, 45
Hall, J., 29-33
Halle, 272, 273
Hamblin, Barry, 192
Hamburg, 37, 111, 112,
 155, 205, 212, 227-229,
 246
Hamilton, John, 25, 26,
 58, 214, 219-221, 223,
 225, 227, 229, 279
Hamm, 14
Hancock, William, 80
Hanover, 29, 200, 212

Harris, MRAF Sir Arthur,
 23, 66, 68, 69, 256
Harris, Gerry E., 216
Harrison, Wilfred,
 122-125
Harsh, George, 127
Hart, Robert, 159
Hart, William, 242
Harvey, H. Thomas, 105,
 217, 218, 241, 244, 245
Hatton, Hyman, 145
Haybes, 113
Heape, John, 138
Hedge, H.G., 29, 30, 32
Heidekrug, 241
Heinz, Feldwebel, 82, 84,
 103, 105
Hess, Rudolf, 37
Hewitt, Peter, 194, 196,
 198, 265, 267, 268
Hillier, E.B., 14
Hilton, Paul, 75, 76, 110,
 168, 169
Hind, Peter, 41, 42
Hitler, Adolf, 23, 34, 46,
 47, 98, 121, 122, 154,
 192, 206, 209, 232, 247,
 251
Hobbs, Geoffrey, 190-192,
 197, 198
Hoerback, Hermann von,
 105
Hoffmann, Kapitän zur
 See, 50
Hogg, Geoffrey, 37, 39
*Hood*, HMS, 45
Hoogerswilde, 66
Hunt, Francis, 90
Hunter, W.J., 51
Hurrell, Stanley, 148

Insterberg, 101, 122
*Insterburg*, SS, 150, 152,
 167, 201

Jackson, Padre Arthur,
 154, 279
James, B.A., 133, 204, 205,
 279
Jennens, William, 191
Jensen, Frank W., 140
Jersey, 163
Jodl, Alfred, 120
Johnston, R.G., 177